THREADS, KNO⌐

Threads, Knots, Tapestries

How a Tribal Connection is Revealed

Through Dreams and Synchronicities

Tess Castleman

DAIMON
VERLAG

An earlier edition of this work was published by Syren Book Co.,
St. Paul, Minnesota, in 2003.

Second, revised Edition 2004

ISBN 3-85630-697-8

Copyright © 2004 Daimon Verlag and Tess Castleman

*To order additional copies of this book,
see the information at the back of this book.*

for Marjorie, Janie, and Ernie—
whose vivid ribbons
have given unmistakable pattern
to my tapestry

Contents

Acknowledgments

I would like to thank my professional colleagues who listened to my ideas and encouraged me to write them down: Mary Briner, Sylvia Weisshaupt, C. Michael Smith, Ernie Bel, and Robert Hinshaw.

I also owe a debt to Patricia Barker for careful editing suggestions, Lisa Walls for tireless secretarial work, and all the people at Syren Book Company who believed in this project.

Invaluable support came from son Geoffrey Straw and husband Gary Cason, without whom none of this work would have seen fruition. (Gary says, "But Tess, all I did was stay out of the room."—indeed, all writers know the value of a quiet, uninterrupted day to write.)

Natalie Goldberg and Buena Vista Social Club also provided untold inspiration.

But most of all, many thanks to all of my analysands and dream group members who so graciously and generously allowed me to write about their private material.

Author's Note

The following case histories and stories are true but small details have been altered to protect privacy. In some instances, similar cases have been consolidated into one example. Dreams, however, are reported verbatim as they were reported to me.

Foreword

THREADS, KNOTS, AND TAPESTRIES REVEALS THE WAY OUR dreaming expresses and reflects our deep interpersonal and environmental interconnectivity. Our dreams are no longer to be viewed as of personal significance only. My dreams may not only open my heart and extend my awareness, they can open and extend yours as well. Your dreams, your spouse's, or your neighbor's may have important implications for your own life or situation. Drawing upon her decades of Jungian analytic practice, and many years of pioneering in dream groups, Castleman weaves a rich tapestry of dream threads that shows us how we are dreaming with and for each other. Her method is that of a storyteller telling the stories of people and their dreams, of shamans, of individuals suffering from cancer, love entanglements—and, most delightfully, stories that show how dreams are woven together with communal life in other cultures, as well as in our own.

Castleman draws our attention to this deep place of interconnectivity from which dreams spring, and calls it the "tribal dream field." She supports her thesis not only with personal examples and stories of dream group participants, but also with Jung and shamanism. She takes us into the story of Black Elk, the Lakota holy man and healer whose dream-visions were danced and enacted with the participation of the tribe, and shows us how the Lakota understanding of dreams had a larger-than-personal significance. This underscores her own mission of establishing dream groups as a way of doing inner work, weaving it together with our lives, loves, and relationships with the outerworld.

Her method of writing is accessible and clear, and resembles the way dream images, dream series, and communal dreamings interweave and even imply each other. After the first chapter one can dip into the book anywhere for a rich perspective on the power of dreams (our own and those of others) to open the heart and extend our horizons.

Therapists will be delighted to find ground rules for setting up and running dream groups. Laypeople will find new ways to dialogue and explore their dreams with spouses, children, and friends.

C. Michael Smith, Ph.D.
Author of *Jung and Shamanism in Dialogue* and
Psychotherapy and the Sacred
Adjunct professor of psychology and religion,
The Chicago Theological Seminary

Introduction

"Humankind has not woven the web of life. We are but one thread within it. Whatever we do to the web, we do to ourselves. All things are bound together. All things connect."

CHIEF SEATTLE

THE CONCEPT OF THE TRIBAL OR COMMUNAL FIELD FIRST emerged into my consciousness from my initial analysis out of my own dreams. The whisperings and soft hints were all around me, but it has taken years of observations and curiosities to discover a workable model for this almost-ignored layer of the psyche. The communal field is, simply put, the intersection of psyches in the unconscious. It is where we meet—and overlap and interconnect and affect—each other's realities and life path. It is relationship. It is, in classical Jungian terms, referred to as the *objective* level of dreaming, where exterior objective ("real") data manifests in the dream world. The objective approach to the meaning of dreams is in contrast to the ubiquitous, highly symbolic, *subjective* approach to dream images—where all aspects and figures in dreams are understood to be *parts of the dreamer.*

Jung was well aware of this less common, communal, tribal type of dreaming, even if he didn't point to it specifically. One early example is the "compensatory dream" to which Jung referred frequently in his writings. In *Memories, Dreams, Reflections,*

Jung related how he first began to discover this type of dream. The theory of compensation in dreams became a cornerstone of Jungian psychology where the unconscious dream image balances or compensates the conscious ego attitude. Like the scales of justice, the dream maker presents the "other side" of our many one-sided attitudes. Jung dreamed about a woman he had in analysis who "aroused [his] doubts" (Jung 1973, 133). Although he had begun to find their work together shallow and unproductive, in Jung's dream his patient appeared in a castle high on a hill, and in order to see her he had to "bend his head way back." He even awakened with a crick in his neck. From this he realized he had undervalued her and his dream was *correcting* his one-sided attitude. He did not interpret or understand his dream as only parts of himself, that the woman portrayed an aspect of feminine nature, his anima, that he was removed from and so on. Rather, Jung saw the dream as real objective information that was about the relationship between him and her, and he realized how his attitude had adversely affected his treatment. After his dream, the analysis improved. In general, compensatory dreams that confront our one-sidedness can facilitate outer change. We do not live and dream in separate hermetically sealed cells but are woven together in an intricate pattern of relationships.

Jung taught in more detail about the dilemma of the objective or subjective interpretation of dreams in a dream analysis seminar that he conducted in 1928–1930 (Bollingen Series, 1984). In the following quote, Jung addressed the important issue of interpreting the dreams of married persons (and others in close relationships) because the spouse who appears in such dreams often represents him / herself rather than simply portrays the part of the dreamer (also referred to as a *projection*):

> We came here to a most important consideration: the
> fact that when one is analyzing married people, or people

who are in very close relationship even if it is not marriage, then one simply cannot deal with their psychology
as a separate factor; it is as if one were dealing with two
people, and it is exceedingly difficult to disentangle the
individual belongings from the relationship. One finds
invariably that the so-called individual psychology of
such a case is only explicable under the assumption that
another human being is functioning in that mind at the
same time; in other words it is relationship psychology
and not the psychology of an isolated human individual.
[. . .] It is even very difficult to isolate the individual parts
from the related parts. So we can hardly consider such a
dream as his own property; it would be his wife's just as
much. His psychology is in her as hers in him, and every
dream that each one has is more or less an expression of
that relatedness. . . . (Jung, *Dream Analysis,* 559)

Jung goes on to say that "[s]uch a dream is only understandable when you take it as the expression of a relationship. It is as if
he and his wife had come together in the night and concocted a
dream, issuing a statement that was equally true for either side"
(560). And, finally, Jung makes the following impassioned statement that encapsulates the thesis of my book: ". . . according to
my experience a vast majority of the dreams of married people are
of this kind.[1] Also, of course, people who are not married but who
are related to somebody. Or even if they are not closely related to
anybody, they are still interpenetrated by external factors." (561).

Relational, tribal, communal dreaming is precisely what this
book is about—it is dreaming that arises from and speaks through
what I term the "tribal field" or "communal field." It is where
dreams inform the psyche about our relationships, not merely
about parts of ourselves (although that approach to the material
is almost always informative and helpful, as well). But it simply

does not encompass the whole picture, just as one would not want to look at a great painting with pieces blocked from view. Besides seeing dreams as factually corrective in relationships, when one looks at dreams from a tribal view they take on a host of meanings and indications. Most of these clues about our unconscious tribal psyche arise in dream groups. Some emerge even in one-on-one analysis. The experiences that most reveal the complex intersections of our dream time often involve synchronicity.

BLACK ELK AND THE LAKOTA DREAM-FIELD

I owe the Lakota a great debt for this work because without the brave elders' willingness to tell their stories to biographers, none of this may have come into my consciousness. I feel certain I would not have realized the importance and power of the dream-group experiment. The Lakota people knew their dreams and visions were meant for the entire tribe, not just for individuals. They also were aware that dreams hold important literal information about events and relationships, as well as the sacred realm. In fact, in their belief system, if one kept silent about an important vision, one would become ill or even die because the vision was meant to be a gift to the community. There are numerous examples of people following and not following the spiritual urgings from their visionary process, but perhaps the single most poignant example with which I am familiar is Black Elk's.

I vividly recall reading *Black Elk Speaks* as I lunched by myself at Little Shanghai restaurant in Denver sometime in 1980. As I read Black Elk's words, I was seized by such a powerful emotion that I broke down and started crying. It was unusual for me to cry then—even in sad movies—but there I sat, sobbing, shaking, and acutely aware I was making the waitress and myself highly uncomfortable. And yet, I couldn't seem to help it. I couldn't read Black Elk's story of the Horse Dance without my feelings coming to a crescendo. The climax of his long suffering, which resulted in his people honoring him with a three-day ceremony that became a permanent part of the Lakota tradition, moved me to tears. Young Black Elk, alone with the power of his remarkable vision, was perplexed and dismayed by what he had experienced. At the early age of nine he had been in a state of visionary grace that lasted days. His parents thought he was going to die, but finally he came back into his body and back to consciousness. Afterward, he felt tormented, depressed, even mentally unbalanced. To a much lesser degree I identified with his depression, confusion, and lack of purpose. I too had experienced deep personal self-doubt about my sanity, my value, and my worth as a person. I had not experienced Black Elk's vision or anything like it, but I knew the same feelings of alienation and aloneness. Unlike me, however, Black Elk (dismal as his history is in its full context) had a supportive community to help him bring his vision into the world. He had friends, relatives, teachers, and mentors who devoted three days in complex preparations and time-consuming activities to pay homage to the gift Black Elk and all of his people had received. For several years Black Elk had held his vision inside, close to his breast where it only tormented and troubled him. But when he finally shared his vision with a teacher, it was received so gently, so respectfully and kindly, that his life's purpose became clear. His doubt slipped away, and his spirit was lifted. As I read and wept, I knew neither I nor anyone else I knew had the community to support such a vision. I knew the church declared visions heretical, psychiatry declared them pathological, and regular folks usually just shook their heads and said, "weird." All of this disparagement had kept me closed off—until I entered Jungian analysis. But even Jungian analysis, with its healing emphasis on dreams and inner soul life, cannot substitute for living in a tribal community where the presence of the sacred is part of the culture, where visions are enacted and honored, and where discovering the meaning of dreams is a daily occurrence.

Unfortunately, to buy (once or more each week) the time of a professional, someone to whom we tell our secrets, our hopes, our sufferings—someone who by law is emotionally and relationally distant—is not the same experience as having a tribal elder stay up all night to learn the songs one has been given in a vision. So I was saddened—for myself by what is not present in my culture, and for Black Elk and other native people whose magnificent customs have been lost due to oppression from the larger people and culture. Even then I wondered if there might be a way for a community to honor a person's dream or vision without the process turning cult-like or psychologically dangerous.

In my analysis that began in 1979 I became acquainted with other people who were also in analysis with the same analyst. We met at classes and parties and became a community of sorts. Before long, a great deal of discussion about our dreams, our analysis, and our analyst ensued, and we formed a tight-knit group. We spent many evenings and weekends in activities designed to manifest the unconscious. Through no fault of the analyst, I then became involved with a few of these people in what I can only describe as a difficult and even dangerous boundary invasion. The friendships all blew up and the close times seemed to be over. It was a frightening and confusing experience. Consequently, from the experience of letting people participate in my analytical inner life and from seeing the negative effects it could have, I developed a cautious style as an analyst candidate and later as an analyst. I did not encourage starvation vision quests, ritual bloodletting, or drug-induced initiations that some healers/shamans seemed to invite. Tossing people into contact with the unconscious was not a favorite emphasis of mine. Rather, I focused on how to process one's ever-present, rich, unconscious material that, to me, seemed ever-apparent and accessible in the psyche. Having the vision is not the trick, it is what the vision means and how it changes one's life that is the more significant issue. The unconscious venue is quite seductive, and one can easily be inflated by the magic and mystery of the manifestations that come forth so easily. The earnest seeker knows his / her experiences are not the end—they are only a window or clue to greater consciousness and understanding.

Unfortunately, modern culture, as I have experienced it, does not provide a place or space to understand, honor, process, and digest this rich unconscious matter. In fact, it seems to deny it, label it, and condemn it over time. This is why Black Elk's community touched me so deeply. Here a connected tribal culture was well able to integrate the young Black Elk's vision into its collective religious mythos.

What also made a profound impression on me was how dreams and visions were experienced as tribal phenomena and not solely as an individual event. I found examples in the written accounts where one person's dream would be understood as a message to someone else, and instances in which a dream could be seen as crucial for the tribe's survival. I read about a person's name being changed because of someone else's dream, a ceremony altered or adjusted because of a person's vision, two people dreaming of each other on the same night being initiated in the "twin dreamer" lodge, or a community forming around people who dreamed of the same animal.

Imagine you are a Lakota, about twelve years old, awakening one morning with a stirring dream. You tell your father you dreamed the night before of being a wolf. You were in the forest, on all fours, and when you looked down at yourself you were surprised to see your furry legs and paws instead of hands and feet. You experienced fully being a wolf, the heightened sense of smell, of hearing. Never before had you dreamed like this. Your father is reserved, but you can see he is pleased. He sends the tribal messenger to tell every teepee that his child has had a great wolf dream. Then he selects the finest of your family's horses and leads it into camp, announcing a give-away. Then your grandmother appears with one of her best deerskins, tanned and soft as velvet, to add to the horse-gift. Next, a group of elders comes to your teepee to fetch you for a special meeting—and you realize they are all wolf dreamers and members of the wolf lodge. You gather together, and they listen intently while you repeat your dream in detail. They ask questions. They desire to know every aspect of your dream—did you receive a song, a message, an object? Your dream and all the information contained in it is memorized and thoughtfully pondered. Then, in a secret ceremony that you never reveal to anyone who is not a wolf dreamer, you are initiated into this lodge of which you will remain a member until you die.

It seems clear that the Lakota's approach to their interior soul was vastly different from Western-European religious attitudes, as well as from the modern psychological approach to dream material. The Lakota people already knew, in their own way, about Carl Jung's discovery of the collective unconscious—and perhaps they understood it at a more significant level.

Jung asserts there is a personal and a collective unconscious. To state it briefly, the "personal unconscious" contains a repository of our memories, wishes, fantasies, and personal experiences—it is uniquely an individual's own material. Additionally, Jung rightly noted the existence of a "collective unconscious"—the field of inner archetypal existence where psyches encounter the common ground of reality. His theory explains why there are vast similarities in disconnected cultures regarding their art, myths, religious beliefs, and so on.[2]

But what Jung wrote less about is the space in the middle—the territory that lies between the personal and the collective unconscious. This is the field of psychic reality the Lakota knew well. It is the place where relationship affects the unconscious. It also involves a precognitive dimension (to know ahead of time) that is baffling to the ego that we Jungians call synchronicity. It contains material about "we" rather than "I" or "one." It is the communal level of the unconscious, or, in other words, the place where two psyches, or groups of psyches, intersect in a colorful complex tapestry.[3]

The tribal field clarified itself when I began my analytical practice as a candidate to become a Jungian analyst. Right away, I noticed oddities that other therapists and analysts I talked to said they experienced as well; for example, the embarrassing way my clients would mirror issues I was currently working on. Again and again people would begin therapy or analysis with me only to outline my own process in the first session. Issues that were not public knowledge, some very fresh, would land in my office. I noticed, too, how similar certain sessions were over a day or a period of days. Peculiar synchronicities would occur from one session to the next without clients' knowledge. I might hear three very similar dreams in three different sessions over the course of a day or an issue like a mother's birthday gift might be mentioned several times in a week. Only recently I heard the image "amphitheatre" mentioned in analysis or in dream images four times in one week One week seven of my clients traveled to New York City for holidays in the same week of October. Currently I am seeing three terminally ill clients, all of whom had begun seeing me long before the illness or prognosis was known. Other oddities occurred, as well. I noticed my clients would wear similar clothing on a given day, or sometimes I would be dressed almost identically to one or two of them. Then, other synchronicities occurred. I ran into clients in unexpected places, and some had connections to people in my past from another part of the country, connections that defied rational explanation; others would bring a dream in that I had had myself that morning.

My thoughts returned to the Lakota people. They lived a tribal life. They shared diet, customs, geography, religious beliefs, daily activities, a gene pool. They dressed alike, lived in similar structures, participated in similar daily activities and religious rituals. I cannot imagine what tribal life would be like, but when I think about it I sense a longing in myself. I have an instinctive feeling that alienation and much modern "loss of soul" would diminish. Human beings couple, form family groups, extended family groups, and tribes or clans. In modern life our tribal connection is severed. An entire development of human social behavior has been lost to modern civilization.

In the modern and postmodern era we have lost connection to the tribal life we social beings have operated within since antiquity. The ring of relationships, including initiators, mentors, teachers, shamans, spiritual advisors, and dream interpreters, was once contained within the tribal social structure. This layer of relationship does not exist in the same sense in modern times, but it still resides within the psyche and within our souls. It is the area where we intersect in dreams, where our psyches meet and interact in the most powerful ways. It is the archetypal realm of connection that includes love, hate, war, and procreation. We are modern men and women in search of a soul that is nearly impossible to discover because we have lost a significant and essential layer of our social structure. According to anthropological studies in Ireland, Africa, North and South America, as well as all over the world, tribes and clans have been a part of human social development for most of human history (about two million years) and hominid history (five million years). Tribal life is also evidenced in the mammalian world. Thus, one can surmise that the tribal existence is very old in our brains. In our modern era, however, all of this is lost. We don't speak the same language, come from the same gene pool, wear the same clothing, have history together, travel together, live in community together. Within the tribal life of antiquity, one could find his first teacher, learn his first medicine songs, learn to hunt, bead, sew, weave, plant, and seek the inner spirit's voice. This type of social support is only recently lacking in the modern age. It is missing now even though humans lived with it for thousands of years. Currently we are scattered and dissipated into fragments, short relationships, fractured encounters, piecemeal connections. But the dream world does not know we have given up tribal life. Our psyches still operate in the old way; the authors of our dreams pick characters from our connecting tribe to use in our nighttime dramas, which inform us about ourselves, about the persons in whom we dream, and about our relationships.

Analysis, it seems, is an individual container, and is not to be tampered with by the messy stuff of relationships. However, this individualistic attitude is challenged by the Lakota approach to dreams, because, as I have been arguing, many dreams are meant for the whole tribe, or are at least important for all the characters in the dream, regardless of who dreamed it. I asked myself how something, anything, could be provided for people to create a safe, grounded, yet deep enough process for a community vision to manifest? Dream groups came to mind. I had seen various types of groups throughout my graduate school and Zurich educations. I had seen how powerful and bonding they could be. I knew they were potentially dangerous, too. But my thoughts returned to the Lakota. Could people together bring their dreams to a group setting and find support as well as illumination? Could one person's dream impact another's? Would dreams about each other be relational information or would we be stuck in the subjective interpretation box where all characters in dreams are parts of the dreamer? Would we have the courage, and did I have the skill, to take people into a psychological and spiritual place that would manifest healing and understanding? I didn't know, but I wanted to try.

What follows are the stories and tales of forming dream

groups, their failures and successes, the questions and perhaps some answers they bring to the analytical table. I have also included tribal, synchronistic, and relational stories from my individual cases in this discussion. My hope is that the mystery of our meaning to each other, for each other, among each other, can be, ever so slightly, illuminated here.

Part One

Threads

CHAPTER ONE

Structure of Dream Groups

STRUCTURE

IN THE YEAR 2002, ON AN ORDINARY TUESDAY MORNING, I came to a regular dream group meeting—regular because it had met every week since 1990 or so, and this Tuesday was no different from all the other times we had sat together in our dream community. The week before, N. had shared a long dream, entitled "The Girl in the Tub." To quote:

> . . . *In a back room there was a large tub . . . a marble tub and about 6–8 candles sitting across the back wall. In the tub was this fat bleached-blonde girl, naked with a lot of water and bubbles, rubbing water on herself. . . men were sitting and standing and leaning against the back wall and on the floor masturbating. The men were totally focused on her.*

The week before, this dream had captured the group's attention, and we spent the entire session exploring its meaning, its twists and turns. For the most part, the focus of the dream work was N.'s life experience as a sex object. N. is classically attractive, as well as warm and open, and most men do a double take when she walks in the room. But as we started this group, A. was clearly eager to share something. She announced, "I have a 'dream group' event to tell about." Then she described her weekend—a quick trip to L.A. with her husband and a visit to the J. Paul Getty Museum. Then she showed us a print she had purchased from the museum shop of one of their paintings. It was Cézanne's "The Eternal Feminine" which depicts a naked, plump, blonde girl lying in / on a white bed / floor / tub being watched by an assortment of men. The painting well represents in image form the plurality of the masculine element as well as the singularity of the feminine element—so prominent in dreams. In addition, the art reveals the fascination, the spellbinding dumbstruck intrigue, that women and the feminine archetype hold as a power over the masculine. She is the focus, she is the center, and she is the "object."

With A.'s synchronicity (so common in dream group, yet ever an experience that produces an awe and respect for life's mysteries), we amplified this event, an event the group saw as significant for everyone present—in part because the group field constellated the process. This group of men and women explored and delighted in N.'s dream, in A.'s art discovery, and in how these issues were universal and pertinent for each one of us.

But it takes some time on the potter's wheel before the vessel is ready to sit on the fire. Dream group is much like crafting a cauldron; it needs to be watertight, able to withstand high heat, and ultimately fulfill its purpose of being able to "cook the stew." The recipe for this stew follows—with full acknowledgment that all good cooks vary recipes and all fine potters make their own distinct creations.

Dream groups can be structured into various formats. I have explored three possibilities: meeting every week for an hour and a half, meeting alternate weeks for three hours, and meeting once a month for an all day retreat. I have formed groups that were all women, men and women, all clergywomen, all therapists, all families that have suffered a recent suicide, and all women incarcerated in jail. I have not facilitated an all-male group. I have used a male co-facilitator in one group, which has been enriching and exciting. Each of these models works and probably other variations could be successful too. Each model has its own plusses and minuses, of course. Meeting weekly keeps the group members in regular touch with each other's lives, and a personal familiarity forms rather quickly; however, there is less dream material covered in this model because the time taken to report life events on a weekly basis necessarily erodes the dream process time. The same "catching up" occurs in the other models, but more time then is left for dream work. In the weekly group usually only one dream is processed per session, but the lack of dream process time is fully compensated for by the significant and enduring relationships that develop.

In the second model, meeting every other week for three hours certainly provides an intimate container as well, but more time is spent on dreams. Often, the dreams will be compared and contrasted to each other, common themes mentioned, and other connections noticed. By processing so much dream material at one time (usually around six dreams), the group moves to a quieter, more reflective state. It's easier to stay hidden longer in the first model, but like all of the dream groups I have experienced, people who hide eventually come out of hiding or leave the group voluntarily. The second model produces a pondering introspective tenor; occasionally members feel they have entered into an altered state of consciousness during dream group.

In the third model, the pattern of deep reflection is amplified even more. After seven hours together, the members report an intensity that is almost unbearable. I have only used therapists as participants in this last model. The members see each other just once a month, so there is less ongoing personal interaction regarding their waking world activities, but much more emphasis is placed on their inner realities. Sometimes they report feeling exhausted or "blown away" at the end of the day. All who have a dream to share are most often able to, and the entire group does other inner work as well as dream work. I use active imagination, art tissue paper collage, writing exercises, meditations, and so on. Again, time is spent not only seeing themes and congruities between members' work, but also congruity between individual member's dreams and art processes. One begins to see each person's process (overarching unconscious issues striving to attain consciousness) manifest in the variety of modalities explored throughout the day. In this model, dreams are anchored with art or writing and thus amplified.

Curiously, I find seven participants is usually an ideal number in all three dream group models. This way, if one or two members are absent, the group still has enough synergy left in the remaining participants to constitute a group field. And seven allows time for all of the members to be included in the group process. Even if participants aren't working on their own dream with the group, there is still significant participation from all of the members that allows dream group to be therapeutically significant for each member. Seven allows inclusion and comfort. A large dream group can become chaotic, and reticent members remain uninvolved for long periods. Another therapist may find a different number ideal for him / her. I am familiar with groups that are as small as two participants, and they have been quite helpful for the members. The difficulties tend to arise when groups become too large, and ultimately the facilitator has to decide what the right number is.

The following description is how one dream group might look, but please note that all of the dream groups, regardless of their size, gender composition, or type of participants, always develop their own unique character. Over the past seventeen years I've noticed that some groups are more formal than others, and some focus more on Jungian concepts and use the time as an opportunity for group study. Some focus more on dreams than others. However, the description that follows is a window into a typical dream group.

Members gather in my inner office, the consulting room where I hold analysis and dream group meetings. The room is painted a dark mossy green to evoke the sense of entering into a cauldron or vessel. The carpeting is deep purple, and the wall opposite the entrance door is a wall of floor-to-ceiling windows that reveal a garden filled with mature live oaks, maples, Japanese maples, and rhododendrons. I have a leather sectional, leather chairs, and a wicker rocker grouped in a circle where eight or ten can sit comfortably. One wall is covered with four library shelves, and the back corner is taken up by my computer desk. It is a cozy room with some cloud paintings, an alchemical etching, and a marble sculpture of a nude woman's torso.

As the members file in, they start to "catch up" or "get current," as one group liked to put it. They may tell updates on a grandchild's health, how the new remodeling is coming, or what the dean said in the last faculty meeting. They may discuss the war, the Academy Awards, a book, or Anna Nicole Smith. Politics and other collective issues are usually processed in group. The sociological level of stress is a real one that necessitates a group in which to process. A war is difficult to think about all by oneself. It almost cries out for community to tell the story, to ponder the consequences, and so on. Therefore, all of the main events that have occurred in the last seventeen years have been discussed in my groups, and that is often how the group gets started. If it is September 11th or a presidential election that is sent to the Supreme Court, it may even take the entire group time. But most often the outer events processed are wrapped up in around fifteen minutes.

At this point I ask the group to set the agenda for the meeting. In a group that meets for an hour and a half weekly, we review where we left off the week before, see if the dreamer wants to continue to work more on his/her dream, and if not, conclude the dream with thoughts from the dreamer and the group about how the dream "percolated" over the week. Then the group decides who the next person will be to work on a dream. How is that done? Oddly, I have not experienced anyone demanding or posturing or acting out around "sharing the dream" time. The group members naturally take turns based on who has not worked on a dream lately. Occasionally, when I sense someone is hogging the time a bit (usually a new member), I simply turn to a long-term member and say, "We haven't heard a dream from you in a while, do you have one to share?" But this is the most proactive I've been and have only had to say this a few times over the years. I even feel a little hesitant to take this much leadership, since I prefer to let the group process dictate the tenor of the group. Naturally, if one person is hogging, it is material that is useful to process. The person taking too much time would eventually be confronted by another member and feelings would come to the surface. This is how traditional therapy groups are run, and they are extremely useful. Sometimes, I dodge this approach just a bit to keep the emphasis on dreams. But there are times, in each and every group, that I have had to run a classical process group so relationships and issues between group members and issues with myself were given an open and trusting place to process. With some groups of people, it might be necessary to "take numbers" so that people have a place in line. They can defer if they don't want to work that day or haven't remembered a dream in a while.

In my group that meets for three hours and in the group that meets for seven hours, it is my intention that each session cover one dream per member so the issue of who gets to work is not germane; however, the order of turn is. Sometimes I run out of time and one person gets shortchanged, so who gets to go first or second is important. When one member continues to go last, he / she invariably gets confronted by the group about what is going on with the behavior. When someone gets left out, I try to start with that person the next meeting. Again, the groups are mature and generous about the dream time, partly because all the members gain from hearing the dreams, not just the person who has had the dream. Also, many of the people in my dream groups are therapists themselves, and this may skew my experience.

Next, the dream work begins. First, issues are brought up that the member wants to work on or simply share which may include anything from a job search to a divorce to feelings about the group or me. Then the dream is told to the group. Some bring their journals and read straight from them, others simply tell the dream, and still others type them and bring copies. My style is to lead the discussion at this point. I ask for associations to the dream images as well as any pertinent data in the outer waking world that may affect the meaning of the dream. Context is especially important in dreams, and all of the surrounding life issues need to be understood to hear the dream with some clarity. Members help in this process, asking a lot of questions about areas that need to be clarified. Together, we sort of "pump" the dreamer. At some point, an indeterminate one, but one that "feels" right, I ask the dreamer to make an attempt to say what the dream is revealing. Sometimes I help a little, but with the statement that my thoughts are only speculations, not interpretations. Other members may suggest *possible* meanings or thoughts or insights, too. Then, when the dreamer is ready to stop, we let the dream "rest." Finally, other members may say how the dream or the work affected them as well, or how the dream may have provoked her / his own process. I may ask the group, "Why did you need to hear this dream?" Or the group may simply want to react or celebrate or support or ventilate about the material that has been discussed. Then, the next person takes a turn.

I close with a wrap-up, homework, comments on the common themes for the day, other thoughts of insight or gratitude for the openness and courage of the participants. Sometimes in groups we have closed with prayer, laying on of hands, energy work, chanting, a meditation, a joke. Just anything goes, but there is an ending, a closure similar to an hour of analysis. The members leave, filing out of the office. Almost all of my groups have augmented dream group with lunch after group or breakfast before. As I will emphasize in this book, the community and the relationships formed in dream group are the most significant aspects of the work.

APPROPRIATE MEMBERS FOR DREAM GROUP

Over the years, I have seen a surprising variety of people benefit from dream group. People from their twenties to their seventies, married or single, well-to-do or struggling financially, gay or straight, male or female. I have included artists, actors, clergypersons, therapists, attorneys, homemakers, nurses, secretaries, financial planners, engineers, corporate executives, retirees, physicians, teachers, exotic dancers, as well as many others in dream group. My experience is that most people who make the effort to seek information about joining a dream group are "suitable" individuals for the work; i.e., relatively open, honest, searching people with an interest in dreams or in understanding their interior self.

There are, however, people who have no business being in a dream group since their presence may be injurious to the group, or even to themselves. Some people are not suitable simply because they are too afraid to encounter their "essential self" (see glossary) that dream work demands. The general public carries the attitude that dreams are fun or entertaining or "cool," and thus learning about them is a curious parlor activity. Nothing could be farther from the truth. Dreams sear to the bone and open us to a vast and vulnerable territory that closed, supercilious, or defended people cannot tolerate. If, in an initial interview to determine whether a person would be a good fit for a dream group, the defended personality is not fleshed out, it will quickly do so. Such new members will remove themselves because they find they are "too busy" or "there is too much traffic" or "I need the daylight to weave" or "dream group takes too much of my time."

The population that is most unsuitable for dream groups consists of individuals who suffer from serious emotional disorders. Poor "ego function" is the key. Without a stable ego, digesting material from the unconscious as presented in dreams is too frightening. Examples of such persons are those with histrionic, borderline, or narcissistic personality disorders. In general, these people take too much of the group time and energy. They may lack empathy (which is necessary for group cohesion), be obsessed with envy or competition, or be prone to wild displays of emotion. Their ego or conscious known self is weak. This results in an unpredictable, unbalanced personality. When unjustified, raging, attacking viciously, running out of the group room in a temper—all are unfortunate examples of what may happen when unstable people start poking around in their interior psyches.

The first level of work is to establish ego solidity. This includes the ability to be self-reflective, the willingness to acknowledge responsibility where appropriate, the ability to feel and express compassion for others, and a sense of sharing the group space without needing to dominate or control others. When these attitudes are present, the person is ready to encounter a rich and fruitful experience from participating in a dream group.

Perhaps surprising to some, women incarcerated in jail have been some of the most "suitable" people I've encountered. People who have survived the suicide of a loved one and people with addictive issues have proved likewise suitable. The personality traits most required by dream work encompass courage and humility, compassion and curiosity, and are present in a vast number of people, quite separate from their life circumstances.

Expressing emotion, however, is vastly different from wild acting out—and yet it is not the only evidence of deep interpersonal work at hand. In dream group the explosive emotional personality is detrimental to the goal of the group. In some ways it is almost dictatorial. In the presence of strong emotion, other members tend to feel muzzled. Additionally, it can be difficult for an overly defended person to try to integrate into a dream group. The type of personality that is devoid of imagination, that cannot see anything beyond the facts, may be stunted in its ability to leap to the symbolic expression of meaning. Indeed, training analysts have noted the existence of persons who are incapable of thinking symbolically, no matter how much we endeavor to teach it to them.

THE FACILITATOR

The dream group leader is an essential ingredient, perhaps the most significant variable in whether or not a group solidifies. I define group solidity as: regular, consistent participant attendance; generally long-term commitment to the group with a minimum of members coming and going; and the development of mutual trust, openness, and vulnerability among the participants. The facilitator sets the tone that encourages or discourages this solidity. Quintessentially, he / she must have a connection to the Self—a significant encounter with the unconscious—that is not unlike a shamanic initiation. This results in, among other things, the individual being able to understand the metaphorical realm of dreams. The work of a dream group leader is that of a storyteller and a storykeeper—a person who tends the fire of transformation. This is not an intellectual pursuit or accomplishment. This is not something one can learn from reading about it. This is not something in which one can become skilled without substantial involvement in one's own dreams and one's own process.

The leader needs to be assertive but nonjudgmental. Dreams have to be "worked," and someone needs to lead the process. This requires being able to handle some strong-minded adults and at the same time maintain an attitude that is kind, rather than one that bullies. The dream group facilitator's skill level with dreams is a significant aspect of forming group solidity. Understanding dreams is a life-long pursuit; they are complex, contradictory, and not nearly as apparent as they appear. It follows that since dreams are sophisticated, the facilitator's knowledge must be so as well. However, being a master of all the subtleties of dream work is not necessary to facilitate a fruitful dream group. Many seasoned analysts I know, myself included, would not claim to be "masterful" at dreams—they are far too mysterious and mercurial for most to ever make that claim. But exposure to dream work is a necessary preparation for any facilitator. There will be exceptions to my assertion, but they are the exception and probably most often relate to extraordinary individuals with innate talent to understand the metaphorical language of dreams. I have met a few of these people, and their abilities and gifts are significant. But most people, including most therapists, have to experience dream work firsthand to become proficient in the complex, enigmatic language of the dream maker. Making a dream analysis, attending a dream group, or reading informative books about the subject are ways to begin.

For the most part, the facilitator's skill with dreams will lie more in what not to do or say, rather than the contrary—not to judge, not to advise, not to inject one's own opinion or attitude, not to fall into a complex, not to jump to canned symbol interpretation, not to use pat answers, not to be disgusted about anything in a dream, not to label, but to listen and follow the process of the dreamer's dream. What follows is guidance for the facilitator, acknowledging that some statements have exceptions, since dreams and dream work can almost always be turned upside down, resulting in an entirely different perspective.

CHAPTER TWO

Keys to Understanding Dreams

THE MAGIC OF THE DREAM MAKER LIES IN THE WORK THAT can be uncovered by examining images, feelings, metaphors, and symbols that appear in dreams. This is the language of our deep, archaic, ancient brain—which is also the language of literature and poetry. It is from the framework of literary devices that one can begin to understand dream stories. The use of puns is widespread, hyperbole is almost an ever-present element, and metaphor is the stock in trade. In addition, the images have to be decoded through the technique of making personal associations and (occasionally) archetypal amplification. All of this information has to be put into context regarding the dreamer's current situation, past issues still tickling the psyche, future concerns, trends that loom ahead, as well as all of the relationships that weave in and out of this intricate life pattern. Dreams may have within them body sensations, emotional outbursts, "clear as a bell" insights, knowledge that bursts forth right in the dream, or even a voice that utters a direct message.

Most dreams and their messages have to be teased out, coaxed out of hiding like getting the cat to come out from under the bed. Like cats, dreams are quick to scamper away. One forgets or dismisses dream material because our modern culture does not allow for this aspect of human life to be integrated and validated. Dreams, experiences as common to all people as a change in the weather, are nonetheless largely laughed at or forgotten. It is for this reason that the facilitator's patience and gentle attitude are so important. Cats don't come out from under the bed in response to our aggressive actions but by quiet, safe coaxing. Likewise, in dream work the dreamer has to be invited repeatedly to "go on, jump in and be brave."

Dreams do not come from a rational plane; therefore, it is inadvisable to reduce a dream to a small simple meaning. "A" does not equal "B" and "this" does not mean "that." Some dreams simply remain a mystery, which is preferable to driving toward "meaning." Mystery trumps meaning in the dream world. All books of symbols are suspect until the dreamer gives personal associations to dream images; even then it takes finesse and skill to ascertain the meaning of the dream. Personal associations have to do with the collection of memories, attitudes, and opinions around an object, issue, or figure in a dream. For one person, a red car may evoke adolescence, power, and autonomy since that was the color of a first treasured car. For another, it may have been the place of a first sexual encounter—and whether it was positive or negative will greatly affect the significance of the image of a red car in a dream. Or the red car could be the color of a car the dreamer was rear-ended by last week—then the image might represent a crash or relate specifically to the recent experience of the car accident.

Dreams are to be absorbed, taken in by osmosis, not reduced to a fine point or two and then dismissed. The natural tendency of ego consciousness is to reduce, encapsulate, generalize, and basically diminish the quality of the dream. The dream is just fine if it brings more questions than answers, more confusion than clarity, more uncomfortable feelings than reassurance. The dream is like looking at a fine piece of art in a museum. A painting can lose effect if the tape player in one's ear demands we see the painting or sculpture as meaning this or that—the meaning is something for the viewer to gain for him / herself.

Additionally, it is natural to make symbols mean patent things. It is common to forego all data and revert to what we believe is true—most often the ego is looking for corroboration rather than challenge. Therefore, it is easy to rely on clichés in dream images. Red does not mean anger or sexuality unless the dreamer agrees it is so. Houses do not necessarily represent the self until the house image is deconstructed. Perhaps the dreamer is an architect, and houses have a very different meaning for him or her. Jumping to conclusions and not leaving the door open completely to possibilities is a certain error.

Here is a simple protocol for working on a dream:

  1. Date and record the dream thoroughly.

  2. List all of the images, characters, props, as well as the setting that appear in the dream.

  3. Make personal free associations to each item listed in #2. Take the time here to "get" the association. This is when the dreamer (no one else) has a clear certainty: "Oh! I know what that is about!" This step is hard to do all by oneself, which is one reason analysis or dream group can be vitally instructive. One can also use a "dream buddy," where two people trade off telling their dreams and associating aloud about the dream images. For some reason, just saying the words aloud is quite helpful in revealing the association. In the red car example, it would be necessary for the dreamer to sink back into the image and "open the red car file" by taking an inventory of the image; for instance: "I do or do not like this image;" "The history about this image is _____;" "This image (or person, animal, figure, etc.) reminds me of_____;" "The emotion I have about this dream image is _____." Some dream images are quite easy to decode; others remain elusive for

years. Most, however, can be brought to consciousness by following the coaxing method outlined here, as follows:

> *I dreamed I was in a job interview and there in the room with us was a tree that had chocolate kisses on it like pieces of fruit. I asked if I could pick one.*

In association to chocolate kisses the dreamer said:

> *Chocolate kisses, candy, sweet, a treat. Silence. Oh! Chocolate Kiss was the name of the hair color dye I bought for friends last weekend. They wanted to have their mother's hair dyed for her open-casket funeral and asked me to buy the hair color. A few days after the funeral the father called me and offered me a job.*

Now the chocolate kiss begins to make some sense. Before this, the image was seen as odd, mysterious, and not meaning anything. In this case, the chocolate kiss tree suggests bounty and fruit, since through association it referred to a literal job offer just days before. (Much more could be said about the chocolate-kiss tree, including the death-rebirth motif.)

4. Take a weather reading of "what is up" in the waking world. What is the dreamer aware of that is a current issue? Jobs, health, relationships, finances that are current difficulties or successes will be important background information. This is the conscious foundation from which the dream emerges. Dreams tend to be corrective or informative, so the current events of the dreamer's life are necessary in order to factor the dream's significance. Current events are not necessarily outer events. If a dreamer is thinking/feeling a lot about some childhood issues provoked by any number of things, this would be an "inner event" that would be a current event, and just as important as an outer event.

5. Connect the dots. After all of these steps are taken—steps that deconstruct the dream—then reconstruction is the next process. What is the overarching story the dream is telling? What is the plot or the "big picture" of the dream? What is the point? In dream work one benefits from looking at fine detail, then the big picture, looking at fine detail again, then the big picture again. Steps four and five can occur simultaneously, especially after the facilitator and/or dreamer become more adept at dream work.

6. Finally, a conclusion can be drawn: "What did I learn from this dream that I didn't already know?" or "What is this dream telling me?" or "How is this dream guiding/warning/correcting/encouraging me?" or "What is the good news/bad news in this dream?" Even after all of this work, the ego, or conscious self, remains in submission to the ultimate dream meaning. Some dreams prepare us for things we cannot know ahead, so "the meaning" is not necessarily "the point." For instance, a woman with an acute illness had the following dream:

I walk into a great house. It is old and beautiful. There are enormously tall ceilings, a grand carved staircase, antiques, and tapestries all about. As I survey the living areas I notice all the magnificent furniture needs to be recovered.

She was in chemotherapy at the time and hoped the dream meant she would get well. She understood recovering the furniture was a dream image that did not signal a "serious" problem—as if her dream house had burned down entirely. But sadly, as it turned out, this was a death dream. Here, her unconscious evidently portrayed the psyche or soul as grand and fine, but portrayed the ill body as only the fabric on the furniture that needed to be changed. Nonetheless, her dream did provide hope for her. As she declined and seemed to accept her death (although rapid and untimely), her dream was a beacon—it helped her approach death as a passage rather than as an end. The dream clearly elucidated the image of the eternal, the timeless, or out-of-time essence that remains—beyond life, beyond death.

Dreams are brilliant at producing situations and images that console, confront, and give hope simultaneously; for example, a common dream is one where the dreamer enters a house (that is my house in the dream but not my real house in my outer life) whereupon he / she discovers all kinds of space and rooms heretofore unknown. Often this dream is seen as a pat on the back for the ego: "I'm a lot more interesting than I thought, and there is so much potential in me." Actually, the dream has a sharp side too. The dream points out an enormous amount of unconsciousness on the part of the ego—unconsciousness that manifests as unlived life, resources going stale and left in storage. This dream may appear in the classic puer / puella psyche—the eternal youth who lives out both an aspect of irresponsibility in life commitments, as well as displays high energy for a number of heroic and creative endeavors. Their lives tend to be continually viewed in terms of potential rather than measured by accomplishment. The folk tale "The Tortoise and the Hare" illustrates well the puer personality that races ahead with confidence and verve but doesn't have the sustenance to finish the task.

One becomes more adept at understanding dreams with practice and patience. The dream world is an alternate world, a "separate reality" as Casteneda described, and with commitment to crack its code, one will eventually achieve a greater consciousness.

CHAPTER THREE

Tracking Complexes

ANOTHER NECESSARY INGREDIENT FOR THE "DREAM STEW"
is that the facilitator of a dream group should track the process[4]
of the members of dream group. Tracking the process is similar to
acting as a mirror. The mirror reflects, simply revealing back only
what is shown. This is similar to reflective listening. Reflective
listening is a counseling technique in which the therapist repeats
what the client says, sometimes rewording, sometimes abbreviat-
ing the client's statements as a way of listening empathetically.
This technique is powerful and artful when used by a skilled
therapist. Tracking the process, however, involves not only playing back to the subject language content, but also "reading" and
then checking out the client's feelings and attitudes the therapist
is sensing. One attends body posture and movement, breathing,
face color, what is being said, what is not being said, and, *especially
important,* the attitudes and beliefs of the subject—the subject's
world and reality. As an example, if a friend said to another
friend, "Oh, I'm so worried about finding a job," the response
might be, "Oh, I'm sure you will find a good one soon. You are
so talented at your work." This can be comforting and reassur-
ing, but it is not tracking the process. Suppose a client or dream
group member said the same: "I'm so worried about finding a

job." Then the facilitator would remain quiet or support the statement with a reflection: "Looking for work is anxiety provoking." This validates the statement rather than attempting to comfort the anxiety. Here is the mirror. The anxiety is the process, not the job, so a facilitator would not want to enable the anxiety to crawl back under a rock but would rather help shed light on it. The process is a force; it has emotional tone and tends to follow a path if the parties attending will notice the clues carefully. The dreamer or subject ultimately gives the clues about whether the process is being tracked. An analogy would be sailing, for those who have experienced this unique way to travel. The wind carries the boat because of the dynamics and position of the sails. The wind is the force and cannot be a contrary force—one has to use it to proceed forward. Likewise, the progressive force in the psyche is the wind; it has to be tracked and followed with directional integrity. The client or dream group member will usually give straightforward feedback about whether the facilitator is on target or not. Anytime one finds oneself disagreeing or arguing with a client it is pretty certain the process has not been tracked. When the facilitator is arguing, no doubt a complex has been hit.

Complexes are critical to track in working with dream groups; I have included a brief description of the phenomena. My hope is the reader will be curious enough to explore this notion further. Complexes are one of Carl Jung's remarkable contributions to the field of psychology, a concept he is often not given credit for, as well as one that is undervalued. Complexes and their understanding in oneself allow a level of consciousness that is significant. And it takes courage and persistence to affect this level of inner awareness. What is a complex? One definition is: "a feeling-toned, autonomous aspect of the psyche"[5]—which is, simply put, a part of us; one of the committee of voices and attitudes within that direct behavior. A complex will seem somewhat like an alternate personality in which our facial expressions, vocabulary, and postures are proscribed and repeated each time the complex is activated—quite unlike the primary, conscious, known personality. The complex is repetitious; the same phrases, feelings, and thought patterns take over the primary personality in a sly fashion. Usually the "I" one considers as his / her identity is the last to know a complex has arrived, raped, and pillaged before dawn breaks. Those who are in contact with the individual who is under siege will know well: "Mother is in that *mood* again."

Complex indicators abound, and it is helpful to know general ones as well as particular indicators unique to each person.[6] Emotional outbursts, fidgeting, not hearing, blushing, and changing one's tone of voice are some examples of indicators. Memory blocking is a favorite: when one "forgets" an important date or meeting, name, or responsibility. For those who aspire to consciousness, "forgetting" is not a *reason* to excuse behavior; it is only a *description* of how the complex tricked the ego into expressing unconscious feelings.

An illustration of this phenomenon: A woman and her family were invited to join her husband's extended family for a holiday dinner. When the hostess called, the woman asked if she could bring anything for the meal. It was decided she would bring Swedish meatballs. The two women planned the menu on the phone together, and Swedish meatballs were to be a significant feature of the meal. The families lived forty miles apart. So when the guest arrived late, "forgetting" the Swedish meatballs, there was no time to go back for it. The dynamics between the two women were tense and complicated but all went entirely unex-pressed. Competition and envy were the chief issues between them. When the Swedish meatballs were "forgotten," the woman was able to express hostility, anger, and a need to sabotage the meal. Naturally, her ego knew none of this. What she experienced was shame and frustration at "forgetting."

One who strives to know oneself will not let the complex get away with this trick of rationalization. I have often heard: "Since this created so much embarrassment for me, and I certainly didn't want to be embarrassed, I must have just forgotten it." This explanation is full of faulty logic because, of course, the one not bringing the meatballs to the dinner is exactly the same one who wishes not to be embarrassed—and the part that "forgot" won. Actually, this is an opportunity to see more clearly into one's genuine feelings and attitudes that the ego is resistant to knowing. Here is a window into the unconscious. The woman could have asked herself, "Why on earth would I have done that?" What feelings underneath might have contributed to the unconscious set-up that enabled her to foil the meal? If honest enough, she might then be able to acknowledge envy and anger for the in-law.

Another clue that one is in a complex is how those around us behave toward us—most often with complete exasperation. The complex wants empathy and sympathy but will not get it; instead, others are annoyed or turned off. In the case cited above one could imagine that the one who "forgot" would want comfort, but instead would find an icy assurance, at best, that the meatballs weren't that important. I find it quite informative to "read" my environment and let it tell me if I am in a complex or not. Dream groups can provide invaluable feedback for individuals in this instance. The feedback has to be delivered with tentative compassion, however.[7]

Complexes are tricky and elusive, but they can be mapped and tracked. Invariably, they are associated with strong feelings and emotional outbursts. The meatballs woman felt burning humiliation when she realized her mistake—and had a miserable time for the whole evening. The feelings a complex activates are so strong they have a residual effect that can last for days. Anytime one finds oneself overreacting, or feeling later that one expressed or felt too much emotion about an incident, one has tracked a complex. Then one knows an autonomous part of the self "took over" the reigning ego and was in charge for a while. Complexes are not terribly unique. A negative father complex can seem similar in many people—which is another way complexes can be tracked to determine if one has been hit: "Am I saying anything new? Is this information or feeling leading to a creative outcome, different than other times? Am I only repeating things I've said to myself for years? Does this emotion seem old, perhaps being triggered by past events?"

Let's take an example of a complex that doesn't involve others, but only manifests as an internal process. A dream group member shared the following story, which illustrates the pattern of the banal repetition a complex activates inside one's psyche. She was searching for a job in a difficult field, and, after a couple of years of her arduous quest, she finally made it into the short list of applicants for a fine position. She was flown out of town, interviewed, examined, and queried for a day and a half; then she flew home. Her complex was activated when, a few weeks later, she received a rejection letter. Naturally, one argues, this would bring up feelings in anyone—we are only human. Yes, she felt hurt and rejected, which were appropriate emotions given her circumstances. But then came the attack: the voice in her head said, "You're a loser, you're never going to get a job, you shouldn't have tried this pipe dream, you are an idiot, something's wrong with you that these interviewers see, and you will never, never be able to get a good job." By now she's in a terrible funk—in a very down and dirty place in the psyche. Her inner voice isn't very different from negative voices others have, too. In fact, I joke with group members that we could all trade this particular voice and no one would know a switch had been made. The behavior we are possessed by is a banal cliché—one has been in this space many times before. The voice is collective, non-unique, and has not once resulted in any positive behavioral change. In fact, at times it drives one to self-destructive behaviors: drinking, overeating, obsessive thoughts, and so forth.

Tracking these internal rumblings allows for a plethora of awareness and freedom. Finding victory and winning over the inner cruelty is a genuine way to transform. The facilitator of a dream group needs to track the complexes not only in the participants, but also in her / himself. A passion or fury is a warning sign. Any emotion that is "louder" than usual is one about which to be circumspect. Sometimes the client or group participant is "erased" in these furies, and no amount of consciousness can creep into the session. An emotion is, in part, a complex, and when one is in a complex, one is almost entirely deaf, dumb, blind, and follows a proscribed track that has no creative or new information in it. Bringing the emotion into the conscious process is a way to clarify it, as the following example demonstrates:

THERAPIST: I'm feeling outraged as you tell me your dream and your memories of your grandfather taking photos of you bathing nude with your cousin when you were both ten years old. I feel like saying you were sexually violated!

CLIENT: I can feel your anger, but I do not share it. I grew up in Scandinavia, and this was not a violation as I experienced it my culture. Here in the U.S. it would be unheard of.

THERAPIST: Well, I see I still have my own rage about experiences I had in childhood—as well as anger from many client's stories I have heard over the years. Tell me, what feeling does the bathing recollection bring up for you?

One can see this is a vastly more helpful dialogue than the therapist simply labeling the client sexually abused prompted by the therapist's personal history. That would miss the client's reality in favor of the therapist's. The best way for the therapist to avoid this all too human trap is to have a significant understanding of one's own issues and complexes. Without personal reflection and consciousness, it is nearly impossible to midwife someone else's.

Another warning sign of falling into a therapeutic prescription rather than a creative process (which signals a possible complex) is when one repeats oneself to clients. It is possible to be different with each client, especially the ones who have the same issues. Although syndromes do create similar issues for clients, each one is still unique. Dreams are the best route to facilitate the essential self of the client. They are completely individual and unique. Similar dreams don't mean the same for each person either. In dream group this is a special challenge. The members have to be coached over time to not project onto other members but to let the members discover on their own the rich jewels coming from the dream world. It is disappointing and painful to have one's sacred process perceived formulaically by well-intentioned (albeit misguided) group members.

COACHING THE LISTENER

The dreamer must be free to let the dream speak freely, free from the set notions of the facilitator or the members of the group. No one cares, least of all the dreamer, if one thinks this dream means one has to: (fill in the blank) confront mother, get more exercise, let go of anger about an old relationship, and so on. This is the judgment function that appears often in connection to hearing and listening to dreams. We human beings tend to advise, control, guide, and direct when it is of absolutely no use whatsoever. It is imperative that the listeners not tell their own stories as they listen to the dream material from a dream group member. This requires consciousness and patience. There will be plenty of time later to share how one's own process is evoked by the dream of another person, but initially the meaning or experience of the dream has to be ferreted out by the dreamer and the group acting as facilitators. The listeners need to be aware of their own current issues; otherwise, they are instantly plastered onto the dreamer with zeal and conviction. This is experienced quite negatively by the dreamer, who tends to feel unseen, controlled, and misperceived. Just because a person shows resistance to a possible hypothesis to a dream image, it does not necessarily mean the dreamer is resisting. Very often it means the listeners are on the wrong track and need to go in a different direction.

Years ago, quite reluctantly, I made a late-night call to my pediatrician. My infant son was ill with a high fever, and I called to ask the doctor if we needed to come into the emergency room. His response was to ask me what I thought about coming in or not. I queried him about asking me—how could I know, someone with no medical training and a new mother, if my child needed medical emergency treatment or not? He responded by telling me that over the years he had learned that mothers pretty much knew instinctively how ill their children were, and if he followed their gut reactions, he handled the case the best possible way. This is much like dream work. Let the dreamer lead the way.

Unfortunately, it is impossible to adequately cover even the rudiments of dream interpretation and the theory of complexes in this venue. The chief reason is that there are so many important exceptions to the rules—and exceptions to exceptions. The best way to listen to dreams, as well as all unconscious information, is to create an open, trusting, curious field. Then, both facilitators and dreamers can hear more creatively with their nonjudgmental attitudes. This is a skill that is hard to learn by reading about it. Furthermore, very different and yet equally valid experiences and interpretations can come from the very same dream. A dream is like a kaleidoscope with a myriad of facets to explore. The main point, however, is that a dream reveals to the ego something it does not already know. There is new information to be processed from the dream. This is the nugget, the jewel, the morsel that is fed to the ego each morning it has the discipline to recall an image, no matter how insignificant, brief, vague, silly, stupid, or pointless. I have never yet met a pointless dream. In this way, dream group is especially helpful in breaking down one's natural resistance, because there are so many people urging the dreamer to break into consciousness.

However, dream groups have their special challenges as well. Ideally, the group helps the dreamer not to edit or censor parts of the dream work. The group support can also give structure for the individual's fears to be explored. Within the group a safe place can be developed for awareness and insight to come forth. Another important skill for a facilitator to acquire is knowledge and awareness about psychological projection. A basic key is that group members must be coached and guided to keep their projections in check. "Making people up" out of our own imaginations usually results in negative experiences for all parties. Jungian psychology is especially helpful in this arena. "Shadow" and other projections within the group are rich fodder for members of dream group, but safety and openness are requirements for consciousness. Dreams pull one into a psychologically vulnerable area and to share them in a group is an enormous risk of trust. It is imperative the leader makes dream group a safe place for dreams to be shared and fully explored. As I have emphasized, it simply is counterproductive for group members to jump in with interpretations, accusations, and personal judgments. The therapist is not advised to create a Sunday school environment that is so guarded and superficial no real emotions can emerge—quite the contrary. The dream groups that provoke the most healing and awareness for their members have a solid foundation and a strong structure upon which an individual has the opportunity to explore the process of individuation. Safety is the key. Few things tear at the fabric of the group process more than allowing persons to become scapegoats or simply not mirrored when they are being their most revealing.

Moreover, the person doing the projecting has to be handled compassionately, not slammed into submission. This is where the Lakota history is so helpful. They understood that dreams could come from one person for another—or for the whole tribe. We don't dream today substantially differently than they did then. The person who is provoked in some fashion by another's dream has been so for a reason—not for the dreamer but for the listener. The listener needed to hear the dream in order for the material to be provoked—which is the heart of the matter in most projections. The facilitator can (kindly, playfully, curiously—whatever one's style is) ask: "Why did you need to hear this dream? What is coming up for you?"

A body therapist told me long ago that hunched shoulders will produce an attacking energy from a person with whom one is having conflict. Likewise, an open, exposed chest with shoulders back will produce respect and good will from the other. Perhaps the "kick me" sign from junior high gets branded into a person's signal system and victims are forever victimized. In dream group it is important to notice and track this energy in a way that does not constellate a group attack or scapegoating. "Poor me," overly self-critical, and personally degrading people will eventually produce a like-process from the group. If this is acknowledged and elucidated by the facilitator, it can be worthwhile for a person who tends to get picked on. Scapegoating and splitting are real possibilities in all groups, and facilitators can be most helpful when they seek to make this unconscious pattern conscious in the group.

Jeremy Taylor (1983) has contributed some important and groundbreaking work with dream groups.[8] One of his techniques is to let group members say, "If this were my dream . . . ," and then fill in what the dreamer thinks the dream may mean or mean to him / her. Although at first glance this appears to be identical or at least very similar to what I am describing, actually it is quite different. First of all, images in a person's dream are digested, amplified, associated to, and discussed in my dream groups with thorough detail. Dream group members are fond of and adroit at saying, "but what about the possibility of . . ." over and over until the image has been looked at from all angles. The process of looking at images from various angles is paramount to understanding the meanings or feelings or thoughts or insights that the dream images may convey. It is not as if all dreams can be boiled at a high temperature and reduced like chicken stock to one or two elemental meanings. Quite the contrary; dreams often simply open up the psyche for more questions, more awarenesses, or more possibilities. The dream work has its own integrity. This is why dreams can be re-worked over time with new insights coming forth, or different therapists and dream groups can help a person take an entirely new and different direction with the material. The important factor is to track the dreamer, not to track the listener. If the dreamer feels the suggestions from the dream group members have pertinent meaning, then the group has successfully facilitated the dream process. But for the therapist to impart his / her own meaning onto the dream is premature and discounting if not preceded by extensive exploration by the dreamer. Even then, projecting one's own material onto another's dream is risky.

Recently, an analysand of mine told a new friend about a dream series he and I had worked on for over a year. Immediately she said, "Well, if it were my dream . . . ," and then told him about the mother being a symbol of the earth, which *sublimated* (a process of the psyche where difficult issues are falsely elevated to grand proportions) the painful content the dream was presenting. He was offended by this intervention into his dream process. And the understandings he had gathered from our dream work together were not my interventions, but his own careful, measured inspections of his images, his feelings, his history, his current situation, his upcoming process, and so on. Another example of this occurred when a nurse who worked in a treatment center told her dream to the director. He also immediately told her what the dream meant as if it were his own. She found the interaction less than helpful to enable her to explore some of the essence for herself.

Another similar yet quite different dream group model is "social dreaming matrix." I have experienced this work, and it was thoroughly interesting and enjoyable for me. Facilitators in this process record all of the dreams and comments with only a bare minimum of interventions. People share dreams and all can associate to the dream or tell a dream of their own. Collective universal issues *are* noticed and dealt with, much like my dream groups. However, social dreaming matrix has participants talk into the center of the group, where they may be responded to or not, whereas my participants engage in hearty dialogue and relationship.

Dreams are extraordinarily complex, and they necessitate a slow, careful, and expansive attitude to develop fully. Dream group members are best suited to this work if they carry the approach of helpful listeners, curious supporters, or friendly guides to the path within. Better to say, "Tell me more about your mother," than, "If it were my dream, I would think of the mother as a symbol of the earth." Later, it is therapeutically essential to let members of dream group explore how the dream discussed may have related to their own process or illuminated issues that tend to be universal. There are some dreams one cannot help but be affected by when one hears them. At such times, one is gifted with the opportunity of being part of the dream process. In the model of dream group I am exploring here, each dream told and heard is everyone's dream; the question is not "If it were my dream?" but "How is it my dream?" or "Why did I need to hear your dream?" The dreams we hear are synchronistic to our own process and do speak directly to the heart of our own issues. It is this exploration of and participation in another's dream that can clarify one's own process. The missing piece is this: dream group forms a tribe, and our unconscious speaks to us out of the tribal mind. We dream of each other; we dream in similar images; we experience a group dream as well as an individual dream. The danger in saying, "If it were my dream I would be angry with my father" is that the question can be heard as, "I think you're angry at your father, but if you want to deny it, I'll be cool about it." In the dream group model I have developed the exchange might be dealt with like this:

LISTENER: I think you're angry at your father.

DREAMER: Well, I don't think so (frowning). I was so sad when he died in the dream.

FACILITATOR TO LISTENER: Perhaps some father stuff is coming up for you. Maybe this dream will help you connect to your issues around your father. Let's explore that when we finish discussing this dream—let's all think about our father issues and talk about them when the dreamer is at a stopping point.

Later, all of the members should be invited to reflect on the subject of fathers, anger at fathers, fathers dying, the inner father, the outer father, being a father, and so forth. Then, after the group has reflected on the dream and the ways it provoked all the members' father issues, the dreamer invariably will have at least two reactions to all of this dialogue: 1) greater clarity about the dream's meaning; and 2) being pleased and touched by the experience of having one's dream genuinely facilitate so much awareness for others. Thus, the dream group does not aim to systematically share and analyze all dreams of each participant, but 1) uses a few dreams each session to open things up for the dreamer; and 2) allows the dream themes to motivate reflection or focus attention on similar themes or issues for the participants.

RESPECT AND DETACHMENT

In order for dream groups to experience "cross fertilization" in each member's process yet, at the same time, maintain each member's individual integrity, the climate of the group is essential. The facilitator shows respect and curiosity for the one sharing a dream; then the group members follow in kind. The attitude of respect is one that avoids shaming, judging, discounting, interpreting, or giving advice. For all of us, judgment is ubiquitous.

As an example, a dreamer in discussion about her dream had provoked sad and guilty feelings about abortion. She mentioned she had had three abortions over the last twelve years. Instantly, the therapist rescued the dreamer from her guilt and suffering by not reinforcing the emotion the dream had brought forward for the dreamer but, instead, pointed out a number of reasons the abortions were good decisions. Regardless of the lack of edification of guilt, this missed the important potential in the dream: the opportunity for the dreamer to discover and access the suppressed feelings that were unconscious to the waking self. By recognizing these feelings existed, some healing was possible. Maintaining therapeutic neutrality on abortion or other emotionally charged topics takes an extra conscious effort for the facilitator.

Once a depressed teenage male client told his therapist that he had gotten angry that week and had accidentally (rather than intentionally) broken a table by slamming his fists down and breaking the glass tabletop. This outburst even required a few stitches in his hand. He felt enormous relief at his display of anger to his stepsister, anger that had been building and was entirely unexpressed for years. But the therapist only got angry at the young man and lectured him about the cycle of abuse. She implied that breaking the table was only a small step away from hitting his stepsister, and this display predicted a violent future. Later, the therapist confessed she used to break her daughter's toiletries when she got mad. The young man was thoroughly shamed, and his emotional content was ignored.

To be a therapist is to be objectively professional. A professional is someone who can track the process of the client regardless of how close the issues hit painful personal hot buttons. It is the client who needs his process illuminated, not the facilitator. But to complicate this even more, most therapists I have talked to notice the phenomena of like attracts like in their practices. In fact, I do not personally know of a successful long-practicing therapist who has not observed this remarkable coincidence. That is to say, if a therapist has an eating disorder, more than the usual eating-disordered clients will come for therapy. If a therapist has trouble making a long-term commitment, then the clients will be inordinately weighted in that direction. It can get silly, too. Clients may take the identical vacations as the therapist without prior knowledge, buy the same make car, and so on. My experience is that these so-called "synchronicities" are not necessarily opportunities to share personally with clients—or to project and assume conclusions about the client. They are, rather, challenges to stay even more focused on the client to remain objective, keeping the therapist's issues out of the way as much as he/she is capable. Staying clear of the client's process is fundamental to good therapy, but know that the overlap between the therapist and the client is a signal the work can be good and fruitful for both parties and that a tribal, unconscious connection is at hand. It encourages a level of empathy that is significant and genuine.

This personal detachment is a form of respect and professionalism that allows the process to remain vital, hot, transformative. Identifying with clients and sharing too much personal material can diffuse the "hot pot" of therapy, like letting the air out of a balloon. Of course, clients love it when therapists are personal, in part because it takes the heat off the endeavor of making the unconscious conscious—both with individual clients as well as groups. The therapist's job is to dive deeply and carry the resistant client ego into the depths where soul and life lie in the realm of potential.

Curiosity is another necessary spice for the dream soup. When the therapist feels enormously curious about the client's life, psyche, past, present, fears, hopes, and so on, then this attitude encourages a client's trusting vulnerability. An analyst mentor of mine, Sylvia Weisshaupt, taught me a small phrase that encapsulates this notion: "Tell me all about it, dear." The Buddhist notion of *compassion* is relevant. It is from a greater kindness and depth of our own being that we are able to listen with our hearts open, our minds clear from preconceived notions and cumbersome judgments. Here is where the process is ideally attended and tracked. It is in a client or dream group member's own open, vulnerable state that he / she is ultimately able to connect to the healing passion that allows one to understand oneself in a new way, to make the courageous changes necessary for full, new life.

CHAPTER FOUR

Goo

DREAMS—WHETHER THE EGO REALIZES IT OR NOT—ARE extremely *gooey*. *Gooey* is a word I use to describe the part of us that comes from the fertile self, the self where we are creative, spiritual, sensual, heroic, saintly, and passionate. People can fall in love easily when they enter the gooey realm together. The gooey realm is quite sensitive and shy. Of course, modern culture has ignored and suppressed goo for so long, it isn't surprising to find goo a bit reticent. Goo is mercurial and will quickly disappear if it is not honored and invited to be integrated into the psyche. It is a primary and significant task for the therapist to notice and encourage goo.

The following client / therapist dialogue is an example of how goo is discouraged:

> CLIENT: I had a stupid dream where I was being chased by banditos. I was out in the middle of nowhere—perhaps it was Ghost Ranch in New Mexico. Just as I rounded a curve and the hostiles were gaining on me, I came to a very deep precipice. There, standing on the edge of the cliff, were a man and a woman poised to jump. I woke up.

THERAPIST: Why didn't you try to stop the man and woman from jumping?

CLIENT: I'm not sure, I don't know.

THERAPIST: Well, you see, that points out your socio-pathic tendencies.

This is an overt example, but one that actually occurred, so I include it here. One can easily see the client would have been deeply reticent about ever sharing a dream in this therapy again. Labeling and judging chased away the opportunity for the images to be illuminated.

When analysands are in the dream goo I find they often use the word "stupid." This dream is stupid, this relationship is stupid, this experience I had on the mountain top sounds stupid, and so on. "Stupid" is a real sign one is near goo.

Another time I presented some drawings that my analysand had produced in analysis to a group of mental health professionals. My client was a clergywoman who was breaking ground in her denomination. I respected her process quite a lot. She was becoming a bit miserable with institutional church. She drew a number of pictures during her work with me; one was of a river with precious stones dotted under the surface. I presented this drawing to the class and asked for reactions, thoughts, insights. A highly respected professional asked what the blobs in the river were; I told him gemstones. He remarked he was certain they were actually all the pills she was taking since she sounded like a borderline personality disorder.

Incidentally, the clergywoman client/artist became the dean of a well-regarded spiritual studies program—the stones were undiscovered elements of her process, jewels hidden in the river of life that were to be mined and brought to consciousness through the exploration of her soul. But this happened later—her drawing was a prospectus of the process that was emerging in her psyche. It saddened me that the attitude of the therapist, like some others in the mental health profession, was one of disgust toward the inner work. It seemed almost as if he needed to assert his power to diminish the artistic images her soul work had produced. Devaluing the client's process is harmful. It shames clients and blames them for the tender gooey self that so much needs a safe place to emerge. Labeling patients, throwing medication at them for every possible uncomfortable symptom, disregards their process, as well. It is through exploring and courageously finding the messages in our suffering that we are able to become new or whole. The therapist must carry the safe "you can tell me anything" attitude for the mystery and healing to unfold.

The superior, powerful "one up" attitude of mental health professionals is not theirs alone. It was apparent in the teachers' lounge when I was a schoolteacher. There, making fun of students and their parents was a favorite lunch time activity. Not all teachers are like this, nor are all therapists; however, this attitude is popular in quite a number of circles. It is simply disrespect. It partially comes from an element of fear on the part of the helper. As I have mentioned, the clients and students we encounter often mirror our own issues, and thus getting "hooked" is a pretty common experience. The challenge lies in what one does with being hooked. This is why I am so attracted by Jungian psychology. Throughout Carl Jung's work with the unconscious, he maintained an attitude of respect, even awe, toward the psyche of all individuals. He amplified and studied the images his analysands presented to him, in a way that informed him about their psyches and all psyche. This is one cornerstone of his work with people. The process of analysis and therapy requires one to feel sacred honor, respect, and curiosity about being a part of a person's psychological journey.

Less obvious examples abound in how a facilitator may unwittingly discourage the gooey realm. Telling a dream is like undressing. Pictures, poems, musical compositions, and other creative pursuits within the container of analysis or therapy are all naked revelations of the self. Dream work requires the therapist to be ever mindful of the great responsibility he / she carries when a dream is offered. Receive it gently and kindly.

Empathy is a word that I don't hear in therapeutic circles as much as I used to. Now the focus is on treatment plan or diagnosis. Plain old-fashioned empathy goes a long way toward letting the healing process take place. It can be the foundation of trust and caring that allows the pain to emerge and move on. In fact, a facilitator does not have to know much about dreams but can be extremely helpful with them if he / she can practice simple empathy and keep personality out of the way of the dreamer's explorations. But empathy is not a simple concept. How many of us have thought or said, "I didn't know what it was like until it happened to me"? How many of us have helped dozens of clients with divorce, breast cancer, bankruptcy, or the death of a spouse only to discover that when we suffered a similar fate, the experience was quite unlike looking at it from the outside? This doesn't mean therapists cannot significantly help clients even when they have no similar life experience; however, it does mean that the therapist has to be extremely careful to fully experience the event as much as possible. A beneficial way to uncover this profound empathy is to practice the meditation "as if."

"As If" Exercise

Sit with eyes closed. Center oneself or do whatever techniques one has developed to become relaxed, open, and in a meditative state. Then imagine you have the same difficulty or dilemma as your client. Ever so slowly feel into this experience. How would you feel hearing the news of this circumstance? What effect would this have on your job, your sleep, your relationships, and your daily routine? What would be the worst part for you? How would this experience impact you spiritually, creatively, artistically, financially, physically, psychologically? The more time and patience spent on this exercise the more enlightening insights one can have.

This exercise has other benefits as well. It combats narcissism, however briefly, and it helps dispel negative projections. It is possible to experience empathy for those you dislike—or anyone you have collected negative energy for—by simply spending as much time as it takes to imagine being that person to see what compassion, empathy, and insights can develop. In dream group, empathy for each member is imperative.

Clearly, dream group does not work very well unless there is an underlying foundation of trust, but harmony is also an important factor. The personalities of the most productive dream groups are patient and gentle, respectful and reverent, since most who participate quickly perceive the sacred space that dream group constellates. The time together is meditative, introspective, and relational all at the same time. The space is respected. The style of group therapy where individuals confront, even fight and scream, is in contrast to gooey dream group where harmony, not conflict, allows for a productive atmosphere. Raw conflict without introspective insight tends to shut down the process rather than open it up.

The dream maker, the teacher within each one of us, is generally a kind teacher. We only get confronted harshly (as when one has a terrifying nightmare) when we absolutely ignore obvious data. Sometimes this data presents itself in a dream, a synchronicity, an "omen," a vision, or possibly an insight. Sometimes this confrontation appears from those around us as corrective feedback or sometimes in a slow progression of awarenesses. In dream groups, the whole of the group, with some individual exceptions, is a body that mirrors truth for a member if the trust and bondedness has had a chance to develop. Attacking and accusing styles of confrontation are rarely helpful, but the base foundation of love and respect are. Love is the great healer and teacher of all human experience, and dream group is largely about connecting to that energy within ourselves and the members of the group. Clever interpretations of dreams are far less important than the attitude and atmosphere of the people participating. Despair, violence, "inappropriate" sexual fantasies, anger at the facilitator or someone in the group are all delightful pieces of the puzzle that give one clues to the unfolding process. There are no taboos, none that I can think of, that are unacceptable in the discussion and amplification of dream images.

The group is the frame. It is odd to me how much a frame can do for a painting. The painting may be a B-, and the frame may be a C+, but put together they create a B+ piece of art. The frame is the structure, the container, the outer edge that gives rise to the *temenos,* the sacred space where the spiritual transformation can occur.

In ancient days people would dance around a fire at night, deep in the forests of Europe. After they danced and danced, they would form what was called a "cone of power." When the power cone was fully formed, they would enact their rituals. Similarly, the dream group forms a cone of power. A frame for a painting, a sacred space for the altar, a meditation garden where the process can congeal and shift to its next evolution. But the gooey realm—trust, safety, and love—are the essentials for this magic to take hold.

CHAPTER FIVE

The Shadow

INEVITABLY, CONFLICTS CAN ARISE, CONFRONTATIONS DO occur, and difficult moments can and do emerge in dream groups. Sometimes negative feelings are revealed in dream figures, when one group member dreams of another member or of the facilitator. Sometimes hostilities arise during discussion, and this creates a rich opportunity for negative feelings to be explored. The negative ruminations one holds onto in a secretive fashion can be ultimately destructive. Secrets are not contained well in a dream group, anyway, because the work is too revealing. Thus, it is beneficial to treat anger, hurt, hostility, resentment, envy, disgust, and so forth, head on—again, with curiosity rather than shame. Dream group members may interact outside of group as well, and invariably relationship will bring conflict. In general, *shadow projection* is an invaluable concept that can unravel most of these difficult knots some relationships develop. A brief explanation of the shadow and an exercise follow.

First of all, shadow is dark matter (unconscious in the psyche) that is being collected and manifested onto another individual— not one's self. Theoretically, this occurs with the same sex person. (I will discuss projections on the opposite sex in chapter six.) Think of shadow as energy. Look at a group of persons—upon whom does the energy land? For our discussion, we will presume the energy is negative: "I don't like her;" "He's too coy with women;" "She's manipulative." Within a dream group, it is imperative that shadow projections occur. Why imperative? Because the shadow projection indicates the psyche is active and alive; the Self is "talking" to the ego, and the group process has entered the rich dark matter—the *prima materia*—that at first appears to be vile but is actually the seed of one's new growth. Dream group is about making the unconscious conscious. Shadow projection is an avenue for the psyche to begin to communicate with the ego that there is something here to know more about. Fundamentally, it doesn't matter if "I don't like her." Who am I to pronounce people likable or not? What is useful though, is: "Who have I made her up to be, and what is it this activates in myself that I don't want to know about?" It is far more comfortable to give that part away to someone else than it is to see it in ourselves.

Most resist the notion that all people we dislike are portraying parts of ourselves we don't want to own. Somehow this is too simple or pat or degrading. But, for the most part, it is so. Of course most dislike Hitler—this is not shadow projection. Most dislike individuals who have betrayed us, and this is not shadow projection, either. Shadow projection is, however, ubiquitous, fascinating, and can be remarkably psychologically illuminating. The following exercise is designed to assist in developing awareness about one's shadow. It is useful for dream groups to participate in this together when shadow issues need addressing.

Shadow Exercise

List several (five to ten) public figures or people one does not know personally, people that seem annoying or distasteful. These are people that one "can't stand" and has no intimate knowledge about. Movie stars, news casters, and unfamiliar neighbors are excellent material. Be sure all persons listed are the same sex as the person engaging in the exercise.

Next, list at least one quality, preferably the quintessential quality, which is most unlikable. This is the difficult part of the exercise. Like finding the exact point of pain in the body, identifying the particular point of irritation takes some thought. Then list these qualities next to the name of the person.

Here are some examples that come from generous workshop participants. Please note these descriptors are fiction, not fact, and not the opinion of this author:

WOMEN:

Barbra Streisand	pushy, arrogant
Goldie Hawn	ditzy, insincere
Demi Moore	cold, angry

MEN:

Bill Clinton	untrustworthy
Warren Beatty	womanizer
Kevin Costner	pompous, takes himself too seriously

Next, write for each name listed how the figure is one to envy. Envy is a painful longing for something—a quality or aspect one does not have. Envy lies behind the shadow projection.

Barbra Streisand	enormously talented, powerful, focused
Goldie Hawn	appealing, sexy, funny
Demi Moore	beautiful, successful, strong, mysterious sexuality
Bill Clinton	powerful, able to withstand enormous difficulty, popular
Warren Beatty	A sex object for women
Kevin Costner	Young, handsome, successful

This is a nonthreatening way for people to begin to see their shadow (yes, the negative qualities listed are one's own). But the negative qualities are also encapsulated by envy—that which the psyche desires. In other words, the psyche is trying to move toward integrating what it envies. Not all qualities are enviable in all people—some desire recognition, some power, some wealth. But the envy gives us a clue where the psyche wants to move, and where libido is in reserve. If consciousness can begin to shed light on the psychic situation, then the shadow can begin the shift toward integration. Shadow projections are like arrows that point in a direction—as soon as we decipher the projection, the more chance we have of living our potential.

"Nonsense," you may say. "I can't stand Barbra Streisand, and I have no singing talent whatsoever." This is not an exercise to take literally or concretely. I imagine the person who has trouble with Barbara Streisand does have an unlived creative or effective self. Creativity doesn't necessarily reside only in the arts—one can be an imaginative mother, an office worker who has passion about the contribution the company is making, and so on. Simply watercoloring a few hours on the weekend can immediately soften the envy one might feel for people living their talents and gifts. Nor does one have to become rich and famous to deal with the envy—one does need to challenge oneself, however, to grow or to take a risk, and then the envy will abate. Our previous shadow projections can become neutral or even fascinating subjects in our minds, whether they are remote public figures or a neighbor down the street, when acknowledgment and integration begin to occur.

There is a relief in letting go of the resentment and seeing one's shadow projection as a teleological function of our psyche. Teleology is what is emerging or coming into light in our life. It is our river—it is where we are going. Teleology is similar to the biological process of evolution. Our psyche pushes us forward toward greater consciousness and differentiation—a process that is moving ahead, wanting healing, awareness, and resolution in our personalities. The God image, the most common and consistent archetype, perhaps exists *because* we have evolution to prove it. It is ironic to me that some groups are offended by the theory of evolution, as if this theory of scientific observation could somehow undermine the existence of God. I find quite the opposite to be true. In fact, I think it is more likely that evolution "implies" the theory and reality of God. Just where does this energy force come from that allows organisms to differentiate, to adapt, to survive and thrive and become more complex? Is this only by accident or random selection? Just what is the driving motivation behind the process of evolution? Here is the God manifest in creation, and the creationists want to discount it. Perhaps change is the largest aspect of resistance. Change is what evolution is all about. A static, rigid, unflinching attitude is not the way the soul or the incarnate body works.

The teleological function in the psyche, like the process of evolution, pushes us toward greater differentiation and complexity. The annoying emanations from the psyche (which cover desire, envy, and passion) want to be claimed for the self. One may desire a slimmer body, or a more creative life, or a more secure job. The phenomenon of shadow projection is actually a remarkable gift that speaks to us from the unconscious process in which we swirl about. Many times clients say to me, "I just wish I knew what I wanted. I don't have any idea what my passion is." Here is a beginning. Here is a start to finding the passion, to collecting our energy into a focused will that can begin to actualize the unlived self.

Perhaps one resists this exercise by saying, "I envy youth, and since I am long past it, there is no point in integrating something I can't ever have." Again, one cannot be too concrete. Youth has to be deconstructed as a symbol for vitality, freedom, options (or whatever the person with the shadow projection sees as the essence of youth, much like an image from a dream). When these issues are identified and allowed to be a part of the conscious ego, the wrinkles around one's eyes are less significant.

Possibly an aunt didn't invite you to a family wedding. Or a brother swindled part of your inheritance. Maybe a sister slept with your husband or you and a best friend have had a dreadful falling out. These people are too close to us to be good shadow projection material. One needs more of a blank slate (upon which to project) rather than a complicated relationship to discover the essential shadow projection. This is why public figures or people we don't know very well work the best.

Here is a personal example that illustrates the surprises and fertile possibilities hidden in shadow projections. In the late 1980s, just back from Zurich, I received a surprising phone call inviting me for dinner at a woman's home. It was surprising because the woman, who had taken a class from me, had been obviously disgusted with my teaching and level of expertise I provided to our class. About three years before, she had let out an audible groan in the middle of my lecture and hid her head in her hands for the rest of class after I couldn't answer a question she asked.[9] I was embarrassed when I couldn't answer this piece of data I probably should have known and was doubly shamed by her reaction, especially since this was my debut teaching event to the Jungian community in Dallas after arriving from Zurich. I was hoping to begin a private practice. Further, over the ensuing three years I had heard from not a few people how poorly she thought of me. "Badly trained," "uneducated," "a young whippersnapper" were all comments that had found their way back to me. So you can imagine my surprise when I received her invitation. I hesitated; she jumped right in with an explanation: "Well, you see I'm in analysis, and it has become clear I have an enormous shadow projection on you, and my analyst insists I invite you for dinner and see what this projection is all about." So with that, I accepted. What an evening! At three A.M., I finally returned home. We began a friendship then and later spent several evenings having splendid, riotous times together. She was a corporate attorney at the time, and her desire for a different life had provoked the shadowy envy. Not long after our dinner, she began a series of life-changing decisions that included re-educating herself and changing her profession altogether. Currently she is an ordained clergyperson—a profession better suited to her passion for people, as well as her expertise in Jungian psychology.

Some of the members of dream groups will collect more projections than others. Likewise, some members will be dreamed about more often than other members of dream group. Such persons are known as "Projection Collectors." They possess an energy or presence that is more vivid than ordinary. It is not about clothing, good looks, or even intelligence. One can make this observation in groups of all types and in all quadrants of relationships and families. These people are gossiped about more than others and have natural charisma.

In dream group it is important to deconstruct all of the projections members put upon each other, as well as the projections the leader carries. As in all productive therapy groups, the ideal attitude is one that is a nonthreatened, objective approach to the negative material, just as one must be objective and non-threatened about neutral or positive material. It is all projection and, therefore, all interesting in the process of uncovering the underpinnings of the psyche. I have witnessed experienced and seasoned therapists, especially ones that have made a career of group work, be masterful at this process. Whatever the members say about the leader is okay and acceptable. This alone—that is, the leader's ability to receive negative material from group participants without getting defensive—can be magnificently healing for the person brave enough to share the material. What results, in part, from this approach is that the members of dream group are actually coached and taught in a subtext to learn how to experience and express emotion in a way that is beneficial to self and other. It does not have to be delivered or received in a cruel or defensive way.

The following is an example of a shadow projection from a dream grouper where personal, hurtful emotion was omitted from the work:

CLIENT: I had a dream about you.

TESS: Let's hear it.

CLIENT: I dreamed you had a bunch of suitcases in your waiting room, and they were crowding all of us waiting to come into your office for dream group.

TESS: And how did this feel?

CLIENT: Well, aggravating.

TESS: And what are your feelings and thoughts about me?

CLIENT: Well, I do think you have a lot of baggage that interferes with our group. I think you're angry about your divorce and it takes up room in our group. And your personal issues are like baggage that shouldn't be in here. I don't think you have good boundaries.

TESS: Any other feelings or thoughts?

CLIENT: Well, I envy you too. I think you have a really easy life. You don't have a bunch of kids to take care of or a husband either. You're a Jungian analyst and your life looks pretty perfect to me.

In exploring this dream, the client uncovered a real need to adjust her over-taxed life as a mother of five, a college professor, and an artist. She needed much more support for her life rather than support for her family and students. I will admit, this was a painful dream for me to hear, and I took it to heart. As Jung said, all projections have a hook, and I sensed I needed to listen to what her dream was telling me. I certainly became less personally revealing after that. This exchange took place in 1991 or so, and I learned then that being less personal is usually more effective. But I refrained from sharing with her my personal material and the emotion of feeling hurt. I felt that would divert her work onto my work, which is not the purpose of dream group. To defend, apologize, disagree, or display any other reaction would have resulted in dropping her process—this was a window for the client to see into a part of her life that wasn't working. Since then, she has cut down on her teaching, spends much more time on art, and the issue of envy or annoyance about me has not resurfaced.

Sometimes a negative projection that emerges in a dream about the leader can indicate the work is not destined to go well; or to say it another way, the projection is too fierce for any progress to be made. In such cases it is better to try another therapist or group. For example, a number of years ago, a woman dreamed:

> *I came to Tess' office for our first appointment when I no-*
> *ticed she had a large spider on her shoulder. I was horrified.*
> *In the dream this meant Tess was an evil witch.*

In our conversation amplifying the dream images in her second session, she could only say the salamander pin I had worn on our first meeting had disturbed her. It seemed pagan or evil. No amount of cautious exploration of evil, her mother, feminine dark energy, or how this could be an aspect of herself would soften the strong sense that she had been given a message from her dream that I was a witch. I referred her to someone else. I'm relatively certain our work would not have been productive.

A friend also had a disturbing dream the night before her first session with a popular analyst in Zurich. She had been on his waiting list many months. The entire dream was this:

"Don't work with _____!" a voice resounded.

She reluctantly took that dream to her first session. She knew what it meant but didn't want to accept it. His interpretation: "Kick your husband's anima out of the relationship." They proceeded to work together, and she acknowledged she learned a number of important things from him, but the analysis failed badly and ended in a traumatic, destructive fashion. I learned from that something then I hope I never forget—to listen carefully and intently to my own dreams, as well as to my client's. Not every dream is about projection. On somewhat infrequent occasions our dream maker speaks to our ego straight from the truth center, and it is imperative that we listen. How does one know the difference? The dreamer most often will know after discussion about the images. One clever aspect of dream work is the dreamer can confirm or deny any hypothesis set forth just by tuning into the interior self and "testing" the information the dream is providing for its truthfulness.

All three dreams reported here are examples in which the tribal level of the unconscious, the place in the psyche where the intersection of dream characters creates real objective information or clues about relationship, is revealed. My friend dreamed about her analyst (or their work together), not a part of herself. (And my dream group member dreamed I had too much personal baggage in my office—true!) Just as my client dreamed I was a witch (not true!—most of the time), she did receive accurate information that we did not constellate a healing relationship together. Not entirely projection, but also information. I have reasonable certainty that the spider dream predicted a poor outcome for our work. I am quite able to fail and am sure I would have done so, unfortunately, with the best of intentions. By honoring her dream reality I can only hope the analysand was better able to see negative possibilities ahead of time. This was a chance for her to use more of her instincts of survival rather than be forever maligned by the constellation of negative feminine forces.

My friend's analyst might have explored her dream this way:

ANALYST: Is it possible you need to start working with someone else, then perhaps later we could see if there is something we could do together?

CLIENT: That feels right to me.

A strong, authoritative voice appears in dreams not infrequently. Jung discussed this phenomenon in several of this writings: ". . . the 'voice' in dreams always has for the dreamer the final and indisputable character of the *avros eoa,* ('He said it himself.' The phrase originally alluded to the authority of Pythagoras.) i.e., the voice expresses some truth or condition that is beyond all doubt" (*Psychology and Alchemy,* 1944, paragraph 15). In other language, the "voice" is the voice of the Self, the center and totality of our psyche out of which our dreams come. Some analysts and Jungian scholars call the Self "God." Whether this authoritative voice is God or not, it is important to explore the images and information that come in dreams from a mind that is totally open, because the "voice" often is in opposition to the desires of the ego. One has to be free from attachment as well. The most uncontaminated information one receives is from dreams, whether the dream comments on the appropriateness of one's analyst choice reveals a shadow projection or any other issue. Dreams confront and challenge the waking, known, conscious "I." The "I" is full of illusion, ergo the need for "corrective" information.

CHAPTER SIX

Animus / Anima

IN ADDITION TO SHADOW PROJECTIONS, THERE ARE PROJEC-
tions of the opposite sex, too. These projections are as common
as shadow projections—where our reality is cleverly disguised by
our beliefs about people, rather than based on facts. We "make
people up" to such a regular degree that consciousness can
resemble a bubble of existence, unconnected and unrelated to a
more objective reality. Naturally, it is dangerous psychologically
to base one's life on fiction. In addition, to help break us out of
our set notions, the dream maker is extraordinarily politically and
socially incorrect. Frequently our golden idols are mocked and
ridiculed, our disdained images exalted. The ego, for example, no
doubt would prefer that emancipated, educated, powerful women
not dream of men as such profoundly creative and exhilarating
models, but that is just how the psyche often presents men in the
ancient dream language. Gay women, straight women, young
women, older women, single women, married women, women
of all colors tend to project their emerging potential onto the
opposite sex. Why? It is simply the nature of projection to attach
unconscious qualities of ourselves to people who are "other"
than we are. They are not us, not the conscious us with which
we identify. In addition to that, nature has divided us into two

groups—male and female. We are physically quite different, and this division extends to animal and plant life as well. From birth our gender is a significant feature that divides us into two sets—the first question new parents ask is, "Is it a boy or a girl?" Regardless of the recent progress in American culture to debunk some of the gender stereotypes, we are still two genders. And since our human life is divided into these two most obvious groups, it follows that the psyche will attribute unconscious aspects of the personality to a group that is most different from the conscious self. In a similar way, projections occur on other ethnic groups, other social groups, and other regional groups different from the ego. Whatever one is not will produce an opportunity for projection. As a result, men tend to operate for women as a handy catch-all for the projection of what one is not yet, but what one is beginning to *find* in the personality.

Naturally, men dream women in the same way; that is, they systematically project onto women the qualities they are struggling to make conscious and integrate—often those regarding relationships. But these projections cannot be stereotyped or generalized. Each person's process must be carefully and cautiously unraveled for its individuality. That is why it is important to associate personally and fully to dream figures. It is not just any man or woman carrying the projection, but a particular individual that represents qualities and aspects one needs to explore to understand the push the dream maker is giving the ego.

The following exercise will help explore specific rather than generalized projections:

List five to ten people of the opposite sex (whether one is gay or straight). List people that are largely personally unknown—movie stars, people from work, the neighborhood, church, art class, the gym, and so forth. These are people that one finds attractive, the attraction ranging from feelings of mild interest to a full-blown

THREADS, KNOTS, TAPESTRIES 57

crush. Again, watch where the energy goes. In a crowd of men or women, which one carries a fascination? After listing these people, try to determine the exact nature of the attraction by listing the one or two qualities that are most interesting. "I really like her because . . ." "I find him irresistible because . . ." In this exercise it is important to include not just personality characteristics, but aspects about their lives too; for example: Paul Newman may be on a woman's list, and she may think he is attractive to her because he's handsome. But we all know dozens of handsome men—both famous and not. So the question is: why him? What sets Paul Newman apart from other nice looking men? After more reflection it might be revealed that Paul Newman is actually admired for his charity work or for his relationship with his family. Then one begins to understand the projection. For women and men, respect lies under the attraction or fascination. (This is why this exercise works for gay and straight people. Attraction is not necessarily sexual; it has more to do with unconscious desire.) Just like envy and shadow, one asks, "Why do I respect her?" And, just like a shadow projection, the projections of the anima / animus (known as the contrasexual) are arrows that point one toward emerging potential.

Attraction: Jewel
Cute, nice figure
Respect: Jewel
Hardworking, talented, survivor against odds

And yes, the qualities one admires in Meg Ryan, Jewel, or Goldie Hawn are one's own. "Cute" is not necessarily about how one looks. "Cute" may be defined as approachable, friendly, or funny. These would be qualities that the man with the projection also has. But like the qualities we envy, the ones we admire are pointing us in a direction which encourages conscious integration.

In a dream group some years ago, we all participated in this exercise. My co-facilitator, Ernie Bel, entertained us for some minutes explaining his long-term, rather profound feelings about Sophia Loren. What was funny for the group was that all of the qualities Ernie described as hers were his own as well. He described Loren as warm, sexy, inviting, nonjudgmental, luscious, and so on. Ernie was also this way—warm and engaging to almost everyone. He was pretty surprised to hear the dream group comment that it sounded like he was describing himself. In his case, he had her qualities already integrated into his personality but was nonetheless unconscious about it. The projections that land on people around us give us information about aspects that desire and need to be a part of us.

Jung postulated that, in fact, each woman has a "male" personality that lives in her called the *animus,* and each man has a "female" personality that lives in him called the *anima.* To understand these vastly unconscious parts of ourselves is daunting. This part of our Self is even farther from consciousness than our shadow. It takes some digging to ascertain the traits of one's contrasexual.

The following exercise should illuminate the process:

Sit quietly and completely relax. Spend whatever time is necessary to feel centered and connected to a deep place within. Then, go back in time and imagine you were born as the opposite sex. How did your parents and siblings feel about you? What was your name? Then travel slowly throughout your life and see what might have been different for you as the opposite sex. What would your early days of school have been like? What would you have been like in junior high? high school? What would have been your interests and hobbies, your sporting activities? Who would have been your friends? Continue to progress to the present. What would you be like now? What would be your style of dress? Your style of hair? Profession? Who would be your lover or husband or wife? What kind of lover would you be? What would sex be like for you? Who would you be friends with? What kind of parent would you be?

After all of this reflection, one can begin to imagine aspects of the contrasexual. The more we become conscious, the less we project. As some of these traits are integrated into the personality, it becomes larger, fuller, and has more options.

The dream maker is also politically and socially embarrassing, especially when dreaming about ethnic groups or cultures that are different from his / her own, because projections of all kinds don't fit with what society has trained us to say, think, or believe. Years ago, I studied the Psychology of Prejudice under a gifted African American professor, George Tate. It was a revelation to me to learn that the basis of prejudice is fear—fear of what we don't know and that with which we aren't familiar. So it follows that these fearful projections will play an important role in our nighttime dream dramas. We project all kinds of hates and dislikes onto people we fear—this way, whatever they may mean to our process is sure to stay unconscious. The ancient people were necessarily territorial and defensive, so protecting oneself may have a primitive root—one that hasn't caught up with the consciousness of inclusion.

However, it is necessary and ultimately healing—both personally and societally—to understand that the qualities attributed to other groups are parts of the self that need to be honored and integrated. It was handy during the Cold War for Americans and Russians to project evil onto each other. It is far more psychologically mature to see both sides as gray, rather than black or white, and to acknowledge the part of self that fears knowing who one actually is. Additionally, the resistance to being so "politically incorrect" during free association of the dream images is a real issue. The embarrassment and cultural taboo against telling an analyst one's stereotypical generalizations about an ethnic or gender group (especially when the analyst belongs to such group!) is formidable.

What a challenge I had one session when an analysand brought a dream with an Irish family in it. She had entirely negative associations to this ethnic group stemming from her childhood East Coast "ghetto neighborhood" as she described it. I identify enough with this ethnic group that I felt stung by her generalizations—a reminder to me how powerfully destructive blanket stereotyped projection can be. In this case, her dream image was pushing against her old worn-out attitude, encouraging more consciousness.

For women and men the opposite sex attraction is one of the most informative aspects of the psychology of projection. It is fashionable currently to discount the "classical" Jungian approach that refers to anima/animus by replacing this concept with a unisex hybrid archetype. All women and all men have both anima and animus. Perhaps that amalgamation can be argued convincingly but nevertheless, the projection one delivers to a member of the gender one is not is different in quality than same-sex projections. Quite obviously, it is farther from consciousness.

Why it is, I don't know, and certainly it is not always so, but a majority of women's attractions for men revolve around their professional/spiritual development, while men's projections on women tend to encourage them to integrate more feeling, more vulnerability, and more relationship into their personalities.

DIAGRAM OF THE PSYCHE

Here is a diagram to illustrate the paradigm of the tribal field in an individual psyche:

Persona
Our mask or outer personality, the roles we play.

Ego
One's conscious "I," i.e., who I am and believe myself to be.

Complexes
Emotionally charged autonomous "mini personalities" that are quite different than the ego's perception of self—rooted in personal biography but have an archetypal core.

Shadow
Unconscious aspects of the personality—usually obvious to others, to which one is blind. These are aspects that one excludes from self-identity and thus projects on others.

Anima / Animus
Inner man and inner woman in psyche—the ultimate bridge to the Self, our essential wholeness of being.

Tribal Field
The dimension in the inner self where one's psyche intersects with other psyches—evidenced by objective dreams, synchronicities, ESP, and other visionary phenomena.

Archetypes
Vast, unknowable, universal images that are numinous and undeniable—e.g., "God," "Mother," "Father," "Death."

The Self
The author of dreams, visions, the organizing principle of the psyche, both its center and circumstance, one's inner numinosity.

Collective Unconscious
The universal soup out of which each psyche manifests.

Another way to conceptualize the tribal reality as it relates to the individual psyche and the collective unconscious is in the following description: one can see the personal psyche—*my* memories, *my* experience, *my* uniqueness—as a *stream* that flows into the next layer of the psyche, a *river* where I become larger and progressively less conscious. Our experience, our relationship, our love / hate leads to the final deep territory of the unconscious—the *ocean*—where the archetypes and the collective unconscious and all unconscious processes are collected in permanent storage.

The Stream
Persona, Ego, Complexes, Shadow, Animus / Anima
Personal
Individual
Unique

The River
Tribal Field, Communal Dreaming
Relational
Tribal
Groups
Clans
Families
Communities

The Ocean
Archetypes, Self, Collective Unconscious
Universal
Collective

Part Two

Knots

CHAPTER SEVEN

Aspects of Dream Groups

SPONTANEOUS RITUAL

DREAM GROUPS TEND TO BE MORE PERSONAL AND FAMILIAR than other support groups—at least, the tendency is for greater intimacy. The level of closeness is astonishing at times. I have seen permanent, significant relationships that may even include marriage develop and endure over many years. This is not the exception. I have pondered this because I don't consider myself to have any skills at matchmaking, and because the "group business" is not conducive to romance in any obvious way. Most of the time, the members are quite serious about understanding their dreams, and since this is a time-consuming activity, they are focused and task-orientated. But, nonetheless, gooey relationships seem to spring up out of the dream-group air.

The act of diving into the gooey realm of dreams with others is the glue in these groups. Dreams are the intimate, revealing, bonding, illuminating, connecting, and magical goo from which relationships naturally form. Not unlike a theater production or a civic cause or some group endeavor that involves creativity and risk, people find they fall in love with each other. I was often excluded entirely in the intimacies, since they regularly occurred outside group time. I knew I didn't want to forbid or control outside interactions, but not knowing about developing relationships or people's personal behavior between group members can certainly affect group dynamics. Generally, I learned over time to be patient because the dreams quickly revealed the group process.

Besides romance, ritualizing behaviors also spontaneously spring from the dream group field, even though I feel certain I have not specifically encouraged them. One evening, in 1989, I came into my office and was asked to wait a few minutes because there was a surprise. Later, when I was ushered in, I encountered a breathtaking sight—a dream altar. A member had chosen to honor her dream by bringing trinkets, talismans, and other ornaments and objects to signify symbols from her dream. She had dreamed of a treasure chest on the ocean floor, chock full of pearls, gemstones, gold, and glowing objects. For her altar she seemed to have brought every piece of jewelry she owned—pearls, broaches, rings, necklaces—that all cascaded from a chest lined with a satin cloth. This had been planned by the members that week over the phone. It became a frequent part of that group's activities, a spontaneous ritual of sorts. These creative thoughtful activities succeeded in developing significant bonding and closeness, as well as developing a type of dream group personality. Some of these rituals or ceremonies would take hold and have energy in them for years, as the groups repeatedly performed traditions they had developed out of their own dream time together. I was reminded again of the Lakota who could adjust their religious ceremonies when a member had a vision or a dream that suggested a new way to express a traditional spiritual rite. Ritual seems to arise naturally out of the group tribal psyche. When a cluster of people discover common themes amongst themselves, the natural outcome is to concretize or symbolize the connecting thread. A number of such events come to mind—some of the ones that stand out are as follows:

1. "Charlatan Graduation": In a dream group it was discovered over time that each member suffered from what came to be known as the "Charlatan Complex." This is the deep secret that one is only fooling the world about being a professional or even an expert in some areas. All degrees happen purely by accident, special honors are really mistakes, and any achievement in the world occurs only from good fortune, not by a manifest effort. One group member was inspired to honor this crippling absurdity by printing diplomas on her computer for each group member. She designed an elaborate, realistic-looking diploma, complete in old script Latin, on parchment paper. Each name was lettered in calligraphy as receiving a "Ph.D. in Charlatanism." Additionally, she brought gowns (old choir robes), and we had a ceremony where each received her diploma, had her name announced, and shook hands with all members of the "graduating" class.

2. A lesbian couple met and fell in love in dream group. They weren't "out" yet, so the dream group gave them an engagement shower when they decided to live together, even though their grown children thought they were only roommates. The dream group felt somewhat responsible for the relationship and was delighted about it. The women were "straight" before they met in dream group, so the whole experience signified radical change. One member was disgusted about it and left, which only managed to bond the rest of the members more tightly around the couple and their desire to celebrate their union. They received small romantic gifts, and the group gave them a blessing and fixed a meal for them. They were, of course, touched because they had no other container to tell about and celebrate their love.

3. One group designed a ceremony around abortion. Each of the women in the group had some history with abortion: one woman worked in an abortion clinic, one member had been an abortion

counselor some years before, several members had themselves had an abortion or had contemplated it, and so on. One woman had had an abortion when she was quite young and this was something she had shared with no one. Over time, a ritual grew out of this common connection. The members (unbeknownst to me) brought a dark velvet cloth one evening and displayed all types of paraphernalia related to abortion. On the cloth were a coat hanger, a rabbit skin, and even some surgical instruments used in the procedure. Several members had devised a liturgy, and we all participated. It was an extraordinary event—difficult, painful, healing. This ritual was the most shocking one from my memory bank. But the woman whose process provoked the abortion ritual afterward had a magnificent dream that seemed to indicate a substantial psychological shift. Her dream was:

> *I am pregnant and in the dream group. All of the members are there; one holds my head, one holds my hand, and so on. I am surrounded by the women, and they are assisting me. The baby is born. Tess cuts the umbilical chord with golden scissors. I know I have given birth to a new part of myself.*

4. Another example of spontaneous ritual involved a group member who was quite ill. The dream group opted to meet at Church of the Transformation in Dallas where a replica of the labyrinth at Chartres Cathedral has been permanently installed in the church narthex. We walked the labyrinth together to honor and participate in our member's healing process. Afterward, another member of dream group had a series of dreams that seemed to indicate she had latent healing abilities with her hands. Even though the dreamer detested fundamental religion of all kinds, her dream presented a potential that took a courageous risk to integrate. As a result of her dream, our sick dream group member

requested that the group lay hands on him and pray for him to honor both their processes.

5. Another evening when I arrived for dream group I was instructed to answer a few questions before I entered the meeting room, because a surprise was being planned. I was to name which cardinal direction I most identified with at this time in my life, to say which direction I was moving toward, to choose an object from my office that I felt special attachment to, and to pick an animal I thought helped me most in my dreams. Then I was ushered into my own office and asked to lie on the floor, where the group proceeded with a brief yet very touching ceremony to prepare me for the hysterectomy I was having the next week. They blessed me for a safe surgical procedure and honored the crone stage of life I was now entering.

Dream groups often honor transitions in their members' lives. Going off to graduate school, moving to another area, the death of a spouse or parent, a marriage, a surgery—all have been opportunities to express the event in ritual. It remains astonishing to me to remember how often and in what detail some of these experiences manifested. Repeatedly and without encouragement, in all of the groups, spontaneous ritual emerges as part of the dream group process.

CONFRONTATIONAL DREAMS

As I have emphasized, dreams by the uninitiated do not at first glance appear to be all that revealing, intimate, or sacred. Usually, this is the attitude novices have when a dream group experience begins. Quickly, however, even very new members experience the nakedness dreams reveal from the beginning. Dreams are also confrontational—just as a therapist might be—often using humor and exaggeration to make a point. In training candidates to become Jungian analysts, I have often stated, "You don't have to confront the analysand directly. The dream will do so and far more effectively than you can, because it comes from the dreamer himself." Dreams have the sting of being one's own creation.

Let me share an example: An analysand had a bad crush on a much younger woman with whom he worked. In four years of analysis this was his fourth or fifth debilitating crush that brought on obsessive feelings, fantasies, irritability, not to mention trouble with his long-suffering wife. The pattern of his crushes was one of unrequited love. None of the women was the least bit interested in him, which fueled a resentment, bitterness, and even dangerous rage toward them. I was getting impatient by the time the last one emerged in his life. He was sarcastic, invasive, obtrusive, and accusatory to the previously mentioned young woman. But eventually he brought a dream that allowed a shift, albeit a painful one, as follows:

I stood up, turned around, put my butt right in D's face and let a huge fart on her.

He was embarrassed by the dream. I said, "What do you suppose this could mean for you?" (Dream facilitator tool kit uses "play dumb" for sensitive moments.) He said, "I think I've let a big emotional fart on her." I was relieved to see this dream changed his conscious attitude entirely. He immediately let go of the relationship, even though he still felt the pull of attraction, and most of his anger and harassment toward her ended.

Additionally, he showed insight about his entire psychological makeup after this dream—insight of which I had not known he was capable. He said, "You know I'm angry all of the time. I imagine grand visions about myself, like becoming a famous actor at 50, and then I retreat to vicious sarcasm and resentment when the fantasies don't come true. It's like I'm riding an inflation / deflation roller coaster. The women I project on are designed to make me end up feeling like shit."

This is one of the delights of dream work; here, all by himself, he found insight, through the dream's confrontation, that set him free from a psychological injury that had tormented him for years. His defensive structure would not have tolerated so much confrontation from me, as he had fired other therapists before. I knew his resistance was strong to having me address his behavior directly. Confronting directly doesn't work, anyway. If it did, therapists would have been out of their jobs long ago because all suggestions would have been taken to heart, resulting in the desired change. Yelling at and shaming clients doesn't work, even if the therapist is on the radio or T.V. No amount of telling a person how to live is effective. Alanon has well articulated the futility of trying to control another's behavior. But most know that when one decides to make a change, then it is possible to succeed. Our own dreams are our own—they make their point much more effectively than another person could. The dream cited above occurred some years ago, and it remained a turning point in the dreamer's analysis.

Dreams are quite revealing, even the ones members believe are "safe" to share in a group. For example, a dream group member seemed to be having a difficult time integrating into the group partly because she presented an entirely happy and "I'm satisfied with life" façade. Her children, marriage, parents, volunteer activities were all entirely "wonderful, great, and fulfilling." Even though her positive attitude was commendable, there seemed to be a false edge to her cheery demeanor. She brought in the following dream:

I am with my husband in our kitchen getting dinner ready. As we prepare a soup together, suddenly he turns to me and says my lips are too thin. I feel hurt.

This dream contained a multiplicity of directions in which to explore: the dreamer's feminine side, her self-esteem, her sexuality, her relationship with her husband, as well as the negative projection she had attached to her husband. However, the avenue the dream discussion took involved how her husband treated her, since, until then (perhaps six months), the group members had only heard how wonderful he was. In the classic rule book of Jungian dream interpretation, this dream compensated the ego's overly positive view of the husband or husband complex. The dreamer was shocked and embarrassed to be caught by her own dream. The discussion revealed her husband to be rather critical and tyrannical. There she was, not as happy as she liked to portray herself and surprised a little dream could bring up such a flood of naked, undefended, unconscious feeling.

In another case, a dream group member shared her dream with not a small amount of chagrin. She had been working with her dreams for some time and therefore knew well its meaning as soon as she awakened.

"I am in my daughter's house. I look down at my shoes and see they are muddy." She laughed and blushed as she told the group that she had been "caught" by the dream maker. She and her daughter were having difficulties because the dreamer was trying to influence some life decisions for the daughter. In other words, old fashioned mother-meddling. She immediately realized her shoes were muddy, her actions were bringing a destructive aspect to the relationship, and she was entirely responsible. Even before dream group met, she called to apologize to her daughter and remove herself from the controlling position she had taken.

Confrontational dreams could fill an entire volume alone because nearly all dreams contain some element of difficult information. But my observation is that the dream maker gives a constructive critique—one that is designed to improve our lives and relationships, even if the knowledge may be painful. One knows that looking inside the box hiding in the attic is risky.

ARCHETYPAL DREAMS

"Archetypal" (see glossary) elements are one of the chief features of dreams. They are rich, potent, mysterious, and yet easily trivialized images that must be handled with circumspection. Besides the subjective and objective approach to dream interpretation, archetypal dreams fall into their own category. As earlier stated, subjective dreaming is where characters in a dream represent aspects of ourselves. For example, the terrible men breaking into our house generally can be distilled to fears, anxieties, or negative self thoughts involving the psyche of the dreamer. In objective dream interpretation, the actual data or fact the dream presents informs our waking reality. For example, in the dream "Thin Lips" previously cited, the dreamer realized she carried too positive a view of her relationship with her husband. Other times, usually infrequently, one may have archetypal or collective dreams. Archetypal dreams are somewhat rare but do account for a percentage of dreams one will experience.

The following is an example of an archetypal dream:

> *I dreamed an East Indian woman met me on a dusty path.*
> *She had full lips and was dressed like the ancient statues,*
> *full of jewelry and flowing fabrics. Her navel was showing.*
> *I felt intense love and attraction. She kissed me full on the*
> *mouth. Her lips were like a vagina. She had cows or oxen*
> *and showed them to me.*

The dreamer had no specific knowledge of Buddhism, the oxen motif in Buddhism, or of the archetypal feminine goddess he encountered. But this dream did begin a course of study and practice in Buddhism that changed his spiritual direction permanently.

In Zen Buddhism, a series of ink drawings dating back hundreds of years, called the "Zen Ox Bearing Pictures," serves as a template for *Satori,* or enlightenment. These remarkable painting are the subject of much commentary and study in Zen. Roshi Phillip Kapleau states in *The Three Pillars of Zen:*

> Among the various formulations of the levels of realization in Zen, none is more widely known than the Oxherding Pictures, a sequence of ten illustrations annotated with comments in prose and verse. It is probably because of the sacred nature of the ox in ancient India, that this animal came to be used to symbolize man's primal nature or Buddha-mind. (Kapleau, 313)

Furthermore, after beginning his religious exploration in Tibetan Buddhism, the analysand eventually settled into Zen—apparently his true path. He found in Zen practice a home unlike any he had encountered before. He entered into the Zen emptiness state of mind relatively easily and found innumerable positive benefits from his meditations. His Zen discipline developed three years after his dream.

Archetypal dreams come from a level "below" the personal unconscious in a realm we all share like the underwater rivers and table water below the earth's crust. Each of us is part of this great soup. When dreams are deeply moving and profoundly perplexing one might go to the library or to symbol books to see if the universal amplifications shed light on the dream images, only if, of course, one has no distinct personal associations.

In the archetypal oxen dream one also can see the prospective nature of this dream. Here a "prospectus" of the psyche's process is shown. Not a prediction of the future, but an invitation to a possibility, which is why and how looking at dreams in retrospect seems to indicate they have predictive features. In the case of an archetypal dream of this sort it would be inadvisable for the dreamer to ignore the inherent beckoning toward Buddhism the dream reveals.

In the beginning of my practice a significant session occurred that brought into focus for me the ease in which one can make the classic mistake of jumping to archetypal or collective conclusions before the proper personal associations have been explored with the dreamer. In this session, I was told a dream in which Ken Kesey appeared. Being a bit of a beat literary fan, I right away saw the Kesey figure in the dream as an archetypal anti-hero, a myth of collective consciousness and the revolution of culture that had taken place in the 1960s. Luckily, something told me to ask first if there were any personal associations to Kesey. To my surprise the dreamer said, "Oh well, he's kind of got a little pot belly and he doesn't say much. . . ." Before she could go on, I asked incredulously, "Do you know this man?" "Oh yes," she said, "He's been a sound engineer for our band for a while." So what I was all set out to make into a "romantic, heroic, quest for meaning and the new order" archetype was actually a rather confrontive dream image about an animus projection that wasn't entirely positive. To her, he was a fatherish figure and not at all the hero I made him up to be. Over-romanticizing dreams, archetypes, and all symbolic images is a common error amongst those who work with dreams. It is easy, as one can see in this case, to leap or race off to preconceived pretty notions that fulfill one's need to be optimistic, meaningful, helpful, wise, literate, metaphorical, and so on.

In another case during my training, an analyst criticized my poor posture and indicated my analysis should have helped it. At my next session, my analyst was quite outraged by this story. He jumped around the office (being a bit on the dramatic side) and squealed in a high voice, "I'm going to call her right now and tell her I love your back, your back is perfect, I wouldn't do anything to change your back!" I asked him to explain. He told me my back was important psychologically to hold the homeostasis of my psyche—change the back and another worse symptom might appear. As he put it, "Your back is very smart, and I know your back is smarter than I am."

Later it began to occur to me that all material that emerges from the unconscious is "smart"; it has its own integrity and is part of the play in the whole system of the incarnate body-soul-mind. Most of the things we don't like about ourselves are there for a good reason and won't go away, in any case, just because we want them to. The offending or confusing attitude, whether it be sadness or defeat or mania or loneliness, is more able to be understood if it is validated, explored, or even exaggerated.

A member of a dream group felt wretched and despondent after graduate school because she hadn't succeeded in securing employment. She studied a dozen years to complete an undergraduate degree, then received a master's degree, as well as a doctorate in Divinity. She wanted to serve a church in her denomination in which she was ordained. Her church had ordained women pastors for years, but it was still difficult to find a congregation willing to accept a fifty-ish woman to fulfill the duties of pastor. Year after year, no job came. She interviewed, sent out her vita, and guest preached. Still, no job. Meanwhile, she developed a strong solitaire habit and frequently would stay up until four A.M. playing cards. She hated herself for it and regularly chastised herself for such aberrant behavior. I figured the solitaire might be saving her from something much worse and likened it to the rote and repetitious activities often described in fairy tales where the hero or heroine is being required to perform endless tasks before resolution occurs in the tale. But I was concerned when she reached seven years post-graduation with no employment. I began to wonder if she would ever work. The solitaire got worse, of course, and her shame along with it. I asked her to be kind to herself, thank herself for having the energy and creativity to stay up all night to play solitaire and to PLAY IT MORE. She was to celebrate solitaire completely, get a really fancy deck of cards and put herself on a compulsory diet of lots and lots of solitaire. The dream group gifted her with a new deck of cards. Perhaps coincidentally, but nonetheless, within a few weeks we gave her a good-bye blessing because she was off to a new job in another state as a head pastor of a church near a large state university. She has been well received by the people and, as of this writing, has been employed over eight years with the same congregation.

The amplification of the dark, the unknown, the shameful, and the frightening is just where the psyche needs to go, because this is precisely where the energy lies. The emotional "charge" is where the trapped libido lies in latent potential.

One can imagine the following metaphor: suppose ego consciousness—that is, our self or the "I" as we perceive it—is a vast prairie. From a distance it appears to be a flat grassland with no outstanding features. But upon closer inspection, one can see prairie dog holes, creek beds, a few trees, sunken and raised areas of ground—an entire ecosystem. This is like the psyche; it appears mundane and ordinary, but actually it is complex and quite unique. To discover one's unique self is to "individuate" in Jung's term. Our adaptations aren't especially unique, nor do they contain strong medicine from which one learns. It is in the sufferings, the phobias, the obsessive attitudes, the addictions, and depressions that one can find the unique self, the part that is wholly individual, the part that is complete.

It, of course, would not be admissible to amplify behavior that is destructive to self or others. I would not suggest an alcoholic drink more. Common sense needs to prevail. In all psychology common sense, ethic, and the grounded nature of things are paramount for effective treatment to occur. But tired, clichéd, therapeutic formulae only smooth the surface. It takes risk and courage to transform the psyche.

CHAPTER EIGHT

Self Disclosure

FOLLOWING A PROCESS OR TRACKING A CLIENT IS NOT MEANT to rob him or her of their emotional self, however. Sometimes I have to contain my outrage so the client can have his own and not be erased by my passion. Validation of feeling may not always be as effective as containing the feeling—sometimes supporting the dark is just being silent. To take a case in point, a demure woman with an impressive education and career came for treatment of depression. She suffered significantly. Since she was somewhat socially isolated, I suggested she join a dream group. She agreed. Early in our conversations she revealed a long-term ongoing relationship with her former priest. To our dismay, dream group learned she began the affair while in marriage counseling with the priest. The marriage, not surprisingly, didn't survive. Then she implored us not to judge this relationship with her former priest because it was the only intimacy she had—albeit infrequent since he struggled with staying in their relationship. So we agreed. I held my attitude in check, coaching the dream group to do the same, keeping quiet while we learned disturbing details about their relationship.

I could almost bet this man had no real concern or feelings for my client even though she fantasized a significant love affair.

Over time, however, she began to acknowledge her disappointment when he didn't call and his distance and unavailability when she called him. Eventually she confronted him, and he lived up to every one of my tainted expectations.

In retrospect, I believe that if I or dream group had lectured, persuaded, or bullied her into outrage and fury, she would still be defending him to herself, as well as to all of us. By containing her process rather than directing it, she herself found the feelings that were hers from the beginning.

This is only one case illustration but many more could be cited. Perhaps each day I have the challenge to contain or detach from my own feelings so that the feelings of the analysand can emerge. These are precisely the feelings that can allow the soul to transform. This is highly disciplined work; it includes holding attitudes, theories, beliefs, and models of psychology in abeyance. It is simply not helpful to imprint one's therapeutic training and outlook onto a person who is struggling to find his / her own voice.

Much has already been written about the phenomena of projected self-identification. This is the experience in which the therapist has emotions or fantasies that are attributed to the client rather than the therapist. Theoretically, the therapist has "caught" the unconscious process of the client and, by bringing it into the session, can aid in making the material conscious. The same occurrence works in groups when the group mirrors the unconscious feelings of the person working.

This is quite different than just blurting out declarations, however. Consider the following:

> THERAPIST: Can you shed any light on why, all of a sudden, I am having profound anxiety? As I sit here, I feel an actual pain in my heart, as if it is cut in two. Does this image mean anything to you or is this only about me?

Or:

THERAPIST: I find I'm very angry as I listen to this
story—where might these feelings be in you?

Helpful as this technique is, "tracking the client's process" must
take precedence. I am curious about my emotional and imaginal
self in the analytic hour or in dream groups, but always there is
the opportunity to lose the client's process by falling into seductive narcissism. It can be a great relief to talk about one's own
feelings after listening carefully and objectively, but this is not
projected selfidentification. Rather, projected self-identification
is an experience not unlike a shamanic trance in which the
therapist (or sometimes a dream group member) experiences an
urgent, loud, uncontainable feeling. The person who describes
his child abuse in a flat monotone will likely arouse this response
from the listener. Seductive pitfalls exist in many forms in group
work, as well as in analysis. Group is the largest challenge because
there are so many personalities with which to project. Often I do
make personal comments—and am frequently surprised to hear
just what is coming out of my mouth. Then again, I am silent
at times when it would be "okay" to make a self-disclosure. I
imagine instinct is at work; sometimes I make the right choice,
sometimes not. On two or three occasions in my practice I have
been compelled to be quite personal in ways that made me terribly uncomfortable. I hated the way "my process" was imploded
into theirs. But then, this is what my book is about, and in almost every case "my process" really was "our process," after all.
However, one must be circumspect about giving information—it
cannot be taken back.

     As an example, I offer the following experience. I have vol-
unteered off and on for a number of years at the Dallas Suicide
and Crisis Center. In fact, in 1976, I received my first taste of

counseling by participating in telephone crisis work and thereafter decided to leave school teaching to attend graduate school in psychology. Additionally, I became very interested in suicide in my early career and spent time lecturing to groups about warning signs and prevention. Currently, about once a year, I hold a seminar on grief and dreams for families who have survived a suicide. I tell you this so you can understand the energy and history I have for the subject of suicide. The coffee cup I use in my office is a gift that all volunteers from the organization received one Christmas.

A woman I have worked with commented, "I just don't see how families could ever cope with a suicide" in response to our discussion about her spouse's untimely, accidental death. This would have been an ideal opportunity for the seduction of self-importance to hit (which, unfortunately, I am still able to fall prey to!). I could have launched into all manner of authoritative lecture material about suicide, families, grief experiences, and statistics. Instead I sat quietly, letting the moment pass. It did not seem to mirror her process for me to carry off on my own free association. Furthermore, in this case, the client was clever about trying to get me to reveal personal facts so I was hyper-vigilant about not being seduced. But occasionally clients are more tenacious and clever than I am at out foxing me to obtain personal details.

One day, to my horror, an analysand walked into my office with a bouquet of a dozen violet roses the size of pears. She smiled a Cheshire cat smile and said, "Happy Birthday." I must have looked puzzled. She said, "Oh, when I called Gini about my bill, I asked what day was your birthday, and she told me." My humiliation was complete when I asked for her check at the end of the hour, and she told me the roses were my payment. And I found myself unable/unwilling to confront this outrageous act so simply let it go. The case failed shortly thereafter.

Naturally, tracking the process does not exclude self-disclosure.

Quite the contrary, extremes are usually never the right path. To reiterate, self-disclosure is imperative for analysis to be human and real. Refusing to self-disclose appropriately is a way of making the analyst too important—it cloaks him or her into a secretive mystery that is counterproductive. What follows is an example of an analyst's refusal to self-disclose:

CLIENT: I read that book I talked about last session this weekend, then dreamed about it. Have you read it?

ANALYST: *(Silence.)*

CLIENT: Rather than tell you the detailed plot of the book in order to set up my dream, could you tell me if you've read it already?

ANALYST: *(Silence.)*

CLIENT: Can't you just tell me if you've read the fucking book?

ANALYST: *(Long silence.)* Why don't you just tell me the plot of the book.

I find this "macho analysis" archaic and insulting. Relationship and humanity are necessary and vital to the trust and understanding that group members or therapists and clients must have for one another. Tracking the process does not mean that on a given day I won't disclose personal or significant details in an analytic session. These moments seem to arise in the fertile soil of analysis quite spontaneously and unexpectedly. The analyst and analysand carry on a dance. The analysand is leading; the analyst follows. All persons who know how to follow on the dance floor know what an art and achievement it is—and how sublime an experience when it works. The closer the analyst follows the client's lead, the better the dance will be.

Twice I've heard analysts say they refused to work with dreams in their practices, because after a fashion it became clear the analysand intuited too much personal material about the analyst. Often this spooky intuition will come up in dreams; in other cases it appears in the analytic field whether one works with dreams or not.

Actually, there is validity in the concerns of these analysts, but I feel they have taken their caution too far by cutting off dream work entirely. One does have to be careful about clients who have too much innate curiosity and factual data about an analyst—it begins to feel like a terrible invasion of privacy. Additionally, the analyst can be in danger. Clients like this take a psychological and emotional toll on the analyst, a toll that may have a debilitating physical component, as well. One can experience fatigue, depression, confusion, anxiety, physical pain, insomnia, and a general burned-out feeling. It is as if the client's psyche has invaded or trespassed on the analyst's privacy and personhood. It can have a deep effect in the unconscious since the client has entered a sacred tribal area that may be an unwelcome intrusion. Through jealously, envy, power needs, or destructive tendencies, the analysand may be set on betraying or destroying the analyst, in part, out of an unrequited love experience or general unresolved transference.

Several cases I know illustrate these unfortunate phenomena. One involved a therapist who was being sued for a frivolous allegation. The paperwork and bureaucracy were expensive financially and emotionally. Although the experts on both sides agreed no harm was committed, she lost her malpractice carrier and, more importantly, her trust for the people who came to her for her care.

In two other cases, clients ran off with the analyst's / therapist's spouse. This is quite a betrayal on several levels. Amazingly, these things can and do happen without the therapist breaking any "boundary rules." For example, when all parties are therapists, they might cross paths professionally. Or, a psychotherapy practice in a small community could make crossovers almost inevitable. It is just as important for the client to understand the container of trust and self-preservation as it is for the therapist. The analysis can fail in any number of ways. Clearly, the therapist must behave ethically and professionally so that he / she might establish a safe professional field within which the client and therapist can work. So be it! But let one not ignore the other component of the professional relationship—the safety and health of the analyst. So far, this part of the therapeutic relationship has been largely ignored, however subtle or extraordinary the invasions may be. On a few occasions, therapists have even been murdered by angry or disturbed clients or group members. And yet the analyst has only his / her own intuitions and diagnostic skills to determine if the therapeutic relationship will be beneficial to the client, as well as safe for the therapist.

These determinations are, in part, made in the tribal field; however, the client "knowing" the therapist's personal material before it has been shared is not a good sign, even though it may seem like an indication of a positive connection. Again, if the therapist feels a particular type of exhausted affect that emerges after the session, this can be an indicator that the client has unconsciously invaded the therapist. Some examples follow.

During her session, a client told her therapist that she had had a vision in which the therapist was being sexually abused by her father. The client wanted to know if the therapist was aware of this fact! Naturally, the therapist was appalled. First of all, the father had not been a perpetrator at all; it was all a projection and fantasy from the client during the time when repressed sexual memories were fashionable to discover. Second, the client's clear inflation and lack of appropriate boundaries were disturbing to the therapist. But this case worked out well. In the early stages, the therapist maintained a strictly private and anonymous demeanor, so eventually the client developed appropriate boundaries. In this way, she was forced to focus on herself and to find a self rather than project all of her imagination onto the therapist.

In another situation, I was interviewed by telephone for a prospective case. The father called inquiring about work for his twenty-year-old daughter. He started calling every other day or so to ask more and more questions. They became increasingly personal. During our last conversation, he wanted to know what my worst shadow characteristics were, since he felt it necessary to understand this in order to approve my working with his daughter. Believe it or not, he was also a therapist. I told him that information was really none of his business, and that was the last I heard from him.

While I was still in training but beginning to work with analysands, I discussed a case with my analyst, Mary Briner. I was concerned but also fascinated by a new client that had an extremely uncanny ability to invade my personal process. A number of synchronicities had occurred, including her calling me at the exact moment she crossed my mind. Mary told me to terminate with her, that she was violating me unconsciously, or at the least to be very careful not to let her in to my personal life at all. Unfortunately, I didn't respect the importance of that advice nearly enough; this case ended as perhaps the worst of my entire career. Connection and relationship and synchronicity are what this book is all about, but even so, one has to contain this energy with a strong ego structure. Suspicion is appropriate—especially when danger is possible. One cannot go off the deep end by being seduced and sidetracked from too many mysterious experiences.

One must acknowledge that the interior, deep work with people is a vulnerable and risky undertaking for the analyst as well as for the client or dream group member. It is a gooey, relational, magical, funny, sad, enlivened place in which to sit in sacred space together. The analyst also has to trust—to believe in the value and worth of the client. To take him or her on, the process requires loyalty and commitment from both sides of the experience, and when the therapist senses a disturbance in the field, it must be attended to. In working with therapists and their failed cases, or even disastrous ones (as well as my own), rarely have I heard one say he / she hadn't received loud clues that flagged trouble from the beginning, clues that were patently ignored chiefly because they came from this mysterious connected realm.

KNOWING / NOT KNOWING

One can think of the ego and unconscious as separate, sometimes opposing, forces within the larger structure of the personality. A row boat on a vast sea offers a helpful image. In this paradigm, a little rowboat is the ego; the unconscious is the ocean. The boat is the tiny island of consciousness the ego has made for itself. The ocean is the base, the great support, the vast space upon which the boat rests and travels. The ocean is in charge, as any rower knows. If there is wind or weather or a current greater than the capacity of the rower to conquer, the ocean will win. The ocean is vast and more powerful than the boat, and yet the boat is supported by this vast sea. When the unconscious experiences a disturbance or upheaval, the ego can only go along, just like the rowboat—no matter how strong the will or desire.

A middle-aged woman came to analysis disturbed by her inability to perform household tasks with the vigor and certainty she had exhibited in the past. Terrified, she was unable, no matter how hard she tried, to sort through the attic and closets or to keep the refrigerator clean and stocked. She bemoaned this frightening and embarrassing symptom. What previously had given her meaning and purpose now had utterly failed her, and all energy or libido for housework had left. Her rowboat was in waters too choppy to navigate.

She thought by coming to see me this problem could be fixed, and she would be able to return to her routine, undisturbed and uninterrupted. Unfortunately (or fortunately) this was not likely the case. Here was an example of the unconscious—the far greater force in the psyche—winning out over the ego attitude which believed maintaining the status quo to be the safest and best course. In therapeutic sessions, the analyst would instinctively wish to explore the symptom of "laziness," and perhaps validate it or find its root motivations. If we think of the lazy self as "smart," one can see a woman who is at a crossroads in life, desperate to find fulfillment and a sense of meaning in the absence of such. Although housework satisfied her earlier years, it no longer supported the Self's need for autonomy. Her system had completely shut down in rebellion. Her desperate statement, "I just can't do this anymore," suggested the ego was beginning to acknowledge the greatness of the unconscious—whatever "this," for her, turned out to be. Her quest, then, was not to find a way to clean the oven but to discover how she really wanted to spend her time—time free from conventional expectation.

But the ego needs are not insignificant, and civilization and ethic do have to be considered. Naturally, following the emergence of the unconscious has to be tempered with reality and common sense. Most mistakes occur when the ego overly concretizes the images from the unconscious and loses its bearing. It is something like a sailor abandoning ship to jump in the ocean and swim to a faraway shore, a shore that could be purely illusory. Sometimes middle-aged men or women develop a strong attraction to a person other than their spouse. Additionally, they often feel that to truly honor the process emerging, an affair or leaving the marriage is essential. One must look at the images first, however. What does this new person symbolize in the psyche if he / she were an aspect of self? What part of the feminine self or masculine self or talented self (the possibilities are infinite) needs to be recovered and "made love" to? How can one become more spontaneous, wild, fun, sexual, uninhibited, alive, creative, or spiritual? This is often (but not always) what these mid-life affairs tend to be about. Too many years of toiling at work, achieving goals, and fighting dragons can make the psyche vulnerable to outrageous emotional compensation. When the energy for heroic accomplishment begins to subside at mid-life, it can be a critical and difficult time for a man or woman. The energy can land on a person who, ultimately, may have nothing at all to do with the process of becoming rounder, fuller, or more complete as a human being.

Simply shaming oneself for the attraction and suppressing the sexual feelings are not the answers either. The life and energy that have emerged need to be validated and brought into the light of day for close examination and understanding. On occasion, the "smart" aspect of the attraction is moving one toward acknowledging that the marriage is dead, lifeless, and no amount of fear about family obligations or finances will change that. The unconscious has a way of demanding our cooperation until it becomes essential that the ego adopt different values and beliefs about itself. Plenty of people have gone on to marry and have long-term happy marriages from these "blow up the family" attractions—that is why one has to be especially cautious about jumping to conclusions and making generalizations based on preconceived judgments, one's own experience, or one or two previous cases. In each instance, the analyst must approach the psyche of the analysand with curiosity and openness. Not all fat women are the same, nor are all middle-aged men. And so it is a subtle walk—that of honoring the client or dream group member by making him / her the center of the work, yet allowing the therapist's unconscious to be part of the mix as well. Then, the emerging "process" can develop in a container of courage and new possibilities.

One has to walk a tightrope, balancing between not knowing on the one hand and knowing too much on the other. The not-knowing side is open, curious, has no thoughts or judgments, has no ideas or motivation to fix, heal, or change. It is the contemplative, void Self. It is compassionate, receiving, a pure vessel in which to contain the emerging process. The knowing-too-much self has experience, insight, intuition, and education. This self has spoken hours to persons who suffer, struggle, and search. Additionally, the knows-too-much self has had his/her own process to evaluate and experience through his/her own therapies and analyses. This side is also quick to see a pattern or a syndrome, to judge, to categorize, to label, to compartmentalize. This side is not knowing, as well.

CHAPTER NINE

Synchronicity Emerges

SOMETIMES THE IRRATIONAL PROCESS EMERGES SO COM-
pletely in analysis or in dream groups that one cannot dispute the
complexity and mystery of the work, no matter how much one
believes it has all been said or experienced before. Synchronicity
(see glossary) is one way the ego gets a bump on the head that not
all of reality is as it seems. Following are two dreams I had that
were both identical to dreams of two of my analysands:

*1. I am at a beach in India. Giant stone statues lie on the
beach. They seem to be ancient gods and goddesses.*

*2. I am married to Kevin Bacon. He is unfaithful, and
I am sad and angry.*

The first dream was brought into analysis by a male analysand a
few days after I had dreamed it myself. The second dream came
from a female analysand, and was also the same dream I had had
a few nights earlier.

I relate the specifics of these dreams to make it clear that they
are not common variety dreams. This coincidence is referred to in
Jungian Psychology as *synchronicity*—a meaningful coincidence.

91

If an analysand and I, or two dream group members, both dream we are trying to find a classroom, or our teeth have fallen out, I would certainly take note, but not with the same intensity and curiosity that these two dreams produced. Synchronicity is an overused word in recent years. It appears in newspaper columns, *Time Magazine,* talk shows, and other common places where the word has entered into everyday vernacular. Synchronicity is not a "garden variety" coincidence that the ego can easily dismiss with the thought, "Oh this is just a coincidence," but rather, synchronicity is shocking and poignant. Synchronicity signals a confrontation for the ego, because it reveals an undeniable truth.

The shocking coincidence, almost impossible to believe, has a way of breaking the ego's set attitude that it sees all, knows all, understands all. There, right in my consulting room, the mysterious magnificent process reveals a potent magic. One races to explain or justify such an experience. Perhaps there is no teleological meaning. Perhaps the experience speaks for itself—it stands as the mystery against a backdrop of the banality and routine of life. It is at such times that I know we have entered sacred space. It is here transformation and change occurs. Synchronicity in analysis and dream groups reveals a connection between two or more persons attempting a task together—the task of individuation, wholeness, meaning. It reveals an irrational level of the unconscious that is even more common and prominent in dream groups. It suggests that we are unique selves; we live on a foundation of archetypal truth, and in between lies a tribal, relational field where psyches intersect in a mysterious yet rather common way.

This is not an ability of an oddly gifted psychic or some peculiar hoax that can be exposed as a fraud if only enough effort is put into investigating it. Rather, this is an ordinary, everyday experience that our ancestors knew well. It literally helped them to survive. Through the development of understanding dreams, visions, and omens, this asset was used to assist in providing safety and nourishment for the tribe. Now it is buried, forgotten, or defended against.

Lakota history documents a shaman named Clown Woman. She could tell where buffalo herds were from her dreams. Since she was a "contrary," she spoke in opposites, in the morning she might say, "There are no buffalo over the next hill." Then her hunters would know to travel over the next hill to hunt. Reports are that she was skilled in this art, and her people revered her highly for her ability (among other things) to keep the tribe well stocked with fresh meat.

Exercise

For those who find these stories ridiculous, I offer the following experiment. It takes a rather significant commitment, but it is well worth the effort.

1. Record every dream you have for one year. Do not skip any dreams or omit any detail, however insignificant, unimportant, too short, too vague, confusing, or ridiculous. Do not skip dreams that are "stupid," "shameful," "frightening," or "only a snippit." They are almost always the most important.

2. One year later, read all of your dreams. Notice the patterns, the recurring images, the dreams about your family members, your friends, and the people with whom you interact. Are there any clues in your dreams ahead of significant events? Are there clues ahead of time about relationships and how they may have transformed over the year?

Jung was said to say, "Dreams prepare the psyche for the events of the following day." Sometimes they prepare us for events in the weeks, months, or even years to come.

Synchronicity, in general, is a much more common phenomenon than is ordinarily accepted by current attitudes, and yet it is not "commonplace" in the sense that synchronicity is only a mildly amusing irony. But synchronicities occur regularly in people's lives when they begin to watch for them and take note. When one experiences outrageous connected events that may cause the jaw to drop, a deep gasp or sigh to expel from one's chest, or even feel an electric sensation that penetrates the body then synchronicity has manifested. Over time, even remarkable synchronicity becomes more "ordinary," just as the "ordinary" becomes more remarkable.

Synchronicity can emerge in a myriad of ways. Another example involves friends who told me a story that illustrated the tribal field—a story that is commonplace, yet still remarkable if one asks how or why these things happen. In a small group of people, invariably one or two will share a similar experience. After a professional picnic, several of us gathered by White Rock Lake to watch the sunset and visit awhile longer before the weekend was over. One individual began to tell about his ring that helped him find lost objects, which led to the following tale. He and his wife lived apart for a time during which this event occurred. One night his wife, "S," was unable to sleep, so she went downstairs to watch television at 2:30 A.M. Suddenly, she heard a loud noise and feared someone was breaking in. The noise continued. Terrified, she was certain intruders were breaking into her home. Then, she did the only thing she could think of at the time—she banged pots and pans, made a huge racket, and hoped to scare them off. She did. But later, when she spoke to her husband, she discovered he had awakened at exactly 2:30 A.M., distressed, oddly frightened, and unable to go back to sleep.[10]

The tribal, relational element in the couple's psyches had not let go of each other yet, even though they were estranged and apart from one another. However, synchronicity of this sort does not automatically mean that all couples will reconcile. We are just as likely to experience synchronicity surrounding negative or painful manifestations. Synchronicity is only an indication of energy. But it is important to ask the meaning of these experiences, to understand them as clues or guide posts to our lives that often are perplexing and confusing. In this case, the psyche presented a compensation to the outer situation (marital separation) by constellating connection. This "psychic" event occurred for two people, each one participating in the numinous experience of it.

The following is a personal story that further illustrates how the tribal unconscious is not only apparent in therapeutic settings, but can be observed in regular life as well. I have a friend who was a college roommate of mine who has no psychological interests or particular abilities. This is one reason I have enjoyed her company—she is a total vacation from my professional self. We have had some rocky times, however. One night when she was very drunk, I heard her proposition my husband. After that party she quit drinking, but I had a hard time forgiving her. Periodically, anger would resurface, and I would distance myself from her. I decided to discuss this issue in a therapy session of my own, since it seemed to me I was experiencing a type of paranoid anxiety. I still had fears two years later that she was plotting to seduce my husband. Just as I walked into my session, my cell phone rang, and, of course, it was my old roommate. I didn't answer the call. In the session I became aware of a viscous anxiety that attacks my peace of mind especially when I am enjoying myself—a complex (deeply unconscious) that sabotages my joie de vivre. "Hmmm. This was interesting, chewy stuff," I thought as I left the session to go to my office. The idea that my existential suffering was a neurotic trick to rob me of life's gifts was an exciting idea; exciting because it was a breakthrough, and something perhaps could be done to change it. After I got to my office, I flipped on the computer to check email—fifty-four entries, because I had been off-line for a few days. Buried amongst the jokes, advertisements, and brief notes was a letter from my friend. Receiving an email from her was nothing unusual; I had one most of the time I checked my mail, but never before did I remember her sending me a dream. In fact, in almost 30 years, I had heard only one or two of her dreams, because, besides her lack of interest, I had made it clear I could not work on her dreams with her.

The email said:

I had a dream about you last night. I was cleaning out your closet, and all of your clothes looked like they came from Bangladesh. You were wearing a necklace of nettles.

I was decidedly provoked by this dream—it seemed to echo the session I had just had, a session that was in turn largely provoked by my friend-dreamer. She had dreamed about me as impoverished, without proper clothing, and wearing a necklace of nettles. Nettles are stinging plants, and I well remember accidentally brushing against them on Vashon Island in childhood. My hands burned and stung for a long time from just the slightest contact with the plant. In one fairy tale, a kidnapped princess has to weave shirts from nettles to throw on her cursed seven brothers. This is how she is able to change them from bird form back into her human brothers. The nettles are like a stinging, painful sacrifice one makes for transformation to occur. I think anxiety is a lot like weaving a necklace of nettles. Anxiety is a punishing painful fog that can cloud perception, reality, trust, and joy. And yet it seems to be a process many individuals have to experience. I don't have to wear the necklace anymore—I can take it off and choose to live with reckless joyful abandon. The need for the nettles is gone, the brothers are transformed. Or to put it another way, "Since we all are booked on the Titanic, one might as well go first class!"[11]

In accepting new analysands, I prefer two items surface in the first session or two for me to feel the indication our work together might be productive. First of all, I must experience the emotions of like / compassion / curiosity for the individual. This is sort of like a bonding experience toward a child or creature at the animal shelter. I know when I have connected to the caring place in my heart I have a chance, at least, of facilitating an encounter with the numinous process.

Second, I am even more encouraged about the prognosis of an analysis or a dream group when a synchronicity emerges early in the work. For example, once I returned a call to a young man looking for analysis. After a brief introduction by telephone, I asked what, in general, he was interested in accomplishing. He told me he had just broken up with his African American jazz-singer girlfriend, and he was in quite a mess over it. I did not share with him but noted that in my previous session I had just heard a dream about an African American jazz-singer woman.

In spite of the fact that his finances didn't allow him to pay very much, I agreed to see him. In the course of our work a number of synchronistic events occurred that continued throughout the analysis. Overall, I think our sessions were clarifying and meaningful to him. It seems as if synchronicity indicates the Self is alive in the work, that the potential for transformation is indicated because the fire is already burning under the pot. A couple of years before this man called me to begin analysis, I had an experience that was a profound one for me.

I have studied and admired Native American spirituality since the late 1970s. So I was interested in the pipe ceremony that was announced at a local church. Additionally, I was hosting three friends from the Santa Fe Indian College of Art—an Iroquois shaman, a Hopi man whose parents were both shamans, and a Cherokee / Washo man who practiced his native religion. We decided to attend the ceremony together. I was concerned because the person holding the pipe ceremony was charging ten dollars to participate. This did not seem quite right—something akin to a priest charging for the Eucharist. Immediately, when we entered the room where the pipe ceremony was being held, I smelled a bad air. The whole experience screamed out "charlatan." Dozens of people were crowded in the Sunday school room, few I recognized. They seemed to know each other, however, and the protocol of the "ceremony." In the center of the room all faces were on the leader who, on a blanket, was surrounded by rattles, drums, a longhorn skull, crystals, a glass ball, and trinkets of all kinds. His pipe was wrapped in yellow and bright blue ultrasuede and from it hung garishly painted blue turkey feathers. He was dressed in matching blue and yellow ultrasuede clothes, a vest and pants cut with fringe down the side seams. He had a blue suede headband with ponytail. He glared when the four of us joined the group and seemed to become visibly nervous. He was Anglo, like I am.

The three Native American men who accompanied me lasted fifteen minutes or so before they walked out in a unison protest. But we were there long enough for my Iroquois friend to become so angry about the inauthenticity of the "ceremony" that when he received the talking stick being passed around the circle, he spoke only in his native language. My other friends passed the stick silently. After we left to walk around the church grounds to talk and share the experience, I felt pain, sadness, and outrage. I wanted to throw up. I was ashamed of my ancestry—how my people had stolen and pillaged everything we could from the indigenous culture we obliterated in a few decades. And now we were stealing and mocking their religion, too. I felt helpless. Native American culture has been commercialized and exploited widely. And what could I do? I did call the church office to complain about allowing an inauthentic person to masquerade as a holy man in order to charge money for a religious ceremony. My view of the evening was not well received by the staff member with whom I spoke. My reaction that night resulted in Sheldon, the Iroquois shaman, carving a pipe for me. The next day he presented it to me but told me never to use it publicly; it was only for my own private use. I was deeply touched.

Now to return to M., my client who dated the jazz singer. During our first session he discussed an additional issue that was troubling him. He had gotten himself into a cult-like group in the college town where he lived, and he was worried about how to extricate himself without suffering painful consequences. He mostly feared humiliation and pressure from the leader, with whom he felt quite uncomfortable. The leader of the cult turned out to be the same man who led the pipe ceremony at the local church (over forty miles from M.'s college town) that I had attended with my Native American friends.

It was two years before I shared this "coincidence" (aka synchronicity) with M.—it would have been far too much self-disclosure, as well as too much opinion from me for the first session. I had extremely "loud" feelings about the cult leader that were entirely my own. I do admit, though, to allowing the experience I had had with this charlatan to help me support my client to break free from the cultish group. I have discovered, over time, that most unusual experiences or pieces of information that cross my path eventually make sense. As an analyst I knew well used to say, "If you live long enough you get to see the end of so many stories."[12]

However, in dream groups synchronistic phenomena occur amongst all the members, not only to me, so holding back is often not even possible. Consequently, this results in a powerful, magical, and mysterious tone to the group process. One of the reasons I wanted to try the dream group experiment was the sense I had that the drama, the passion, the tears, and the miracles I heard each day in my office were too much for only me to hear. Surely there was a larger audience this was meant for. The metaphor and humor of the dreams, the hyperbolic characterizations, the archetypal stories that encompassed aspects of mythology, literature, and ancient traditions were almost more than I could absorb. (Sometimes I yearned for other persons to help me "hear" the enormity of the process.) Also, at least weekly, I heard a dream I knew could benefit others if they heard it too. The interconnectedness of group members was something I suspected could happen but didn't know for sure. Indeed, as the people united and bonded, life began to unfold the complex synchronistic tapestry of their lives and how they wove together and impacted each other.

The Group Field

The power of groups is a magic long noticed and acknowledged by many observant professionals. When individuals come together to share a common goal, understand a problem, or support each other, the power is greater than an individual can manifest by him/herself. Fritz Perls is credited with saying, "The whole is greater than the sum of its parts," which characterizes this notion succinctly. One cannot underestimate the power and legacy groups manifest. No one person can find the motivation and passion that several can constellate together. In groups, ideas can become companies, thoughts can become a revolution, heartache can become many working together for change and the evolution of society. Just a few people together can form Alcoholics Anonymous, a group that succeeds in battling alcoholism with group support as one of its cornerstones. Those suffering from eating disorders, multiple sclerosis, female pattern baldness, men seeking intimacy—all have formed groups to heal, to motivate, to change. Dream group also has the powerful synergy of people working together interested in achieving a common goal, which is to learn to understand the language of the dream maker, to make conscious some of the mystery of the underworld, to weave stories of its members into a pattern, and to connect to and support one another.

The group forms a field—it is a base or background—a solidity from which ideas, love, energy, focus, creativity, spirituality, and passion can emerge. The field is the space that is often ignored because the object is so often the focus. The space between the notes in music is a field; it is the emptiness that allows the melody to take a shape, a pattern. The thought behind the thoughts is another way of conceptualizing the field. The thought behind provides a base, a base of deep thought accessed through meditation, writing, or working with dreams, as examples.

There is a legend in the Maritimes of Canada that only once in a person's lifetime might he / she see the shadow of the star of Venus. In order to see this shadow, one has to be present during the following conditions: a new moon, a clear night, and a freshly fallen snow. Only then is it possible to see this most subtle of shadows cast by the first star on a pitch-black night. (I cannot resist pointing out that this star / planet is named after the Goddess of Love—the archetype that brings the first glimmer of consciousness in the darkness.) The shadow is there at other times; we just don't see it, because it is obliterated by brighter realities. But it is there. It lies quietly behind in the subtle substance, in the background.

We are affected by each other. Ordinary observation tells us that we create wars, fall in love, and form families by our contact with each other. When adults come together to discuss dreams, they too are affected by each other, and the entirety of the group forms a personality. Educators observe how classes are different from each other based on the mix of personalities of the participants. Dream group is the same way. Generally, because the group is interested in something personal and vulnerable such as dreams, the goo is strong. As stated earlier, some people enter dream group far underestimating the power of dreams and groups; they are surprised or even dismayed to discover that dream work is a naked experience, totally defenseless and emotionally raw, even with the so-called "unimportant" dreams. The field, then, is of a raw vulnerability, a shocking intimacy rarely touched in our daily lives, and bonds form that are deep and permanent. Additionally, the field produces a foundation that can be thematic or similar to having a unique personality of its own. I recall the divorcing-women dream group. The field in that case was splitting, separation, division, destruction. Another group I worked with for a number of years was grounded in the field of love; not only did a couple form in the group, but at the same time one of the members formed a love partnership and brought her partner to the group. The group was composed of significantly wounded people: physical disabilities, family tragedies, loneliness. The group members became a loving support for each other and developed into an extended family. They shared holiday dinners, attended their children's weddings, helped each other find new jobs, bought symphony tickets together, and traveled together. After I terminated my participation in the group to stay home with my son in the evenings, they continued to meet and still do as of this writing, which is now about twelve years after I was involved.

The field can also be observed in the form of synchronicity. Dream group members have an uncanny habit of dressing in the same colors or in the same clothing on given days. Dreams will be congruent beyond the average level of coincidence. In one group I have led since 1986, we almost always identify a theme for each time we meet. Sometimes everyone's dream will actually be about the same issue.

This commonality, or theme as it might be called, lies within the tribal field that modern life has almost completely annihilated. Like the shadow of the star of Venus, it remains a part of the background even when society has become too individualistic to recognize it. The themes succeed in providing a sense of belonging. It is significantly amazing to realize that the human condition has a common ground. Then, one may begin to lose the sense of alienation and isolation that the modern and postmodern eras have encouraged.

Some of these events are nearly impossible to describe fully, rather like taking a black-and-white photograph of a three-dimensional colorful sculpture. Additionally, some of these occurrences are so fantastical I can't fault anyone for doubting their credibility. Dream groups laugh together when these events occur, because we all postulate no one could possibly believe any of this is real. Furthermore, I have lost many of the nuances and subtleties over time; they have washed down the river of lost memory. Even some of the most remarkable events have been lost for me. Only recently, two former dream group members were incredulous when I didn't remember a specific dream and synchronicity regarding a misplaced purse. One member dreamed the contents and the location of another's missing purse. I had and have no recollection of the dream and surrounding events; however, the members assure me it happened. So many mysterious things have occurred, I postulate my psyche can hold only so much; the rest is stored in a place too far away for me to retrieve. I find it interesting to reflect that the specifics have faded, with the exception of a few examples, but the flavor has remained. However, the landscape of the field is intact in my encounter and the encounters of those who participated in this experiment.

Thus, with this disclaimer, I offer an example. Two members of dream group went hiking together over a weekend. Both women, in their early forties, were gifted intuitively and attempting to integrate the spiritual into their lives and professions. One was attending seminary; the other was a grant writer who later also attended seminary and went on to become an ordained clergyperson. The first woman ultimately became a licensed therapist. During the hike, they decided to take separate paths for a period of time and meet back at the wide space where the path forked. Later, they reunited and shared their solitary hiking meditation time apart. Both had selected stones to take home. Each woman, as she was walking on her fork of the path, had decided to bend over and select a rock that somehow attracted her attention amongst all the rocks and pebbles on the trail. When they examined their respective stones, they were astonished to see the two rocks were part of one large stone that had been broken into two pieces. One woman had picked her rock up at the start of the walk, the other as she returned to their meeting place.

At the next group meeting, the two members brought their rocks, their story, and their amazement. We passed the two slivers around the circle. The rocks fit together perfectly like a jigsaw puzzle—two freshly cut pieces of the same rock, the edges still raw and sharp, the inside flesh of the pieces paler and lighter than the outer, darker skin. We marveled over this fantastical synchronicity.

One may point out this phenomenon did not occur in the dream group proper. Therefore, how can one claim any synchronicity fueled by dream group? Over time, in groups, I have witnessed a number of alliances, relationships, coincidences, synchronicities, and inter-weavings of the members that didn't necessarily occur within the confines of our biweekly, three-hour meeting. The field that is created by the interaction and risk of dream telling goes beyond the manufactured set time limits of modern civilization. The groups fostered intimacy, contact, lunches, phone calls, and other gooey transactions. As previously mentioned, I didn't discourage outside contact between members as some group leaders suggest, or even require. Quite the opposite, I supported the interaction of members partly because one of the objectives of dream group is to encounter and become related to the tribal field in which one finds oneself.

Synchronicity can manifest in a variety of ways. For example, it became evident as a sweeping event in which six women all became divorced in a dream group over a period of two years—all women who had only been married once, who had children, and who were married between fifteen and twenty-five years. Another example of a broad synchronicity that spanned a two- or three-year period of time was the years I had seven women in my private analytical practice, women who were all moving from heterosexuality to a lesbian lifestyle. Since then, I have had no such similar cases, nor did this curiosity reflect movement in my own process in any literal way. On the other hand, synchronicity may manifest as a single, pointed event like the two women who both chose pieces of the same rock to take home from their hike. Synchronicity might be evident immediately or over an extended period of time. It might be humorous, frightening, or inspiring. In dream groups the most common manifestation is in dreams. Similar dreams, dreams with the same characters, dreams about similar or the same issues all have become some of the "ordinary-extraordinary" occurrences in dream groups. During the time the divorcing-women dream group met, they experienced a rather unforgettable synchronicity of an entirely different type. The connecting link of this group was the way in which all of the members were exploring a vast new territory of spirituality. In the late 1980s, they were spontaneously devising rituals, building dream altars, and delving deeply into the goddess movement. Snakes, of course, were and are a significant symbol in a number of myths—the women were fond of snake jewelry, carved wooden folk art snakes, even rubber snakes found in science shops. The snake was thought to be the primary symbol of the Great Goddess, and therefore, the snake creature was highly revered among these women.

My office, at that time, was on the first floor of a two-story traditional Dallas office building. It was part of an office building corridor along the giant "LBJ 635" highway, and the area remains a rather industrial corporate part of Dallas. There were four entrances to the building: north, south, east, and west. My office was at the end of the hall, just at the corner intersection where two of the hallways met in the northwest corner. The corner offices were the ones farthest from the exterior doors, which were locked at 7:00 P.M. The hallways were about one hundred fifty feet long. Additionally, I had a waiting room that was separated from my inner office where my groups and individuals met. Imagine our surprise one evening when we packed up to leave at 10:00 P.M., only to discover a two-foot long snake slithering across the gray office carpeting in my waiting room. We blessed her and put her outside. I have had an office in this same building for over fifteen years, and I have never again seen a snake anywhere around the building or grounds, much less all the way down the hall into my own office waiting room.

This group did not last as long as some have. It exploded, or perhaps imploded, within two or three years. The energy was intense, and the boundaries between friendships within the group were complicated. Perhaps we all came together for the divorce time then the group was over.

Currently, I am far more circumspect and don't encourage groups to go out so far on the edge. But that was then. It was a significant time, personally and professionally for me, and it was a clear opportunity to begin to observe the complex dynamics of psyches mingling in groups and how the tribal field of the unconscious works.

As aforementioned, the tribal field reveals a rich area for transference. Once, a woman brought me her "initial dream" in analysis. The "initial dream" is considered vitally important in the Jungian approach since it so often prospectively describes the issues and prognosis of the analysis. In her dream I was distracted, had many people in my consulting room during her session, and I called her by the wrong name. When I probed for associations, it came out that a coworker of hers knew me. My new client thought her coworker was "a bad therapist," so she thought I might be a bad therapist too. After another session, the client confessed she couldn't really pay the (already deeply discounted) fee I had arranged with her. She was apparently expecting me to see her for an "as you can pay" basis. She confessed she had lied to her husband and told him I had agreed to see her with this arrangement, so he would approve. This information followed interviewing her, putting her on a waiting list, and asking a long-term analysand to change his time to accommodate her schedule. After pondering all of this, I came to believe her dream was a warning for both of us that the work would not go well. Further, her dream had motivated me to consult with three colleagues, and we all determined I had to terminate the work—indeed, there were far too many people in our analysis, just as her dream revealed.

My temptation was to become the positive, providing mother— to make fibbing okay, to reduce fees, to arrange schedules according to her needs. This is the downfall of a pleaser, a person who abhors conflict and desires harmony at nearly all costs. What happens, though, is that the providing mother merely reinforces bad behavior, and, in the end, she builds enormous resentment. The Self knows when it has been violated even if the ego wants to deny that reality.

The positive / negative mother is well represented in the Grimms tale "Hanzel and Gretel." In this case, starving lost children (like many of us when we enter analysis) come upon a vision of abundance and plenty deep in the woods. It is a refuge made of candy and gingerbread and sugar pane windows—all sweet stuff, which is like the quick fix one yearns for by following addictions or materialism. Inside the house, just behind the pretty exterior, lies the devouring witch—the part of the negative feminine archetype that will control, demand, and imprison the psyche from autonomy, consciousness, and emancipation. This is like the analyst / therapist / mother / father that makes it all feel good. Underneath that persona, however, is a shadow that wants payment in full for the "feel good." In the tale, the witch fattens the captive children in order to eat them, to "feed" herself. Payment in full might be "love me," "don't leave me," "flatter me," or "be my personal friend."

The self-indulgence portrayed in this fairy tale gives a clue to addictive behavior. Just as Carl Jung stated, addictions are a cry for the spirit, *spiritus*. But the addictive personality, especially in people that spend their lives helping others, can set up just as great a need for matter, mother, earth, nurture, *matre*. This is where indulgence feels like the only thing available—eating, smoking, drinking—these are all for me! Never mind that they are self-destructive at the core—hence, the witch that lives inside. She is the devouring aspect of the addiction, the indulgence, the unconscious hunger that sets up the destructive binge.

It takes vigilance to know if an analysis or dream group participant will work out well in the first few sessions. Unfortunately, introverts tend to know how they feel later, after the fact. I can tell how a friendship is going by how I feel after the lunch is over—am I energized, pleased, content, satisfied? Or do I feel moody, disconnected, tired? The same holds true for clients. After a hard session I use the "how do I feel after" test. Then I can better tell even if the material was painful or difficult. Other times, I feel bored and crabby when things are too sweet or superficial in sessions. It is quite exhausting to carry on a session when all of the important issues are being evaded, rather than discussed or addressed. A therapist "hears" this anyway, even if it's not directly talked about, and it is hard work to comply with the avoidance.

CHAPTER TEN

Caution

APPROACHING A GROUP PROCESS CONSERVATIVELY IS NOT so difficult, and, when done properly, loses none of the depth and rich work possible. It is akin to how an analyst might approach sexual transference. This process (which always needs to be acknowledged and integrated into the analysis) nonetheless can, however, be subtly encouraged or discouraged by an analyst. Perhaps placing so much emphasis on a lengthy obsession about sexual transference is not as productive psychologically as traditional psychoanalysis has led us to believe. I find it can be unnecessarily painful (sadistic / masochistic) and sometimes even harmful. Furthermore, I suspect it can and does unconsciously feed the narcissism of the analyst who may not be entirely conscious of his / her need to be important. After my own training, as well as my experience gained in training and teaching candidates, it has become clear to me that sexual / romantic transference, in most cases, can be respectfully honored without requiring an obsessive focus. Naturally, there are exceptions to this assertion. Sometimes one simply has to obsess about the therapist—this is part of the process. However, analysts can be caring, attentive, humorous, and even playful without being seductive, mysterious, or mesmerizing. As an analyst, one has to continually question one's motives and needs in this work. Analysts have to find their needs met outside the consulting room or they will be victims to so-called flattery, attention, and fascination from analysands. Being an analyst is a dangerous ego trip, anyway. It is an enormously inflating profession; people pay the therapist dearly to simply talk and listen. Focusing on sexual transference is a way some analysts feel validated, attractive, effective, powerful, excited, and interested in the patient.

Similarly, outrageous shock only for shock's value in a dream group can be appropriately avoided without a loss of intensity or healing. Again, the facilitator has to examine motives and needs within him / herself. Is this a voyeuristic thrill? Is it exploitation and emotional abuse of vulnerable or fragile clients? One must find and identify appropriate limits within group behavior. As odd as it may seem, piercing screams, exposing genitals, and bloodletting are all examples of activities that would have manifested had I encouraged them, but would in fact only have detracted from, rather than encouraged, the depth work.

When delving into the mysterious, complex, morally neutral unconscious, one has to recall the purpose of analysis, therapy, and dream groups—that is, to facilitate consciousness, healing, and individuation. The result of this delving may frighten, decompensate, or entertain either client or therapist, but it is not the inherent purpose. Thankfully, gooey synchronicity can be honored and validated gracefully. Since dream group synchronicity often revolves around dream material—the dream allows a natural container or boundary for the work—it fuels passion the ego needs in order to have consciousness shifted by the synchronicity. For example, I awoke one morning with a dream about a member of dream group that was scheduled to meet that morning. I dreamed T. and I were at a religious retreat. I pondered this dream and decided I might need an introspective respite. My association to T. was "tired therapist, needing to connect to her creativity." Then, in dream group that morning, she told her dream:

I am at a religious retreat and need to urinate. I can't find the bathroom.

Urine can be a symbol of creativity. It relates to "making water" from the body and is an act of creation in a literal sense. In T.'s case, she didn't have a container—she had no place to put the urine and no creative process through which to express herself. She planned to make a retreat to pray and meditate about this issue. This dovetailed into my own process, as well, because I was beginning to write for the first time. Writing was not something I thought I could do, but my dreams were encouraging me to try. T.'s dream only seemed to make my dream even louder.

Synchronicity has that effect. Like a neon flashing sign or loud shout, it forces one to see a point, recognize a message of sorts. In this case I shared my dream that morning with T. and the group. This was a self-disclosure that felt "right" to me. It did not lead us down dangerous explorations that constellated acting out behavior. It was a process germane for the whole group that is knitted together by the desire and need to connect to creative self-expression. But synchronicity, just like dreams, does not always indicate what, at first glance, one may imagine.

Mistakenly, the ego will interpret a synchronicity as a green light, a pat on the back, or an indication to take a particular action. This is dangerous thinking. Especially if one bases one's faith on this approach to reality, hardship and suffering are almost a guarantee. For example, an analysand who was a recently divorced mid-fifties woman was quite smitten with a man who wanted nothing to do with her. He seemed unable to be close emotionally. A two-time cancer survivor, he lived in fear of a recurrence. Additionally, he had become a fundamentalist Muslim during his illness and decided sex was only for marriage. This woman had been married over thirty-five years; her husband had just left her, and marrying so soon was not what she wanted. But she could not shake her fascination with him. Furthermore, she ran into him repeatedly all over town to the point it was almost ridiculous and laughable. In line at the bank, in the produce section at the grocery store, next to her at a stoplight—he was there. She took all of this to mean the relationship would work out, that it was, in fact, ordained by God. These omens were simply too much to ignore; she thought he would see this and come around to give the relationship a chance. But he didn't. And I had one despairing analysand on my hands. "What's the point?" she kept asking me. "What does any of it mean?"

She had mistaken meaning for positive outcome—or the outcome the ego desires. Clearly, the relationship and her feeling for this man were richly significant for her psyche. He constellated an enormous process, one (perhaps you have guessed) that brought her elusive animus issue squarely into focus. The husband who left her, the father who had just died, the male friend that wouldn't make love—this was her process, and her psyche was putting it out in front in the loudest way possible. There was energy here. There was stuff stirred up. There was something cooking and getting hot. But that was all we knew. One's ego immediately wants to rush to conclusions (usually awful or wonderful) that may or may not have had anything to do with actual outer occurrences.

A Freudian psychologist friend asked me recently, in a baiting way, what the meaning of synchronicity is. I told him I had no interest in metaphysics or defining reality. What interests me is observing events that occur, rather than ignoring them due to preconceived notions devised to defend our rigid realities. It is just as aberrant to jump to candy-coated "meaningful" connections between unremarkable occurrences as it is to patently ignore, discount, and rationalize the peculiar oddities of life's mysterious process.

The ego, or conscious self, uses doubt and skepticism to support its small position in the face of the enormous unconscious. Snide dismissal, believed to be a solid, rational mindset, is really a poorly disguised part of self that feels frightened and threatened about losing its dominion in the psyche. The ego is usually energetically—continually—defending its position to the detriment of creativity and learning, both of which are activities that require an open mind.

The conscious personality of the therapist is an important aspect of analysis and dream group leadership that is just as significant and can be just as defensive as the client's. Favorite ego-driven biases are sometimes referred to as "counter transference" (or the feelings a therapist has for the client). For example, as I have stated previously, sexual transference can foster dependency in analysis. It can prolong analysis and reinforce the complex some men and women have regarding autonomy, emancipation, and power.

Invariably the male analyst who has more than his share of women in love with him also has an unconscious shadow part that demeans women, is afraid of being annihilated by them (castrated), and uses his position of authority to meet power and aggression needs. These men frequently had strong mothers who were unable to let their sons emancipate and separate from them.

Men are not the only ones to get picked on when it comes to counter-transference, however. The counter-transference for women can become sexual, but more often one sees evidence of emotional dependency—both the dependency the client has on the therapist as well as the therapist's dependency on the client. This can be observed by the complex called the "Positive Mother" syndrome, which does not mean the feelings for the therapist are positive in terms of their goodness for the analysand. Rather, it implies the analysand has his/her projection on the therapist couched in a falsely positive attitude. This is when a client idealizes the therapist and thinks she can do no wrong. Her opinions are gifts from the gods; she has ultimate wisdom, perception, and intuition. For the therapist, this can be just as intoxicating as a client finding the analyst the object of passionate love. How difficult it is not to believe these grand projections—or at least be affected by them! Hence, the dependency. It puts the analyst in an all-too-powerful position. Just a word or glance from the analyst can result in the analysand ending a relationship, changing a job, relocating, adopting a baby, ad infinitum. So the therapist and client become trapped in an unconscious pattern: I need you for guidance and direction because I don't trust my judgment nearly as much as yours (client). Or, I need you because you validate me and make me believe I am helping you by asking for advice (therapist).

This can evolve into the "Sunday School Teacher" syndrome, as I call it. All apologies to sunday school teachers, but the syndrome involves advice giving, correcting behaviors, making goals for therapy, and "confronting" clients when "they need to be." This type of thought process has, as its foundation, a belief structure that "I know best for you better than you know best for yourself." Often in the current era, I miss the insights of Carl Rogers, a groundbreaking pioneer in the field of client-centered therapy.

It is easy to see how ultimately dangerous and destructive this attitude is. Grandiosity mixed with unconsciousness has resulted in acts of pure evil throughout history, and the potential is no different here. Even with all the protestations about meaning well, helping, or setting limits, what can happen is the darker shadow part of self that needs to be right, to be better, to be more powerful than the client takes over. We are all capable, whether one is a therapist or not, of making horrendous errors when we set out to guide and coach other people down paths we think are the right ones. Certainly, it is challenging enough to just try to coach oneself.

A client or therapist might rightly question the purpose of therapy if coaching from an expert is not advised. This is where dreams are especially helpful. Dreams are forthright, confrontational, and often wickedly humorous in how they point out our foibles. Additionally, they are our own unique creations—our nighttime dramas that set us on a correction course in which our deep self is the author. A therapist who begins to work with dreams will quickly find this is so. As an example, a woman dreamed:

> *My son and I are lovers. Somehow, in the dream, I realize this is not an appropriate relationship.*

This dream could be examined in several different ways, but, after all of the discussion about the images, working context, and associations, the dreamer clearly felt that her relationship with her son was being confronted as being too close, dependent, and enmeshed. Often, the dream maker uses hyperbole to help the ego "get the point." The messages are sometimes exaggerated to compensate the ego attitude, or the images may be simply colorful, frightening, and extraordinary, so that a particle of consciousness might creep into our dark minds.

This dream helped the woman begin a necessary separation as her son headed off for the university. She desperately needed to begin to see how letting him go would help him become a man. The mother didn't realize that she was robbing her son of his male effectiveness and energy by smothering him. A week later, the son had this dream:

> *A voice said: "In order to slay the dragon, you have to gently kill the pig."*

The son had no associations to this dream and was quite puzzled by it. After reflecting with his analyst, it seemed he was dreaming about the same issue as his mother. Pigs are a symbol of the goddess or great mother representing fertility and abundance. (Archetypal amplifications are used when the dreamer has no personal associations.) The son needed to become separate from the pig—but in a gentle fashion. The dragon was a symbol of his heroic quest, his myth, and his position in the world that he was beginning to search for at this time in his life. The mother/son separation was hard work for both of them. The mother, I feel certain, would have taken much longer to realize this issue had it not been for her dream. A therapist would have had to build trust to find a way to confront this delicate issue effectively and gently. Again, here is an example where a client is simply more able and willing to make changes when they come from their inner beings rather than as a result of being "corrected" by me. The mother/son dream was also an example of relational, tribal-field dreaming. The son and mother were both dreaming about aspects of their relationship. Furthermore, both dreams were in agreement about the unconscious psychological situation. This synchronicity, or "tribal overlap," is a way the ego's defenses are confronted.

Dreams cannot be over-concretized, however. It is tantalizing to jump to the objective conclusion; for example, a dream about breast cancer means the dreamer has breast cancer. Or, if a loved one dies in a dream, that means he/she is really dying. These objective, concrete, and literal reactions to the symbolic language of the dream maker are natural emanations from the ego that fears almost everything—especially consciousness and change. To complicate the matter, every once in a while dreams are literally true. But for the most part, the unconscious is far more surreptitious. Breast cancer or other illnesses can appear in dreams in a literal way but more often will appear in code. For example, a middle-aged woman dreamed:

I am in my garden, walking toward my favorite tree. As I move closer, I see the bark is alive, moving even. But upon closer inspection, I see the tree is filled with worms and they are eating the tree from the inside.

Here is another example of a woman who had breast cancer that had recurred (but she was not yet aware of it):

My son has a spot on his lung, and it is cancer.

In the first dream, the worm-infested favorite tree was the symbol for breast cancer. In the second dream the code was the woman's son, and she was dreaming about a part of herself played by the son. Also, it was not breast cancer, but lung cancer that her dream maker used to prepare her ego for the recurrence. (Lung cancer was the illness from which her husband had died.) Dreams often use symbols to communicate in code, as if A equals B, B equals X, and so on. Both of these dreams occurred prior to the dreamers' knowledge of health problems.

In another case a woman awakened with this dream:

I was driving my old Ford LTD and had a wreck. The front left fender was smashed.

That day she had had her yearly mammogram and discovered a problem. Within a few days she underwent a mastectomy on her left breast. The dream maker, regularly, is interested / knowledgeable about our health, our relationships, our inner life, and much more.

The tribal field manifested in dream group one day in the following way: as dream group met for its weekly session, we circled the room checking in with each other about waking life, and one member was excited to tell about her new dachshund puppy. Another dream group member also had a new dachshund puppy—the brother of the first pup. Then, a third member said he had a dachshund joke, which he told. We worked on one of the dachshund puppy owners' dreams. The third member who told the joke appeared in the dachshund owner's dream in quite a positive way. Her association to the joke teller was, "He has iconoclastic humor and the ability to 'puncture balloons.'" She had had a terrible nightmare about being under constant critical surveillance from a camera that followed every move she made as she vainly tried to escape this type of imprisonment. The resolution of her dream involved the joke-teller dream group member showing her the way out of the imprisonment that the dream illustrated. Sometimes, I have to just shake my head at these complexities; what is the actual nature of reality? What is linear time, an illusion? Later that day, humor emerged quite unexpectedly again in my office. A client who has suffered depression had "fallen to pieces" when she learned of a colleague's wife's suicide. This brought back her own mother's suicide twenty-one years before. It was an issue she had not dealt with in our work together. In fact, she seemed devoid or blocked of feeling about it altogether. Her dream went as follows:

> *I am running across an icy dirty field, getting my shoes and feet cold, dirty, and wet. Then, Daffy Duck pops up from under the frozen ground.*

I was a bit concerned. I hoped she wasn't suddenly going "daffy," but her associations were entirely positive. Daffy Duck was the "funniest of them all," she asserted. He carried her trickster energy. This is how the psyche often works; just as she uncovered terrible grief and horror about an incident she had never let herself feel, humor that was frozen beneath the surface emerged as well.

I know her to have a wicked, black sense of humor not everyone can appreciate. But this dark, earthy laughter can balance the terrible suffering that one occasionally has to face. Like the masks of theatre, comedy and tragedy always appear together, two parts of a whole that bring balance to the drama of life.

CHAPTER ELEVEN

Repressed Emotion and the Critical Voice

SO, IN ONE DAY I HEARD TWO FAMILIAR THEMES WITH humor as the strong medicine to combat the negative internal process. Depression can be emotion-repressed. Some people may experience being flattened out, disconnected, and lifeless as a result. The repressed feeling finds its way to the critical voice, feeding it like a well spring. If emotion is not experienced consciously, it reverts into other more familiar channels in the psyche. If one is feeling particularly fat, stupid, or worthless, it is time to ask what feeling has been avoided. This requires a mental exercise of reviewing the past day or so to determine where the glitch occurred. One might say, "How did I feel this morning? How was I on the way to work?" and so forth. It will become clearer, with a little bit of examination, where the "complex" was activated. Then, it is up to the individual to feel, deal with, process the glitch, and go on from there. The negative grip can be abated substantially. This is psychological triage.

In life, however, it is ideal to have a deep bank account when it comes to resources to fight negative thinking. Humor is among one of the most valuable assets. Oddly enough, almost any positive action will improve the ego's stance against the internal negative construct. When my frustrated clients implore me with the question, "But what can I do about this critical voice?" I usually answer that almost anything will work, even the smallest thing can be enormously helpful. The list of possibilities is endless and individual; some medicines work better for one person, other medicines for others. It is important for a person struggling with this dynamic to determine for himself/herself which activities and actions are most effective, including ones that are entirely one's own creation.

Here are only some of the items on the list my dream groups and clients have tried with success:

Journal writing
Painting, drawing, sculpting
Listening to music that evokes the joyful excitement
    some pieces inspire
Engaging in a compassionate act for a person less fortunate
Aerobic exercise
Connecting to a person with whom one has a significant
    and nurturing friendship
Attending a religious service or twelve-step meeting
Meditation/prayer
Reading inspiring materials or listening to them on tape
Committing a courageous, outrageous act
Spending a block of time for significant self-care
Reading a novel, turning off the phone, doing nothing
    "worthwhile" for an entire day
Getting in the car without a plan and seeing where one
    finds oneself
Doing one dreadful task one has been avoiding
Changing something: whether it's a daily schedule, the
    color of the bedroom, or which route one drives to work
Changing hair style or style of dress

Initiating and choreographing a lovely evening with a
  spouse or partner
Reading poetry, writing poetry
Pulling weeds (symbol of yanking out the unwanted in
  our psyche)
Allowing / demanding oneself to be foolish in a way that
  is frightening
Spending time participating in an activity where one
  loses time
Dancing
Writing creatively
Singing / whistling

It can be a tremendous emancipation to remain creatively free
each time we feel hurt or angry or anxious or sad. The psyche then
becomes more spacious and less regulated by previous behaviors
and patterns. This is freedom.

When women, especially, find some spaciousness from the
internal critic, their focus of development often turns from relationship toward capability and effectiveness. Projects, degrees, creative
pursuits, and, in general, accomplishment fed from the inner Self
take over as the passion of life. Women who can't make this transi-
tion by mid-life become increasingly empty and pointless. It is not
as simple as whether to work outside the home or not, but rather
to connect to the unique "I" within, to let it guide and direct a
meaningful course of action—however that may unfold.

Interestingly, men more often take the opposite path and find
relationships and feelings are the parts of themselves they are
fascinated by in the second half of life. This may seem to be a
broad generalization, but nonetheless, it is ubiquitous that men
become softer with age while women become more focused. Letting go of the critical voice can allow both men and women more
psychological freedom which leads to a deeper self discovery.

Following Impulses

Death is more acceptable when we have lived our life our way, with courage and conviction. To live life for someone else or as someone else would want is to deny the true nature of self. Indeed, all one actually has is his/her true self contained in the present moment in order to experience consciousness.

How to discover what we truly want and who we truly are is a depth process that is sacred, profoundly frightening, and enormously fulfilling. One cause of our resistance to discovering our true nature is that it will surely require change of some sort or another. Change threatens the status quo, our equilibrium, our safety and security, our balance and routine. This resistance is not entirely without a favorable side, however, since without it one might run headlong down paths that are untimely dead ends or discover aspects of the psyche that can lead to madness or the absence of ethic.

Self-discovery is a balance. One has to push a bit if one has turtle nature, and one has to quiet and slow oneself if one has rabbit nature. Sometimes we have both natures, so one of the first lessons to learn is when to push, when to pull. Jung writes about following impulses and tracking libido as an essential way to begin to uncover the unique self. This is the difficult but necessary work of self-discovery. Tracking libido is simply asking in a moment, "What is it I really have an interest in doing, being, feeling right now?" This is as simple as being mindful about one's favorite ice cream flavor or knowing which job offer to accept. The question "Who am I" is too big; it is a grand sweeping generalization, not a question that one can easily discern. One has to begin with the smallest awareness possible, such as "Which movie would I really prefer seeing?" Then, as one becomes more in tune with the wishes and desires of small things, the larger discernments become apparent as well. Some clients say, "I know about movies and ice cream." Perhaps they do. But I think it is important to take an open-minded and curious look at all pre-determined behaviors and inclinations. Some of these behaviors are actually performed just out of habit. They can be old family messages, or ideas (wherever they may have originated) based on what we think we are or what we think we should be, rather than what the actual self desires.

Later, one can plan a period of time—a whole day, perhaps— where only one's impulses are followed. Short of hurting oneself or going to jail, the rule is: no previous obligations, no external interruptions, only pass the day doing exactly as one feels pulled to do. The day might begin something like this: I am getting out of bed. I put my feet on the floor. I have the need to use the bathroom. My next instinct is to travel into the kitchen to have a cup of coffee. I will use cream this morning. I love the color of coffee with cream, and I want to see it. I want to taste the coffee slowly, with appreciation and consciousness. Or the day may begin differently: I awaken. I remember this is the day to follow my impulses and energy. I am excited and want to fly. I put my feet on the floor. I dash to the closet to get out clothes to take a jog. I want to move.

If one practices this much conscious activity even over a short time, awarenesses and surprises will erupt into the waking mind to inform the defended ego about secret and veiled treasures hidden within.

In Zurich in the early 1980s, when I trained at the Jung Institute, this was by and large the process many of us who were in training at the same time followed. One day of following energy can extend to weeks or months—or even years, if the commitment to the process is strong. Perhaps the day of following impulses only brings one to the television or the movie theater. Maybe the day is dull or empty. Outcome is not the goal here; it is the process. Learning to track the nuances and subtle clues, "psyche's gifts," are the ways one can recognize the more substantial signposts for our life and our work.

R. comes to mind. When I met her after I first arrived at the Jung Institute in Kusnacht, I didn't feel much interest in pursuing a friendship. She was twenty years older than I, dowdy, and she seemed negative. She was old, dried up, sour—the type of personality that almost everyone naturally avoids. But we often rode the same train, so I saw her frequently. After a few weeks of small talk, she told me during one of our train rides that she was deeply depressed and that her analyst was encouraging her to "follow this depression process." All of a sudden she wasn't unpleasant to be around anymore. Her honesty and vulnerability made her appealing to me. I began to look forward to running into her—partly because I knew when I asked her how she was, she would tell me the truth. Truth can be like a drink of fresh spring water after a long hike. Over time she would tell me how she was doing. Each answer was about the same. "Terrible;" "I hate it here;" "I see no point to things;" "I'm miserable;" "I'm lonely." A few months later, I saw R. and said, "Hi, how are you doing?" She answered, "Terrible, awful." I asked, "Depression not any better?" R. answered, "No, I'm just trying to stay with it. Not push it away." She was like that for about a year. She stayed conscious of her pain and misery continually.

Later, at Thanksgiving time, the American students splurged and gave a large dinner for the entire Jung Institute. Swiss as well as many other nationalities were represented in the student body and faculty. The Americans had an especially festive time locating and shipping a turkey from a New York deli and, over a period of months, acquiring canned cranberries and pumpkins by ferrying these American foods back to Zurich each time one of us visited the U.S. It was a huge success and, like all Thanksgiving dinners, a wallowing mess. I peeked into the kitchen to survey the damage, and there was R. She was wearing a white apron tied around her waist, rubber gloves that came up to her elbows, and a delightful smile as she seemed to be single-handedly tackling all the dishes. She had told me she didn't have the energy to perform even the smallest tasks, so I was quite surprised by the scene.

R. said, matter-of-factly, "Well, the depression lifted. I feel so much energy, I just decided to come in here and do the dishes." I said, "All by yourself?" R. said, "Why not? Sure." But soon there were many helping R. She became the center of all the activity, managing the clean-up project. It was perhaps the most fun I've had doing dishes.

Future train ride encounters indicated the energy held. R. passed through depression and moved beyond it to passion and fire, verve, initiative, and humor. Her wit and clever mind were revealed in a way that was previously clouded by negativity (the unexpressed pain gone into the critical voice) which became depression (all affect flattened, no libido); then the libido exploded into a creative, energized, witty personality.

Not all of these stories end so gloriously, but this one did, so I tell it to you. The process can bring divorce, illness, even suicide. It takes enormous courage to follow the deep Self—like Abraham who was ready to sacrifice his son because Jahweh told him to do so. We, too, have to give our entire lives and selves to our journey.

R. found her way out of depression by following the process of depression, by being honest about who she was, rather than simply trying to make it go away. This is a form of honoring melancholia, a state of mind we moderns avoid at almost any cost. Since my training in the 1980s, antidepressants are the common and accepted treatment for depression based on the notion that depressed people suffer from chemical imbalances. Although this pharmaceutical development has helped many people maintain functioning lives, there are other natural and situational events that demand sadness or hopelessness as the response of integrity.

In R.'s case, she rode the horse of depression until the ride was finished. The libido didn't have any more energy for negativity and inertia. What happened to her? Through her dreams and analysis she probed deeply into old pain. She faced it, felt it, made meaning from it, blessed it, and let it go.

Contrary to the criticism that inner work is "navel gazing" or pointless self-absorption, actually facing disappointment and resentment that is well buried under years of denial can allow one to be far more connected to family and community in a significant way. Just as R.'s energy returned to her, it was directed toward helping others—cleaning up the mess left by a dinner that fed well over one hundred people. This can be one of the crucial differences between some therapies and analysis. One seeks to fix and erase painful symptoms; the other desires understanding about their cause and lets the symptom tell its story to the psyche, which frequently will lessen or even eliminate the symptom. Most skilled Jungian analysts I have known and who have been my mentors recoil at the "goals for therapy" approach to exploring the psyche. The ego writes the list of the goals, or in some cases, the therapist's ego writes the goals. This is a current trend in psychotherapy that threatens to rob the individual seeking help for the meaning of his / her suffering. Rolling Thunder, healer and shaman, said that it is important to understand the meaning of an illness before one can be healed.[13]

During this time, the tribal community of Zurich supported the process of diving into the dark until consciousness could transform or shift the energy to a different territory. It is possible that without tribal support this work is almost impossible. It requires courage and commitment to follow what often seem to be the pointless, stupid, self-absorbed, and banal musings from the dark corners of our inner beings. It can be truly humiliating to "follow one's process or impulses," because it necessitates amplifying and acknowledging unflattering aspects of ourselves that have great control in our personalities, albeit unconscious control. It is painful to see how foolish, cruel, negative, fearful, or controlling one can be. The awareness that punctures our rigid ego results in enormous affect, usually shame and humiliation. Currently, shame is often misunderstood. It is characterized as a "bad" emotion, one that should be eliminated as quickly as possible, and one that is pointless to have. Surely shame is not a pleasant emotion, but like all emotions, it exists. Rather, one could discover what is driving the shame, then make the necessary adjustments. Just telling ourselves that shame is a bad feeling is like forgetting to connect all of the dots—without which one cannot see the whole picture. Many emotions have hidden within their core a desire for action—the change which is most often resisted. The "change" could be anything—monumental to inconsequential. But erasing or repressing the emotion that is confronting the ego is like receiving a letter that one does not open, as Jung is reported to have said.

CHAPTER TWELVE

Knots Form Patterns

THE COMMUNAL, TRIBAL FIELD IS INTERESTED IN RELATION-ships, in the interactions between friends, lovers, family, foes, clients, therapists, members of dream groups. One could say the social layer of human behavior fascinates the psyche. Over evolutionary time we humans have developed complex society and interchange. It is through this vehicle that our consciousness has developed and differentiated. It is only natural, then, that the dream maker has a unique presence in the tribal territory.

It is false to believe or perceive of ourselves as islands, disconnected psyches with consciousness and language that does not connect in some vital and significant way with the field of relationship upon which we emerge, change, and individuate. Jung states in *Dream Analysis* (1984), ". . . a reaction may reach you through your fellow beings, through waves in your surroundings. The reaction is not only in you, it is in your whole group." (p. 77). The following is a personal example:

My mother developed what was initially diagnosed as Alzheimer's disease but later, in 1996, was called dementia with Lewy bodies. The failure of her mind and physical abilities was a painful and difficult experience for the entire family. She disintegrated in stages; by fall of 1998, she lay in a nursing home bed, hardly able to put weight on her feet to stand, confined to a wheelchair, mentally nonfunctional. She did speak in metaphorical language, however, and often would talk about trying to get on the train that was waiting for her or ask why we were at the airport so long, because she was ready to fly home.

Over Labor Day that autumn, my husband and I took a trip to visit his daughter in Arizona. It was a lovely time of year, and I was moved by the stunning beauty of the paprika-colored stone outcroppings that seemed like an ancient eroded rock race of people, and the night sky was a vivid navy blue sprinkled with powdered sugar stars. Nevertheless, I experienced a profound depression while I was there that I couldn't seem to shake. The first night I woke up crying from a dream in which my mother had died. The third night I dreamed again that she died.

At the airport on Monday I decided to buy a mindless book to read on the plane after discovering I had the dreaded middle seat. I scanned the Phoenix airport kiosk and picked out something I hadn't read that didn't look too awful. The book was *The Notebook* by Nicholas Sparks.[14] The blurb on the back cover said it was a Literary Guild Selection, so I thought I might even enjoy it. Nowhere on the cover of the book did it mention Alzheimer's disease—in fact, the novel was presented as a love story. It seemed to be just the thing to get me through the flight and pull me out of my sadness. But I was not honoring my sadness, only trying to avoid it—so of course, I had chosen a terribly sad book.

The book was a love story, but the lovers were facing Alzheimer's disease at the end of their lives. These passages were poignantly written, and powerfully explicated the overwhelming suffering this illness brought to the family. It hit my sadness squarely. The dreams—clearly showing me I was not yet fully conscious of the loss of my mother—were compensating what I was shutting off. And synchronistically, I had chosen a book (or the book had chosen me) that also brought the feeling to the surface.

When I arrived home, I called my father to see how he was doing. I check messages frequently, even when I'm out of town. I hadn't heard from him.

"Oh, you're returning my call," he said.

I said, "What call?" Right away I felt the dull alarm of pieces coming together.

"I called you three days ago and left a message for you to call me. I have something to tell you about your mother."

I assured him I had not received the message (there is a trickster in every phone service I have ever used that evaporates certain messages with the most uncanny results) and implored him to tell me how my mother was doing.

"Oh, she's not too good. She got a lot worse about three days ago and can't sit in the wheelchair anymore. All the staff are very concerned about her."

Then I understood the intense depression I couldn't shake off, the persistent dreams, the book I read. My mother was ill and deteriorating, and the tribal aspect of my psyche knew that and was letting me know—preparing me, sending me the message. This may sound like "only a psychic experience," but I observe this type of event regularly in my office. Most everyone is "psychic," in a sense, "connected" to a tribal / relational field in the psyche. This is a natural, ordinary experience. Saying something is "only a psychic event" is another way to discount or ignore it. One has to ask where these psychic events come from and what we can learn about them from observation with an objective attitude.

After writing about my mother's illness on September 9, 1998, I drove to my office to start my day with a dream group scheduled at 10:00 A.M. I called my son, impulsively, at 9:55 A.M. to say good morning. I woke him up, then apologized, but he assured me the alarm had just gone off as I called. Then he said, "Oh, I just had a terrible dream. I dreamed Nana died, and I was devastated. I sobbed and sobbed in my dream in a way I haven't cried in a long,

long, time." He had dreamed this at roughly the same time that I was writing about my own (nearly identical) dream and the tribal field of the unconscious.

Here again was an example of what I observe regularly. The only difference between my son and me and many other families is that we often discuss our dreams as a matter of course. This type of occurrence happens regularly; it just goes unobserved.

In fact, as a relationship field, our circle affects consciousness and interconnects us in more ways than dreams. In a death, awareness can emerge of a spiritual or psychological nature for those close to the person who died. I find in grief work there is usually an epiphany, a clarity of direction, or a re-assessment of priorities that occurs around the loss of someone significant. Remarkable events or a significant illness can affect the field in the same way. Sometimes we simply learn how many good friends and family we have. Sometimes these disastrous events give us an opportunity to make things right with old hurts and resentments. But sometimes the effects of a tragedy are more specific or far-reaching. The MADD (Mothers Against Drunk Drivers) movement was formed by women taking action from grief—as if purpose and meaning accompanied their loss. They have positively affected our attitudes about teenage drinking and about drinking and driving in general.

The change does not always result in a "positive" or "sweet" outcome. Sometimes families disintegrate when a tragedy occurs. Most are familiar with the high divorce rate among couples who lose a child. The change in the tribal field is only that—change, process, movement. The quote attributed to Jung a few days before his death comes to mind, "To this day God is the name by which I designate all things which cross my willful path violently and recklessly, all things which upset my subjective views, plans and intentions and change the course of my life for better or worse."[15]

The following story is one with which I am personally familiar.

Many years ago, a young minister and his wife gave birth to an eagerly expected child. The baby tested positive for Down's Syndrome after early tests in the hospital. Following a day or two of euphoria, the couple went into seclusion when they received the test results. They dealt with their choices and their fate in the seclusion of heartfelt privacy and introspection. The congregation was, in a word, devastated. After a long weekend, they emerged—clear, focused, and committed. They would keep and raise their son, have no more biological children but possibly adopt, and commit wholeheartedly to the latest medical and educational advances to enable their son to have the best possible life. They squared their shoulders and stepped up to the plate.

The effect on the congregation was profound. Inspired by this young couple, many were touched and energized to make similar commitments in the face of adversity. At least one young woman changed her course of study and decided to become an educator for the handicapped. Awareness and open acceptance of this malady affected the entire church. This tribe's collective consciousness was significantly altered by an event that affected so many.

To reiterate, sometimes dreams do predict events that are significant (both tragic and fortunate), but it is best not to get into the habit of seeing dreams as oracles or fortune-telling devices. This is where recording and dating them is helpful. Then, the predictive elements become obvious, indisputable, and are quite curious. Why one may dream months in advance the name of a street one may later live on is a curiosity, but it happens. Through this exercise one can get a "feel" for the predictive dreams, as opposed to the majority of dreams which use characters and action to mold a metaphor that bears little literal resemblance to outer events and waking reality.

Once, many years ago, a relative told me a disturbing dream. In it he was forced to watch his young son be tortured by evil kidnappers. He was terrified that somehow this dream predicted an early end for the child, or worse, that his son would become the victim of a crazed madman. This child is now an adult—educated, established, well adjusted, and productive. The dream was about the dreamer, for the most part! Always, one has to be tentative and open-minded with dreams. Absolutes don't apply to the vast mystery and territory of the unconscious.

In this case, the dreamer had projected his own young vulnerable self onto his son. The son would also represent his potential, vigor, youth, and creativity—the self that is "in potential," the "not yet complete" part of ourselves. The kidnappers were a part of the dreamer as well. They were the aspects that are rigid, fault finding, controlling, confining, and cruel to the dreamer himself. This is a vicious part of the personality that is driven and unfeeling. During this time the dreamer was experiencing terrible stress at work, in a job he had devoted himself to for seventeen years. His "mean inner voices" were working overtime.

But does this dream have anything to do with the boy who turned out so well as an adult? Not in any literal sense. The dream showed the son was carrying a projection for the father that was potentially harmful. The father would want to watch the pressure and criticism he might place on the son, because the dream indicated his "father complex" could spill over onto his son—then the father might act the role of the kidnapper. The confrontation about these disturbing dreams is that they are about us—we are the bad guys! Not only does this manifest as an internal critical ideation, but it comes out in our personalities in the ways we relate to others. The "kidnapper" is in all of us, a kidnapper who not only robs us of our own child energy, but can also rob us of our compassion in dealing with those around us. Interestingly, in this family the father consciously played the opposite role—that of a supportive, cheering coach for his children. This probably was a natural compensation and a healthy alternative to letting the "kidnapper" take hold.

Once again, the dream maker used the field to make the point. The dream wouldn't be nearly as affective if the boy were anonymous and not the dreamer's son. It is when we are gripped by affect (fear, sadness, horror, or anger in a dream) that the ego can begin to assimilate some of what the dream maker is presenting. Think of the ego as a failing, elderly person, a person hard of hearing, nearly blind, and uninterested in change. The dance the dream maker must perform for the old ego has to be loud, colorful, exaggerated, and dramatic. This is why dreams are often nightmarish or so vivid and intense. The dream maker cares enough to try to get our attention.

It is lamentable at times, to see how resistant the ego is to the patterns and forces of the unconscious, even though the resistance is probably a necessary aspect of the evolution of consciousness. One can observe this especially in the cases of severe, even terminal illnesses. Those who face imminent death feel connected to life and its meaning in a way almost impossible to achieve otherwise. This immediacy of the end (which is the actual case for all of us; we just don't know when exactly death will appear) heightens the connection to the Self and reduces the distractions and attachments of human existence. Most of us live each day believing (or at least behaving as if we believed) a big lie—that we will live forever or at least long enough to get it all done, all resolved . . . tomorrow. When death is encountered, life is experienced and rejuvenated. In one's tribe or circle this can have a profound affect on the ego's insistence s/he is everlasting. The sting of death must provoke one to live life with more integrity and passion or else death's confrontation is wasted.

Additionally, "The Kidnapped Son" dream is an example of how dreams can be relevant and instructive for more people than simply the persons who dreamed them. For example, in a dream group, "The Young Son Kidnapped and Tortured" dream would benefit and make an impression on all that heard it from the ensuing therapeutic conversation surrounding the dream work. Who has not felt the pain and limitation from the internal critic that kidnaps our happiness, peace, serenity, creativity, productivity, and passion for living? This horrific dream has an impact on listeners, not just dreamers, because it so aptly depicts a collective issue as well—that is, how negative aspects of self that are dangerous to our potential must be made conscious, confronted, and depotentiated. Negative archetypal masculine elements—those of patriarchy, violence, and control, for example—overwhelm positive archetypal masculine and feminine aspects—those of vulnerability and creation—whether in the personality or in the culture as a whole. Thus, "The Kidnapped Son" is the type of dream that I ask my groups to make their own, by asking, "Why have you needed to hear this dream? What in this dream is new information? How does it reflect your process synchronistically as well as the dreamer's? Where are you in this dream and in this painful discussion?" This dream is an important reminder to all of us. It is a manifesto to stay protective and vigilant toward the younger less-developed parts of ourselves, lest they be kidnapped by our own self-destructive attitudes.[16]

CHAPTER THIRTEEN

The Psychoid

MANY OF US REPORT THE UNCANNY, UNEXPLAINABLE EXPE-
rience of "feeling a person's stare." How many times at a party has
it happened that one "feels" a look from across the room, only to
turn and catch a person staring? This can happen anywhere—at
the stoplight from the driver in the next car, in a classroom, at a
meeting. How is this explained? Even the most concrete thinker
must acknowledge this is a true and common human experience.
So far, I don't know of any scientific explanation for being able
to feel a person's curious stare. There are no measurable brain
waves, electric impulses, or flying sparks that, up to now, have
been identified and gauged. Often, it is almost impossible to be
the starer and not get caught. I have developed a technique of
quickly shifting my stare to an object near the person as soon as
the person turns to look, so as not to get too embarrassed. Even
then, I doubt I get away with it very often. If one thinks about it,
the power of "the gaze" is a mysterious phenomenon—as if *will*
can direct energy to some degree. Evidently, we have the ability to
"shoot" energy, whether we believe in these things or not.

Similarly, the tribal field is in the same energy plane. We have
the ability to direct energy and will toward people and groups that
are of fascination to us. Notice the next time you stare at someone,

139

how curious and pointed your energy must be to get the attention of your object of fascination. This is like the dream maker. It picks the people and situations that you have energy for, the significant events where there is still libido surrounding the image. We, in the tribal field, experience a type of connectedness to ourselves and each other that is both irrational and commonplace. It is comforting yet disturbing, a part of us but not very conscious. It is a common experience, yet it still evokes respect from the mysterious phenomenal universe in which we all participate. Part of our psychological and spiritual being, synchronicity is one of the evidences of the tribal / psychoid field. It is a part of the manifest phenomena that we all can experience if we pay attention. The "psychoid" (see glossary) realm is the blending of the psychic and the physical—a paradox, because it is neither of these things, yet both at the same time. The tribal unconscious is one way the psychoid reality manifests. It is all around us in the mundane matter of life, wanting to be seen, apparently, since it never abandons us no matter how we may try to ignore it.

Larry Dossey has been known to say that not only does prayer positively effect healing, based on research he has performed for ill patients, but that the most effective prayer of all is, "thy will be done." Consequently, the notion of negative prayer is an important one to consider as well.[17] The energy we "send" has an effect— especially if it has significant positive or negative qualities.

Just as positive thinking and healing prayer uplift and bring wholeness and understanding to a situation or to a person, negativity does the opposite. Not unlike the power of the gaze, if one is a worrier or a negative thinker, it can bring about the worst. If prayer works in the positive, it follows that the negative has power, too. The shamans of ancient times were aware that they had to be stewards of their thoughts. They knew the powerful effect thoughts could have on a ritual or healing ceremony. This is part of the tribal field where the interconnectedness of our realities, our thoughts, our feelings, our actions, and our destinies all converge to produce a complex phenomenal interweaving that defies any rational explanation, roadmap, or phenomenalogical theory.

Many people have experienced the communal field through synchronistic contact with friends or family with whom they converse infrequently. For example, one recent Sunday afternoon, my family and I drove through a smallish town about forty miles from our house. We pass through this town frequently, because it is on the road to our favorite lake. For some reason this particular Sunday, B., a former client, seemed to invade my consciousness with utmost insistence and persistence. It seemed as if I couldn't get her off my mind. I hadn't heard from her in over a year. The next day, on Monday, I received a call from B. wanting an appointment. B. lives near / in the lake town.

Then, two days later in a dream group, a member reported that two long-term friends had called her since our last session, because they both "felt something was wrong." Indeed, my group member had been struggling terribly and even announced she was leaving the group, because she couldn't afford it anymore. Her financial situation had become critical. Both friends had "sensed" a distress and reached out to call—friends that she is close to but only speaks with a couple of times a year.

Here are two "everyday" examples of evidence of the tribal field. Sometimes, this experience is labeled "intuitive," which is too general a term and is just another way to package, label, and discard these occurrences as quickly as possible. Intuition is the ability to see around a corner, to imagine the big picture, to visualize a possibility. Many have observed that brilliant entrepreneurs are often phenomenally intuitive, but intuition is not exactly the same as a "psychic" ability to sense the future. There is, naturally, an overlap between the aspect of personality that is intuition and the gift that is psychic ability.

Psychic people are more connected to the tribal field than

the average person's experience. It is curious to note that psychic people tend to have suffered substantial wounds in early life. Perhaps woundedness fosters a depth in the psyche—perhaps that depth is a way to survive; perhaps this ancient, safer place, the place of the tribe, the greater community, is a support and security for the sufferer. And one finds many therapists that are both intuitive and psychic.

Carol Smith, a therapist and poet in Oklahoma City wrote her good friend, Jane, the following piece that illustrates my point:

> Dear Jane: All day I had been, on and off, memorizing the first section of "Prufrock"—in the car, between patients, just for kicks. That evening a young man came into my office—mild depression, adjustment disorder, red-haired, looking like he just stepped out of an Irish pub. He tells me he loves poetry. Poetry? "Yeah," he says. His favorite poem is "The Love Song of J. Alfred Prufrock." I look at him in disbelief. Then, I simply begin: "Let us go then, you and I . . ." And he joins in. Word for word. We stop at the first "talking of Michelangelo" and just sit for a moment in silence. Driving home, I thought how much you would have appreciated that synchronistic moment. . . .[18]

Another way of experiencing the tribal connection between persons in our field is to connect to "Eros / Agape" (see glossary) and all forms of love energy. Love is, perhaps, the most powerful, transformative, and life-affecting emotion human beings are able to feel. Its archetypal energy has the ability to scoop us away into a far different place of existence from where we ordinarily reside. "Eros / Agape" can be seen in all the cracks and crevices of our lives—church, job, neighborhood, clubs, classes, the bowling league, the consulting room, and so on. This love experience (which necessarily is not a sexual love, although it can be) is the emotional signal that we have found a tribal member. This is our experience of knowing or feeling or being affected by a person to a degree that an attachment is formed so that psyches interweave at a layer that is below or beyond our ordinary consciousness. This is how our good friends sense there is something amiss across a thousand miles of separation.

The tribal field can inform the individual as a type of litmus test. For example, one may ask a close trusted friend advice on a difficult issue. We sense that the people who love us and that we in turn love also see us, know us, and can guide us by their deep experience of us. Some years ago, during my analytical training in Zurich, I became aware of a phenomenon of letting the tribe not only inform me of a correct action, but also predict the future as well. Let me explain. . . .

Even though I had years of analysis deconstructing both a father and mother complex, this did not affect, in any adverse way, my outer "real" relationship with either of my parents. In fact, our interactions improved dramatically over these years. One aspect of our relationship that I found curious was how correct they (as well as my in-laws) were about actions I was considering taking. Over time, I realized that all the times they expressed cautious hesitancy I did indeed live to regret my plans. Likewise, they would show excitement and support for actions that later turned out to be very fortunate events. This is not a case of finally learning to listen to the wisdom of the parents—it was more subtle than that. I'm not even sure their collective "yays" and "nays" were very conscious. More often, I would hear the clues in their initial reactions—silence, immediate positive responses, and so on. These became a type of barometer that I could "read" regarding the appropriateness—or not—of the proposed plan that I was articulating.

Likewise, close friends were able to give me the same, albeit unwitting, feedback. I learned to read these "omens" to let me know if I was following the "Tao" or not and how well something might turn out. Jung states that our field will mirror negatively to us when we have acted unconsciously and unethically: ". . . The reaction is not only in you, it is in your whole group. You may not react, but someone next to you or in your immediate surrounding, someone near and dear to you, your children perhaps, will react. . . ."[19]

Perhaps the decision to move to Zurich is a good example of this. At the time, my husband and I were thirty-one, had a three-year-old severely asthmatic child, leftover debts from undergraduate and graduate school loans, no more than a few thousand dollars to liquidate, and a full private practice and college teaching position to leave behind. In Switzerland, the working laws are very strict, and we were advised to plan not to work during our student course that could take anywhere from four to ten years or more.

My parents and in-laws were horrified to see their grandson move so far away—we had all lived harmoniously in Denver. Additionally, there was so much to leave behind. But behind those human reactions, I could feel the deep support they felt for us. I knew then that we would go to Switzerland, train, and finish. My "number two personality" knew this by their reaction, their excitement, and their support even in the face of such loss. This tribal ribbon of intuition has been valuable for me to recognize and respect. Just as I think (at times) I can see which is the right path for a person I love, so they too can mirror the same for me.

As we were struggling with all of the realities involved in moving to Switzerland—inadequate funds, fear of the unknown, no assurance we could complete the training—three synchronicities occurred that convinced us to push forward, no matter how impossible training in Europe seemed. I heard stories that the Swiss government was cruel and harassing to foreigners (they can be). I heard the Jung Institute could kick you out at anytime (and did occasionally). I heard the weather was bitter, gray, and depressing (it is). I heard a lot of people who go to train get sick (we all three did).

After I called the Swiss Consulate in Denver in the fall of 1982, I was discouraged beyond words. He explained to me that attending school in Zurich would require a passport, a visa, additional permission from the Canton of Zurich, fifty thousand Swiss franks deposited into a Swiss bank account, and that they still might not let our three-year-old son accompany us. The conversation lasted about thirty minutes, during which he outlined, detail after detail, points I hadn't even considered. He made it clear it was a unique privilege to be allowed into his country, and people as ill-prepared as we were not the types to be given that permission.

I put the phone down and held my head in my hands. I experienced a physical sensation or feeling of loss that all my dreams, my future, my focus was being taken from me. I stumbled into the living room. Our son was watching the program *Sesame Street* on PBS. The program ran for a moment or two, but then was, almost immediately, interrupted with a "we are having technical difficulties" message. After another minute or so, an entirely new program was broadcast in which a loud booming voice began the narration, "Switzerland, a land-locked country in Central Europe . . ." I was shocked. Ninety seconds before I had hung up with the dour and dismal Swiss Consulate only to subsequently witness a shocking synchronicity. My son and I watched, completely transfixed. We learned from a crackly old film (that reminded me of geography films shown on Friday afternoons in my public elementary school) that Switzerland produced cheese, watches, and chocolate. I watched the entire thirty-minute program standing, frozen, with my mouth gaping open.

Earlier, in August 1982, we had begun to suspect that Switzerland might lie in our future. I had just spent a week attending a seminar with a visiting Jungian analyst from the Jung Institute in

Zurich and had met students of his who lived and trained there. After the seminar, my husband and I went on to Aspen for a few days of vacation. We stayed at the Jerome Hotel. Those who have been to Aspen (at least in 1982) know that the village was impacted by the Bavarian, Swiss, and Austrian European influences that date back to the beginning of the ski industry. The city had chalet-type buildings, German gingerbread, a lot of Alpine kitsch. One could not help but be reminded of Switzerland. I was in the coffee shop of the Jerome Hotel, eating a muffin and reading the newspaper by myself on the first morning there. I couldn't seem to release the idea of moving to Zurich. It invaded my concentration to the point I that couldn't even read. I put the paper down and said, as a "prayer" to the Self, "Unconscious, I wish you would clarify this Swiss issue; is this a symbol of something, or are we literally to pack everything up and move to Zurich?" This was my prayer, or petition to the Self, the part of me that dreams and seems to give me clues about my life if I tune in and listen. I made this plea with a bit of desperation; the ambiguity was driving me to distraction—whether the energy around Zurich training was just a symbol or something to be taken concretely.

Then, immediately, only a second later, a man at the table next to me said so loudly that all the surrounding tables could hear: "Zurich is the ONLY place to live!! You can buy cheese and beer from a local farmer, then take it down to the lake to cool, go for a walk, only to come back to find it will still be there, ready for a picnic."

I was amazed, thrilled, ecstatic, moved, dumbstruck, on fire. Never before had such a thing happened to me. I still did not then believe I had to move to Switzerland, but I was entertaining the thought with increasing certainty.

Finally, on the way home from this trip, we stopped at the Denver Public Library to check out some books about Switzerland to begin to do research on this country we really didn't know that much about. Then I heard my husband shout excitedly, "Tess! Tess!!"

As I roamed through the stacks, he had randomly turned on a microfiche machine—one of six or eight—and "Switzerland, Travel and Adventure" popped up on the screen. He said my name over and over, pointing excitedly and squeezing my arm. The microfiche apparatus back then was a scroll of all the library contents on a tape device. One had to press a button, then listen to the hum while the machine scrolled through all of the entries. Wherever the last person had left off was the place in the alphabet where one would begin. Somehow, the person who had used the machine right before us had turned it off on the only frame that listed the books the library carried on Switzerland. Furthermore, every book listed that day was on the shelf; we took them all home and read every one.

Later, in analysis with Mary Briner, who trained and analyzed with Carl Jung, I discussed these events, still puzzled and awe-struck—even though I was now in Switzerland, training at the Jung Institute there. But Mary wasn't awestruck at all. She told me Jung had said that synchronicity simply indicated the ego had libido (energy) for a matter and that was that. The energy was neither good nor bad, nor was synchronicity any actual predictor of outcome, fortunate or unfortunate. Synchronicity is neutral in and of itself; however, it does accurately reflect the amount of energy one has for a task, accomplishment, relationship, and so on.

Going to Zurich with a young asthmatic child, no employ-ment, and very limited funds is an undertaking that necessarily would require a vast amount of libidinous drive. Perhaps success is, in part, determined by how ernestly a person desires it. But then again, one is forced to speculate about the origin of synchronicity, the nature of it, the meaning of it, the metaphysical implications of it. As I have stated earlier, synchronicity in and of itself does not necessarily predict outcome, but it does reflect canalized libido, and it is possible that energy can affect outcome.

It seems as if we operate not only from our own psyche—its wishes, dreams, memories, and drives—but within a larger context as well. The universe, as it is often referred to, is an ultimate container, an inclusive one that indicates the whole and the totality of our existence. This vast great vessel holds us—those of us who now live, have lived, and are yet to live.

But within this vast inclusive wholeness also exist cells, networks or pockets of connectedness. Within these smaller cells lies our "world"—the events, relationships, history, geography, and interactions of our smaller universe. And these cells contain a number of human beings that seem to live, operate, and exist with determined effect on each other. Within these cells of life, the tribe, and the occurrences that exist in relation to the tribe, are the synchronistic events that press us on toward greater consciousness and understanding of our nature, our will, and our desire.

As Jung asserts, energy is neutral; it carries no inherent positive or negative features. It functions as a natural raw force without judgment, but without which we, perhaps, could no longer survive. It is energy, will, and desire that motivate the human psyche to progress. Therefore, energy is extremely valuable for a person to track within him / herself. This is why one knows instinctively that to ignore or discount synchronicity doesn't seem quite "right." Joseph Campbell said "Follow your bliss," which Jung articulated earlier in different language when he advised that if one were to "follow one's impulses" one could individuate very quickly. Bliss, energy, libido, impulses are all terms for the same human experience—desire. Where does the will go? Where does the drive want to take you? This is not a license to live outside the structure of civilization or legal and ethical constructs. But most of us could agree that stepping outside of and challenging a life of duty and obligation is not going to threaten the moral fabric of society. It is far more important to locate the libido and to track it.

Like a flashlight in a dark cave, our impulses can help lead us out of total darkness and unconsciousness. Our libido is a valuable resource, much like the dream world is a resource to inform the ego about where the psyche's energy is. Synchronicity, those outer remarkable coincidences that emerge out of our tribal, connected self and existence, gives us even more data to help us find a path, one's own path—not his or hers, but yours. The life lived uniquely is a gift for those who don't or can't. Discovering the Self and having the courage to live the discovered Self is the individuation process Jung has articulated for modern men and women.

So often I hear the frustration from people struggling to discover and clarify their dream, their vision, their goal. It's as if they know they desire something but don't know what that thing is. Recently, a well-to-do young woman said in analysis, "It would be wonderful to know I wanted to be an artist so badly that I would move to a small, cold, roach-infested apartment in New York and sacrifice all the pleasures of life to pursue my dream of creating art."

The tribal or communal field, one's inner desire, the movement of the Self, does not reveal itself in drop-dead-jaw-agape synchronistic phenomena alone. It may just as likely emerge as a mild, quiet, connecting link, like the notes in a melody that flow one into the next in a chain or matrix of meaning and music. Noticing the tribal field necessitates one to see and hear subtle nuances.

Similarly, the tribal field is subtle, present all the time, noticed by few, because it isn't loud or obnoxious, but quiet and mercurial to catch. This becomes, inherently, part of the difficulty in describing it. It is exceedingly soft and gentle and often easily missed entirely. To point to it and say, "See! There it is!" is a lot like getting a friend to see the shooting star you have spotted before it fades into memory. Loud messages can come via extremely quiet means—by a slight sensation or an intuition or an impulse. This most subtle of perceptions, this elusive, vague, easily discounted experience is where the magic and meaning live within the psyche.

The small moments, the soft inclinations, the brief insights are how we discover who and what we are. This mystery of Self that emerges after we have the courage to set aside duty and obligation to collective norms needs a calm quiet ear to hear its pleadings, its concerns, its desires.

The tribal field is the rich fertile soil upon which this small seed can sprout and grow; it is the fecund emanation of the dream maker and the Self, the beginning of the journey upon which we can take a first step—a step toward wholeness, fulfillment, and meaning.

Part Three

Tapestries

CHAPTER FOURTEEN

Time, Space, Reality

ONE ASPECT OF SYNCHRONICITY IS THAT IT CONFRONTS EGO consciousness with its linear understanding of the nature of time and space. When one dreams in preparation for events that occur the following day, it baffles the rational understanding of reality. Dreams can present events and issues that manifest days or even years later. Breaking out of preconceived notions is the first and foremost challenge—the benchmark of the gifted scientist. How time lives up to reality as the ego experiences it is not yet entirely explained or understood. Einstein fifty years ago poked a big hole in our set notions of time and relativity; his work encouraged new thought regarding physics and particle relationship to space, causality, and linear time.

Recall that Jung said, "Dreams prepare the psyche for the events of the following day."[20] I have experienced this countless times, both for myself as well as my analysands. It is remarkable to even entertain the notion that dreams prepare one ahead of time for actions that cannot be known by ordinary consciousness. The following is an example. . . .

A woman dreamed:

I was in an unfamiliar house but knew it to be my own. I descended some stairs down to a garden room, a space on the ground level with French doors leading to the outside. One door was ajar, and to my dismay I saw a squirrel scamper in. I tried to shoo it out but when I did, it bit my hand on the finger. The bite was laden with affect in the dream; it was horrifying, it stung, it felt something like an electric shock.

The next day after she had this dream, she received an angry, accusatory phone call from a colleague with whom she had a difficult relationship. This call was particularly unpleasant, because the colleague was quoting other colleagues as supporting her anger and accusations. The dreamer felt attacked and betrayed by people she thought were her friends.

"Coincidence," one might immediately say. Perhaps, but this dream and the resulting events (particularly the very next day) are ordinary dream occurrences. It is hard for me, after a number of years of observation, to discount these phenomena by calling them merely coincidences.

In another example, a young man living with roommates away from home for the first time, had this dream:

I dreamed my roommates were all ganging up on me and planning an attack. I felt terribly betrayed and hurt.

When he awakened in the morning there was a note on his door: "Please talk to us at your earliest convenience." Of course, they were all mad at him and instigated a cruel discussion after which he ended up moving out of the apartment. In fact, biting, attacking, pursuing dreams are important to notice—they can operate as a protective device, which is perhaps one reason why we have them.

Here is an additional example. A Jungian analyst and friend of mine had the following dream:

I am in the bayou in Louisiana and two crabs jump out of the water and each bites one of my hands.

Shortly after, he discovered he had cancer in both lungs.

The dream maker "makes ready" the process as well as uses these warnings to reduce his / her resistance and denial. With a numinous dream to help prepare the way, the fight and energy necessary to deal with cancer is abetted.

It is well documented that several of the Lakota people, including Black Elk, had a number of precognitive visions and experiences that foretold their demise as a great nomadic Plains culture. One can imagine that in earlier times, native people could have dreamed or envisioned or sensed a coming attack from a warring tribe, a catastrophic weather condition, or a hostile animal encounter.

One can also imagine, since the anthropological literature is full of examples, that these dreams and images were received with utmost sincerity and concern, and that appropriate defensive measures were taken. One can easily conclude that this talent or ability allowed the human being to survive and thrive and that it still exists within the modern psyche as well.

In Littleton, Colorado, on the farthest southern edge of the city, I often watched the horses that were boarded in a prairie behind my house. Sometimes they would gallop and whinny together in a magnificent circumambulation that created a cloud of dust we could see a mile away. I asked my father why these usually docile and somewhat boring creatures could behave in this erratic fashion. He said, "Just wait—in about two hours we will have a nice storm." And so we usually did. As predictable as the clock, the clouds and thunder would roll in and a great rainstorm would follow.

I noticed a similar phenomenon while teaching elementary school, especially in the primary grades. If, on the playground during recess, I observed an extraordinary amount of running, screaming, thrashing about, and general chaos, I usually would hear the thunder an hour or so later.

We still have this brain function, although it is now clouded and coated by doubt, education, propriety, and conventionality. We all still have an instinctual brain even if we aren't very much in touch with it. And this function has a predictive feature that boggles rational understanding. Just how does linear time really function? How is it that one thing seems to follow another without our previous knowledge or intent?

The tribal field is not bounded by linear time or by external reality as we currently understand it. The surrounding events and relationships of our lives operate in a swirl or tapestry of energy and design that encourages us to develop, grow, and become more conscious.

An inherent force exists within the soul of a person, a force that pushes one toward greater awareness and understanding. This force has at its core an instinct to survive and thrive. The life force is a strong energy, and it permeates and affects perhaps all cells of physical reality.

The North American native people knew rocks, as well as plants, mountains, and buffalo, had spirit. They were perplexed by Western European attitudes that saw humans as viable creatures with soul and other life forms as soulless. These two views of the sacred—the European and the Aboriginal—could hardly be more divergent. This split that Western thought has perpetrated—the split between matter and spirit—has led to a host of difficulties—spiritual, social, ecological, political. I recall years ago a young woman who came in for a session with a distressed air. . . .

"How are you today? Did you enjoy your visit to California to see your relatives?"

"Yes . . . but they think I'm listening to the devil by coming to you to work on my dreams."

Then she produced a book—one that has thankfully disappeared over time. The basic premise was that no new revelation was possible after the Bible was written; all new ideas (and especially dreams) are evil, because they are in direct opposition to the only real truth—Christianity as interpreted by late-twentieth-century American Protestants. Such an ideology, of course, denies change, evolution, transformation—all of which are suspect because they challenge the status quo.

Jung relates this interesting vignette in *Dream Analysis* (1984):

> . . . it is quite possible in the case of a person living in a hotel that in the next room lives somebody with a peculiar kind of psychology and a certain amount of that filters through the walls into his dreams. I know a man who had a terrible murder suicide dream when sleeping in a certain room, and it turned out that he had got into the room where that happened, so he was penetrated by the atmosphere. We can get infected in the same way where living people are concerned. A mental contagion is amazingly strong; we hate the idea and repress it as well as we can. (561)

Example

The C. G. Jung Institute of Dallas gave exams the weekend of February 7, 1999, during which a rather clear example of the tribal / communal field emerged that was not within the classical analytical setting. The people involved have kindly allowed me to write about this occurrence, and I am indebted to them for their generosity since I have to use their real names to tell this story.

The story began two years earlier when Nicholas French, a candidate taking his final exams for the Diploma in Analytical Psychology, had begun to think about who might be on his thesis-reading committee. Part of the thesis involved presenting a proposal and selecting a reading committee as well as setting some dates for completion of the first draft. The Dallas Institute used "outside" analysts to read and examine our candidates' papers. Thus, candidates might have an examining analyst from any institute, in any part of the world.

Candidates were not "allowed" to choose their examiners, but their suggestions were taken into consideration. Nicholas French had requested John Beebe from San Francisco to be one of his readers. Beebe was an analyst he had never met but one whose work he admired. Since Beebe was a highly respected Jungian analyst, the Dallas analysts were in agreement with French's request. No one thought, however, that John Beebe, a busy analyst, would agree to read, critique, and examine the thesis. It can be a long drawn-out process, including spending a weekend in Dallas for the oral examination—all for a mere $200 fee. So when John Beebe said he would be willing to be a part of the exam, both Nicholas and the Dallas analysts were surprised and pleased.

Next, French wrote his first draft, sent it off to his readers, and while waiting for their initial reaction, he received this dream:

> *I am high in the Andes. I see a magnificent eagle flying*
> *alone. To my dismay, I realize a small man in a leather suit*
> *is shooting the eagle with a rifle. Somehow I chase him off,*
> *and then I notice a tail twitching under the man's coat, and*
> *I see he's really only a monkey. Furthermore, when I pick*
> *up the rifle he's left behind, I see it's really only a beebee*
> *gun. Then I see a burro whose liver has been cut out. Other*
> *animals are with him and are going to take him to a safer*
> *place.*

Meanwhile, John Beebe, a careful and tactful man, wrote his critique of French's thesis to a Dallas analyst, not realizing the fax would be passed on—unedited—to Nicholas. It was fairly brutal. Beebe didn't think the thesis was good at all and even questioned if this candidate was ready to graduate.

Naturally, Nicholas was disappointed, but he couldn't help but recall his dream. John Beebe and the beebee gun. Just like the dream, Nicholas felt his soaring eagle-like intuition / inflation was shot down by Dr. Beebe. Nicholas knew he was in the midst of a rich and vital time. He worked tremendously hard, read and reread literature, rewrote, edited, and virtually began anew. His second writing was vastly improved, and all of his readers, including John Beebe, were satisfied he was ready to be examined.

During the thesis exam, the majority of time was devoted to Nicholas's dream: how the flying eagle became the wounded burro, the healer / analyst that carries the burden of his clients. The suffering the healer experiences as a result of the deep soul work s / he is involved with was explored. The liver is the "seat of the soul" in some traditions, so this dream was viewed as an initiatory dream—the eagle transmutes into the lonely wounded burro who has discovered and differentiated his soul, and also needs the other animals for safety. All three of the examiners were profoundly touched by this synchronistic dream of the beebee gun, the suffering that followed in the agonizing rewrite, and the fine thesis that resulted.

Thus, French was initiated by an analyst that he had never met, one that he had intuitively wanted on his exam committee, one that delivered the painful and correcting message regarding the first draft, and one that appeared in code in a precognitive, synchronistic fashion in French's dream. And one who processed his dream thoroughly and sensitively in the exam. And here we were. All of the analysts present had often observed and been party to synchronistic events, yet we were still touched, still awed by the emergence of our mysterious connection to the Self, to the unconscious, and to each other.

RELATIONAL DREAMS

Sometimes dreams reveal clues about "the relationship" that is not the same as dreaming about another person in objective reality. And it is not necessarily "warning" the dreamer. To illustrate: a middle-aged therapist was having a devilish time getting her thirty-ish son emancipated and independent. He had always been a poor student and was now a low-functioning young adult. Off and on, he would "camp" at Mom's house—never with a good outcome. During one of the "just until I get on my feet" stays, Mom had this dream:

> *I dreamed of a bird in a nest taking care of her chicks. One chick, however, was huge—much too big to still be in the nest. Then I saw the mother bird just push the big bird out.*

I asked her what happened to the big chick and she said, "I don't know and don't care. It was time for him to go." When she had awakened, she felt she knew exactly what this dream was about—her relationship with her son and what needed to happen. Thereafter, she told him he had to leave and was firm about it, with a conviction she had not felt or ever communicated to him before. He did leave and began his first substantial steps toward adult independence.

Here, the dream revealed how mother and son related to each other. It provided the information as well as the conviction for the dreamer to take the hard step to not "over-mother" any longer. The dream provided a type of knowing that allowed the ego to act courageously.

Another dream that commented on a relationship is one a forty-year-old had at the time she and her husband separated. She was a naïve yet contented wife. She married a man a little older, more experienced, a bit "wild." She loved his good looks, his charm, his arrogance. But after they were married about twelve years, he began an affair with a much younger woman. The dreamer had no idea about his new relationship. He had even set up a second household and introduced his girlfriend to some of his family. But even though she eventually learned about the unpleasant details of their affair, she remained optimistic he was going to return any day and that they could regain their marriage. Then she dreamed:

> B. and I are holding each other in an embrace. There is a
> huge thick rubber band around us. I know in the dream the
> rubber band is what holds us together. But I see it has bro-
> ken and now is only tied. I know we are still held together,
> but that a rubber band broken and tied is never the same as
> the rubber band when it is whole.

The "rubber band dream" confronted the dreamer to see and accept the permanent damage the relationship had suffered. She was better able to begin the slow painful experience of admitting her loss. He went on to have a child with the younger woman, and he and the dreamer divorced. Now they have practically no contact; and he has even severed ties from the daughter they had together.

CHAPTER FIFTEEN

Dreams for the Entire Group

ONCE A WOMAN HAD A DREAM ABOUT A HERD OF HORSES galloping on a beach. They were in a line, as if they had a leader, and the others followed. I didn't think much had come of our discussion about the dream—mostly, we amplified the horse image and tried to understand what that might be for the dreamer. But the next session, two weeks later, gave me a better clue about this abstruse dream. Another member, not the dreamer but one who was talented artistically, had been moved to paint the dream image. She produced a magnificent scene of several horses all in line, traveling together, on the beach. Suddenly, it seemed as if it were a painting of dream group—of course, the horses were the same in number as the participants, and here we were, moving together at the edge of earth and water, on the transitional space between two realities, together, free, wild.

In this case it took one member to dream the image and another one to paint it before we could see part of its significance. We were moved and humbled by this interesting gift-image. My own dreams were also informative during the process of dream group and one especially comes to mind. I had the following dream a few months after I had begun facilitating dream groups:

One of my dream groups is to raise a "cone of power"
around a magnificent blue bowl. The cone is raised and
the bowl breaks. I know the ritual has worked. "B." goes
after the shards and waves them menacingly in a child's
face that is also attending this ceremony. I get scared. I scat
her away and pick up the shards. They turn into Rosetta
stones, crystals, and jewels. I put them in a box and give
them away. Then I make Scotch whiskey in a bucket for
the group.

At the time I had this dream I didn't have any overbearing concern about B. Later, however, "B." turned out to be destructive for the group process. I think this dream, which I can still remember vividly today, gave me a clue about a personality of which to be careful. Not all people are suitable for dream group. This clue was a hard one for me to catch, because at this point in my training and studies it was virtually sacrilegious to see a dream like this as anything but a shadow projection I needed to make conscious. In other words, the only dangerous person is me, and I have a dangerous projection onto someone else. Truly, one cannot expect dreams to always be oracles of inner truth about other people. Suffice it to say, I had had plenty of hints about B. but was ignoring them due to my own pathology—that of eternal optimism, expecting the best, and trusting people entirely too much. So this dream compensated my outer attitude about the member of dream group, but it also gave a clue about how the relationship would turn out later.

Dream images can speak to many, if not all, members of the group in remarkable ways. In a dream group I facilitated in the Dallas County Jail, a woman had this image:

I dreamed I was outside in the free world, but I was still in
jail living in a hut with all of the other inmates.

The women in jail struggle with various issues of self-destruction, substance abuse, violence, poverty, and lack of education. It was crystal clear to all of them that life on the outside is like a jail, just as much—in some ways—as literally being in jail. Especially if the old patterns of behavior are continued, the "prison" is still intact. The dream confronted them with the fact that even though they all will be "free" at some time in the future, without a new attitude and mindset, they will still be incarcerated. The women knew that jail was a metaphor and until they could break out of their own cages of self-destruction they would be in literal jail for some time. Perhaps it is not so easy to put into words the effect an image like this one can have on a group. It was cementing, bonding, touching, amazing, connecting, revealing, insightful, meaningful, faith-producing, illuminating. Both the dreamer and the listeners felt the power of the experience.

During this writing project, a member of a dream group had a circumstance evolve in her life that mirrored my own. That is, we both resisted writing as if it were a painful dental procedure endured without the benefit of modern painkilling medication. This is a curious mode of rebellion that almost every writer I know (as well as Natalie Goldberg) can relate to. Writing is satisfying, creative, challenging, great fun, and brings enormous pleasure to our otherwise-insignificant existences. But we avoid it. We shun it. We discount it. We ignore it. We are afraid of it. We gnaw and gnash and scream and kick rather than be led to the altar of writing as a way of life.

My dream group member was in a pickle. She was in that dreaded state of being "ABD" (all but dissertation). In other terms, she had completed each and every requirement for a complicated Ph.D. but had only her dissertation left to write. The problem was that her time was running out, and some of her committee members had or were retiring. She had already let it sit on her desk for three or four years and had only written sixty-five pages so far. Her advisor wanted the final product to be about two-hundred-fifty pages. Another person in this dream group wrote as well. She was a clinical psychologist who had almost entirely given up her practice to write fiction. She was in the middle of a novel but also found it exhaustingly challenging to carve out the time and energy to write. I too was trying to write. I found all the excuses known to resistant writers and maybe even a couple I made up on my own to deter me from a task I felt compelled to do, yet did not seem to be able to do. To myself, I said, "Tess, if you come to the natural end of your life and find you have not had the courage to write this thing you've thought and dreamed about for years, you're going to be one mighty sad and disappointed person." But still, I didn't write much.

Finally, a crisis of sorts evolved in dream group around the Ph.D. project. I cannot say for certain how it happened, or exactly what happened, but one day, in group, it was clear S. really wanted to write. She really wanted to finish. She had about ten weeks left until a rough draft was due; otherwise, she was going to have to give the university authorities an explanation about why she hadn't produced a product. During this time, she had the following dream:

> I am at a chili cook off. There are eleven contestants but
> only ten place ribbons. Everyone places in the contest except
> me. Next, my little camping stove that I make my chili on is
> lost. I find it in a hotel lobby, pretty beaten up, but it's mine
> and I'm relieved and excited to have it back. Finally, three
> unknown women and myself make ecstatic love together.

In this dream blatant clues were given about the loss and retrieval of the creative process. In the first scene of the dream, the Grimm's Tale "Brier Rose" elucidates a germane point.[21] In this story the long-expectant daughter is blessed by only twelve of the thirteen fairies in the kingdom, because the King only owns twelve gold plates. The thirteenth fairy is furious and curses the child. To be left out, excluded, is a painful psychological experience—particularly when we do it to ourselves!

In this case, the dreamer had set up a judge in her head that was finding her woefully inadequate—others can achieve goals, write, find happiness, and so on, but not her. It was a chilling condemnation. Then one can see the problem presented by the dream, a problem that develops from too much competition and comparing to others—the stove is lost! The fire, the passion, the heat, the heart of the transformative process—the stove. It is a creative vessel because it is where we mix and concoct our magical, tasty, nourishing formulae for the soul and body. Heat changes elements from one form to another.

But S. found the stove "beaten up." I've heard her say, "Well, I've been beating up on myself pretty badly lately." We know who the perpetrator is in this case. But then the magic re-emerged in a new form, that of sexual love for women, four women, a complete set (four directions, four elements, four seasons)—an image of feminine passion and connection.

We ALL decided to write each day. S. figured she might be able to write two pages a day which could produce a rough draft in time to meet her deadline. The novelist, myself, and the other members who write in their journals all combined in one connected effort to create together, to break the resistance, to find the stove, to fuel the heat and fire that produces the fine soup.

This is another example of how processes overlap, intersect, weave together and, in general, act more like notes in a symphony than individual solos that operate independently one from another. Dreams and group issues seem to emerge in parallel, in harmony, and with congruence.

CHAPTER SIXTEEN

Death in the Community

"When I die, God isn't going to ask me if I was the best Moses I could be, he will ask if I was the best Marty I could be."

MARTIN BUBER

MUSIC AND LITERATURE HAVE A NUMBER OF CORRELATIONS to the larger life process. Sometimes when an analysand is confused about making a decision or wants to know the outcome of a stressful event I will ask, "What would make a good story?" Usually the good story (one with plot, action, foreshadowing, metaphor, hyperbole, puns, and a satisfying resolution, both tragic and comedic) can be sensed within the life process. As stated in chapter two, the language of dreams and the unconscious is the foundational language of poetry and literature. Similarly, our outer life is a dream story, too. It unfolds before us like a long ribbon furling out into the distance—we follow its path, and over time we begin to understand the nature of the path a little bit. We begin to notice road signs and "curve ahead" warnings, and, if we are lucky, we gather some clues along the way about where the road ultimately leads and why we are on it.

As mentioned, the death of a family member or close friend has a way of showing us some of our path if we listen to our innermost feelings about the death. Each death brings with it a number of gifts for the persons surrounding the one who died. Their lives and how they lived them are framed at death—put in a perspective that lets one see the entire picture: the beginning, the middle, the end, the successes and failures, the tragedies and celebrations. Each death is like a nudge to look at life closely and examine it with pointed clarity. Mourning is a human emotion that doesn't allow as much ego resistance and denial as our usual common outlook does. Of course, we all die eventually. Some die earlier and therefore carry a bigger frame to their life. The life is more closely examined, the loss of it felt and acknowledged by more people. It becomes a marker for the rest of the tribe—one warrior falls first and thereby leads the rest into the most unknown journey. In our tribal field certain individuals lead in this way. By experiencing their deaths we learn how to experience our own. Death is another way the tribal field talks to us, bringing us into that layer of relationship, interaction, and connection that shapes us, guides us, teaches us, and leads us to the next step in our human learning school. Within the tribe we suffer losses and struggle to find the meaning or purpose of these painful events. Sometimes the meaning lies within the tribal field itself. In death, closeness is sought and achieved by tribal members. It becomes a great, gooey healing connection for some, bringing stories and history to the wake, leaving resentments behind. Death is the great leveler, the one human experience that best manifests our humanity.

Recently, someone I worked with for a long time died. She was diagnosed five months before her death, and, in the context of her analysis, such a shocking and sudden death was not anticipated. This was not the first analysand of mine who has died or has struggled with severe illness, but her death reminded me again of how utterly unconscious we are most of the time. I do not mean to suggest that consciousness can save one from a life-threatening illness, but I do know that as a general human condition, it can take a fatal blow to get us to live. As my analysand who died put it, "It has taken me suffering a terminal illness to be able to hear my story."

The gift I think I received from this remarkable woman was to pay careful attention to all information, in all its forms, that comes to our consciousness. It is to keep life compact, framed, not so leaky that energy cannot build and transform in areas where we can affect change. To be extended hither and yon, to have a yard and house and bills and family and work and volunteer activities and projects may result in a life that doesn't heed the one true thing calling out for attention and energy. An artist needs a studio and time to paint.

Above all, I have learned that if a person detests some aspect of life, whether it is a job, a marriage, an apartment, or an extra fifty pounds, after a fashion something has to be done about it or it can become dangerous. Sitting with chronic unhappiness is unhealthy for the psyche as well as for the body. When we receive every piece of necessary data that change is essential, then proceed straight to unconsciousness, trouble lurks. It can appear in the form of depression, anxiety, stress-related disorders, or any number of physical symptoms. Change is what we most resist and what we most need.

I recall a case from a dream group of several years ago. M. was morose and detached from the group. No amount of dream group seemed to thaw her out; she was profoundly frightened of all of the members. She also had a job that terrified her—if she lost it she was certain she would be homeless, and yet her boss was harsh and ridiculed her at work. Moreover, therapy did not touch her depression, either. It seemed to me that there wouldn't be any improvement until she sought alternate employment. But she held on to that awful job like a dog with its teeth sunk into a juicy bone. She developed paranoid ideation (thought she would open the morning newspaper one day to find herself incriminated in print) and slept fourteen hours a day, in total social isolation.

Eventually destiny helped her and our work together. She got fired. Her countenance the very next time she came to dream group was dramatically changed. She looked fresh, younger, had better coloring, and she even smiled. I was grateful she had constellated what she needed for herself, albeit unconsciously, so at least she could worm out from under the blanket of depression. She did.

But my analysand who died was not fired from her job; she was fired from her life. And she too exhibited an odd sort of ecstasy when she received the news. She said, "I don't have to work anymore. I don't have to diet or exercise anymore. I don't have to do anything I don't want to!" This was spoken by a person who had lived her life feeling oppressed by various institutions and individuals.

I do not suggest that this illness was the analysand's creation to escape the outer reality she felt smothered and wounded by, but I am curious if it perhaps could be a factor in a long list of ultimately speculative conjectures regarding why we die when we die. Death also gives us the gift of remembering the impermanence of our physical existence. All of our current reality will be dust someday. All of us have a limited time to be incarnate. One can choose to ignore that glaring fact quite easily since current modern society ignores death and runs from facing it. Like the fairy tales where the hero has three wishes and then it's over, our lives are temporal and fragile as well.

I ask my groups sometimes to imagine the end of their lives and to list a few important items they would regret not accomplishing or experiencing. This is the backdoor route that sometimes can open a passageway to a vein of passion to be followed or explored. It is not unlike the exercise of listing the people about whom we have envy, since they too bring up latent, unlived aspects of ourselves yearning for integration somewhere in the conscious psyche.

"Yes but" is a poisonous phrase for the Self that yearns to be heard and acknowledged. Many courageous decisions tend to be complex and difficult. Aspects have to be carefully weighed and measured; however, chronic unhappiness will drift back into the unconsciousness of depression if it is not held up, seen, and validated. It's so easy to rationalize staying in an abusive relationship (I want to keep the family together) or going for holidays to parents' houses rather than take the trip one has longed for (my mother would never get over it). I am not advocating utter selfishness as an approach to life, but one must not ignore the yearnings of the soul, either. Our heart's desire is all we have to begin the journey of insight, awareness, and understanding. And it is our own unique lives, after all, we are best able to live, not the prescribed behavior that society or family has dictated to us.

One group asked themselves the dangerous question, "If there were no consequences to consider, what would I really want to do?" This question came from a dream that touched the whole group—the sense that we are, much of our lives, imprisoned and living out of duty and obligation, that there are rare moments, if any, when one is allowed and encouraged to be free and real.

This question and its answers led to some dramatic life changes—a romance, a degree, a move. This is precisely why the conscious self, the "I," the ego, will resist dreams with a passion; they demand change because each day, in many ways, we fall so short of the mark, we live half-lives, blanketed over with denial and ignorance.

In the smallest ways we die each day through denial, fear, ignorance, discounting, and simply not paying attention. We, as a culture, look to the external to validate ourselves—beauty, wealth, social position, and power. But it is the internal that truly drives our significant development of soul. It is the inside, the emanation of our unique self that manifests the goodness of our being. Existence occurs in the quietest moments, in the smallest detail. Each moment has opportunity—and failure—imbedded within it.

The tribal field is, in fact, all of the relational energy one feels, energy that is at its base, the stuff from which our histories are made. War is an example. Hate coalesces into fear, multiplied by many individuals, and violent conflict erupts. These remarkable historical events occur with a tangle of energy driving them—energies about which we are only slightly conscious. I recall a graduate school lecture about group hysteria from my behaviorist professor in Abnormal Psychology. Our text cited a passage recalling Mesmer's demonstrations wherein patients would break out in perspiration, twitch convulsively, scream, laugh, moan and, like a contagion, it would spread to other members of the experiment.[22] This was a lecturer who could explain any human behavior both logically and scientifically, yet when I asked him how this mass hysteria could happen, he shook his head and said, "I don't know."

I frequently see evidence that the tribal field is ignored and discounted by collective consciousness. Somehow human relationship and its interactions are thought to be a "lite psychology" or a frilly nonacademic study. This bias (a patriarchal one) only increases our continued stupidity about the aspects of life that carry the most meaning and most affect our existence. With a community, the human being can survive almost anything.

Much is written and discussed in Jungian psychology regarding one's "process." This is a difficult concept because it is three dimensional and largely irrational as well. Process is about theme, story, meaning unfolding. It is current and present for all people all of the time. It involves the messages being presented in dreams, the experiences of the body, jobs, relationships, synchronicities, odd feelings, intuitions, our current developmental phase of growth, and much more. It is the story being told at a moment of our existence. Sometimes the stories overlap, and an analysis can help clarify all of the data. The analyst is much like a data catcher, trapper, classifier. It is important to identify and illuminate the information being presented. Novels are about characters' processes. They are the best example of how the psyche works: a problem emerges, is identified, various attempts are made toward resolution, transformation occurs in the end. We live within many tales—we are the protagonist in some, a minor player in others, the foil in a few. Some stories take years and years to develop, some have an epilogue decades later, some are finished in a short time. There is at least one big, overreaching story that tracks us all our lives. Jung called it one's personal myth. It is arduously difficult to discover one's myth, yet valuable beyond description to achieve this element of consciousness.

Likewise, groups have a process, as well. Groups can be a set of factory workers, a neighborhood, a third-grade class, a graduate school practicum, a political precinct gathering, a First Baptist Church. A group is a family, an extended family, a clan. The group process is the evidence of the tribal field in the unconscious that has purpose, intent, and evolutionary movement just like the individual psyche.

A story about Einstein goes like this: once someone asked if Einstein knew anything for absolute certain. He thought about the question for a long time. Weeks. Finally, he answered, "The only thing I know for certain is that something is moving."

The Lakota knew well the power of dreams—these rich sources of information with their pointed, sometimes humorous, messages that guide and direct. They present the information the ego most needs. In twelve-step circles there is a slogan, "Just do the next right thing." This is much like the overall purpose of the dream; it is the next right image or insight one needs to move forward. In this way the dream is an oracle, because it portrays the emerging image that is right underneath the surface of consciousness. The movement in consciousness is like the seed sprouting; the natural growth process sends it up for air and light and existence. It could be a confrontation about a debilitating complex—perhaps the dream shows the ego how futile and narcissistic perfectionism is—or the dream could be a tap on the shoulder to truly embrace a creative spark within.

Dreams operate much like the *Heyoka* clown of the Lakota people.[23] This shaman is one who is specifically called and initiated into his tribe as a contrary. His backwards upside-down antics bring forth laughter in some cases, hence the translation "sacred clown." However, the *Heyoka* shamans are enormously powerful and feared because they carry the opposite, compensatory attitude of the tribal consciousness. Just like dreams, they are funny, sobering, and intensely confrontational.

Dreams are passionate as well. They seem to care or "give a shit" in modern vernacular. Like a good parent, they continually correct our course, monitor progress, reward good behavior, coach, encourage, and punish. Nightmares are like getting grounded or losing privileges—this is when we need some important lessons, and we are so resistant the dream maker has to nearly frighten us to death in order to get our attention.

Actually, when the system improves, the individual experiences more distress psychologically. For example, a person may enter a therapeutic relationship with a whole set of problems— unhappy love life, dissatisfying job, financial uncertainty. Over time these symptoms usually ameliorate. Then the real trouble begins. No longer can the external circumstances carry the angst of existence—one has to face and deal with the soul, only the soul, without distraction.

Family-systems professionals have long pointed out the dynamic of one person in the family who plays the role of the identified patient. This phenomenon was noticed by Carl Jung when he cautioned parents to not project shadow or other qualities onto their children, because the children have a way of acting out their parents' unconscious selves with a most accurate and exasperating mirror. In systems analysis, these dynamics can be seen in families and groups of all sorts. Interesting work is being developed, for example, in churches. Family dynamics can be seen in some of the problems congregations and ministers have together.

To return to our dream group member who was struggling to write her Ph.D. dissertation, she continued after her "Lost and Found Stove" dream to write and progress on her rough draft. I and others, too, in the dream group found writing easier and more fluid. Is it possible that people can increase their chances of health and improvement more in a group than through a singular effort? Sociologists have already accurately pointed out that the ethics of a group can quickly sink to the lowest common denominator amongst the participants. This gives some explanation how ordinarily upstanding citizens, good husbands and fathers, could commit something as heinous as a lynching. In crowds, people will do incredibly evil acts that they would never commit alone. Likewise, groups can have the opposite effect as well. The power of a group to support and to heal is psychologically phenomenal contrasted to individual effort.

Years ago I was struggling with a difficult case. The young woman I was counseling had a wretched case of bulimia, the first time I had heard of such a disorder. Additionally, she exhibited a host of problems—promiscuity, job instability, financial insecurity, exercise addiction, estrangement from family, and serious health problems resulting from her bulimia. I saw her twice a week for over three years. My current recollection is I didn't help her at all. It could be argued (as my supervisor kindly pointed out) that she could have been much worse without my care, nonetheless, she exhibited no significant improvement during our work together.

Our work terminated when I moved to Zurich to train at the Jung Institute. When I visited home a couple of years later at

Christmas time, I called her to see how she was doing. Much better, it turned out. She reported her bulimia was all but gone. The vomiting, bingeing, food shoplifting, destruction of her teeth and jaw, the scars on the back of her hand, the compulsion to run six miles or more a day, as well as the constant comparing and competitiveness around body size had all but evaporated. "How did this happen?" I inquired. "Oh, I joined a group for bulimics, and somehow it just worked itself out." A humbling piece of news for me—I had tried as hard as I knew how to help her find a path out of her hell. Nothing we had done made any overt difference.

Together, with a common purpose and focus, humans can accomplish almost anything. History and civilization well support this notion. What one is seeing here is the intersection of psychology and sociology. The group carries with it a mysterious element of power—which can work for the benefit or the detriment of society.

The tribal field can also manifest in the body process; that is to say, physical symptoms and illnesses can be linked to disturbances from the tribal field. Physical illnesses are not only related to disturbances but they also account for a correction the unconscious is working to manifest. The following illustration is an example:

A couple I've known and respected for years ultimately divorced some time ago. Many in the relational field of this couple were hurt, shocked, confused. The husband had become involved with a younger woman, someone also in the relational circle. The first wife was angry and expressed it freely; it was painful to hear her rage, even after she met and became connected to a kind man who seemed to love her deeply. She, however, refused to marry him—a testament to the pain and suffering she still endured. Her ex-husband went on to marry the younger woman, and after a few years the second wife became pregnant. At the same time, the first wife became ill with breast cancer and died within the year. In a last conversation, she told me that the second wife's pregnancy had done her in—"It was something I could never get over." Then, her robust, athletic ex-husband became chronically ill after his first wife's death.

Here, betrayal, loss, grief, and anger all coalesced into a wad of suffering that was extended to the members of this family in the form of illness and death. The second wife suffered too. Their infant had serious health issues. Ignoring the psychological aspects of illness and only treating symptoms is like ignoring the house's foundation problems and only repairing the cracks in the wall. Just as illnesses signal trouble, they also can provide us with affirmative images that truly inform the ego about unconscious developments that are significant and positive. It is important to view the illness from a tribal perspective in these cases. One misses the mark if each element of the illness is only seen as a part of the self.

Marion Woodman, in her book *Bone* (2000), a story about her own journey with cancer, provides this remarkable example of tribal dreaming between two of her analysands:

> . . . I'm also going to talk about my two analysands who were friends. When Ruth was diagnosed with cancer, she came to me because she had had a dream in which she saw her own tombstone. On it she read, "Beloved daughter of . . . , beloved wife of . . . , beloved mother of. . . . Her own name and birth and death dates were not there. She herself had not lived. About the same time, Lyn became pregnant. Astonishingly, Ruth began to dream she was pregnant, and Lyn began to have fearsome death dreams. As she realized she was pregnant with herself, Ruth glowed with energy, her radiance increasing as she approached death. Her final dream was of a golden child being born from her crown *chakra,* gently and relentlessly

pushing through the crown of her head. Lyn stayed close to Ruth, even sometimes experienced the darkness of Ruth's tumor growing within herself, a darkness which Ruth did not experience. Lyn saw the Light in the room in which Ruth was dying. She knew Ruth was being initiated into her own wholeness. She also knew such a journey was somewhere in the future for her. That journey began some weeks later, when Lyn gave birth to a stillborn child. (Woodman, 166–7)

CHAPTER SEVENTEEN

The Dream Maker's Fascination with Relationship

DREAMS ACT AS CHEERLEADERS TOO, ESPECIALLY WHEN one is being unconscious of one's assets and accomplishments. A woman with an important career had this dream:

I go to a meeting with all of the heads of companies I work with. They tell me they can smell me before I come and that my scent will always change the direction of the meeting. My scent is described as lemony and woodsy.

What the dreamer had failed to acknowledge to herself was her effectiveness and power in her work circle. Furthermore, her effect was "lemony and woodsy" which by association the dreamer described as "clean and natural, fertile." The heads of the companies could be described as parts of herself, but I think that view does not entirely satisfy the intention of the dream. Rather, the image is clearly a tribal one in which the dreamer was being shown her relationship (somewhat unconscious prior to the dream) to her circle, her group of peers, and her colleagues. The dream was about how she related to those around her, not particularly how she related to herself. The objective reality is that the dreamer had no conscious awareness of the level of power she had in her work group. Actually, she tended to diminish her role and presence.

Dreams and the dream maker tend, in general, to be quite fascinated by one's relationships, groups, clans, and gangs. Often, images in dreams occur around other people in clusters, like dream buddies.

TWIN DREAMS

In one anthropological account of the old Lakota society, the twin dreamer lodge was identified. In this case, two people who dream about each other on the same night are initiated into the lodge with special ceremonies and medicine. Clearly, the Lakota were cognizant of the importance of double dreamers.

Recently, I had a "typical" anxiety dream that I was ill-prepared for a presentation, had overslept, was without makeup and had left my notes at home. Rather than slough that dream off as a "common anxiety dream," I decided to apply my theories to myself that the ego continually discounts the message of the dream, and, in any case, dreams do not present facts of which we already are well aware. I certainly knew I was nervous about presenting a three-hour seminar to therapists in a few weeks. Through association, thought, and processing, the dream revealed itself to me with a new type of clarity. The dream was not "obvious" or two dimensional at all. In fact, it hit on some core and chronic issues for me regarding facing the work, getting ready and being willing to communicate my own passions, and having the positive creative confidence to "assemble the personality and assert it!"[24]

This dream was all about laziness, just getting by, hiding, diffusing my focus, and continually rationalizing why life can just sweep on by and somehow circumstances have left me missing it. "It" in this case was creation, myth, voice, focus. It was the small

unique part of self that yearns to be expressed against the background of mundane and banal normalcy. Feminist theologians
talk about sin in a way that evokes this issue. Sin is defined as not
telling the truth, lack of focus, denying self.[25] That is what this
dream was about.

Later in the week, at my office, an analysand brought in a dream
he had about me on the same night I had the "anxiety dream." In
it, I have left a portion of my practice to spend time writing in a
library room at Southern Methodist University. Neither he nor
I had attended SMU, in fact he traveled in from another city for
analysis. His associations to SMU were unremarkable. I, however,
have a strong association since SMU is where I uncovered some
important anthropological research for my Jung Institute thesis
that I wrote several years ago. In particular, I found an article
entitled "Clown Woman" that made quite an impact on me.[26] My
analysand was a writer as well, so the dream could be all about
him if one wanted to pursue the safe road here in the analytical
transference. But I knew I was in his dream when he told it to me,
because I could feel it.

I was noncommittal about it when he brought it into the
session. The dream was viewed as only his dream, namely the
subjective approach. Eventually, I decided to tell him about
"Clown Woman," a cornerstone piece of research for my thesis,
which was the first time writing was an utter joy for me. He was
grateful for the disclosure and said it was helpful. I tend to agree
that it was.

As I have stated, these disclosures have to be tempered with
restraint, privacy, decorum, and propriety. A little of it goes a
long way. The analysand has to be the primary focus and feel
the session and the work are about him, not the therapist. But
for an analyst to "sit on" pertinent information from his own
dream is a therapeutic failure as well. It would be like tossing out
a letter that said he had won a writing contest. It is unfair not to

let people who are earnestly seeking an inner journey know the power, impact, and synchronicity of their process.

DREAM DRESS CODE

Sometimes it is hard to hide the overlapping elements of the analyst and the group's process. For example, Tuesday, March 30, 1999, I decided to go the office in casual dress. About once a month I decide to wear blue jeans or some other casual attire. This day, I wore faded blue jeans, a black v-neck tee shirt with a black linen collared shirt worn open and over the tee. I had on black shoes. My first client came in wearing faded blue jeans, a charcoal gray v-neck sweater with a black shirt over it. She had brown shoes on. Next, I had dream group. "A." was wearing a black tee shirt, a black shirt worn open and over the tee with a black skirt and black shoes. "B." was wearing blue jeans and a black shirt. "C." was wearing black leggings and black shoes and a blue denim shirt. "D." was wearing blue jeans, black shoes, a black shirt, a blue jean vest with some leopard print on the pockets. "E." was wearing blue jeans and a light blue and gray shirt. "F." was wearing gray slacks and a light blue and gray dress shirt.

My next client came in workout clothes—all black; the next client (a man) was wearing blue jeans, black shoes, and a black shirt; the next client (a woman) was wearing blue jeans (the second time in three years she had worn blue jeans to analysis) and a white tee shirt with a light beige sweater over it. The next client was wearing black slacks, a matching black soft jacket with a black and white shirt underneath. The last client was wearing a black shirt, black soft jacket with a blue tee shirt underneath.

This exhausting detail is necessary in order to establish the exact phenomena I refer to when I say the group members and the clients who haven't even met each other often come into analysis in strikingly similar colors or styles. A dream group member who is active in her church as an usher reported that the ushers notice the same curiosity. In fact, the congregation teases that they must get on the phone Sunday mornings to plan together what they will wear, because it is all so strikingly similar.

Blue with black may be popular colors and blue jeans as common as a furniture store going-out-of-business sale, but not on the same day, hour after hour, with such remarkable congruence. Moreover, this phenomenon occurs again and again—not just with denim, blue, and black. Curious, too, is the apparent way this oddity applies to all of my practice, not just dream group, and it suggests that there is an unconscious connection amongst the entire practice. In fact, I see this "rule" apply in public, as well. Clusters or pairs of people shopping together often appear remarkably congruent in their dress and style of dress. At a small jazz festival only recently, I saw three attractive women who appeared to be in their sixties, all dressed in black and white print capri pants with tee shirts in shades of grey. Two of the three were wearing straw hats. Perhaps getting dressed, unless planned in advance, is one of our daily activities that manifests an unconscious process, like choosing the items for a sandtray projection²⁷ or letting a person "draw or paint whatever comes to mind" in art therapy. Our clothes reflect, also, a "not fully conscious" process that has a clue about what is in the underneath world of the psyche.

Tribal Social Living—Karma and Community

The image I see is a connected universe of all types of beings—some live here and now, some live in other realities, some have died and may exist in ways not fully understandable for people still living. The animals and plants participate in this matrix of complex interconnectedness. Surely it is not original to me to make this observation. What I see in addition to this "six degrees of separation" is a concentrated set of relationships that operates within the complex universal connectedness. It is what I refer to as the tribal field. Human behavior tends to mirror the realities of the inner psyche, and for centuries humans have formed tribes all over the globe. The nests or knots or concentrations of relationship reside within the larger field, also in relation to one another. Some groups may be loosely or tightly connected to other groups with a complicated mixture of inner connectedness. This is all compounded by circumstance, chance, fate, and destiny since outer events contribute to these tribal formations. Synchronicity is only part of how this can be observed. One can play the game (*It's a Wonderful Life*) "What if I were never born?" or (*Groundhog Day*) "What if I could live my life over?" to see convincingly how far-reaching and impacting our lives are to one another. The tribal field is who we are affected by, who we love, who we hate, with whom we have "learning relationships"—sometimes referred to as "karmic relationships."

Karmic relationships are fuzzy to define or describe, partly because almost all relationships produce the opportunity for growth. However, some relationships reign supreme in the ways they permanently affect and change us—sometimes for better, sometimes for ill.

Jung was reported to say that suffering leads to two roads: one, a road of bitterness; the other, a road of wisdom. Karmic relationships often involve a substantial amount of suffering. It is up to the individual to process the experience as a growing one or as a thwarting one.

It is within the tribal field that psychological evolution takes place. It is here one can individuate (which Jung said wasn't possible unless one was in a primary relationship) to allow the karmic suffering to work its necessary corrective movement in our being. Dreams and relationships are the most honest mirrors of our personalities; they don't lie or soft-pedal the truth.

Marriages and divorces are examples, often, of teaching relationships. They include love, hate, betrayal, abandonment, suffering, and breaking apart. They manifest powerful emotions for people—especially the type of marriage and divorce where both fire and ice are experienced or many years of history, children, and extended family. Many divorcing clients have told me they don't miss the spouse as much as the family. That small cell, the first cell of the tribal organism, is ancient and primitive in our relational souls. To be pulled out of it is to experience an alienation, disconnectedness, and aloneness that perhaps defies language to articulate. The tribe exists, but like almost everything else in existence, it evolves—it changes, it moves. What may have been a vital life connection then is now merely smoke wafting and disappearing from a fire that has gone out.

To be disconnected from the tribe is to experience profound isolation. Many so-called neurotic complaints can resolve with community and social support. In the late seventies, when I attended graduate school, the course that affected me most was Community Psychology. It dealt with seeing individuals' therapeutic issues in the context of the whole—their families, jobs, and neighborhoods. The focus of this class was to see the community, not the individual, as the system that was ill.

In today's world the tribe is ill. The tribe that carries both the conscious and unconscious support of the individual is fractured and disbursed into a distant web rather than a contained pueblo of community life.

The internet is a connecting device much more than a tool of isolation, as some claim. It presents a peek at how modern society will evolve back to a more tribal system—in this case, technology helps to accommodate the sheer numbers of persons alive on earth now. Technology will succeed in bringing people back into connection, albeit a substantially different interaction than living and working communally.

However, communal living could well make a comeback. It is possible an emerging faction of Americans will explore new and different ways to co-exist. Trends in architecture and real estate reflect this. Dallas, Texas, for example, has been a sprawling city for many years where the center, the heart of the downtown, nearly died as larger and more vital commerce and residential neighborhoods formed numerous miles out in greater and greater concentric circles. Currently, however, a plethora of new developments are forming within the inner city. In addition, many of these refurbished structures have a multitude of uses: retail on the first floor, residential on upper stories that are suitable for home offices, exercise gyms, small theater rooms, and so forth. This will result in the tenants and owners having far more interaction than they would have had in traditional apartment buildings or in the isolated suburban-designed homes of the past. Already I have encountered women who talk of living in clusters as they become older and less interested in the fierce independent lifestyle popular since 1900 or so. Lifestyles might become more orientated toward relationship; in other words, living with persons that one enjoys and with whom one shares common interests. Our outer behavior reflects the inner psychological reality—that we live and dream within a matrix of relationships.

DREAMS INFORM REALITY

As I pointed out in chapter five, part of the ancient tribal aspect of the psyche is its way of informing the ego about impending danger. Not infrequently, the dream maker operates as one who warns or as one who prepares the ego for a difficult path ahead. In a curious fashion, dreams will occasionally alert a person about an unsafe situation or an unsafe *relationship*. In particular, dreams portray people in our field in a flattering or unflattering light—often to clue us in on relational elements we are consciously ignoring. One could explain many of these dreams as being compensatory, or, in other words, the waking ego is simply ignoring obvious data about the relationship that the dreams balance by presenting the other point of view. But occasionally these dreams appear in a fashion that seems to be about preservation and protection, instincts ancient human beings must have developed since they survived into the modern age. Many anthropological anecdotes suggest aboriginal people were able to ascertain dangerous future situations. One well-documented example is the Native Americans' awareness that their culture would end and be annihilated, before white Europeans invaded the continent.

People who sense the future have frequently complained to me, "It's always bad stuff I know about ahead of time, it's so punishing. I've learned to just shut it off entirely." The burden of being the seer is a real one—in antiquity, as well as now. But possibly this aspect of psychic development harkens back to a time when imminent danger sensed ahead of time could mean the difference between life or death that day or the very next day. I include two dream examples:

> *I am on a boat with people from work. A shark jumps out of the water and bites my arm. I bleed profusely; the shark won't let go.*

Next dream:

> *I go in my kitchen at night to get water. When I turn on the light to open the cupboard for the glass, several black lizards shoot back into the crevices of the woodwork where I can't see them. It is terrifying.*

In the first dream, the dreamer knew immediately who the shark was. He had been on a week-long working boat trip with people from his office, and a woman on the cruise was trying to sabotage a deal he and she were working on together. The dreamer saw the dream as an important indicator not to discount or overlook the power of this relationship to destroy his job.

The second dream had an interesting twist. At the time of the dream, the dreamer was involved in a difficult romantic relationship. The dreamer's partner was a manic-depressive recovering alcoholic who had shot himself in the chest attempting suicide a couple of years before. He was also an artist and an intuitive personality. She told him the dream, and he said, "I'm the lizards." When he said it, she knew he was right. The relationship terminated shortly thereafter.

It is curious to note that in my recent analytical practice I can think of several (a dozen or so) examples where frightening animals actually play the role of dangerous people in our lives. This cannot be taken too literally, since one could easily miss the intra-psychic elements of these dreams and end up projecting all reality onto others. Perhaps inner reality and outer reality intertwine, and to ignore one in favor of the other is to miss half of the picture.

The following example from a dream group illustrates how inner and outer realities weave together. A dream group member had had recurring dreams about shoes, socks, feet, bare feet. In each case, the images were frightening, almost like a life-and-death conflict. The dreams had a common theme—the dreamer was frantically searching for shoes or something for her feet. If she didn't find the shoes, she felt that she would die. The dreamer had come to a crisis in her career. As a therapist, she had been struggling with managed health care for a long time, watching her practice dwindle and require more work and effort for less money. Week after week, she searched frantically for a new direction. Absolutely nothing opened up. Eventually, she decided to give up her office and train as a spiritual advisor. It was a great risk, but she felt peace about her decision. Then, she brought a startling dream to dream group:

> *I am in a church sitting behind another member of dream group who is a clergywoman. She is wearing beautiful blue shoes with pearls on them as a special adornment.*

The dreamer's association to the clergywoman was entirely positive—she saw her as dynamic, focused, and "able to make things happen." Here the recurring shoe image was resolved and the nightmares were over. But it was in the tribal field that this resolution occurred. Meeting and knowing the clergywoman helped the dreamer to perceive personal power for herself. To see another resolve conflict helps us. As Jung has stated, projection has a hook. The dreamer saw herself in this image, but certainly the clergywoman "deserved" the projection.

The tribal field is evidenced in many nooks and crannies throughout Jungian psychological works, anthropology, literature, and films. It is peppered among many case studies, but is not named or explained directly in most cases. Curiously, however, it is the phenomenon that often will take precedence when Jungian analysts get together at meetings and conferences. Inevitably, the stories about the tribal field emerge and are spoken of and shared orally. Almost like a gooey secret place, the analysts relate and detail instance after instance of synchronicity, analysands dreaming about them or vice versa, and events in the dream world that defy rational explanation.

In a case I have worked on for a number of years, my analysand had begun to dream in a more objective way. Recently he had this dream:

> *A fellow worker has crashed into a brick wall.*

Naturally, the coworker being dreamed about was in trouble at work, despite the fact that the dreamer knew her to be a fine employee. However, another manager was bent on firing her. My analysand collected his dream in the dream net—like fish in the deep ocean. He pulled up this image—why? In the history of this case, it had been apparent the analysand had a peculiar, almost mythic connection to his career and profession. To begin with, he left a fine, solid line of work to go heavily into debt to seek the necessary education for his new career—in spite of being a man who had suffered from depression and had difficulty taking risks.

Then, in the course of his career, he had been laid off twice due to business closings and downsizing. In both instances, these difficult times led to a transcendent type of psychological growth for the analysand. In the face of his anxiety and depression, he found peace, trust, and detachment about outcome. For years, his worst fear had been of becoming homeless, but during a real financial crisis he discovered faith.

At the time of the "brick wall" dream he was safely employed, but his company was in an ownership shift. His intuition caught the tribal turmoil and played it back to him in story form. He felt close kinship with the dream figure under attack and believed his dream to be helpful in order to devise a possible plan to assist the woman in trouble.

Tribal/communal dreams, almost as much as anything, help one take action because they present aspects of concrete reality that the conscious self either cannot know or *will not* know. In the remarkable book *The Sacred Heritage*, Norma Churchill shares her own buffalo vision. In the spirit of the Lakota approach to dreaming that directly inspired my dream groups, the editors summarize:

> This is a report of a single vision from a visionary in our
> own American middle class culture, in which there is no

community support for such visions. It is powerfully poignant, and it contains a warning for the whole culture.
Such visions are ignored at great peril. They reach far
beyond the individual who has them, and they are meant
to be heard by all. (Sandnor & Wong, 1996, 203)

In this vision, Ms. Churchill saw the ground water poisoned, the
buffalo dead and dying, and the earth in great peril. This is an
example of the danger that one person senses for the whole community—the whole earth, in this case. I suspect her dream is one
to be taken literally, as well as symbolically.

She received an image that is a confrontation for the culture,
the society in which we live. Without acknowledgment of this
issue, future peoples could be in grave peril. Ms. Churchill is the
shaman for the community; the poisoned water, both actual and
metaphorical (living water, the deep feminine, the life-giving
force of nature that is necessary for abundance, growth, and
nurturance) is symbolic of the attitude we must correct in the
next generation.

In Jung's discussions on active imagination, a technique that
involves retrieving material from the unconscious while remaining awake, he made a point to admonish people from using this
practice with any living, real persons. The reason, he noted, is
that one doesn't know how much affect these imaginations might
have. Jung knew these visualizations have at least some affect in
outer reality, because he had observed and studied these matters
in his encounters with shamanism and anthropological studies.
What the shaman does is enter into a tribal arena where psyches
connect; there he/she can effect a healing, a cleansing, or a retrieval that can change objective reality. These tribal field events
were common among the more natural people who had not yet
left the deeper realms behind.

CHAPTER EIGHTEEN

Synchronicity Weaves
an Intricate Pattern

A VETERINARIAN CALLED FOR ANALYSIS IN JANUARY A FEW
years ago. He had been referred by a friend for dream work and
thorny mid-life existential issues. He couldn't start immediately,
so he asked for homework to do during the time we needed to
work out a schedule together. I suggested he begin a discipline
of dating and recording dreams each morning, no matter how
stupid, insignificant, frightening, meaningless or embarrassing.
He also began reading *Memories, Dreams and Reflections.*

In May, we began regular sessions. After a couple of sessions, he
brought his dream journal and said he wanted to discuss the first
dream he had had after contacting me for analysis. The analysand
was married, had two sons and was in his mid thirties. His dream
was as follows:

> *My eldest son has brought home a rabbit from the neighbor's*
> *house to care for during the weekend. I am horrified to*
> *discover in the morning that the creature is dead in its cage,*
> *lying on its back with its feet straight up in the air. There is*
> *a terrible gash in its belly.*

As he related the dream, he became quite excited when telling me the context that accompanied the dream. In April, his younger son had brought home another neighbor's cat to care for over the weekend. To the vet's horror, the next day he ran over and killed the cat in his driveway. He put the cat in the freezer, the only thing he could think to do, so he could return the body when the neighbors came home. Later, the neighbors assured the vet that the cat was quite elderly, deaf and blind, and her death was imminent and expected.

This illustrates the curious path our dream maker takes to convey a complex intricate set of clues to the unique puzzle of time, synchronicity, fate and tribal relationships. The dreamer's woundedness, as well as his connection to his sons formed a rich beginning for our analysis.

The analysand thought this dream was telling him he was damaging his sons. Certainly one must consider this factor, since it is well determined that parents' woundedness negatively impacts their children. But making bad parenting the focus of the dream would be missing several salient points. Clearly the analysand was deeply wounded at an instinctual, primal level. The family pet suggests an underdeveloped elemental aspect of the psyche. The gut wound was the dreamer's. He was the youngest child raised by a mentally disabled father, the last sibling who was left alone with his father after his mother skedaddled and all of his older brothers and sisters had left home. He was quite affected by the emptiness and chaos of this environment. As an adult it had manifested in two ways: 1) a rigidity about behavior, attitude, values, and doing the "right" thing as determined by society; and 2) a sense of unworthiness.

How does one explain or at least begin to understand the meaning of this interesting synchronicity? Certainly, it is not possible to understand fully the meaning or purpose of synchronicity. The easy way out is to deny it any significance at all. Those who experience these events or are party to them, however, sense there is meaning to be mined like the careful and tedious process of panning for gold.

Mystery is at the heart of synchronicity. It is the unknown, that which puzzles us and defies our rational approach to reality. Mystery is the archetype—the "not knowing" place in the psyche that carries numinosity. It is common to hear people imagine death as a resolution to mystery—an experience where all questions are answered, where one "knows." Knowing, then, is equated with meeting God or encountering the divine mystery. This is the territory where synchronicity takes one. In the case of the rabbit synchronicity, three observations can be made. First, the dreamer (like most analysands) was rigid to the degree that a synchronicity of this sort was needed to disturb the ego's resistance to make conscious his deep woundedness. Synchronicity is compensatory just as dreams are—they operate in direct contrast to an attitude that is one-sided, and the ego mightily defends this side. In this case, the analysand was given a substantial jumpstart for his analytical process. Second, the dream indicated a significant bonding with his two sons. He was strongly connected to them and consequently had projected his woundedness onto them in such a way that the sons "carried" his pain. Third, the dream prognosis was neutral for the analysis and the process the analysand had decided to pursue; the pot was hot, the soup was on, and he was in it—but I could not predict from his dream whether he would have the courage to resolve the early gashes to his essence he had experienced. Still, the acknowledgment of the wound remained his first step toward a necessary consciousness; the dream indicated he was ready to face it—hence the discovery of the dead animal. Ultimately, the case went well.

To fully describe the "oddities" that occur in my practice would require breaking too much confidentiality—even with the permission of the analysand—because often other people are involved in the connections that would quickly identify all of the parties. In the following examples, as well as throughout this book, care has been taken to obscure identities. Nevertheless, I include them here because they illustrate the complexity and mystery of the dynamic play between inner and outer reality.

An attorney came to see me for analysis, and we began our work in a difficult, awkward fashion. In our second session, he complained that I wasn't asking him enough about feelings and that he didn't understand all of my questions about his dreams (he was used to a Gestalt approach to dream work). Later in the session, when I asked him why he thought he might be so afraid of a relationship, he answered brusquely, "You're the therapist; that's your job to know." I quickly began to dread our sessions together.

But he persevered, as did I, and we developed a trust of sorts. I could see his process was at hand—he moved his home to another part of the city, began to examine career goals, changed his style of dress, evaluated his leisure activities (the housecleaning inventory that often accompanies the initial stage of analysis). I noticed, like other processes I have observed, his process began to take on a life of its own. Suddenly he began socializing with some friends, went to a few parties, and began jogging. He had several flirtations brewing simultaneously.

In general, he was warming up or melting a bit. His armor was softening. Even so, I still found him challenging, and I felt tongue-tied and stiff in our sessions. But then he began to tell me about a new woman he had met, and before long I realized I knew who she was.

I have been in a study group in Dallas for several years. We are a group of friends and fellow supporters. We have traveled together and regularly meet for evenings together. Unfortunately, one of our members developed ovarian cancer and died a year later. When Jane received her diagnosis, she made a full-time attempt to get well. My mother-in-law was also ill with cancer at the same time, and she and Jane sometimes saw each other when we would go to the cancer center for treatments and check-ups. My mother in law and Jane died less than two weeks apart.

Jane's sister was the woman dating my client. Recently, Dallas and its suburbs (not including Fort Worth) were listed at a population of five million. I don't know what the odds are of something like this happening, but they must be pretty slim.

Of course, I didn't tell my client about this connection. If he were to discover it through conversation with his new friend, then I would openly discuss it with him. But then it seemed like a message for me, not him. It told me that he and I were on the road together, that we had constellated the Self, to some degree, and the bonding I didn't feel consciously was at hand unconsciously, and it sought to connect us, to bring us into relationship, to interact, to love, and to heal. In fact, this is precisely the direction the case took. What began as an awkward guarded attitude on my part developed into a genuine love and affection for him. Within a short time, I began to look forward to our analysis and enjoy, particularly, how much laughter was in our work together.

Again, I see the process of the psyche as like a river. There is an undercurrent to all of it that the ego can be trained to notice, acknowledge, and track. The current is the movement, the teleological process, the story of one's life, the relationships that are formed, and the outer events that occur. Many have commented before me how things become easier (or "feel right" which may not necessarily be easier) when we are in the *TAO*—when we follow an inner knowing and wisdom that tends to guide, direct, and teach us. Often, the challenge in one's path is to follow the current of the river rather than try to fight it. When the rapids are coming up and the white water is foaming, it is entirely futile, even dangerous, to try anything other than follow the current's path. It is quite like the times when life offers extraordinary challenges—times so difficult one is plummeted from illusory castles of sand to stony ground. Somehow it doesn't take many years of living to realize we are totally out of control for most of the major occurrences of our lives. Life, death, illness, weather, other people, our bosses, spouses are not for us to direct. The powerful inflation of the ego can deter the process, and then life tends to get even more painful and difficult.

The current is quiet, yet powerful. It takes some insight, personal reflection, and the courage to listen to one's insides to discover where the current is leading. Life and its events offer clues and hints along the way. Sometimes we can feel certain we are on a right path, only to discover later it was a wrong turn. Dreams offer (perhaps the quintessential) direct clues; however, as all who have worked with dreams know, the clues are puzzling and cryptic and often don't reveal their true meanings easily. In fact, there is an entire category of dreams that appear in opposite symbol or language—death means transformation, a wedding is really about a death, and so on.

Likewise, the clues offered can easily be misread. Once, when I lived in Zurich, a wealthy Swiss acquaintance invited me to London for a week. She agreed to pay for the trip if I would go with her. I didn't think I could refuse such a generous offer! But by going as her guest, I felt compelled to let her set the agenda. She had read some books that referred to an 18th century woman who was the wife of an early religious leader in England. Somehow she had decided she had been this woman in a previous life. She also had a "hunch," she told me, that she would find some of the woman's obscure writings in one of the rare book stores in London. So you can well imagine what we did for two or three days. London is a fascinating town, but one old bookstore is pretty much like the next one. The ones we visited were small, dusty, and piled high with extremely brittle, old, faded books and papers. They didn't categorize topics or papers in a way with which I was familiar.

Well, we searched and searched, but found nothing. It seemed clear to me by the first day of our search that this was a dry well we were trying to pump, but then, I was not the one with the "hunch." Later, this same person pursued for years the hope of a relationship that seemed unlikely. When the man she sought after died, she suffered a terrible blow—chiefly, how to deal with the awful experience of having been certain something will work out, only to discover she had been utterly wrong; or to put it another way, the resolution of the issue does not mirror in the least what the ego was expecting or wanting. Ouch.

It is still possible to discover the current, however. Perhaps one cannot be aware every moment, but over time it is a practice or discipline that can be fostered and encouraged.

Here is another example of a process that may have benefited from more courage. Since the early sixties, a woman wanted to train to be a Jungian analyst in Zurich, but she waited until her children were grown—twenty years. She felt the move to Europe would be too traumatic for them. Then, when she finally arrived, two things happened. First, she wasn't accepted into training (which doesn't mean she wouldn't have been on the second try). Second, she discovered she had a terminal illness. She left, went to the U.S. and died not too long after. I don't believe her rejection from the institute "caused" her illness; that way of thinking is too concrete and simplistic for me. But I do wish she had gone to Zurich twenty years earlier, where she could have realized her life dream and goal long before her illness struck.

For me, the lesson in this story is about the attachment to blinding collective values. Unfortunately, one of her children had a great deal of trouble growing up. Who knows if it might have been different or better in Europe, but not uprooting her children did not give her family the security and safety she was trying to provide. Security may have been better served by pursuing the fire and passion she had for Jungian psychology.

It is too simple and too irresponsible to think that finding and riding our current is only a matter of casting off all collective attitudes. This is how people like Hitler and Jim Jones emerged in our cultures—they thought their inner realities superceded what we have come to know as ethic, compassion, civilization, order. These basic elements cannot be overlooked, which is the reason the current has to be explored and evaluated. The individual current, ideally, is a flow that has as its foundation the structure of common sense.

One has to discover one's compass to make appropriate changes in one's life decisions. The river, the current, the process—all point in a direction that leads one toward greater consciousness, meaning, and fulfillment. Aimless existence is unconsciousness whether one is living from hedonistic gratification or basic survival. The compass is the point of orientation that nudges one in a particular direction.

Some dreams may point toward physical death—this, of course, is a direction as well—one each of us encounters eventually. An analysand was ill but had been valiantly defying odds, courageously facing every type of "cutting, burning, and poisoning" with some hope of remission. Recently, in fact, her prognosis, although guarded, had seemed about as hopeful as possible. But she arrived for her session that day dejected. Chemotherapy was taking its toll. Bald, nauseated, thin, this lonely, extraordinarily brilliant thirty-year-old woman told me she wanted to die. Usually, when she had shared dreams in the past, she prefaced them with either of two remarks: 1) "Oh, I already have this dream figured out" (often she did); or 2) "Please tell me this dream doesn't mean I'm going to die" (which would elicit from me a pep talk about death as a symbol of transformation in dreams). This day, however, she said neither of these things about the dream that follows, but only, "I don't know what this means."

My mother and brother were at the airport terminal. They went into a bookstore because they realized they had an hour left before their flight. I tossed a treasured book I had brought for the trip into the trash to find a new book. I don't know why I did this. Then, I encountered a coworker (a man, "all around great guy") who helped me realize I had missed the plane and that my mother and brother had gone on. I selected a book at the terminal where I saw construction going on, but I couldn't tell if the terminal was being remodeled or being torn down. I either bought Death of a Salesman *or* To Kill a Mockingbird.

As clever as this analysand was, she had entirely missed the puns of "terminal," "gone on," the metaphor of the missed flight, the tossed book, and the subject of death in both book titles. The image of confusion, here about the terminal being built or torn down, is one that has been told to me in two separate cases in which analysands were gravely ill. I felt a chill from this dream, as well as from her hopeless attitude. It did not seem natural for a young person to accept the end of life, possibilities, and hope. I did not tell her the dream concerned me—first, I know nothing as certain as whether a dream indicates a death or not; second, it is unethical to "predict" to clients in such a way that it can be experienced as a curse or a self-fulfilling prophecy. When therapists declare absolute truth, they too, can be unwittingly offering a type of curse. In other words, telling a woman her marriage will fail, predicting depression if a client wants to leave therapy, telling analysands if they don't change a job they could get cancer or die of a heart attack are all examples of cursing (albeit unconsciously) the people who come to us for healing.

Labeling, predicting, setting ultimatums—all are avenues for the therapist to experience an unconscious power shadow in the analytical work. The revelations made open to the client should be cautiously thought through before they are shared. Much better to keep hunches, attitudes, concerns, and predictions in reserve, especially since dreams will reveal the issues much more vividly.

The next dream came a few months after the airport terminal dream:

> *I entered a throne room. It was dark and empty but I could see a king sitting on a great throne. I approached and realized I am to marry him even though I can't see his face. I had to receive my ring from behind since I'm not allowed to look at him. When I reached my left hand over his shoulder, I realize I'm to be married to God.*

I hoped I was wrong, but this dream seemed to prefigure death—that the psyche was being prepared for the final marriage—but again, I had no way to be sure. However, the dream helped me face the severity of my analysand's condition. This aided enormously in my work with this woman. I found the imagery so striking it nudged me out of my optimistic complacency that she probably would just get better. Moreover, another analysand had died a few months before this dream, and I had felt quite surprised that she went so quickly. I chastised myself for not knowing the seriousness of her illness—that her dreams had been right in front of me and I had missed it. I felt that I needed to save my current analysand, or at least know clearly the extent of her illness, so that I could have a better grip on the messages of her psyche. I wanted to aid her more effectively on her journey. So this dream was, in part, for me; it let me know the depth and breadth of her struggle. Certainly I knew she was gravely ill, but her doctors were assuring her she could get well if she were to think positively and so on. I have no quarrel with their tactics; perhaps they are the most humane, and it does really work for some people to believe they can heal, but in other cases, it seems to be a blatant denial and sort of a trickery. I saw this approach taken with my mother-in-law who died of breast cancer. As her cancer progressed and became metastasized throughout her body, her doctor continued to tell her we just needed to find a different treatment. Eventually, his new treatment shut her kidneys down, and she died. Now, I reserved the right to be wrong. I could only hope getting married to God would or could symbolize a type of transformation that my analysand was clearly undertaking—whether physical and / or psychological. However, I appreciated the red alert I heard from her dream maker, especially after the recent loss of my other analysand.

The "Marrying God" dream is archetypal, which refers to reality that is mutually shared by collective consciousness. It informs and clarifies for the ego the nature of death. The dream is a jewel. I have collected "God" dreams for fifteen years or so now. My file is thin. I can only tell two or three. It impressed me many years ago that I never heard a "God incarnate" dream; He or She never directly made an appearance in the dreams. That puzzled me since God is such a present image in our psyches, collectively and often individually. Looking at God face-to-face is too powerful an experience for the human to endure. God dreams come from a deep place in our souls where wholeness exists in a sacred numinosity.

Not long after my analysand had her "God as Groom" dream, she reported in a session, a discussion with friends on religion. However, when she said the words "religious discussion" she accidentally said "romantic discussion." Here, her unconscious revealed again the love image surrounding the connection with the Divine. Whether it be death or a spiritual awakening, she was deeply connected to the masculine, divine passion that intersects with sexual romantic love. For centuries, religious ecstasy has been portrayed as a conjugal experience. One thinks immediately of Teresa of Avila who described her passion with Christ in sexual terms. She believed and experienced Jesus as her lover and husband, and she wore a gold ring to signify this commitment. My ill analysand had experienced the same archetype. God was the groom/lover, and religion was romantic or romance was religious.

In Jungian psychology, marriage in dreams is a metaphor that has received a lot of attention.[28] The sacred coming together of masculine and feminine represents a completion, a wholeness, a transformation of some sort. These profound dreams are extraordinarily useful in preparing the resistant ego to the eventual and final reality of death—whether that death is on the horizon or may occur years in the future. The experience of facing death is a transformation all by itself. Although marriage dreams in no way should be thought to only represent physical death, marriage is a ritual, a bridge that indicates a change psychologically, which could relate to almost any aspect of a dreamer's process, but clearly a crucial one.

However, dreams present an untainted image, one that is free from conscious intent, imagination, or wish. They reside within the psyche in the mysterious territory that provides life-giving knowledge, imagery, and symbol that abet the ego in its struggle to integrate the vast richness upon which it rests.

The therapist benefits from knowing the client's compass as much as the client does. The therapeutic work has a direction and energy all its own that results in each case being unique. Sadly, my young analysand died some months after her "God" dream. Her process was certainly one of facing death, of relinquishing vast areas of life that many of us take for granted, and of developing her spiritual life, her friendships, even a "real" marriage partner. The questions dreams bring to consciousness, the curiosities and the imagination needed to receive them, opens a territory within oneself that enlivens and restores the modern soul.

The relational/tribal field is especially evident in the cases of dreams surrounding death and grief. A number of books and articles have attempted to characterize "death dreams" or the dreams of the dying; however, less interest has been focused on the dreams of the loved ones left behind—the ones that grieve the loss. The dream maker seems to be generally quite interested in the grief process, and an endless amount of grief material manifests in dream images. About once a year I volunteer for the Suicide and Crisis Center in Dallas—for Survivors of Suicide, a group of friends and family members who have experienced a loved one's suicide. They meet once a month for grief support. The topic I discuss with them is, "Grief and Dreams." There is one particular type of grief dream that inevitably will be shared at these meetings that I would like to point out as an example of dreaming from the tribal field.

Not infrequently, one member of the family or friendship circle (not always the closest member) will have a vivid dream about the person who has died. Usually these dreams occur a few weeks or months after the death. The dreamers report a sense of actually having had an encounter with the deceased. Frequently, these dreams are comforting to the dreamer and to the rest of the family as well. Often, too, the deceased communicates a message meant for the whole family—the whole tribe—that the dreamer understands is to be shared. In the case of suicide, it might be "I'm sorry," or "Please stop your suffering, I'm at peace," or "All is well, I'm busy onto new projects," and so on. I go out on a limb here raising the possibility these dreams come from a place that is beyond the repository of the wish-determined psyche and from a "reality" that is still unacknowledged.

But so it seems to me. The dreamers are too intense in their descriptions of the experience, the feelings too profound—and their attitudes shift remarkably after these dreams occur. I marvel as well how usually only one of these dreams appears through

only one family member or friend—and that is all. Silence. If
these dreams were a form of wish fulfillment, then why wouldn't
the dream be ubiquitous? Whatever the case, I do not wish to
speculate any further. We all will experience soon enough the
mystery of death. But what does interest me is the field in which
the dream manifests—in the family, in the tribe.

Moreover, not just anyone dreams this, but it occurs among
the people who loved and love the person who died—the ones
who reside in the relational goo together. This is where the energy
lies. But the dream maker has no regard for chronological time. In
the Summer 1999 issue of *Psychological Perspectives*, Ed Edinger,
a seminal Jungian analyst and scholar, is honored. In one of the
eulogies reprinted for this journal, George Elder tells a dream he
shared with Edinger shortly before his death:

> In one of my last conversations with Dr. Edinger, we
> talked of death—his death—which he did not expect so
> soon but for which he was psychologically prepared. He
> said he would not resist Nature's demand and would go as
> quickly and as peaceably as She required. That night I had
> a dream that I do not consider mine alone; Ed has said
> that the event of death opens us up to levels of the psyche
> that are otherwise closed. In this dream, I was with Dr.
> Edinger in a mausoleum that was also a library, but
> there were no books. All was beautiful cool white-pink
> marble, and I had the impression that we were in ancient
> Greece. Ed sat at a little wooden table with a stack of large
> pages . . . and again I had the impression that these were
> documents containing his last will and testament. It was a
> big stack—he's left us a lot. . . . (Elder, 1999, 12–15).

The tribal field is not something that can only be observed in
a few quick synchronistic patterns of interconnectedness between

persons on an occasional or infrequent basis. Inherent within the tribal unconscious is a long serial story that unfolds and develops much like an individual's dreams that form shape and pattern over time. Dreams reveal themes that tend to shift and evolve as one slowly resolves, heals, and matures throughout life. The tapestry begins, then, to form its image.

Likewise, in the tribal / communal field, the themes and connections that emerge may also manifest over a period of years. What follows is an example.

A middle-aged woman joined a dream group even though she did not fit the profile of "clergywoman / chaplain / spiritual director / religious studies scholar / psychologist" that made up the body of this group. She was a curious combination—an architect and dental hygienist. Since her husband was a successful dental specialist, she frequently had to help him in his office, which is what she was doing when she joined dream group. She hadn't practiced architecture for several years; she had burned out after she had her own firm during the difficult market in the 1980s. She brought to this group a sense of the visual that affected the members, both unconsciously and consciously. Over time, her dreams appeared to encourage her to go back to art—she did. After she spent time pursuing graduate studies in the Dallas / Ft. Worth area, she took a risk to apply to a prestigious two-year graduate program in New York City. She was accepted, and we bid her our bittersweet farewell. Through email we stayed connected with her. One member, in particular, (who had also made a risk to leave her job to live more creatively) kept up a regular correspondence with her. A person in dream group who takes an artistic creative risk will often affect others to do the same. Meanwhile P., a new member who was quite artistic, joined the group. Although she worked in the therapy field, P. was orientated toward the visual and was also redesigning and remodeling an apartment. At this same time, my husband and I bought a broken-down old house and were in the process of a complete restoration, making all the design decisions.

After the architect / hygienist left for her art program and had been gone about eighteen months, two women in dream group brought dreams on the same day, dreams in which the same person appeared in both dreams. One of the dreamers, M., was a clergywoman whose son was about to have her first grandchild. He appeared in her dream as a positive male figure full of new life and possibility. Additionally, her son was a fine potter and art instructor. Another dream group member, P., also dreamed about M.'s son, she had met him recently at an art show. She was quite touched by his work and purchased one of his pieces.

We all had a satisfying time with this interesting occurrence of hearing dreams from different people on the same day that used the same person as a character. Some years ago, as the seed of the tribal idea was germinating in my mind, I recall hearing two dreams in a day with the same priest as the main character, and then the next day hearing a third dream about the same local priest.

But I did not expect what happened later that day, in this case of the double dream. In my "snail mail" was a letter from the artist in New York. It was perhaps her first or second correspondence to me since she had left a year and a half earlier. In it she told an interesting story: she said a synchronicity of sorts had occurred around M.'s son. She discovered two things. First, her niece, who had just started a new school, had M.'s son as her new art teacher. Furthermore, he had simply made her come alive about school, art, and herself. Second, the letter stated that one of her sons, after hearing about the art teacher, realized he had attended private high school with him. Then she wrote, "My son is feeling guilty about picking on M.'s son, the potter, and he wants to convey an acknowledgment of regret."

My, what a time we had with this tangled web of intersection! Odd too, these characters didn't all live in one small section of the city but rather Dallas, Fort Worth, and all of the surrounding suburbs.

Yet the story was not over—indeed, it will probably never be "over," since it seems our interactions continue to weave patterns as long as one notices. The architect finished school in two years and decided to re-enter dream group. Her first day back, S. (another dream group member) had a dream she shared. In it, she had an image that was captivating and inspiring. At the centerpiece of the dream, she and a man were looking at a piece of art on the wall. The art was a three-dimensional work of a woman—almost a sculpture within the wall, like a bas relief. In the torso area of the female figure was a hole (an opening) through which one could see into the next room, which was a magical and mysterious space. The image evoked feeling for the whole group—what a symbol of looking within oneself and discovering a "whole new room"! But our returning artist-member was agitated when she heard this dream and after a bit said, "That is just like the art I am helping a woman install in New York. We made holes in the wall through which you can see into the next room where there are figures of Madonnas." In 2002, three years after our artist returned from New York, another twist developed. J., a member of this group over ten years, was delighted to report her twelve-year-old son had won second place in an art contest at his private school in East Dallas. And the judge (who lived in West Fort Worth) had been the potter-son who had been tangled in this group for so long. And so the connections continue. They overlap, intersect, weave, and spiral into a complexity that defies conventional rational understanding. To take notice allows the possibility that the experience may move one to the sacred space of numinous awe.

CHAPTER NINETEEN

It Takes a Community to Individuate

AFTER LEADING DREAM GROUPS SINCE JANUARY OF 1987, I have observed that Jungian therapeutic work, as well as dream work, is benefited by a group container in which members share their process and offer support and clarification to the work. Analysis can be difficult and alienating. Frequently understanding one's dreams quickly leads to actions one might take that necessarily require courage and passion. Divorce, marriage, relocation, changing careers, school endeavors, even taking up a new musical instrument can scare a person into pathological resistance. When the psyche calls for wholeness—whether one is struggling to understand and integrate the shadow or the contra-sexual—fear can impale the process of individuation. In training groups where people cluster together to become analysts, much of this support occurs. In individual analysis where the analysand is not going to train, the isolation of the analytical process can be counterproductive to growth and progress. Therefore, through their training, most Jungian analysts have experienced the tribal / relational support I have described that happens in dream groups. However, their analysands may be required to undertake a solitary journey that the analyst herself has never had to endure!

In Jung's early days, a cluster formed around a study group called "The Psychology Club." This early prototype evolved into the Jung Institutes we have today. These people studied together, socialized, and participated in rich and messy relationships. All of this "currently questionable, unethical" behavior operated as a glue to coalesce the Jungian vision and work into a body of individuals that had a common purpose—to retrieve the unconscious for modern men and women.

This original group that formed around Jung in Zurich was the natural emergence of how Jungian analysis ideally was experienced. The Jungian communities I have experienced in Zurich, as well as in Denver, Colorado, have been invaluable to me for encouragement, confrontation, and understanding. Jungian psychology is complex and arduous at times to even comprehend. Without many late night discussions with friends and colleagues, I would have had a less significant learning experience. I encourage analysands to attend Jungian lectures and take classes and seminars from other analysts or teachers. These lessons are helpful, but the friendships gained are some of the heart and soul of work with the interior self. Ultimately the power of dream group is that it forms a community.

Sometimes the kinship felt with other Jungians is remarkable. Another analyst I know gave a class on the archetype of Sophia. Two of his analysands unwittingly sat next to each other in the class and began to chat. Then they began dating, and eventually they married. It was on the third date or so that they discovered each was in analysis with the same analyst! It is remarkable to me that recent trends in therapy licensing boards, as well as traditional psychoanalytic circles, would have us eliminate this relational aspect on the grounds that it somehow invades, interferes with, or dilutes the process. In some cases, analysts do not allow their analysands to attend lectures or classes taught by the analyst for fear that the analysands will become acquainted with each other.

In Dallas, and probably other places as well, it is fashionable to have an entry door separate from the exit door so the analysands coming and going don't see each other. Never mind the parking lot, elevator, public restroom, and other places in the building where they may encounter each other; the analyst's job, in this school of thought, is to defend against any possible relationship that could sprout if given a chance. To separate psychology from sociology is a split I have never fully understood. To go out of one's way to avoid relationship is to ignore a layer of psychic interaction that is as informative to one's process as one's dreams.

It is possible, even, that encounters with other clients may be psychologically significant beyond the clients becoming friends or lovers. To illustrate, an analysand of mine saw someone out in the parking lot of my office building as he came in for his regular session. Instinctively, he "knew" the public person he recognized was coming to me for analysis, even though my office has over one hundred businesses and this person had never attended any Jungian programs or classes where my analysand might have seen him. Some weeks later he dreamed about the local celebrity. We worked on the dream figure as his own projection. Neither when he saw the man in the parking lot, nor when he brought the dream, did I confirm or deny his "knowing."

However, on the same day my analysand and I worked on his "projection" dream, I received a note from the man seen in the parking lot. He had indeed been in analysis with me, but was sending me a note saying he wasn't interested in continuing. He wrote that he wanted to try a motivational coach instead of analysis. I then decided to review the dream about him from earlier in the day—perhaps it had contained more material than merely projected contents. It was:

> G. is trying to talk, but he's got a speech impediment and can't get the words out.

After a week or so, I called "G." to see how he was doing, as well as to suggest that a motivational coach and therapy combined might be the best strategy. I had some referrals to give him, since it seemed our work was stalled. He was a well-spoken man, had a colorful, dynamic public persona, and had always seemed articulate and charming. But on this call he was tongue-tied! He seemed to stutter and hem and haw with awkward embarrassment. Naturally, one could surmise a call from an analyst with whom one has terminated work by letter would arouse that reaction from almost anyone. I concur. What impressed me, however, was the clue the dream gave me about the reason the case went flat.

From the beginning of our work together "G." was reserved, shy, almost paranoid. I suspected he was harboring a "secret" or needed to confess something he had determined was immoral. He stated too many times how much he loved his wife and that they were best friends. Then, he had written down a dream he "forgot" to bring to analysis, because he told me he was too frightened by it. After probing, he admitted it had something to do with his marriage or being attracted to other women. Finally, he loosened up just a bit and made an uncharacteristic statement during the associations to his "forgotten" dream: "Oh, she is someone you'd like to have an affair with but not someone to marry."

He said no more, and I didn't press any further, satisfied that this was somewhat of a breakthrough. I wasn't surprised but was certainly disappointed when he canceled his next session, saying, "I'll call you when I'm not so busy." Then I heard nothing from him for weeks until my other analysand presented his dream about "G.," and I received the note on the same day.

Clearly, "G." did not want to continue talking about his sexual feelings. I suspected also that he was developing some transference for me and did not have the ego strength to face his feelings. He was tongue-tied. Talking was too risky; thus the defense mechanism saved him—incoherent speech.

In this case, one analysand dreamed about another, without it ever being confirmed. The dream I heard about "G." was helpful, or at least informative to me as the analyst. How odd to imagine one person (the analysand who spotted the man in the parking lot) having a dream for another person (me) about a third person (the tongue-tied analysand).

In another case one person dreamed for another where significant life decisions were made. An analysand entered analysis with her main issue being dissatisfaction with her marriage and what to do about that, if anything. She and her husband had recently given up on couples therapy, as it hadn't seemed to help. She had been married ten years or so, had a two-year-old son, and wished to work out her relationship. But over time it became clear to her that she needed to see an attorney to begin the steps toward separation. The issues in the marriage were: no sex, no affection, and her husband had no relationship with her family with whom she was very close. After she interviewed several attorneys and selected one, she told her family about the decision. Her family was supportive; however, one sister was less enthusiastic than the rest of the family. A few weeks later, the less-supportive sister had a dream that changed her opinion about my analysand's impending decision. In the sister's dream, she saw my analysand being cruelly tortured by her husband and her sister just laughing about it—having no awareness about the pain and no appropriate reaction to the abuse. The sister awakened from the dream feeling totally adamant about her support for the divorce. In the dream she said to herself, "Oh, now I see it, that is just how S. is; she takes it and takes it but never stands up for herself." This dream was about my analysand, not the sister, although one could wring out a few drops of wisdom regarding how the dreamer might have had a similar issue, as well. But the interesting observation for me was my analysand's reaction to her sister's dream. In the office during her session, she cried when she told the dream to me. Her sister's dream had touched her deeply, and she recognized her psychological pattern of ignoring abuse. She "saw" the dream for what it told her—that the marriage was damaging her spiritually, emotionally, and psychologically, and she must acknowledge her pain to affect change. This gave her a resolve, even though she had a young child and had been quite reluctant to pursue the separation. Here then was an example where a sister dreamt both for herself as well as her sister about the ambivalent marriage. Both felt clarity and resolve after the dream appeared.

In the early nineties, a physician came to me for Jungian analysis. She was a wealthy, attractive, older, well-traveled, socially prominent client. Additionally, she exhibited resistance to hearing any interventions on my part. It seemed to me she wanted to talk, do her own therapy, and use me as a casual bystander. I am moderately comfortable with this and have seen this phenomenon in other cases. Sometimes near silence is just what a client needs to develop the necessary trust required for therapy and analysis. Other times it is an indication that the client's prognosis for therapy is not good—some people are too defended for the therapy to work. Eventually, after each and every comment I made was tossed aside, discounted, or debated, I simply went silent and let her carry on. Clearly I was not "tracking the process," so I just shut up. This particular case seemed to get worse and worse, however. Eventually the dreams dried up, and she left.

At our closing session I confessed a sense the analysis had failed. She agreed somewhat, but she did feel I had helped her change her body image, start exercising, and lose weight. Actually, I had just listened to her each time she told me she was going to the gym regularly. Then, just before she decided to terminate, I accidentally ran into her at a local shop. She was there with her husband. I was somewhat uncomfortable with the situation and waited to let her approach me if she wanted say hello. She did. But to my extreme embarrassment, when I said hello and introduced her to my companion, I called her by the wrong name. I had called her by her daughter's quite unusual name and I felt myself curdle with shame. I was certain this *faux pas* had contributed to her termination. I couldn't blame her.

So when she called me six years later to have another go at analysis, I was surprised. Even though the first few sessions were somewhat better than the earlier work, the same pattern quickly set in. I felt silenced, discounted, and unable to make even benign interventions. She didn't like my metaphors, my empathic comments, my questions that probed for a few more details; again, I eventually just shut up. Then, during this second analysis, I saw her at a professional meeting and again made another *faux pas*. It was a holiday party for an organization in Dallas centered around the medical / mental health community. It was at Christmas time. I said, "Oh hello, Merry Christmas—oh no, I mean . . . Then just sank into awkward stuttering, and all of this time I had known full well she was East Indian, a practicing Hindu, and highly involved in the Hindu community. I was especially embarrassed, because I had often heard in sessions the pain that people from non-Christian backgrounds have shared with me about the ubiquitous Christmas season and how they can feel erased at that time of year. Again, I marveled at how humiliating being human can be. I went home depressed and puzzled.

However, instead of falling completely into the complex and letting the feelings rule the experience, I decided to ponder and meditate on this latest occurrence. Two embarrassments in over six years, but not once with any other analysand had something remotely similar happened. Eventually, I realized what the reader has undoubtedly already guessed. Both of these experiences involved my client not being seen, not being acknowledged, being erased. In the next session I saw the pattern of her life as being a non-person, only doing for others, providing for others, her needs rubbed out. Additionally, she was particularly hurt that day because not as many people had attended a gathering as she would have liked.

Suddenly I felt a compassion for her I never had before. Instead of being intimidated by this attractive, wealthy, prominent woman, I felt only love for her. My frustrations dissolved into a heartfelt pain that connected us in an entirely new way. Our session was the first good one we had had. In this case, the so-called embarrassing slips of my tongue were about her process, not about me being forgetful, rude, or bad at remembering names. The tribal field was constellated by both of us, in which a process manifested that broke through the difficulty I had had in our analysis—sometimes this is referred to as *projected self-identification* or being "dreamed up."[29] Either way, it informed our work, and the analysis was permanently changed.

Jungian analyst Ann Ulanov has written an article about her supervisor's role and countertransference in *The Journal of Jungian Theory and Practice* called "Countertransference and the Self." In this interesting article, she gives an example of the tribal field:

> In the clinical field of interaction between client and analyst, Self dynamics arrange both parties to see the un-seeable. Synchronistic events occur that startle both parties. For example, an analyst I was supervising brought to our session a painting his patient brought to him that depicted the patient's gripping experience of the Self. The painting looked like the alchemical pictures of the Sol Terrenus, the sun in the depths of the earth, a fiery bright disk blazing out behind a blackest dark center. (26) At the center of the earth, this solar light illuminates the unconscious, bespeaking an earthy masculine arising from the depths in contrast to the heights of the heavenly solar Apollo. The patient's painting emerged from his

work helping AIDS victims in a residence for homosexual men, hence bearing on the chthonic masculine.

He painted a huge, densely black circle from which emitted thousands of tiny bright rays almost spermlike with their energetic, whipping tails. I gasped when I saw the picture and heard what the analyst made of it in terms of his own image of the Self, because both pictures portrayed a vision of dark and light that had imploded into my consciousness when a little girl and stayed with me over many decades since. The image of deepest dark with brightest light coming from behind it present the ambiguity of light and dark, of good and bad, each being either and both, and neither one overcoming the other. Here were we three—the analyst, the patient, and the supervisor—unbeknownst to each other, each in our own lives beholding a shared image of the fourth. This fourth was a Self-image conveying the numinous nature of reality, its mixture of opposites, which had emerged in this particular form in our separate lives and joined us in this synchronistic moment in the here and now. (Ulanov, 13–14)

In this remarkable instance, the tribal relationship is evident in the triad of the three in the analytic processes together: supervisor, analyst, analysand. During the writing of this manuscript, I visited a favorite shop near my home. I was sorry the owner wasn't there, as we enjoy conversation together. Instead, a new person waited on me. I told her I was "just looking" so she would leave me to my introverted thoughts. The shop was full of ethnic items imported form Peru, Africa, Mexico, and the Far East. I gravitated to the sale table and immediately picked up an art object. During this time I was contemplating moving my office and changing the color scheme. As much as I love purple and green, I was getting weary of the color combination I had chosen in 1992. But the office was still appealing to me, so I was indecisive. The art object I chose was purple and green, which I hadn't noticed immediately because I was so taken with the design of the piece. The new sales clerk approached me, and even though I had given her the brusque message to leave me alone, she told me the story of the art piece. "This doll was made by a woman from Nigeria who was having a terrible time adjusting to the United States. Just as she felt nearly suicidal, she had a dream that she was being supported by a great hand. And the hand had a voice; it said to her in her dream, 'I will support you but you have to do your art.'" The art object was somewhat like a stuffed doll, the face made out of clay and the body fashioned from purple and green cloth in the shape of the great hand from the dream.

I bought the piece, didn't move my office, and have felt gratitude for the clerk ever since. She didn't know me, didn't know what I do for a living, didn't know the colors of my office, or of my passion for collecting "God dreams." I had the sense (albeit no doubt delusional) that the art object had been made especially for me. Certainly I was its profoundly proud new owner. For me, the clerk was an important link to the chain of events that helped me know my direction. She was connected to my tribal essence, and I suspect if I were to pursue a friendship, I would find her a good friend to have.

Conclusion

A FRIEND OF MINE, A JUNGIAN ANALYST IN LOS ANGELES, wickedly teased me at a professional meeting by saying, as I raced to catch an elevator crowded with other analysts, "Oh, here comes Tess. All of her analysands wear the same clothes and have the same dreams." I still smile when I think about it.

Yes, I see connection and relationship as valuable and crucial to the alchemical container of analysis, dream groups, and relationships in general. I see connection and meaning and overlap and commonality where others may not. I see the healing presence of tribal life and interaction as part of the balm for a lost modern and postmodern civilization. But I do not subscribe to an abandonment of the professional sense of boundaries and clinical wisdom that goes with effectively treating clients. This is a fine hair to split. On the one hand, I am critical of analysts who don't allow their analysands to see each other in waiting rooms or to attend classes the analyst teaches. I think this goes too far and controls the persons' lives too much. It creates resentment. I know group leaders who forbid participants from socializing—what is the point of this, I wonder? Clinically, the point is to protect the process that manifests in the group work as separate and uncontaminated from the social strata of relationship, but I think based on the material in this book that this is a futile, impossible, and questionable goal. In addition, I am aware of a case where the analyst required her analysand to terminate her weekly massage because she was "telling" too much to her body worker. These attitudes do not facilitate healing, trust, or compassion. They do not reflect the reality of thousands of years of human interaction. It is certainly none of my business (in my mind) if someone in my practice wants to take a class, get a massage, or go out to lunch with a person of their choice. On the other hand, within these close, tight, and gooey relationships, certain rules and limits have to be followed with analysands and dream group members or chaos results. The groups are powerful, as I have made clear. For example, one limit I follow (that I learned through not a small amount of suffering) is that none of my dream group members is in analysis with me, but if they want to be in therapy or analysis with someone else, that is fine. In fact, it is encouraged. People in analysis with me are not allowed into dream group unless they are willing to terminate analysis. Dream group members do see a more personal side of me than analysands do, but it is cautiously revealed. The material revealed needs to be digested as well, because it is not wise on most occasions to discuss fresh, raw material. Most seasoned therapists have a feel for these limits.

I imagine my analysands think they know me better than they really do—but it is entirely possible they know me better than I know myself. I think many analysts and therapists can relate to this statement and the difficulty in defining the confusing, dichotomous, personal yet professional relationship between analysand and analyst. Perhaps because of my awareness and attentions to the tribal field and so many of the synchronicities I see in my entire practice, as well as some of the outrageous mistakes I made early in my career, I feel a need to be as circumspect as possible in regard to bringing my process into the room.

When analysands know each other, it can become a problem too. Each is affected by events in the other's lives, and naturally these things come up in the analytical discussions. Of course, one mustn't comment about another's process. I know of a case that typifies the mess a therapist can make when good judgment is lost. A man was in a marital crisis, so he and his wife saw a marital therapist. The therapist saw them individually (which is complicated), and then told the husband he should leave his wife—that she was a hopeless borderline and that he should get out. A few weeks later, the therapist took the wife on as an individual patient and eventually told her the husband was a louse to consider leaving her. Meanwhile, he saw the couple in a session with their children during which all of the parties ganged up on the husband / father with no intervention from the therapist. This is not the type of tribal relationship I am referring to when I speak of the tribal dream. Nor is this family field therapy. This is simply bad therapy and bad boundaries and bad countertransference. The analyst, therapist, or psychologist has to remain neutral, see each case on its own merits, and process each individual for his own understanding and mythic life path.

The tribal / communal field lies between our conscious ego and the archetypal realm of reality that Carl Jung so vividly observed and identified. It is the relational area where our social behaviors occur, but evidence of it is seen throughout dreams and synchronicities in persons' lives. Indigenous peoples all over the world knew this reality and integrated it into their religious practices, their mythos, and their belief systems. It is in this tribal element that modern and postmodern men and women can begin to see the ancient seeds of our connection and rootedness to all people in all parts of the earth.

In the new millennium, we are confronted with a starving global population that is more critical than ever. We see the effects of third world hunger, the mismanagement of ecological resources, and the exploitation of workers who are unable to demand better living and working conditions. This is a political and ethical catastrophe that is manifesting in our current environment and cannot be ignored. Perhaps common to many religious traditions and experiences is the belief, the passion that each of us is connected, that all of us are one. We need each other. We need to care about the plight of each other. We are brothers and sisters in the deepest aspects of our psyches. We are tribally and universally connected, and it demands a response from each one of us to know and realize that we are humanly related to all of the people on earth. Our web of relationship goes on and on; it extends to other continents, to other cultures, to other races, to other diverse lifestyles and needs. Clearly, the human experience is one that has much more commonality than diversity—it is our link of unity to each other. Perhaps, if I have been successful at all, these pages will attest to how vital and significant the people in our lives are. One can be comforted and experience the compassionate level of caring that loving those in our field can provide. My hope is not only to illuminate an aspect of the psyche with some clarity and definition, but also to move and inspire those who see and are affected by these things to feel and act with even more conviction our intrinsic value to one another.

Endnotes

1. Here, Jung is referring to participation mystique, which is literally defined as "participation in the mystical." My definition is: "An unconscious fusion between subject and object where their distinction is lost—who is dreaming what for whom?"

2. See *Hero With A Thousand Faces* by Joseph Campbell who has written extensively in this area.

3. Joseph Henderson, a revered Jungian analyst, suggests a somewhat similar notion to mine in an article published in *Psychological Perspectives*, entitled "The Elder's Perspective." He asserts: *"In recent years I have postulated the existence of a cultural unconscious as well as an archetypal unconscious. I have found it useful and, indeed, frequently necessary to classify this area of cultural influence in civilized societies as consisting of four cultural attitudes: religious, social, aesthetic, and philosophic. Such speculations at least open a window through which new patterns, formed by the intersection of psychology and anthropology, may be perceived."* (Henderson, 2000, 10–21).

4. Tracking the process is similar to Carlos Casteneda's "stalking and hunting."

5. Commonly accepted exam definition from Jung Institute of Zurich.

6. See C. A. Meier, training analyst from Zurich, who has written extensively about complexes.

7. See *Heyoka* article in Appendix.

8. See Jeremy Taylor's *Dream Work* (1983), New York: Paulist Press.

9. The question had to do with the name of the French texts referred to in Jung's *Memories, Dreams and Reflections* that discussed the origin of the wind.

10. The couple reconciled and has now been married for almost forty years.

11. From a private conversation with therapist John Stack.

12. From a private conversation with Martha Wolf.

13. As related by Doug Boyd in *Rolling Thunder,* Dell Publishing, 1974.

14. *The Notebook* by Nicholas Sparks, Warner Books, 1999.

15. Op. cit., Edinger, *Ego and Archetype,* (1992), 101.

16. Much has already been written about gangs and cults providing a type of family where there is a social void. These groups are an attempt for the psyche to find a tribal position. The alienation brought on by modern society abates when individuals live communally, dress alike, or subscribe to a narrow belief system. These are not tribes in the actual sense, because they do not arise out of a long cultural and social history, but rather out of group behavior that falsely mimics the fulfillment of relatedness and connection.

17. Gleaned from private conversation with Larry Dossey's associate, Alice Frazier.

18. From private correspondence of Carol Smith.

19. From *Dream Analysis* (1984), 77.

20. Per private conversation with Mary Briner.

21. From *The Complete Fairy Tales of the Brothers Grimm,* trans. Jack Zipes, Bantam Books (1992), 186.

22. Messmer (1734–1815) was a pioneer in the fields later known as psychology and hypnosis; he identified the phenomenon of mass hysteria: a collective psychic infection where groups of people act unconsciously from the archetype of spirit.

23. See *Heyoka* article in appendix.

24. Mary Briner: case seminar, Zurich 1989.

25. See Dorothy Dinnerstein's *The Mermaid and the Minotaur: Sexual Arrangements and Human Malaise,* (1976) HarperCollins.

26. See Wilson D. Wallis, "The Canadian Dakota" in References.

27. Sandtray projections are a form of play or art therapy where a therapist invites the client to choose from many objects to produce a

"picture" in a box of sand. These are then discussed and interpreted as a projective technique.

28. See Linda Schierse Leonard's *On the Way to the Wedding: Transforming the Love Relationship.* Shambhala Publications, 1987.

29. Analysts Marvin Speigleman and Arnold Mindell have published in this area.

Appendix

I

Heyoka Shamanism and Analytical Psychology

Lakota Medicine Man John Fire Lame Deer relates this story:

> . . . we talk about the heyoka turtle and his friend the
> heyoka frog. They are sitting on a rock by a lake. It starts
> raining. "Hurry, or we'll get wet," says the heyoka turtle
> to his buddy. "Yes, let's get out of the rain," says the heyoka
> frog. So they jump in the lake. Maybe these stories do not
> sound very funny to a white man, but they kept us laughing
> no matter how often we heard them.[1]

This is a *heyoka* story, intended not only to amuse, but also
to break open one's fixed perception of reality. The heyoka is the
"sacred clown," the "contrary," or "opposite to nature" shaman
of the Lakota people. It is the most secret, dangerous, feared,
and misunderstood of all their medicine lodge traditions. Family
members may actually mourn when a relative dreams in such
a way that he is commanded to dance the heyoka dance and
become a contrary. The tradition is controversial, challenges
existing authority, and balks at any kind of conformity—giving

it a mysterious and frightening tenor. First cousin to the trickster, the heyoka will alarm, frighten, cajole, and humiliate any or all respected persons of authority.

He lives in the realm of taboo. He is wholly unkind but often funny. Jung, in *On the Psychology of the Trickster Figure,* describes a religious festival held in France around 1200 that points to similar archetypal energy of the Lakota heyoka tradition. The letter states:

> In the very midst of divine service masqueraders with grotesque faces, disguised as women, lions and mummers, performed their dances, sang indecent songs in the choir, ate their greasy food from a corner of the alter near the priest celebrating mass, got out their games of dice, burned a stinking incense made of old shoe leather, and ran and hopped about all over the church.[2]

The heyoka acts as a collective shadow figure so that he / she can bring into consciousness the opposite, the inferior, the shadow. It is through this backwards, upside down, comic performance that he pulls up and sheds light on the collective shadow. Jung writes: "As in its collective, mythological form, so also the individual shadow contains within it the seed of an enantidromia, of a conversion into its opposite."[3]

The heyoka is enantidromia; he creates the tensions of opposites so the transcendent function can emerge and so that the collective consciousness can compensate its one-sided attitude. Black Elk states:

> You have noticed that the truth comes into this world with two faces. One is sad with suffering, and the other laughs; but it is the same face, laughing or weeping. When people are already in despair, maybe the laughing

is better for them and when they feel too good and are
too sure of being safe, maybe the weeping face is better
for them to see. And so I think that is what the heyoka
ceremony is for.[4]

Joseph Epes Brown in his discussion about the deeper meanings of the heyoka clown describes the purpose of his sometimes
shocking behavior:

> . . . once the awareness, that alertness and openness, has
> been achieved through the initial shock, then it is pos-
> sible to communicate on another level through the use
> of humor. As I see it, all this puts the mind of the person
> involved in a frame which relates to the humor of the situ-
> ation, thus serving to open doors to a realm greater than
> that of ordinary life. It does this extremely effectively,
> because all this takes place, as I have suggested, within a
> very serious ritual or dance-drama context, which involves
> enormous concentration, great attention to minute details
> of the rites of the ceremonies that are being carried out
> and the rigors of all this demand some kind of relief, some
> way in which what is being stated through the rites can
> be translated into a much deeper level, transcending the
> activities, or the forms and motions of the rite itself. Thus
> shock and humor open into another realm. It is a very
> Zen-like technique, it seems to me.[5]

As a result of the peculiar antics of the heyoka, the tribal members
are pulled into a perception disorientation that is a contrary experience to the conscious ego attitude and a profoundly different
way of viewing things. This collective shadow serves a vital function, the shadow is not repressed or projected in a dangerous way
but rather is given a sacred position in a ceremonial, shamanistic

culture. The heyoka humor is valued as sacred and extremely important. Joseph Epes Brown says about Black Elk:

> I think he understood that there is no access to a deeper spiritual reality if there is not the opening force of laughter present there. It tends to open the heart for receiving a greater value than that of this world. That is why it was always a happy experience to be with him, in spite of the fact that in many moments of his life he was a very sad, tragic figure, because of his feeling that he had never been able to bring his people together and have the tree of his culture flourish again.[6]

The heyoka is the most powerful shaman in the Lakota religion. This act of pairing of opposites, the archetypal nature of bringing into wholeness the dichotomous reality, is a role that receives the most respect. The heyoka shaman carries the numinous reality of the Self. Lame Deer says:

> I am going to tell you a story about clowns, but it won't be a funny story. For us Indians everything has a deeper meaning; whatever we do is somehow connected with our religion. I'm working up to this part. To us a clown is somebody sacred, funny, powerful, ridiculous, holy, shameful, visionary. He is all this and then some more. Fooling around a clown is really performing a spiritual ceremony. He has a power. It comes from the thunder-beings, not the animals or the earth. In our Indian belief a clown has more power than the atom bomb.[7]

It was well acknowledged that the heyoka path was hard; carrying the shadow for the tribal collective consciousness was a tiresome burden that drained the heyoka clown. It was a life of sacrifice; the individual sacrificed for the good of the larger group. As a result there was resistance to honoring the heyoka dreams and dancing the ceremony as well as a desire to live the life of the contrary until the dreams said it was no longer necessary. The heyoka is the hardest calling with the highest price. Lame Deer says, "He has the power. He has the honor. He has the shame. He pays for all of it."[8] The heyoka shaman is connected to the power of the thunderbirds, the great mythical beasts that lived on the earth at the beginning of time.

> These thunderbirds, they are *wakanoyate*—the spirit nation. They are not like living beings. You might call them enormous gods. When they open their mouths they talk thunder, and all the little thunderbirds repeat it after them. That's why you first hear the big thunder clap being followed by smaller rumblings. When the *wakinyan* open their eyes the lightning shoots out from there, even in the case of the thunderbird with no eyes. He has half moons there instead of eyes, and still the lightning is coming.
>
> These thunderbirds are part of the Great Spirit. Theirs is about the greatest power in the whole universe. It is the power of the hot and the cold clashing way above the clouds. It is lightning-blue lightning from the sun. It is like a colossal welding, like the making of another sun. It is like atomic power. The thunder power protects and destroys. It is good and bad, as God is good and bad, as nature is good and bad, as you and I are good and bad.[9]

The thunder and lightning on the plains in North America are a fearsome power with which to reckon. Known to come up with no warning, it can strike mercilessly. The Indians were vulnerable within their teepees pitched out in the open empty plains, as well

as the riders on horseback. Thomas H. Lewis notes in his article
"The Heyoka Cult in Historical and Contemporary Oglala Sioux
Society":

> Anyone who has experienced nomadic life on the limitless
> prairies can appreciate the palpable dangers of lightning.
> In summer convection storms play nightly, near and far,
> around the circle of the horizons. A man on horseback,
> the poles of a lodge, or an iron-tired wagon may be the
> highest visible objects. On an evening before the 1967
> Sun Dance, a boy, sent on an errand, was killed with
> his horse by an electrical discharge as he rode up out of
> a shallow coulee. There was no rain and the muttering
> clouds seemed safely distant.[10]

Naturally, the lightning and thunder collected many numinous and powerful projections. The thunderbird is one of the few
mythical animals in Lakota mythology. Much of their folklore
deals with the menagerie of beasts and fowl they lived with
daily, but the thunderbirds are wholly mythic, like the dragon
or the griffin, carrying an aspect of the Self, the unconscious,
the Divine. If a man or woman dreamed of the thunder beings
or one of the other symbols associated with the thunderbird, she
or he would have to become a heyoka or risk death by lightning.
An important part of Lakota belief is the punishment the psyche
will inflict if one does not follow one's dreams and visions to
exact detail. Perhaps some can relate to the destructive power of
resistance in our own psyches.

The heyoka calling comes through the dream world. Many
unfortunate stories are told about dreamers who were too scared /
resistant / preoccupied, etc., to dance the heyoka dance. Wilson
Wallis, a well-known anthropologist, collected this story:

About three years ago a woman was struck by lightning because she had failed to follow directions given her in a dream. The other women prevailed upon her to do as bidden; her husband, apprized of her omission, added his voice to their admonitions. To no purpose, however. She was a young woman, about 30 years old. She said she was too young to launch a career as a medicine woman. In the autumn, a few weeks after the dream, there were three days of violent thunder, lightning, and rain. The storm broke at about the same time each afternoon. On the fourth day it came again. While the woman was sitting in her tipi with her husband, she was struck by lightning and was killed instantly. Her husband, although he was in the same teepee, was not injured. The Thunder was angry with her because of her disobedience.[11]

Lame Deer also discusses the resistance to the heyoka life being explained partially because a great deal of shame is involved for the dancer since he is often asked to perform feats that are exceedingly embarrassing. He goes on to imagine his reaction if he had a thunder dream.

I'd know that before the day ends that the thunder will come through and hit me, unless I perform this dream. I'm scared, I hide in the cellar, I cry, I ask for help, but there is no remedy until I have performed this act. Only this can free me. Maybe by doing it, I'll receive some power, but most people would just as soon forget about it.[12]

The calling carries with it the threat of death—the sense the Lakota people have when a person does not follow his dream; he dies, he is lifeless. His life's purpose is of ultimate importance; his mysterious, powerful inner life is ruthless with him.

THE HEYOKA DANCE

After a Lakota had a dream requiring him to enter the heyoka lodge, he would ask a shaman for help. He must dress up for the ceremony exactly as his vision depicts. All the tribal heyokas would participate in the dance since the initiation ceremony involves all the heyokas. They are just as impelled to dance as the dreamer is. They begin by building a sacred teepee for the occasion and heating a pot of boiling water. After offerings are made, a puppy is quickly strangled. The head, spine, and tail are put into the boiling pot to cook. Meanwhile, the rest of the tribe watches while various heyokas may be dancing and hopping around and doing numerous antics. Black Elk tells this story about his own heyoka dance.

> Even while we were singing thus, the heyokas were doing
> foolish things and making laughter. For instance, two
> heyokas with long crooked bows and arrows painted in a
> funny way would come to a little shallow puddle of water.
> They would act as though they thought it was a wide, deep
> river that they had to cross; so, making motions, but saying
> nothing, they would decide to see how deep the river was.
> Taking their long crooked arrows, they would thrust these
> into the water, not downwards, but flat-wise just under the
> surface. This would make the whole arrow wet. Standing
> the arrows up beside them, they would get ready to swim.
> One would then plunge into the shallow puddle head first,
> getting his face in the mud and fighting the water wildly
> as though he were drowning. Then the other one would
> plunge in to save his comrade, and there would be more
> funny antics in the water to make the people laugh.[13]

When the puppy stew is cooked, the heyokas plunge their arms into the boiling water (all the while exclaiming how cold it is) and pull out bits of the puppy meat to feed to the tribe. The meat is believed to be very healing, and anyone who eats it will be cured on the spot. The tribe cannot eat the meat right away because it's so hot, so it gets tossed back and forth while the heyokas show they can hold it with no trouble. Quite a bit of speculation has been made regarding why the heyokas don't get burned during the heyoka ritual. They have an herb they rub on their arms before the ceremony, but Lame Deer writes:

> What is it that makes a heyoka not get scalded? You can go up to him and examine his hands and arms. There's not a blister on him. It wouldn't even show color as when you dip your hand in really hot water and it gets red. It's not even pink. There is a special herb that I know of, a kind of grayish moss, the root of it, called heyoka *tapejuta*. When you chew that and smear your arms with it the boiling water won't burn you. But you have to be a heyoka for that herb to do you any good. A man who isn't a heyoka could never stand that boiling water. He'd have no arm left. He hasn't got the dream and the power.[14]

During the ceremony they may also give predictions, always in the opposite. For example, they tell who's going to die (who's going to get well), that it will rain tomorrow (that the weather will be sunny), or that a bear will not be killed tomorrow (that a bear will be killed tomorrow).

The ceremony is a sacred rite that is considered a powerful healing ritual for the tribal community. The dog, which is not a common food source for the Lakota, carries the heyoka medicine that initiates the new lodge members as well as heals the ill. The boiling pot, the cauldron that the heyoka must dip his bare arms into, is much like the way his psyche must now dip into the boiling collective unconscious by living in an opposite nature.

THE HEYOKA LIFESTYLE

The person who becomes a heyoka may live his shamanic calling in secrecy or he may be known to a few members of his tribe. Some only dance in disguise, so it is not clear exactly who the heyoka may be. They are forever playing tricks and poking fun—some of them all the time, others only during ceremony or as one's dream advised. They are people who live contrary to others. They may wear warm furs and buffalo robes in the heat of summer all the while shivering, with teeth chattering, as they exclaim how cold it is. Likewise, during the winter (when it can reach forty degrees below zero) heyokas may run around only in breech cloths, complaining of the heat and the mosquito bites (snowflakes). A number of witnesses have related seeing hot / cold heyokas covered with sweat in sub-freezing temperatures.

Heat causes their flesh to shiver and their teeth to chatter, while cold makes them perspire and pant. It is said of them that in the coldest weather of the Minnesota winter, when the mercury congeals, they seek some prominence on the prairie where they put up some bushes to shelter them from the rays of the sun, under which they sit naked and fan themselves as they swelter with heat. And in the oppressive heat of summer they fold around them robe on robe and lean over a rousing fire, sniveling and shaking with cold like in a fit of ague.[15]

He also verbally says everything the opposite of what he really means. Yes means no, no means yes, good-bye means hello, hello means good-bye, and so forth. He may actually speak in backwards Sioux language at a rapid clip that only heyokas are believed to understand. He may express happiness and joy by a sorrowful countenance with sighs and groans and pain and suffering by laughter and smiles.

He may walk backwards or go in the opposite direction of where he is intending to be. He faces the door of his teepee to the west, while the rest of the tribe's doors face east. He may enter his teepee backwards, on his hands and knees, or by lifting the skins and crawling in from underneath where there is no door. He may stand on his head inside his teepee as well. He rides his horse backwards with his face toward the tail, and in ceremonies he dances backwards, out of rhythm and tries to trip other dancers. He is believed to be able to erase a shamanic healing or heal someone who has been cursed. He may dress in rags or opposite-sex clothing, or shave one side of his head. He may invite others to his teepee by opening their door flaps, presenting his buttocks, then running away. Lame Deer describes a clown named "The Straighten-Outer":

> He was always running around with a hammer trying to flatten round and curvy things, making them straight, things like soup dishes, eggs, balls, rings or cartwheels. My grandma had one of those round glass chimneys which fits over a kerosene lamp. Well, he straightened it out for her. It's not easy to be a heyoka. It is even harder to have one in the family.[16]

The heyoka can also perform feats that would not be expected of him, e.g. strength for a woman, speed in an old man, etc. Lame Deer tells:

> Let me tell you a story of a heyoka who performed his act the way he dreamed it. It happened in Manderson, back in the 1920's. It happened on a Fourth of July, and this man was real lively the way he acted. He turned somersaults, and there was a bunch of young cowboys chasing him on horseback. They couldn't catch up to him. They were trying to lasso him, but they never came close. He was running in front of them, and sometimes would turn somersaults. Sometimes he would turn around and run

backward, and when they got near him he'd turn around once more and get away. When he was through, when he took off the ragged sack cloth he had on him, with holes for the eyes to look out of, we saw him. He was an old man in his seventies. What was his name? I can't recall it. An old, white-haired grandfather, but the thunder-beings had given him the power to run fast.[17]

One of the interesting phenomena that surrounds the heyoka cult is the synchronistic lightning and thunder that manifest when they perform their ceremonies or talk about their heyoka visions or their inner religious material. Black Elk finished the story of his life and his great vision of healing the broken hoop of his people for John Neihardt, as Neihardt says in his postscript to *Black Elk Speaks:*

We who listened now noted that thin clouds had gathered about us. A scant chill rain began to fall and there was low, muttering thunder without lightning. The tears running down his cheeks, the old man raised his voice to a thin high wail, and chanted: 'In sorrow I am sending a feeble voice, O Six Powers of the World. Hear me in my sorrow, for I may never call again. O make my people live!' . . . For some minutes the old man stood silent, with face uplifted, weeping in the drizzling rain. In a little while the sky was clear again.[18]

Similarly, in Stanley Vestal's book *Warpath,* a biography of White Bull, a Sioux who lived during the Battle of Little Big Horn, he relates this event about White Bull's heyoka vision:

Though the Chief had promised to tell me the full story of his life, he was somewhat reluctant to relate this vision, and requested that I hear it when there was no one else in the cabin. He explained that, whenever he told this story, a fierce thunder-storm followed, and therefore he told it very seldom. The old man does not see well and is rather deaf. He told the story at four o'clock in the afternoon. He had been sitting with his back to the north wall of the cabin, inside, and the sky was cloudless. We finished the conference at seven o'clock that evening and had supper. By that time thunder-clouds had piled up in the north-west, and my interpreter pointed out certain features of the clouds which indicated a storm was about to break. Immediately after supper, a terrific thunder-storm burst upon us. The cloud was small and swept out of the north directly for my cabin, where the story had been told. No rain fell in the adjacent cabins within a few yards on either side, but the wind was so strong that I had to move my car to keep it from rolling over the bluff. The Chief made no comment on this appalling fulfillment of his prediction. He took the storm for granted.[19]

Thus the heyoka lives the fool's life. His nature is not simply supernatural; it is the opposite of nature.[20] He is committed to behaving in an opposite sacred fashion that provides a collective compensation, a tension of opposites.

PRESENT-DAY HEYOKA SHAMANS

In recent times the heyoka shaman is less protected by uncontaminated tradition than before the invasion of the westward expansion movement; however, similar themes emerge—clowning, fear, bizarre behavior. Thomas H. Lewis describes the swaggering, crazy gesticulation and exaggeratedly drunken behavior of the heyoka clowns:

Heyoka are masked and otherwise disguised, in costumes
often seeming to be caricatures . . . The heyoka behavior
is coarse, grotesque, 'contrary.' They stagger about,
gesticulate crazily, and sometimes appear exaggeratedly
drunk. They dance backward or out-of-rhythm and
interfere with other dancers. They frighten, intimidate,
or threaten. They are unpredictable. Although the
dancing may last up to 12 hours, they rarely are present
more than briefly. They are more often than not solitary,
occasionally appearing in pairs or small groups. It is not
always possible to distinguish them from self elected buf-
foons or from psychopathic or alcoholic persons, but they
are always conspicuously different from gravely-proper
and role-conscious Omaha dancers who show a dignified
self-assurance and a sensitivity to social pressures and
forms of behavior.[21]

They are still much feared by non-heyoka tribal members
according to an interview Lewis conducted:

Mrs. C. U. : 'Children and grownups are afraid of the
clowns. They avoid them carefully. Or they run up to
touch them or hit them, then they run away screaming.'
Several adults in group conversation with this woman
and the interviewer agreed they were afraid of heyoka
too. 'You never know what they are going to do!'[22]

The present-day heyoka still has the task of defeating the pom-
pons and poking fun at the arrogant or self-important. Lewis
describes one heyoka's behavior during a political speech, noting
that Native Americans feel particularly cheated by United States
political structure:

During a political speech he lay on the ground and a
crowd of perhaps 50 children gathered, fascinated, horrified, and scared. He lay first on his back, then on his belly,
kicking his heels and gazing idly about. The braver ones
would run up to hit, touch, or jump over him, and all scattered screaming when he stirred dangerously. He would
be quiet, then suddenly roll over several times, or arise and
run erratically about, not threatening particularly. The
speech was ruined; the crowd watched the heyoka.[23]

The modern heyokas have developed a sardonic, bittersweet,
black humor in their antics. Some dancers at festivities wear
cardboard signs on their backs advertising local bars and decorate
their costumes with beer cans. They seem to be acknowledging
the pain and suffering of the Native American alcohol problem.
At major pow wows and gatherings of celebration they remind
people of the destructive nature alcohol has played in their
modern culture. But the heyokas don't carry a sign that says "remember the alcohol problem," instead they wear advertisements.
It becomes a joke which has greater impact.

Modern heyokas seem to be able to make fun of both their
own traditional culture with all the pomp and ceremony that accompanies their Sun Dance gatherings as well as Anglo culture in
their tenacious and absurd misunderstanding of Native American
customs. The heyoka has been seen wearing "Indian Halloween"
costumes for sun dancing: black wigs with long braids, children's
dime-store headdresses made out of paper, and imitation buffalo
horns all contribute to their apparent attitude to not take anything too seriously. In the midst of the serious, important, large,
Sun Dance with all well-known shamans dressed in rich traditional clothing, a heyoka in a dime-store Indian mask (painted
bright orange to represent the red man and intended for Anglo

children to celebrate Halloween) must provide a striking contrast
of opposites and shadow.

The heyoka tradition is present in other Native American
tribal traditions as well as the Lakota. In each story I have collected there seems to be a congruent theme of humor, shock,
absurdity, earthiness, and taboo. In the Navaho culture the clown
is described as one who impersonates fools and is characterized
by his devotion to filth and disorder. "They do not dance, but go
about shouting *wi . . . wi . . . wi . . . !* They are armed with clubs
and stones, which they use upon anything that arouses their re-
pugnance for beauty and order. Excreta are sometimes deposited
in the houses, and the 'fools' fling nasal mucus on one another."

Adolf Bandelier and Julian H. Steward both recorded the
outrageous and sexually explicit nature of the ceremonies among
other North American tribal life. Buffoon is the name given the
heyoka by some anthropologists who are known to stretch the
limits of taboo. He may simulate masturbation or defecation in a
ceremony or "attack" a virgin to enact rape. Bandelier has admitted his own reaction of disgust and amazement while the tribal
people seemed only amused.

And finally, Kinky Freedman, a musician turned mystery
writer, tells this story from his childhood in Kerrville, Texas, to
a Dallas reporter:

> I ask him how he decided to write mysteries. He shoots
> me a dark mysterious look. "I saw a rodeo in Bandera
> when I was a kid. It was a very seminal experience for the
> Kinkster. They had an act called 'Shoshone the Magic
> Pony.' It was this real old man with this horse that looked
> like two men dressed up in a horse suit. The horse did
> tricks, crossed its legs and stuff like that. At the end of
> the act, the old man took his outfit off, and he was a
> young girl. And she took the saddle and blanket off of

Shoshone, and he was a real horse. That really stayed with me."[24]

When I spoke to Kinky briefly by telephone about being connected to the myth of the heyoka, he quickly agreed it was probably heyoka. He represents an example of modern people who are tap rooted to archetypical collective unconsciousness without any obvious awareness. One can discover a peace and validation when the discovery is made of an ancient connection. Alienation and separation seem to be a large aspect of the postmodern "soul loss" problem, a terminally malignant view that we are alone and narcissistically special in our uniqueness. The Native American culture operated in tribal clusters that defy any parallel to modern life. And within tribal customs the heyoka grouped as a lodge. They initiated members together, enacted ceremonies together and found connection with their tradition. Sadly, this entire aspect of modern life is missing and certain to contribute to depression and aloneness.

CONCLUSION

The heyoka deflates the inflated, exalts the underdog, and brings the contrary into the consciousness. He is the powerful lightning that has the instant, intense, shocking, pointed ability to change a situation, a person, a perspective of reality. He is humor, he is the conjunction of opposites, he compensates the collective attitude. He is the vehicle with which the Lakota people honor the dark and the underneath, allow the change and transformation of the unconscious to take place and integrate the opposing pole that can bring wholeness to an experience.

Sometimes I go home at the end of the day and cannot decide if I'm a prostitute, con artist, or a healer. The common ground between the therapist and the heyoka shaman seems clear to me but difficult to explicate. The unconscious process, especially in dreams, almost always compensates the ego consciousness with an opposite attitude so the dream maker as heyoka is one facet of the common ground. Additionally, the overlap relates to the analyst identifying with the analysand's unconscious process; a good practitioner seems to be able to turn the process upside down and see the psyche from an entirely different angle, a view unseen up to now. Sometimes this is just what is needed to crack open the defenses to allow the underlayers to emerge and to inform the process in a new fresh way. And like the heyoka, the analyst suffers his calling.

But it is the process itself that also evokes the essence of the heyoka magic. Breaking out of complexes, finding new possibilities in one's tired, depressed, blah psyche is akin to heyoka medicine. I find if my analysands can successfully identify the exact nature of their complex that is driving them to stereotyped, painful, repetitive behaviors (like spending too much money or fearing elevators) and find the spiritual warrior's courage to act in the opposite, the complex will never again have quite the grip it had before. The transforming opposite behavior has not been properly identified unless fear, panic, and delight are experienced deep in one's core at the very idea of enacting the behavior. It is not a simple process—determining the transforming action that has the lightning energy to change reality; like threading a needle, it may take several tries to discover the magic. An example: A fifty-year-old woman entered analysis with, among other issues, the complaint of lost sexual desire. She was a professional woman, obese, in a long-term marriage with children. She was conservative and judgmental about sexual matters; certain premarital sex, affairs, and just about all sexuality that did not occur within the sanctity of marriage was evil and wrong. In fact, anything overtly sexual was suspect in any setting. Within her marriage all sexuality was evaporated, so she was quite depressed. She was also clever, gifted, and imaginative. Her dreams presented a shadow figure in the form of a Hispanic woman dripping with sensuality and warmth. This figure became my analysand's anchor for her lost self. In the image she could see all parts of herself that had been amputated by culture, church, obligation, and middle age. She took a huge step—one that frightened, excited, delighted, and embarrassed her—she decided to pierce her ears in honor of the heyoka Hispanic woman. For many, this would be a non-event, but for this analysand it unleashed all of her pent-up desire. She and her husband found a sexual and playful relationship that had never before been tapped and was an enantiodromia for them both.

One act of heyoka courage can shake the psyche out of its complacency and banality—a small act, the smallest possible act, has a profound effect on the conscious self.

Heyoka medicine can be seen as a model for the entire process of individuation or transformation one seeks in Jungian analysis. It is through the slow uncovering of dreams and visions that we come face to face with the left-out parts of ourselves, the ones that frighten and cajole us to be more whole, complete. Another case: A thirty-three-year old woman entered analysis depressed, unhappy with no significant other, bored with her job as a therapist. She dreamed about a bad-boy rock-and-roller type who wore a leather jacket, tattoos, and so on. Through active imagination this image evolved into a bass guitarist. Having had no music lessons, she decided to pursue study. The man who gave her lessons had the same first and last name she did—even though they are relatively unusual names. Somehow this all contributed to evoking the opposite, heyoka nature of her process. Before long she was performing as a bass player for a rock band and went on to study music in graduate school. Depression lifted, boredom left, and her personal relationships turned. The élan, the passion of living, is trapped in the expression of the heyoka image—the seed of enantiodromia that brings fullness to the meaninglessness of modern existence.

I like to make wicked heyoka fantasies in analysis with my analysands. Like the gentleman who thinks he's a dweeb and too shy to speak at a party—we envision a life play where he is the star, loudly dressed, obnoxious, rude, sloppy, demanding, and the center of attention at the office gala. Sometimes these fantasies only make the analysands laugh, but sometimes they feel the liberation and freedom of imagining being out of the cage for just a second—a moment of seeing the other side.

Humor is perhaps the most powerful medicine an analyst can use. Norman Cousins and others have written and documented the healing nature of humor in illness. American blues music is also an example of how smiling at our suffering can take the sting out of it. But black humor is possibly the most closely connected to the heyoka and therefore the most potent medicine. A woman in analysis with me suffered from anxiety and chronic depression which had manifested in a number of her family members as well. She dreamed about a snow bird and began to collect tales with this title. She discovered several fairy tales from different cultures, all about the snow bird. But the one that captured her was an obscure Norwegian tale involving a hero who needed to cross a bridge. Unfortunately, the bridge was guarded by trolls who made it impossible for the hero to cross over and complete the task. But he resolved the problem by hiring a rooster to stand under the bridge and tell jokes. This got the trolls laughing so hard the hero was able to sneak across. I asked my analysand if she had a sense of humor (none being apparent prior to this question). She nodded thoughtfully and admitted she had been quite funny on past occasions. Shortly after, I witnessed her tell, in a dream group, a tale so dark, shocking, and comical it had the entire group in the type of protracted laughter that may result in wetting the pants. Her depressions and anxiety did not resolve entirely, but they shifted to the degree she no longer is impaired in functioning.

Heyoka medicine is about celebrating our losses and grieving our celebrations. In my volunteer work assisting family members of suicide victims, I warn them on the first meeting that on our last encounter, eight weeks later, they will have to name one positive outcome from the suicide, no matter how insignificant. This is a hard announcement to make to parents of teenagers who have committed suicide or to only children who have lost a parent to suicidal depression. From the beginning they are encouraged to see a gift that comes from tragedy—a lost kin reconnected to the family because of the death, a sense of who one's friends are and what is important in life, and so on. Likewise, celebrations can be balanced with acknowledging the difficulties they may bring. Success can lead to hubris, divorce, inflation, stress-related illnesses, and the like. When my analysands are gaga over a new man or woman I encourage them to articulate at least three liabilities about the person or relationship.

An aspect of the heyoka shaman which the analyst or therapist may embody is the unpredictable persona, the shape shifter. I like the feeling that in one session I'm supportive, kind, nurturing, the next one silent and uncommunicative, and the following one confrontive and distant; or chatty and stupid, or smart and witty, or inviting the analysand to terminate, or suggesting more weekly sessions. This tells me I'm doing my job, maybe—and these "spontaneous analysts" that come from me are not predictable ones I even know very well. I am often as surprised as the analysand. I was pleased to see the "Gloria" film in graduate school where Carl Rodgers allowed a session with Gloria to be filmed. He didn't seem anything like his writing—much more engaging than reflective listening allowed. The real work with people is too complex to put into a formula or a system; open and endless possibilities are what allows the creative process of the healer to come forward to help the sufferer.

The heyoka medicine is more than just integrating shadow or playing the trickster. It certainly embraces the power of Hermes that changes the landscape, but it's also funny and coarse. Instead of a fat woman going on a diet and encountering her true, thin, self, it is a fat woman buying a bikini and spending a vacation on the beach. It involves the surprise that creativity knows so well. A woman leading a sweat once said, "If your talk doesn't match your walk, try changing your talk."

Truly our lives are our best creative work.

NOTES

1. John Lame Deer, *Lame Deer Seeker of Visions,* ed. Richard Erdoes (New York: Washington Square Press, 1976), 227.

2. C. G. Jung, *The Archetypes of the Collective Unconscious,* vol. 9, I (New York: Bollingen Foundation, Inc., 1959), 257. New material by Princeton University Press, Princeton, N.J., 1969.

3. Ibid., 211.

4. John G. Neihardt, *Black Elk Speaks: Being the Story of a Holy Man of the Oglala Sioux* (Bison Books, 1979), 160.

5. Joseph Epes Brown, "The Wisdom of the Contrary," *Parabola* 4, no. 1 (1977): 55–56.

6. Ibid., 63.

7. John Lame Deer, *Lame Deer Seeker of Visions,* 225.

8. Ibid., 235.

9. Ibid., 227–229.

10. Thomas H. Lewis, "The *Heyoka* Cult in Historical and Contemporary Oglala Sioux Society," *Anthropos* 69 (1974).

11. Wilson D. Wallis, *The Canadian Dakota,* 82.

12. *Lame Deer Seeker of Visions,* 231.

13. *Black Elk Speaks,* 162–163.

14. *Lame Deer Seeker of Visions,* 234.

15. Wilson D. Wallis, *The Canadian Dakota,* 112.

16. *Lame Deer Seeker of Visions,* 226.
17. Ibid. 231.
18. *Black Elk Speaks,* 233–234.
19. Stanley Vestal, *Warpath,* 15.
20. *The Canadian Dakota,* 112.
21. Thomas H. Lewis, op. cit., 18.
22. Ibid.
23. Ibid., 25.
24. *Dallas Morning News,* Oct. 3, 1994, 7C.

SOURCES CONSULTED FOR APPENDIX I

Brown, Joseph Epes. "The Bison and the Moth: Lakota Correspondences." *Parabola* 8 no. 2 (May 1983).

———. "The Wisdom of the Contrary." *Parabola* 69 (1977).

———, ed. *The Sacred Pipe.* New York: Penguin Books, 1987.

———. *The Spiritual Legacy of the American Indian.* New York: Crossroad, 1987.

Day, A. Grove. *The Sky Clears.* Lincoln: University of Nebraska Press, 1951/1964.

Deloria, Vine, Jr. *God is Red.* New York: Grosset & Dunlap, Inc., 1973.

DeMallie, Raymond J., ed. *The Sixth Grandfather, Black Elk's Teachings Given to John G. Neihardt.* Lincoln and London: University of Nebraska Press, 1984.

Dooling, D. M., ed. "The Sons of the Wind, The Sacred Stories of the Lakota." New York: Parabola Books, 1987.

Doore, Gary, ed. *Shaman's Path, Healing, Personal Growth and Empowerment.* Boston: Shambhala, 1988.

Eagle Walking Turtle. *Keepers of the Fire, Journey to the Tree of Life Based on Black Elk's Vision.* Santa Fe: Bear & Company, 1987.

Eastman, Charles Alexander. *From the Deep Woods to Civilization, Chapter in the Autobiography of an Indian.* Boston: Little Brown, 1936. Reprint, Lincoln: University of Nebraska Press, 1977.

————. *Indian Boyhood.* McClure, Phillips & Company, 1902. Reprint, New York: Dover Publications, Inc., 1971.

————. *The Soul of the Indian, An Interpretation.* Boston: Houghton Mifflin, 1911. Reprint, Lincoln: University of Nebraska Press, 1980.

Jung, C. G. *The Archetypes and the Collective Unconscious.* In *Psychology and Religion: East and West.* Vol. 9, pt 1. London: Routledge and Kegan Paul, 1959.

Kehoe, Alice Beck. *North American Indians, A Comprehensive Account.* New Jersey: Prentice-Hall, Inc., 1981.

Lame Deer, John (Fire), and Richard Erdoes. *Lame Deer Seeker of Visions.* New York: Washington Square Press, 1972.

Leach, Maria, ed. *Funk and Wagnalls Standard Dictionary of Folklore, Mythology, and Legend.* San Francisco: Harper and Row, 1972.

Lewis, Thomas H. "The *Heyoka* Cult in Historical and Contemporary Oglala Sioux Society." *Anthropos* 69 (1974).

Mahdi, Louise Carus. "Contemporary Aspects of the North American Indian Vision Quest." Diploma Thesis, Jung Institute Zurich, 1976.

Neihardt, John G. *Black Elk Speaks.* New York: Pocket Books, 1969.

Mason, Philip P. *The Literary Voyager or Muzzeniegun.* Michigan: Michigan State University Press, 1962.

Mawson, C. O., ed. *Roget's Pocket Thesaurus.* New York: Harper and Row, 1966.

Momaday, N. Scott. *House Made of Dawn.* New York: Harper and Row, 1966.

Radin, Paul. *The Trickster, A Study in American Indian Mythology.* London: Routledge and Kegan Paul, 1956.

Sandoz, Mari. *Crazy Horse, The Strange man of the Oglalas.* Lincoln: University of Nebraska Press, 1942 / 1961.

———. *These Were the Sioux.* New York: Hastings House, c1964; reprint ed. Lincoln: University of Nebraska Press, 1985.

Smith, C. Michael. *Jung and Shamanism in Dialogue.* Mahwah, N.J.: Paulist Press, 1997.

———. *Psychotherapy and the Sacred.* Chicago: Center for the Scientific Study of Religion Press, 1995.

Standing Bear, Luther. *My People the Sioux.* Lincoln: University of Nebraska Press, 1975.

Stands in Timber, John and Margot Liberty, *Cheyenne Memories.* Lincoln: University of Nebraska Press, 1967 / 1972.

Steinmetz, Paul. *Meditations with Native Americans—Lakota Spirituality.* Santa Fe, N.M.: Bear & Company, 1984.

Velie, Alan R., ed. *American Indian Literature, An Anthology.* Norman, OK: University of Oklahoma Press, 1979.

Vestal, Stanley. *Warpath, The True Story of the Fighting Sioux Told in a Biography of Chief White Bull.* Boston and New York: Houghton Mifflin Company, The Riverside Press Cambridge, 1934.

Walker, James R. *Lakota Belief and Ritual.* Lincoln and London: University of Nebraska Press, 1980.

Wallace, Anthony F. C. "Dreams and the Wishes of the Soul: A Type of Psychoanalytic Theory among the Seventeenth Century Iroquois." *American Anthropologist* 60 (1958), 234–248.

Wallis, Wilson D. "The Canadian Dakota." *The Anthropological Papers of the American Museum of Natural History New York* 41, pt. 1 (1947).

Applications of Dream Groups

hospice groups
prisons
nursing homes, retirement communities, assisted living
youth detention centers
mental health clinic staff groups
clergy
therapists
couples
families (one)
people in recovery from addiction
singles (especially those having difficulty getting into relationship)
men
women
at-risk teenagers could be combined with an outdoor
    experience—using morning to work with dreams and
    afternoon for physical challenges
churches; Sunday school classes
college students, especially ones newly away from home
disabled, including head trauma
Alzheimer's patients
newly divorced
survivors of suicide or other losses

The Hundredth Monkey

The "Hundredth Monkey" is a popular story. Perhaps animals have a tribal unconscious too. In it, the story tells us that monkeys on an island were doing their typical monkey thing, gathering bananas, coconuts, and so on, when one of them accidentally dropped his peeled fruit into the ocean and discovered it tasted so much better when it was washed. Because monkeys like to imitate each other, other monkeys started washing their fruit as well. Soon there were one hundred monkeys washing fruit. Just at this time, when the hundredth monkey started to wash fruit, on the next island where there were monkeys as well one of them started to wash fruit. This began the whole process of "monkey see, monkey do" all over again. The point of this story is that when enough energy is collected in the collective monkey psyche, it jumps over to all monkeys in general, and their psyche is affected too. Fact or fiction, I don't know, but the story is told as zoological truth among some. It illustrates the point, however, that when a mass movement is afoot, other beings are affected by it. Humans are the same.

Disclaimer on use
of the word tribal

The word "tribal" could have a negative connotation in some instances or circumstances. Clearly, it can and has been used in extremely negative ways. Tribal is not, in this case, meant to foster the nationalism of the Nazis, the chauvinism of archaic patriotism, or the racism of groups throughout history. Closed systems, such as gangs, religious cults, and secret societies that encourage people to feel better and separate from other groups, are exactly the opposite of what I am trying to elucidate with the concept "tribal dream." In this case, a connection that heretofore has been lost is one to reconnect with—the part of the human psyche where intersection lies within relationship. But to build fortresses, whether they be literal or metaphorical, with a sense of exclusion and uniqueness is counterproductive to my point and the purpose of this writing. This book is about connection, inclusion, and a sense of common purpose and community. It is one of the missing pieces of modern life. Tribal exclusion is neither psychologically nor sociologically productive. It inhibits the flow of "new" and "other" and results in a closed system that excludes the process of dynamic change present in the archetypal psyche. Stale air, overbred dogs, Jim Jones and his followers—all are examples of closed systems. They wear out, tire, become contaminated with sameness, and this is a type of death. Tribal dreaming and the awareness of it in one's consciousness are designed to free one from alienation and isolation to a life lived in relationship to others.

Glossary

Agape

Agape is the Greek word used in the New Testament to refer to God's love, as opposed to Eros's more irrational love. Agape has a connotation of transcendence. It is when we as human beings exhibit a deep altruistic regard and compassion for others, without reference to ourselves. "Agape has long been considered God's love. This form of love has traditionally been seen as originating outside the human psyche. Eros would be natural or human love, but agape would be seen as emanating from outside the human being." (McGehee, 58).

Archetype

Archetype is "the most difficult term to define"—as the students of the Jung Institute Zurich would warn each other when preparing for the grueling oral exams. Archetype is a complex and profound concept that has made its way into popular speech—almost always used incorrectly. Archetype does not mean "quintessential," which is how the word is often used. Archetype refers to an aspect of reality that Jung observed and described. It is a vast, broad, powerful organizing theme in the unconscious of all people, a theme that has energy (separate from the will of the ego) of its own. An archetype is not something that can be easily described, because it is unconscious. So, what we conscious humans observe is the effect of the archetype, or its results, and our reactions. As an example, love is one of the archetypes. It is powerful, transformative, unpredictable, frightening, exhilarating, drives innumerable types of human behavior, and, without exaggeration, has shaped history, culture, and mores for the entire time humans have been conscious. Anyone who has been hit with Cupid's arrow knows what Jung means when he calls archetypes "the indisputable value." He also writes:

> "The concept of the archetype is derived from the repeated observation that, for instance, the myths and fairytales of the world literature contain definite motifs which crop up everywhere. We meet these same motifs in the fantasies, dreams, deliriums, and delusions of individuals living today. . . . [the archetype] is an irrepresentable, unconscious, pre-existent form that seems to be part of the inherited structure of the psyche and can therefore manifest itself spontaneously anywhere, at any time. . . . It is also the psychic precondition of religious assertions and is responsible for the anthropomorphism of all God images." (CW10, paragraph 847)

Collective Unconscious

The collective unconscious is the universal soup from which we all come, into which we all will go, and in which we all currently reside. It is the deepest aspect of the psyche where we are all connected to each other, and yet it is an impersonal realm of the psyche because it is mythic and universal. Jung states that the deeper "layers" of the psyche lose their individual uniqueness as they retreat farther and farther into darkness. "Lower down," or as they approach the autonomous functional systems, they become increasingly collective until they are universalized and extinguished in the body's materiality (i.e. in chemical substances). The body's carbon is simply carbon. Hence "at bottom" the psyche is simply "world." (CW 9i, paragraph 291) And finally he summarizes: "Just as the human body shows a common anatomy over and above all racial differences, so too, the human psyche possesses a common substratum transcending all differences in culture and consciousness. I have called this substratum the collective unconscious." (CW 13, paragraph 11)

Dream maker

The dream maker is an aspect of the Self that is the author of our dreams.

Eros

Eros is the Greek god of love (erotic), also known as Cupid in the Roman era. As J. Pittman McGeehee states:

> "Eros in its broadest working definition is the unconscious desire to relate or connect. The concept of Eros is perhaps as old as human consciousness. . . ." (according to Hesiod's 'Theogany.' (8BC / 1959, v. 116–122) Eros existed almost from the beginning of time, being born together with Gaia (Earth) and Tartaros, out of or at the same time as Chaos. Tartaros was a dark region beneath the earth, even beneath Hades, as far beneath the earth as heaven was above it. Eros, Gaia, and Chaos emanated from this region. This places Eros' psychological origins at a place far deeper than consciousness and far more

substantial than the later writers who depict Eros and his Roman counterpart, Cupid, as frivolous characterizations of archers whose arrow could make even gods fall in love." (McGehee, 9)

Essential Self

Who am I really? Without the messages from society, from church, from family—what is my true nature? What if I could operate outside of my complexes, outside of long behavior patterns that diminish and obscure my true self? Then I would be able to begin to know my essential self.

Psychoid

Psychoid is the intersection of neurology and psyche where they blend into each other and form a third, transitional realm. Then, psyche and matter are one.

Synchronicity

Synchronicity is a meaningful coincidence that cannot be explained by cause and effect. Simple physics, science, weather, biorhythms, or anything else one can postulate will not explain how two events could be so meaningfully connected. Some meaningful coincidences can be explained as pure chance, but as Jung writes: "But the more they multiply and the greater and more exact the correspondence is, the more their probability sinks and their unthinkability increases, until they can no longer be regarded as pure chance but, for lack of a causal explanation, have to be thought of as meaningful arrangements . . ." (CW8, paragraph 967)

An example of synchronicity is illustrated in the following story: A woman called my Dallas office for an appointment. She had recently moved from Denver and had been referred by a Jungian analyst that had supervised me about ten years earlier, before I went to Zurich. During the same week that she called me for her first appointment, I received a call, quite out of the blue, from an old Denver acquaintance who wanted me to go on a trip with him. (I was single at the time.) I declined. During the first session with my new client, she discussed being asked out on the same trip by the same man. (Naturally, I kept this synchronicity to myself, but found it "meaningful" in several ways. For one, I realized I wasn't terribly special to him and was relieved I had declined. I never figured out which one of us he asked out first.)

References

Boyd, Doug. 1974. *Rolling Thunder*. New York: Dell Publishing.

Dinnerstein, Dorothy. 1976. *The Mermaid and the Minotaur: Sexual Arrangments And Human Malaise*. New York: Harper Collins.

Edinger, Edward. 1992. *Ego and Archetype*. Boston & London: Shambhala.

Elder, George. 1999. Gathering the embers. *Psychlogical Perspectives* 39: 12–15.

Ellenberger, Henri F. 1970. *The History of the Unconscious*. New York: Basic Books.

Exploring the soul: a challenge to Freud. 1955. *Time,* 14 February, 62–70.

Frey-Rohn, Liliane. 1988. *Friedrich Nietzsche: A Psychological Approach to his Life and Work*. Ed. Hinshaw & Fischli. Trans. G. Massey. Einsiedeln: Daimon Verlag.

Fuller, Fred. 1991. The fool, the clown, the jester. *Gnosis*. 19: 16–21.

Henderson, Joseph. 2000. Jungian analysis: an elder's perspective. *Psychological Perspectives* 41: 10–21.

Jaffe, Aniela. 1979. *C. G. Jung: Word and Image*. Bollingen Series 48. New Jersey: Princeton University Press.

Jacobi, Jolande. 1974. *Complex Archetypal Symbol in the Psychology of C. G. Jung.* Trans. R. Manheim. New Jersey: Princeton University Press. (Original work published 1959.)

Jung, C. G. 1957. God, the devil, and the human soul. *Atlantic*, 200 (November): 57–63.

———. 1967. *Alchemical Studies*. Bollingen Series 20, vol. 13. New Jersey: Princeton University Press.

———. 1959. *The Archetypes and the Collective Unconcious*. Bollingen Series 20, vol. 9.1. New Jersey: Princeton University Press.

———. 1984. *Dream Analysis: Notes of the Seminar Given 1928–1930 by C. G. Jung*. Ed. William McGuire. Bollingen Series 49. New Jersey: Princeton University Press.

———. 1960. *The Structure and Dynamics of the Psyche*. Bollingen Series 20, vol. 8. New Jersey: Princeton University Press.

———. 1965. *Memories, Dreams, Reflections*. (Rev. ed.). Ed. Aniela Jaffe. Trans. R. & C. Winston. New York: Vintage Books. (Original work published 1961.)

Leonard, Linda Schierse. 1987. *On the Way to the Wedding: Tranforming the Love Relationship*. Boston and London: Shambhala Publications.

McGehee, J. Pittman. 1997. Love in the analytic container: the place of eros, logos and agape in psychoanalysis. Diploma thesis, Jung Institute Dallas.

Sandner, Don and Steven Wong, eds. 1996. *The Sacred Heritage*. New York and London: Routledge.

Sharp, Daryl. 1999. The patron and the puer. *The Salt Journal* 2 (1): 29–33.

Storr, Anthony. 1983. *The Essential Jung*. New York: MJF Books.

Szymcayk, Denise M. 1997. Personal power: Shamanic healing techniques and Feminist counseling practices. *Shamanic Applications Review*. 6: 3–15.

Taylor, Jeremy. 1983. *Dream Work*. New York: Paulist Press.

Ulanov, Ann. 1999. Countertransference and the self. *Journal of Jungian Theory And Practice* 1: 5–26.

Woodman, Marion. 1982. *Addiction to Perfection*. Toronto: Inner City Books.

———. 2000. *Bone: Dying Into Life*. New York: Viking.

Index

Ann Belford Ulanov

Spiritual Aspects of Clinical Work

How does the spirit come into clinical work? Through the analyst? In the analysand's work in the analysis? What happens to human destructiveness if we embrace a vision of non-violence? Do dreams open us to spiritual life? What is the difference between repetition compulsion and ritual? How does religion feed terrorism? What happens if analysts must wrestle with hate in themselves? Do psychotherapy and spirituality compete, or contradict, or converse with each other? What does religion uniquely offer, beyond what psychoanalysis can do, to our surviving and thriving? This book is chock full of such important questions and discussions of their answers.

480 pages, ISBN 3-85630-634-X

C. A. Meier

Healing Dream and Ritual

C. A. Meier investigates the ancient Greek understanding of dreams and dreaming, Antique incubation and concomitant rituals.

In this greatly expanded version of his classic work, *Ancient Incubation and Modern Psychotherapy*, Meier compares Asklepian divine medicine with our own contemporary psychotherapeutic approaches to dreaming. He elucidates how the healing cure was found in the very core of illness itself – a fact of invaluable significance today in both medicine and psychology.

In helping us to recognize the suprapersonal aspects of illness, the dream is shown to reveal a transcendental path to healing.

168 pages, illustrated, ISBN 3-85630-629-3

English Titles from Daimon

Harry Wilmer

How Dreams Help

"Growing numbers of people are fascinated by the dream world. From psychological scholars and analysts to spontaneous groups and cults, the dream has a compelling voice. ... I make the point in this book that our dreams are our most creative inner source of wisdom and hope. ... The criterion for selection is simply that each one illustrates a common human life experience that all readers have had or are likely to have."

192 pages, ISBN 3-85630-582-3

Regina Abt, Irmgard Bosch, Vivienne MacKrell

Dream Child

Creation and New Life in Dreams of Pregnant Women

The spiritual dimension of pregnancy has been overshadowed in recent times by the dramatic developments in scientific and medical realms. The sense of wonder and mystery at the creation of new human life is ever more ignored in the wake of so many innovative technical developments.

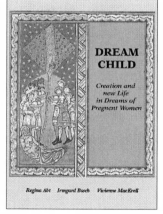

Once-awesome religious rites and traditions that accompanied the dangerous and significant transitions of life – such as birth, puberty, marriage, illness and death, as well as pregnancy – are hardly to be found in much of today's world. A pregnant woman often feels spiritually isolated and at odds with herself.

This book consists of a rich selection of contemporary dreams from many lands, chosen from a collection of some 700 dreams. They are psychologically interpreted and can offer orientation and stimulation not only for pregnant women, but for all who are concerned with the great questions of pregnancy, birth and life's transitions.

hardcover, 480 pages, richly illustrated, ISBN 3-85630-592-0

English Titles from Daimon

R. Abt / I. Bosch / V. MacKrell- *Dream Child: Dreams of Pregnant Women*
Theodor Abt / Erik Hornung et. al. - *Knowledge for the Afterlife*
- *Corpus Alchemicum Arabicum*
- *The Great Vision of Muhammed ibn Umail*
Susan R. Bach - *Life Paints its Own Span*
Diana Baynes Jansen - *Jung's Apprentice: A Biography of Helton Godwin Baynes*
John Beebe (Ed.) - *Terror, Violence and the Impulse to Destroy*
E.A. Bennet - *Meetings with Jung*
W.H. Bleek / L.C. Lloyd (Ed.) - *Specimens of Bushman Folklore*
George Czuczka - *Imprints of the Future*
Heinrich Karl Fierz - *Jungian Psychiatry*
John Fraim - *Battle of Symbols*
von Franz / Frey-Rohn / Jaffé - *What is Death?*
Liliane Frey-Rohn - *Friedrich Nietzsche, A Psychological Approach*
Ralph Goldstein (Ed.) - *Images, Meanings and Connections:*
Essays in Memory of Susan Bach
Yael Haft - *Hands: Archetypal Chirology*
Siegmund Hurwitz - *Lilith, the first Eve*
Aniela Jaffé - *The Myth of Meaning*
- *Was C.G. Jung a Mystic?*
- *From the Life und Work of C.G. Jung*
- *Death Dreams and Ghosts*
Verena Kast - *A Time to Mourn*
- *Sisyphus*
Hayao Kawai - *Dreams, Myths and Fairy Tales in Japan*
James Kirsch - *The Reluctant Prophet*
Eva Langley-Dános - *Prison on Wheels: Ravensbrück to Burgau*
Mary Lynn Kittelson - *Sounding the Soul*
Rivkah Schärf Kluger - *The Gilgamesh Epic*
Yehezkel Kluger & - *RUTH in the Light of Mythology, Legend*
Naomi Kluger-Nash *and Kabbalah*
Paul Kugler (Ed.) - *Jungian Perspectives on Clinical Supervision*
Paul Kugler - *The Alchemy of Discourse*
Rafael López-Pedraza - *Cultural Anxiety*
- *Hermes and his Children*
Alan McGlashan - *The Savage and Beautiful Country*
- *Gravity and Levity*
Gregory McNamee (Ed.) - *The Girl Who Made Stars: Bushman Folklore*
- *The North Wind and the Sun*
- *The Bearskin Quiver*
Gitta Mallasz - *Talking with Angels*
C.A. Meier - *Healing Dream and Ritual*
- *A Testament to the Wilderness*
- *Personality: The Individuation Process*
Eva Pattis Zoja (Ed.) - *Sandplay Therapy*

English Titles from Daimon

Laurens van der Post - *The Rock Rabbit and the Rainbow*
Jane Reid - *Jung, My Mother and I: The Analytic Diaries*
of Catharine Rush Cabot
R.M. Rilke - *Duino Elegies*
Miguel Serrano - *C.G. Jung and Hermann Hesse*
Helene Shulman - *Living at the Edge of Chaos*
Dennis Slattery / Lionel Corbet (Eds.)
- *Depth Psychology: Meditations on the Field*
Susan Tiberghien - *Looking for Gold*
Ann Ulanov - *Spiritual Aspects of Clinical Work*
- *Picturing God*
- *Receiving Woman*
- *The Female Ancestors of Christ*
- *The Wisdom of the Psyche*
- *The Wizards' Gate, Picturing Consciousness*
Ann & Barry Ulanov - *Cinderella and her Sisters: The Envied*
and the Envying
- *Healing Imagination: Psyche and Soul*
Erlo van Waveren - *Pilgrimage to the Rebirth*
Harry Wilmer - *How Dreams Help*
- *Quest for Silence*
Luigi Zoja - *Drugs, Addiction and Initiation*
Luigi Zoja & Donald Williams - *Jungian Reflections on September 11*
Jungian Congress Papers - *Jerusalem 1983: Symbolic & Clinical Approaches*
- *Berlin 1986: Archetype of Shadow in a Split World*
- *Paris 1989: Dynamics in Relationship*
- *Chicago 1992: The Transcendent Function*
- *Zürich 1995: Open Questions*
- *Florence 1998: Destruction and Creation*
- *Cambridge 2001*

Available from your bookstore or from our distributors:

In the United States:

Bookworld Trade Inc.
1941 Whitfield Park Loop
Sarasota FL 34243
Please order on the web: www.bookworld.com
Fax: 800-777-2525 Phone: 800-444-2524

In Great Britain:

Airlift Book Company
8 The Arena
Enfield, Middlesex EN3 7NJ
Phone: (0181) 804 0400
Fax: (0181) 804 0044

Worldwide:

Daimon Verlag   Hauptstrasse 85   CH-8840 Einsiedeln   Switzerland
Phone: (41)(55) 412 2266   Fax: (41)(55) 412 2231
email: info@daimon.ch

*Visit our website: **www.daimon.ch***
or write for our complete catalog

Introduction

Little did we realize when the very first *BLUE BOOK OF DOLLS AND VALUES®* was published in 1974 that our efforts would be rewarded with overwhelming success and that eventually we would actually be bringing out a 7th edition of our book, greatly expanded from the original 194 pages to a volume with over three times as much information and more than 600 photographs. Through the years our objectives have always remained the same. Since every edition sells more than the previous one, we can only conclude that these objectives are in line with the needs of doll lovers, collectors, dealers and appraisers who keep buying the latest editions of our book.

• **Our first objective** has been to present a book which will help collectors identify dolls and learn more about them. These may be dolls that they already own, dolls that they might like to own from the large variety shown, dolls that they are considering as additions to their collection, or dolls which they just might be curious about.

• **Our second objective** has been to provide retail prices of the dolls discussed as a guide for the prospective buyer and seller.

The dolls presented in this book are listed alphabetically by the maker, the material, the type of doll, or sometimes the name or trade name of the individual doll. An extensive index has been provided at the back of the book for the reader's convenience in locating a specific doll. Of course, in a volume of this size, it would be impossible to include every doll ever

German bisque head Simon & Halbig #1249 *Santa* doll on jointed composition body, 23½in (60cm) tall; a "dolly-face" with a distinct personality. *H&J Foulke, Inc.*

made and even all sizes of those discussed, but we have tried to include those which are either available, desirable, interesting, or popular, and even some which are very rare. For each doll we have provided historical information, a description of the doll, a copy of the mark or label, the retail selling price of the doll, and, in most cases, a photograph. For some doll manufacturers we have provided a list of trademarks and trade names, but this is merely for convenience and is not exhaustive for each maker. The historical information given for some of the dolls would have been much more difficult to compile were it not for the original research already published by Dorothy, Elizabeth and

Evelyn Coleman, Johana G. Anderton and Jürgen and Marianne Cieslik.

The data on the retail prices was gathered from July 1985 to February 1986 from antique shops and shows, auctions, doll shops and shows, advertisements in collectors' periodicals, lists from doll dealers and purchases and sales reported by both collectors and dealers. For price information on some of the rarer dolls, we had to dip back an additional few months. The information was sorted, indexed, cataloged and finally computed into the range of prices shown in this book. Hence, the prices used here are not merely our own valuations and judgments, although they must necessarily enter in, they are the results of our research as to the actual retail prices at which these dolls were either sold or offered for sale.

In setting down a price, we use a range to allow for the variables discussed later which must affect the price of any doll. The range used in this edition is wider than that allowed in previous editions because of the greater fluctuation in the current doll market. Collectors are becoming more sophisticated in their purchases by giving higher consideration to originality, quality and condition. Fine examples of a doll can bring a premium of up to 50 percent more than ordinary versions of the same doll. This is especially true of Schoenhuts, Lencis, *Shirley Temples* and American composition babies. Faded and dusty played-with models are waiting to be sold, while collectors eagerly vie for excellent examples. Fine quality bisque dolls which are all original or with period clothes are bringing much higher prices than the same models with poor bisque and new clothing.

This trend is also noticeable in the early papier-mâché and wooden dolls where period clothing and condition are very important and command a premium.

All prices given for antique dolls are for those of good quality and condition, but showing normal wear, and appropriately dressed in new or old clothing, unless other specifications are given in the description accompanying that particular doll. Bisque and china heads should not be cracked, broken or repaired. Bodies may have repairs, but should be old. It is becoming increasingly difficult to find dolls with lovely old wigs, clothing and shoes. Prices of these items purchased individually have escalated within the last few years. Nice old wigs, dresses or shoes can easily cost $50 each; hence, a doll with completely old outfittings will generally be higher than quoted prices. An especially outstanding doll in absolutely mint condition, never played with, dressed in original clothing, perhaps even in the original box, would command a much higher price than those listed in this book.

Prices given for modern dolls are for those in overall very good to excellent condition with original hair and clothing except as noted. Composition may be slightly crazed, but should be colorful. Hard plastic and vinyl must be perfect. Again, a never-played-with doll in original box with tagged clothing would bring a higher price than those quoted.

Certain dolls are becoming increasingly difficult to find and are seldom offered at a show or advertised. If we could not find a sufficient number of these rare dolls offered to be sure of giving a reliable range, we reported the information which we could find and marked those prices "**." In a very few instances, we could find none of a certain doll offered, so we resorted to estimates from reliable established dealers and collectors. These, too, are noted individually with "**."

The users of this book must keep in mind that no price guide is the final word — it cannot provide the absolute answer of what to pay. It should be used only as an aid in purchasing a doll. The final decision must be yours, for only you are on the scene actually examining the specific doll in question. No book can take the place of actual field experience. Doll popularity can cycle, and prices can fluctuate. Even though there are national periodicals and shows, price variations can still occur regionally. Before you buy, do a lot of looking. Ask questions. You will find that most dealers and collectors are glad to talk about their dolls and pleased to share their information with you.

It is interesting to note areas of price change in this edition from previous ones. American cloth dolls continue to rise in price with the Izannah Walker doll still leading with record prices. The early primitive-type American cloth dolls are very sought after, including *Columbian* dolls and *Philadelphia Babies*, early *Babyland Rag* dolls and *Alabama Babies*. Even later dolls, such as the Rollinson doll and those by Madame Alexander are creating a lot of collecting interest. In the foreign cloth market, Lenci dolls have cooled off somewhat but Norah Wellings dolls are very popular. Käthe Kruse dolls continue to be very desirable.

China and parian dolls with unusual hairdos have risen quite a lot;

German papier-mâché head on French pink kid body, referred to by collectors as French papier-mâché as the doll was assembled in France, 24in (61cm) tall. *Private Collection.*

some record prices for these types of dolls were made in 1985 as several "old" doll collections were disbursed. The wood Queen Anne-type doll has also come into her own with quite a few fine examples selling for around $20,000. French fashion ladies are finally coming into their own, as collectors realize that they can buy a lovely old French lady doll for much less than a French bébé.

In the German bisque category, large dolls are still very popular although they have not risen significantly in price. Nice examples of medium and small sized "dolly-faces" are still moving slowly and sometimes can be found for less than "book price." Those with lovely old clothing or original clothing, however, are bringing more than "book price" as noted above. Collectors are paying more for a dolly with an unusual face, but not necessarily for an unusual mark if the face is ordinary. Collectors still do not favor shoulder head dolls on kid bodies. This is particularly true as far as closed mouth dolls are concerned, when the same face will bring much

6

more if it is on a jointed composition body than it will on a kid body. Generally, the prices for closed-mouth shoulder head dolls have slipped making this market more favorable for collectors.

One unfortunate trend is the deep decline in the market for Madame Alexander dolls. This is particularly true of the new dolls which are again appearing on toy store shelves for the first time in about six years. The old cloth and composition dolls, as well as the hard plastic models continue to be popular, but the vinyl models are loosing ground. When buying these, be sure to look around before purchasing because many examples can be found below "book price."

With antique doll prices as high as they are, many collectors who favor old dolls are looking at types which have been less popular in the past, such as Patent Washables, tin heads, china heads and Sonneberg-type papier-mâché, as well as early American composition dolls of the "Can't Break 'Em" type.

Acknowledgements

A book of this type is the result of not only the author's own talents and energies, but also the encouragement, assistance and cooperation of friends, associates and family.

My thanks and appreciation, therefore, is given:

To my husband, Howard, for his lovely photographs, loving support and infinite patience.

To my daughter, Beth, for her willingness to perform many tedious clerical tasks.

To the many supportive friends we have made among doll collectors and dealers who urged us to prepare this new edition.

To those friends who allowed us to use photographs of their dolls or who provided special information for aspects of this edition: Jane Alton, Nancy Schwartz Blaisure, Miriam Blankman, Pat Brown, Elba Buehler, Pearl Church, Claire Dworkin, Grace Dyar, H&J Foulke, Inc., Carol Green, Ralph Griffith, Carolyn Guzzio, Betty Harms, Virginia Ann Heyerdahl, Gail Hiatt, Lesley Hurford, Joe Jackson, Kay and Wayne Jensen, Jackie Kaner, Vicki Lackenby, Catherine Magann, Elsa McCallum, Elizabeth McIntyre, Jean Mettee, Pearl D. Morley, Sheila Needle, Ruth Noden, Joanna Ott, Joel Pearson, Maureen Popp, Roberts Collection, Jimmy and Fay Rodolfos, Mary Lou Rubright, Beverly Schrader, Esther Schwartz, Rhoda Shoemaker, India Stoessel, Dolly Valk, Shila Vanderwalt, Jane Walker, Emma Wedmore, Ruth West, Catherine White, Richard Wright, Carole Stoessel Zvonar as well as several who wished their contributions to remain anonymous.

To the Colemans who allowed some of the marks to be reproduced from their book, *The Collector's Encyclopedia of Dolls.*

To Donna H. Felger, my editor, as well as the staff of Hobby House Press, Inc., who worked on this book.

All of these people helped to make this *7th Blue Book of Dolls and Values®* a reality.

Determining Doll Prices

Doll collecting has become an extremely popular hobby. In the last few years the number of doll collectors has grown by leaps and bounds. This large group of people entering the doll market is reflected within the field in quite a few different ways: there are more dealers in dolls now than ever before; there are more doll shows being organized; there are more doll books and magazines being written. However, the most significant effect this great expansion has is on the increased demand for old dolls. And, of course, since the number of old dolls available is static, the increased demand necessarily raises the prices of old dolls, as a larger number of collectors are vying for the same number of dolls. It is true that some dolls are still turning up from long-time storage in basements and attics, and these are certainly welcome additions to the doll market; yet this increase in numbers of dolls available is insignificant when compared to the numbers of new collectors entering the marketplace.

With the average doll representing a purchase of at least several hundred dollars, it follows that collectors must be as well-informed as possible about the dolls they are considering as additions to their collections. It follows also that if a collector is not particularly well-informed about the doll in question, he should not purchase it unless he has confidence in the person selling it to him. With today's prices, the assembling of a doll collection becomes rather costly and purchases must be made wisely. Actually, very few people buy dolls strictly as an investment, but

most collectors expect to at least break even when they eventually sell their dolls. Unfortunately, there is no guarantee that any particular doll will appreciate consistently year after year. However, the track record on old or antique dolls is fairly good. If you are thinking of future sale of your collection, be wary of buying expensive new or reproduction dolls. They have no track record and little resale value.

Although many collectors rationalize their purchases by saying that they are making a good investment, they are still actually buying the doll because they like it — it has appeal to them for some reason: perhaps as an object of artistic beauty, perhaps because it evokes some kind of sentiment, perhaps it fills some need that they feel, or perhaps it speaks to something inside them. It is this personal feeling toward the doll which makes it of value to the collector.

To what monetary extent a collector will go to obtain the yearned-for dolls, however, is dictated by his financial resources and his willingness to part with them. Unfortunately for most of us, there are enough collectors with the funds available who can afford to purchase the very rare and desirable dolls which cost thousands of dollars each. The rest of us will be content to collect the dolls we can comfortably afford, and even some we cannot comfortably afford, but go out on a limb to buy.

Because most of us have only limited funds for purchasing dolls, we must be sure that we are spending our dollars to the best advantage. There are many factors to consider when

Bisque character head by the French firm S.F.B.J. mold #226 on a jointed composition body, 23in (58cm) tall. *Kay and Wayne Jensen Collection.*

buying a doll, and this chapter will give some suggestions about what to look for and what to consider when purchasing a doll.

MARKS

Fortunately for collectors a good number of the antique bisque, some of the papier-mâché, cloth and other types of antique dolls are marked or labeled. This is particularly helpful to the beginning collector who is trying to sort out the doll spectrum. It also gives the buyer confidence: he or she knows exactly what has been purchased because of the mark or label which has given a trade name or identified the maker or the country of origin or even given a patent date or a style or mold number. With a little study a collector will soon discover that a doll marked "A. M. 390," even though she is in good condition and

well-dressed, is plentiful and should not cost as much as the harder-to-find S & H 1039 doll in the same size and condition. Going one step further, an S & H 1279 girl would be even higher in cost because she has a more unusual character face. Dolls by some makers are more desirable than those by another maker: a Kestner doll, always known for especially high quality, brings a higher price than a comparable doll made by Recknagle. There are even gradations of dolls by the same maker: a Greiner doll with a '58 label is more desirable than one with a '72 label. A *Bourgoin* Steiner is higher in price than a *Le Parisien* one.

Again, fortunately for collectors most of the composition and modern dolls are marked with the maker's name and sometimes also the trade name. A *Jane Withers* doll is higher in price and harder to find than one marked *Patsy*. With so many imitations prevalent in the American doll industry, it is important for a *Shirley Temple* doll to be marked as assurance that the high price being paid is for the genuine article and not for a lookalike doll. Many modern dolls have other methods of identification beside marks on the doll. Some, especially those by Madame Alexander, have tagged clothes, and many still retain their original wrist hang tags.

Of course, many dolls are unmarked, but after you have seen quite a few dolls, you begin to notice their individual characteristics, so that you can often determine what a doll possibly is. After a collector has some experience buying dolls, he or she begins to recognize an unusual face or an especially fine quality doll. Then there should be no hesitation about buying a doll marked only with a mold number or no mark at all. Many fine and unusual dolls do not carry a maker's name or any identifying number or symbol. The doll has to speak for itself, and price must be based upon the collector's frame of doll reference. That is, one must relate the face and quality to those of a known doll maker and make price judgments from that point.

QUALITY

But even the mark does not tell all about a doll. Two examples from exactly the same mold could look entirely different and carry vastly different prices because of the quality of the work done on the doll. To command top price, a bisque doll should have lovely bisque, decoration, eyes and hair. A collector studying many dolls will soon see that the quality varies from head to head, even with dolls made from the same mold by one firm. Before purchasing a doll, the collector should determine whether the example is the best to be found of that type. Even the molding of one head can be much sharper with more delineation of details such as dimples or locks of hair. This molding detail is especially important to notice when purchasing dolls with character faces or dolls with molded hair.

The quality of the bisque should be smooth and silky; dolls with bisque which is rough, pimply or peppered with tiny black specks would be second choices. However, collectors must also keep in mind that many heads were put out from the factories with small manufacturing defects as companies were in business for profit and were producing play items, not works of art. The tinting of the complexion should be subdued and even, not harsh and splotchy, although the

Bisque head bébé by the French firm Schmitt on a jointed composition body, 24in (61cm) tall. *Kay and Wayne Jensen Collection.*

amount of color acceptable is often a matter of personal preference, some collectors liking very pale white bisque and others preferring a little more pink.

Since doll heads are hand-painted, one of good quality should show artistic skill in the portrayal of the expression on the face and in details, such as the lips, eyebrows and eyelashes. On a doll with molded hair, individual brush marks to give the hair a more realistic look would be a desired detail.

If a doll has a wig, the hair should be appropriate if not old. Dynel or synthetic wigs are not appropriate for antique dolls; a human hair or good quality mohair wig should be used. Another important feature is the doll's eyes which should have a natural and lifelike appearance. If they are glass, they should have good natural color and threading in the irises. If they are painted, they should show highlights and shading.

If a doll does not meet all of these standards, it should be priced lower than one that does. Furthermore, an especially fine example with original or contemporary old clothes would bring a premium over an ordinary but nice model.

CONDITION

Another factor which is important when pricing a doll is the condition. A bisque doll with a crack on the face or extensive professional repair would sell for considerably less than a doll with only normal wear; a hairline or a small professional repair in an incon-

Bisque head character child by the German firm Simon & Halbig, mold #150, all original costume. *Joe Jackson & Joel Pearson.*

spicuous place would decrease the value somewhat, but not nearly so much. Sometimes a head will have a factory flaw which occurred in the making, such as a cooking crack, scratch, piece of kiln debris or a ridge not smoothed out. Since the factory was producing toys for a profit and not creating works of art, all heads with slight flaws were not discarded, especially if they were in an inconspicuous place or could be covered. If these factory defects are slight and not detracting, they have little or no affect on the value of the doll, and whether or not to purchase such a doll would be a matter of personal opinion.

It is to be expected that an old doll will show some wear: perhaps there is a rub on the nose or cheek, or maybe a chipped earring hole; a Schoenhut doll or a Käthe Kruse may have some scuffs; an old papier-mâché may have a few age cracks; a china head may show wear on the hair; an old composition body may have scuffed toes or missing fingers. These are to be expected and do not necessarily affect the value of the doll. However, a doll in exceptional condition will bring more than "book price."

Collectors are now paying particular attention to the condition of Lencis, Schoenhuts, and *Shirley Temples* as well as other cloth and composition dolls. A fine example will bring three times more than a played-with model. Certainly, an old doll in never-played-with condition with original hair and clothes, perhaps even in its original box is every collector's dream — and would carry the highest of all prices for that type of doll.

Unless an antique doll is rare or you particularly want it, do not pay top price for a doll which needs extensive work: restringing, setting eyes, repairing fingers, replacing body parts, new wig, dressing — all of these repairs add up to a considerable sum at the doll hospital, possibly making the total cost of the doll more than it is really worth.

Composition dolls in perfect condition are becoming harder to find. As their material is so susceptible to the atmosphere, their condition can deteriorate literally overnight. Even in excellent condition, a composition doll nearly always has some fine crazing or perhaps slight fading. It is very difficult to find a composition doll in mint condition and even harder to be sure that it will stay that way. However, if a composition doll is at top price, there should be little or no crazing, excellent coloring, original uncombed hair, and original clothes in excellent condition; the doll should be unplayed with. Pay less for a doll which does not have original clothes and hair or one which may be all original but shows extensive play wear. Pay even less for one which has heavy crazing and cracking or other damages.

The hard plastic and vinyl dolls must be in mint condition if they are at top price. The hair should be perfect in the original set; clothes should be completely original and unfaded. Skin tones should be natural with good cheek color; avoid dolls which have turned yellow.

BODY

A buyer should inspect not only the head of an antique doll, but also the body. In order to command a top price, an old doll should have the original or an appropriate old body in good condition. If a doll does not have the correct type of body, the buyer ends up not with a complete doll, but with two parts — head and body —

not worth as much as one whole doll. Fortunately for collectors makers such as H. Handwerck, Kestner, König & Wernicke, Jumeau, and J. Steiner, did mark their bodies, helping to remove some of the guesswork from their dolls. As dolls are becoming more difficult to find, more are turning up with "put together" bodies; therefore, it is necessary for the buyer to check all of the body parts to make sure that they are all appropriate to each other. A body which has mixed parts from several makers or types of bodies is not worth as much as one which has parts original to each other.

Bisque head bébé by the French firm Jules Steiner, "A" series, on a jointed composition body, 23in (58cm) tall. *Kay and Wayne Jensen Collection.*

German made china shoulder head on a cloth body with leather arms, 19in (48cm) tall. *Dolly Valk Collection.*

Minor damage or repair to an old body does not affect the value of an antique doll. An original body carefully repaired, recovered or even completely refinished, if necessary, is preferable to a new one. An antique head on a new body would be worth only the value of its parts, whatever the price of the head and the new body, not the full price of an antique doll. It is just a rule of thumb that an antique head is worth about 40-50 percent of the price of a complete doll. A very rare head could be worth up to 70 percent.

If there is a choice of body types for the same bisque head, a good quality ball-jointed composition body is more desirable than a crudely made five-piece body or a stick-type body with just pieces of turned wood for upper arms and legs. This is often the case for heads made by Armand Marseille and Gebrüder Heubach as well as other companies which made only heads and not bodies. Unfortunately, many of the small German character heads came on these crude bodies, and collectors just have to live with them. Only J.D. Kestner, A. Schoenau and a handful of others made both heads and bodies. Other doll factories bought their heads from porcelain factories, some of which were Armand Marseille, Ernst Heubach, Simon & Halbig, Kling & Co, Gebrüder Heubach, Bähr & Pröschild, and Alt, Beck & Gottschalck. Collectors prefer jointed composition bodies over kid ones for dolly-faced dolls, and pay more for the same face on a composition body.

Occasionally, the body adds value to the doll. For instance, in the case of bisque heads, a small doll with a completely jointed body, a French fashion-type with a wood-jointed body, a *Tête Jumeau* head on an adult body or a character baby head on a jointed toddler-type body would all be higher in price because of their special bodies.

As for the later modern dolls, a composition doll on the wrong body or on a body in poor condition which was cracked and peeling would have a greatly reduced value. The same is true of a vinyl doll with replaced parts, body stains or chewed-off fingers.

CLOTHING

A buyer should look at the clothing critically in considering the value of the doll. Because as the years go by fabrics deteriorate, it is becoming increasingly difficult to find dolls in old clothes. As a result, collectors are paying more than "book price" for an antique doll if it has old clothes and shoes. When the clothing has been replaced on an antique doll, it should be appropriately styled for the age of the doll, made in fabrics which would have been used when the doll was produced. Original clothes are, of course, highly desirable and even faded, somewhat worn, or carefully mended ones are preferable to new clothes. However, it is often difficult to determine whether or not the clothes are original or simply just old ones. Many antique dolls came undressed or clad only in a chemise and were dressed at home.

A doll with original clothes is certainly more valuable and higher in price than one with replaced clothing. Unfortunately, because these clothes are sometimes faded or worn or not of a style preferred by the buyer, they are removed and the doll is redressed while the original clothes are lost. This is certainly an unfortunate circumstance, and it is hoped that collectors who feel that they must redress their dolls will show respect for the original clothes and keep them in a labeled bag or box for giving to the next owner should the dolls ever be sold or passed down to another family member. Dolls are heirlooms and part of their charm is their clothing which is also part of social history. Present owners are only custodians for a short time in history.

For the first time, antique dolls are beginning to attract the attention of the buyers in the art market. As these people enter the doll field, they will be looking for the top-of-the-line dolls with original clothing for which they are willing to pay record prices. Doll collectors must realize that some of their dolls are truly works of art.

Composition doll *Barbara Joan* designed by Dewees Cochran for the American firm Effanbee, all original costume, 15in (38cm) tall. *Nancy Schwartz Blaisure Collection.*

They must be treated as such, and in the future many will be sold as such. The art market is currently beginning to buy early French dolls, rare German character dolls, pre-Greiners, Izannah Walkers, and other early types. These buyers want the dolls in pristine condition with original clothes.

To bring top price, a modern doll must have original clothes. It is usually fairly easy to determine whether or not the clothing is original and factory made. Many makers, such as Madame Alexander, placed tags in the doll's clothing. Replaced clothing greatly reduces the price of modern dolls. Also without the clothing it is often impossible to identify a modern doll as so many were made using the same face mold.

Composition doll by the American firm Madame Alexander, all original costume, 14in (36cm) tall. *H&J Foulke, Inc.*

TOTAL ORIGINALITY

Having already discussed body, wig, eyes and clothes, this would seem to be a good place to put in a word about the total originality of an antique doll. An antique doll which has all original parts and clothes is much more valuable than one which has replaced wig, body parts, eyes, pate, clothes, and so on. Collectors try to ascertain that the head and body and all other parts are not only appropriate, but have always been together. Of course, this is not always possible to determine when a doll has seen hard play for several generations or has passed through many hands before reaching the collector. However, sometimes if the original source of the doll is known, the collector can be reasonably sure by using a little knowledge as well as common sense. Totally original dolls nowadays are few and far between, but the determined searcher can still be rewarded.

SIZE

The size of the doll is always taken into account when determining a price. Usually the price and size are related for a certain type of doll — a smaller size is lower, a larger size is higher. The greatest variances of price to size occur at the extremes, either a very small or a very large doll. On the large side, bisque head dolls, especially over 30in (76cm) are in demand and have risen in price; the large 36in (91cm) vinyl *Shirley Temple* and the 30in (76cm) *Patsy Mae* are very difficult to find. On the tiny side, the small closed-mouth Jumeau, tiny German dolly-faced dolls on fully-jointed bodies, and the composition *Wee Patsy* and 11in (28cm) *Shirley Temple* are examples of small dolls which bring higher prices than dolls in their series which may be larger.

AGE

Another important point to consider in pricing a doll is its age. An early Queen Anne wood doll is more greatly valued than a late 19th century penny wooden one. However, curiously enough to beginners, the oldest dolls do not necessarily command the highest prices. A lovely old china head with exquisite decoration and very unusual hairdo would bring a good price, but not as much as a 20th century S.F.B.J. 252 pouty. Many desirable composition dolls of the 1930s and fairly recent but discontinued Alexander dolls are selling at prices higher than older bisque dolls of 1890 to 1920. So, in determining price, the age of the doll may or may not be significant, according to the specific type.

AVAILABILITY

The availability of a doll is based on how easy or difficult it is to find. Each year brings more new doll collectors than it brings newly-discovered desirable old dolls; hence the supply is diminished. As long as the demand for certain antique and collectible dolls is greater than the supply, prices will rise. This explains the great increase in prices of less common dolls, such as the K & R and other German characters, the early French and German closed-mouth dolls, googlies, composition personality dolls, and some Alexander dolls which were made for only a limited period of time. Dolls which are fairly common, primarily the German girl or child dolls and the china-head dolls which were made over a longer period of time, show a more gentle increase in price. The price of a doll is commensurate and directly related to its availability.

POPULARITY

Sometimes, it is the popularity of a certain doll which makes the price rise. There are fads in dolls just like in clothes, food and other aspects of life. Dolls which have recently risen in price because of their popularity are the American cloth dolls, Käthe Kruse dolls and large German bisque "dolly-faced" dolls. Some dolls are popular enough to tempt collectors to pay prices higher than the availability factor warrants. Although *Shirley Temples*, Jumeaus, *Bye-Los,* Heubach pouty characters, S & H 1249s, and most hard plastic and vinyl Alexanders are not rare, the high prices they bring are due to their popularity.

UNIQUENESS

Sometimes the uniqueness of a doll makes price determination very difficult. If a collector has never seen a doll exactly like it before, and it is not given in the price guide or even shown in any books, deciding what to pay can be a problem. In this case, the buyer has to use all of his available knowledge as a frame of reference in which to place the unknown doll. Perhaps a doll marked "A.M. 2000" or "S & H 1289" has been found, but is not listed in the price guide. The price is 25 percent higher than for the more commonly found numbers by that maker and the collector must decide on his own whether or not the doll is worth the price. (Of course, it would be!) Perhaps a dealer offers a black *Kamkins* for twice the price of a white one, but she is not listed in the price guide. In cases such as these, a collector must use his own judgment to determine what the doll is worth to him.

RETAIL PRICE

An important factor which helps determine what asking price goes on the doll in a dealer's stock is the price which the dealer, himself, had to pay for it. In buying a doll, a dealer has to consider all aspects of the doll discussed in this chapter in addition to whether or not there is a possibility of making a reasonable profit on the doll. A dealer, when buying stock, cannot pay the prices listed in the

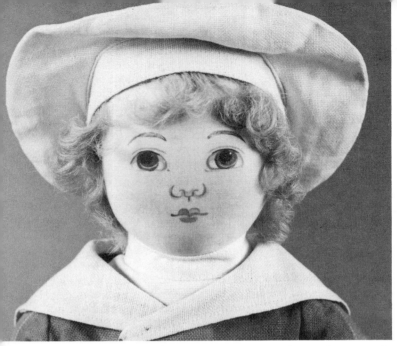

Cloth doll with hand-painted face by the American firm E. I. Horsman from their *Babyland Rag* line, all original costume, 17in (43cm) tall. *Private Collection.*

price guide; he must buy somewhat lower if he expects to make a profit. In order to obtain stock, a dealer looks to disbursement of estates, auctions, collectors and other dealers as possible doll sources — all of which are also available to collectors who can purchase from these sources at the same prices that dealers can. Contrary to what many collectors believe, dealers in antique dolls do not make enormous profits. Their margin of profit is not nearly so high as that of the proprietor of a shop which sells new items. This is primarily due to the availability factor already discussed. Old dolls cannot be ordered from a wholesale catalog. Most are coming from estates or collections, whose owners, understandably enough, want to get as

much as they can for their dolls. Expenses involved in exhibiting at shows include booth rent and travel costs which are quite high. To the price which he must pay for a doll, a dealer must figure in his costs and percentage of profit to come up with a dollar amount for the price tag.

The price for a doll which is listed in the price guide is the retail value of a doll fulfilling all of the criteria discussed if it is purchased from a dealer. Collectors, however, sometimes have other sources of dolls where the price could be somewhat lower. Sometimes collectors will sell to each other at less than "book price" or sometimes a dealer will undersell a doll if he wants to turn stock fast or if he obtains a type of doll which he does not usually carry. Then, too, collectors just might get a lucky price at an antique shop, garage sale, flea market or just about anywhere that there might be an old doll!

Cloth doll with hand-painted face by the
English firm Norah Wellings, all original
costume, 24in (61cm) tall. *Esther Schwartz
Collection.*

A.T.

Maker: Possibly by A. Thuillier, Paris, France
Date: 1875—1890
Material: Bisque socket head on wooden, kid or composition body
Size: Size 1 is usually 9in (23cm); size 14 is 29in (74cm)
Mark: "A.T." and size number (1-14 known) incised as shown or with size number between the A and T

AT·N° 8

Marked A. T. Child: Perfect bisque head, cork pate, good wig, paperweight eyes, pierced ears, closed mouth; body of wood, kid or composition in good condition; appropriate clothes.
24in (61cm)   **$20,000—21,000**

22in (56cm) A. T., composition body. *Mary Lou Rubright Collection.*

Alabama Indestructible Doll

Maker: Ella Smith Doll Co., Roanoke, AL., U.S.A.
Date: 1904—on
Material: All-cloth
Size: 11½—22½in (29—57cm) known
Mark: On torso or leg, sometimes both:

PAT. NOV. 9, 1912

NO. 2

ELLA SMITH DOLL CO.

or

Alabama Baby: All-cloth, painted with oils, tab-jointed shoulders and hips, painted hair and features, molded face, applied ears, painted stockings and shoes; appropriate clothes; all in good condition.

"MRS. S. S. SMITH
Manufacturer and Dealer to
The Alabama Indestructible Doll
Roanoke, Ala.
PATENTED Sept. 26, 1905"

17—19in (43—48cm)   **$800—850**

(also 1907 on some)

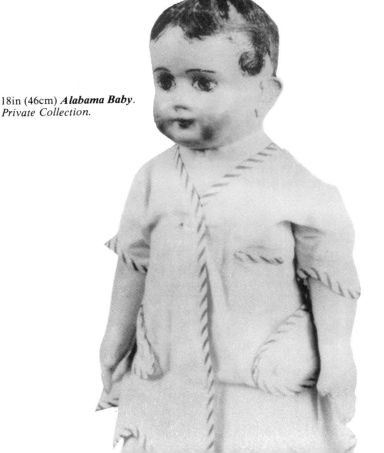

18in (46cm) *Alabama Baby.*
Private Collection.

Madame Alexander

Maker: Alexander Doll Co., New York, N.Y., U.S.A.
Date: 1923—on
Mark: Dolls themselves marked in various ways, usually "ALEXANDER".
Clothing has a white cloth label with blue lettering sewn into a seam
which says "MADAME ALEXANDER" and usually the name of the
specific doll.

CLOTH

Alice in Wonderland: Ca. 1930.
All-cloth with one-piece arms
and legs sewn on; yellow yarn
hair, flat face with hand-painted
features, large round eyes, O-
shaped mouth; later dolls had
molded mask face; original blue
and white dress with apron; all in
good condition.
16in (41cm)   **$400—450**

Cloth Character Dolls: Ca. 1933
through the 1930s. All-cloth with
one-piece arms and legs sewn on;
mohair wig, molded mask face
of felt or flocked fabric, painted
eyes to the side, original clothes
tagged with name of particular
doll. Produced characters from
Little Women, Charles Dickens,
Longfellow and other literary
works as well as storybook
characters.
16in (41cm) Good   **$325—375**
        Mint   **550—600**

Dionne Quintuplet: Brown hair
and eyes, gold-colored name pin
or necklace.
17in (43cm)   **$650—750**

Cloth Baby: Ca.   1936. All-cloth
with molded felt or flocked mask
face, soft-stuffed stockinette body
with flexible arms and legs; yarn
or hair wig, painted eyes with
long upper and lower eyelashes;
original tagged clothes; all in
good condition.
17in (43cm)   **$300—350**

18in (46cm) all-cloth baby tagged "American Baby," all original. *Courtesy of
Carolyn Guzzio.*

10in (25cm) *Little Shaver*, all original. *H&J Foulke, Inc.*

Susie Q and Bobby Q.: Ca. 1938. All-cloth with turning head, yellow or red yarn braids, mask face, large side-painted googly eyes, button nose, tiny closed mouth; striped stocking legs, white felt spats; original tagged clothes including hat, coat and cardboard suitcase; all in good condition. Came in sizes 12—13in (31—33cm) and 15—16in (38—41cm).
All sizes: **$500—600**

Little Shaver: 1942. Stuffed pink stocking body, curved arms, tiny waist; floss wig glued on; mask face with large painted eyes to the side, tiny mouth; original clothes; all in good condition.
MARK: Cloth dress tag:
"Little Shaver

Madame Alexander	7in (18cm)	**$225—250**
New York	10—12in (25—31cm)	**225—250**
All Rights Reserved."	16in (41cm)	**325—375**

Madame Alexander continued

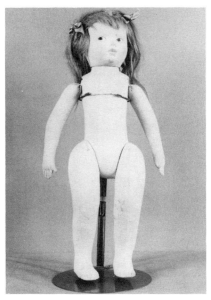

20in (51cm) Alexander girl with flocked composition head, cloth body. *Maurine Popp Collection.*

COMPOSITION

Marked Alexander Girl: Ca. 1920. Flocked composition head, painted eyes to side, closed mouth, original mohair wig; swivel neck on composition shoulder plate, hard cloth body with swivel jointed hips and tab sewn arms; original clothes; all in good condition.
20in (51cm) **$450—500**

Dionne Quintuplets: 1935. All-composition with swivel head, jointed hips and shoulders, toddler or bent-limb legs; wigs or molded hair, sleep or painted eyes; original clothing, all in excellent condition.
MARK: "ALEXANDER" sometimes "DIONNE"
Clothing label:
"GENUINE
DIONNE QUINTUPLET DOLLS
ALL RIGHTS RESERVED
MADAME ALEXANDER, N.Y."
or
"DIONNE QUINTUPLET
(her name)
EXCLUSIVE LICENSEE
MADAM [sic] ALEXANDER
DOLL CO."

7—8in (18—20cm) **$175—200**
10in (25cm) baby **300**
11in (28cm) toddler **350**
14in (36cm) toddler **450**
16in (41cm) baby **400**
Pins **$75 each**

See also color photo on page 250.

14in (36cm) Dionne Quintuplet *Emelie* toddler, all original. *H&J Foulke, Inc.*

Madame Alexander continued

Little Colonel: 1935. All-composition with swivel head, jointed hips and shoulders; mohair wig, sleep eyes, closed mouth, dimples; original clothes; all in excellent condition. *Betty* face.
MARK: On head:
"ALEXANDER"
or none
On dress tag:
"Madame Alexander"
13—14in (33—36cm) **$500—550**

Foreign and Storyland: Ca. 1935 to mid 1940s. All-composition with one-piece head and body on smaller ones and separate head on larger ones, jointed shoulders and hips; mohair wig, painted eyes; original tagged clothes; all in excellent condition. Made children to represent foreign lands as well as storybook characters.
MARK: On back:
"Mme. Alexander"
7—9in (18—23cm)
Foreign Countries **$150—200**
Storybook Characters **200—250**

See color photo *Scots* on page 253.

Dr. Dafoe: 1936. All-composition with swivel head, jointed hips and shoulders; gray wig, painted eyes, smiling face; original tagged doctor's outfit; all in excellent condition; doll unmarked.
14in (36cm) **$675—750**

Wendy-Ann: 1936. All-composition with swivel head, jointed at neck, shoulders, hips; human hair wig, sleep eyes, closed mouth; original clothes; all in excellent condition.
MARK:
"WENDY-ANN
MME ALEXANDER"
9in(23cm) painted eyes **$250**
14in (36cm) swivel waist **350**
21in (53cm) **450**

14in (36cm) *Wendy-Ann*, all original. *H&J Foulke, Inc.*

16in (41cm)
Little Genius, all
original. *H&J Foulke, Inc.*

Babies: 1936—on. Composition head, hands and legs, cloth bodies; molded hair or wigged, sleep eyes, open or closed mouth; original clothes; all in excellent condition.

MARK: On dolls:
"ALEXANDER"
On clothing: "Little Genius", "Baby McGuffey", "Pinky", "Precious", "Butch", "Bitsey"and so on.

11—12in (28—31cm) **$150—175**
16—18in (41—46cm) **225—250**
24in (61cm) **275—300**

Jane Withers: 1937. All-composition with swivel head, jointed shoulders and hips; dark mohair wig, sleep eyes, open smiling mouth; original clothes; all in excellent condition.

MARK: On dress:
"Jane Withers
All Rights Reserved
Madame Alexander, N.Y."

12—13in (31—33cm) **$650—700**
15—16in (38—41cm) **750—850**
21in (53cm) **900—1000**

Madame Alexander continued

14in (36cm) *Scarlet O'Hara* or *Southern Girl*. *H&J Foulke, Inc.*

Princess Elizabeth: 1937. All-composition, jointed at neck, shoulders and hips; mohair wig, sleep eyes, open mouth; original clothes; all in excellent condition.
MARK: On head:
"PRINCESS ELIZABETH ALEXANDER DOLL CO."
On dress tag:
"Princess Elizabeth"

13in (33cm) *Betty* face	**$275**
14—15in (36—38cm)	**300—325**
18—20in (46—51cm)	**350—400**
27in (69cm)	**600**

Scarlet O'Hara: 1937. All-composition, jointed at neck, shoulders and hips; original black wig, blue or green sleep eyes, closed mouth; original clothes; all in good condition.
MARK: On dress tag:
"Scarlet O'Hara
Madame Alexander
N.Y. U.S.A.
All Rights reserved"
Note: Sometimes the name is spelled "Scarlet" and other times it is spelled "Scarlett".

11in (28cm)	**$350—375**
14in (36cm)	**425—450**
18in (46cm)	**500**

Madame Alexander continued

Snow White: 1937. All-composition, jointed neck, shoulders and hips; black mohair wig, brown sleep eyes, very pale complexion, closed mouth; original clothes; all in excellent condition.
MARK: On head:
"PRINCESS ELIZABETH ALEXANDER DOLL CO."
On dress tag: "Snow White"
13in (33cm)   **$275**
16—18in (41—46cm)   **325—375**

Dopey: 1938. Composition character head, cloth body; original felt outfit; excellent condition.
13in (33cm)   **$225**

11in (28cm) closed mouth *McGuffey Ana*, all original. *H&J Foulke, Inc.*

McGuffey Ana: 1937. All-composition, jointed at shoulders, hips and neck; blonde human hair or mohair pigtails, sleep eyes, open mouth, original clothes; all in excellent condition.
MARK: On head:
"PRINCESS ELIZABETH ALEXANDER"
On dress tag: "McGuffey Ana"
9in(23cm) painted eyes   **$225**
11in (28cm) closed mouth   **275—300**
13—15in (33—38cm)   **325—350**
18—20in (46—51cm)   **400—450**
24in (61cm)   **550**

Flora McFlimsey: 1938. All-composition, jointed at neck, shoulders and hips; red human hair wig with bangs, sleep eyes, open mouth, freckles on nose; original clothes; all in excellent condition.
MARK: On head:
"PRINCESS ELIZABETH ALEXANDER DOLL CO."
On dress:
"Flora McFlimsey
of Madison Square
by Madame Alexander, N.Y."
13—15in (33—38cm)   **$500—600**

Kate Greenaway: 1938. All-composition, with swivel head, jointed shoulders and hips; blonde wig, sleep eyes with eyelashes, open mouth; original clothes; all in good condition.
MARK: On head:
"PRINCESS ELIZABETH ALEXANDER DOLL CO."
On dress tag: "Kate Greenaway"
16—18in (41—46cm)   **$425—475**

15in (38cm) *Flora McFlimsey*, all original. H&J Foulke, Inc.

28

Madame Alexander continued

18in (46cm) *Sonja Henie*, all original.
H&J Foulke, Inc.

Sonja Henie: 1939. All-composition, jointed at neck, shoulders and hips; human hair or mohair wig, sleep eyes, smiling open mouth with teeth; original clothes; all in excellent condition. 14in (35.6cm) can be found on the WENDY-ANN body with swivel waist.
MARK: On back of neck: "MADAME ALEXANDER-SONJA HENIE"
On dress: "Sonja Henie"

14in (36cm) **$300—350**
18in (46cm) **400—425**
21in (53cm) **450—500**

Madelaine: 1940. All-composition, jointed at neck, shoulders and hips; dark wig, sleep eyes, closed mouth; original clothes; all in excellent condition.
MARK: On head: "ALEXANDER"
On dress tag: "Madelaine" or "Madelaine Du Baine"

14in (36cm) **$350—375**
18in (46cm) **425—475**

Bride and Bridesmaids: 1940—on. All-composition, jointed at neck, shoulders and hips; mohair wig, sleep eyes, closed mouth; original clothes; all in good condition.
MARK: On head: "MME ALEXANDER"
On dress: "Madame Alexander"

14in (36cm) **$250**
18in (46cm) **325—350**
21in (53cm) **375—400**

Madame Alexander continued

14in (36cm) **Bride**, all original. *H&J Foulke, Inc.*

14in (36cm) Alexander **WAAC**, all original. *H&J Foulke, Inc.*

Jeannie Walker: 1941. Composition, jointed at neck, shoulders and hips, with walking mechanism; human hair or mohair wig, sleep eyes, closed mouth; original clothes; all in excellent condition.

MARK: On body:
"ALEXANDER/PAT. NO. 2171281"

On dress:
"Jeannie Walker —
Madame Alexander — N.Y., U.S.A.
All rights reserved"

13—14in (33—36cm) **$350—400**
18in (46cm) **500—550**

Armed Forces Dolls: 1942. All-composition, jointed at neck, shoulders and hips; "Wendy-Ann" face with lashed sleeping eyes, closed mouth, mohair wig; original tagged clothes; all in excellent condition. Dressed as **WAAC, WAVE, WAAF** and **Soldier.**
14in (36cm) **$350—400**

Madame Alexander continued

Carmen (Miranda): 1942. Composition, jointed at neck, shoulders and hips; black mohair wig, sleep eyes, closed mouth; original clothes including turban and gold-hoop earrings; all in excellent condition.
MARK: On head:
"MME. ALEXANDER"
On dress:
"Carmen
Madame Alexander, N.Y. U.S.A.
All Rights Reserved"
9in (23cm) **$200—225**
14—15in (36—38cm) **300—325**

Fairy Princess or Fairy Queen: 1942. Composition, jointed at neck, shoulders and hips; mohair wig, sleep eyes, closed mouth; original clothes including tiara and necklace; all in excellent condition.
MARK: On head:
"MME ALEXANDER"
On dress: "Fairy Princess" or "Fairy Queen"
14in (36cm) **$250—275**
18in (46cm) **350—400**

Special Girl: 1942. Composition head, shoulder plate, arms and legs, cloth torso; blonde braids. Doll unmarked; clothing tagged "Madame Alexander", excellent condition.
22in (56cm) **$350**

Margaret O'Brien: 1946. All-composition, jointed at neck, shoulders and hips; dark wig in braids, sleep eyes, closed mouth; original clothes; all in excellent condition.
MARK: On head:
"ALEXANDER"
On dress tag:
"Madame Alexander
'Margaret O'Brien' "
14in (36cm) **$450—500**
18in (46cm) **600—700**

Karen Ballerina: 1946. All-composition, jointed at neck, shoulders and hips; blonde wig with coiled braids and flowers, sleep eyes, closed mouth; original clothes; all in excellent condition.
MARK: On head:
"ALEXANDER"
On dress tag:
"Madame Alexander"
18in (46cm) **$425—475**

9in (23cm) **Carmen**, all original. *H&J Foulke, Inc.*

Madame Alexander continued

Alice in Wonderland: 1947. All-composition, jointed at neck, shoulders and hips; blonde wig, sleep eyes, closed mouth; original clothes; all in good condition.
MARK: On head: "ALEXANDER"
On dress tag: "Alice in Wonderland"
14in (36cm) **$275**
18in (46cm) **350—400**

HARD PLASTIC

Margaret Face: 1948—on. All-hard plastic, jointed at neck, shoulders and hips; lovely wig, sleep eyes, closed mouth; original clothes tagged with name of doll; all in excellent condition. All prices for the 14in (36cm) size except *Wendy-Ann* and *Prince Philip* which are 18in (46cm).

Nina Ballerina, 1949—1951	**$275—300**
Fairy Queen, 1947—1948	**250—275**
Babs, 1948—1949	**300—325**
Margaret Rose, 1948—1953?	**250—275**
Margaret O'Brien, 1948	**500**
Wendy-Ann, 1947—1948	**300—350**
Wendy Bride, 1950	**275—300**
Cinderella, 1950	**500**
Prince Charming, 1950	**500**
Cynthia (black), 1952—1953	**500**
Story Princess, 1954—1956	**325—350**
Wendy (from Peter Pan set), 1953	**450**
Prince Philip, Ca. 1950	**500—600**
Snow White, 1952	**400**

See also color photo on page 254.

18in (46cm) *Prince Philip*, all original. *H&J Foulke, Inc.*

18in (46cm) *Margot Ballerina*, all original. *H&J Foulke, Inc.*

Madame Alexander continued

Little Women: 1948—1956. All-hard plastic, jointed at neck, shoulders and hips; synthetic wig, sleep eyes, closed mouth; original clothes; all in good condition. Some models have jointed knees.

MARK: On head: "ALEXANDER". (used both "Maggie" and "Margaret" faces)

On clothes tag: "Meg", "Jo", "Beth", "Amy", and "Marme"

14—15in (36—38cm)

Floss hair, 1948-1950	**$300**	
Amy loop curls	**350—375**	
Dynel wig	**250—275**	
Little Men: Tommy, Nat and		
Stuffy, 1952	**750 up each**	

Godey Ladies: 1950. All-hard plastic, jointed at neck, shoulders and hips; lovely wigs, sleep eyes; original period costumes; all in excellent condition.
14in (36cm)   **$600 up**

Glamour Girls: 1953. All-hard plastic, jointed at neck, shoulders and hips, walkers; lovely human hair wigs; original period costumes; all in excellent condition.
18in (46cm)   **$600 up**

Maggie Face: 1948—1956. All-hard plastic, jointed at neck, shoulders and hips; good quality wig, sleep eyes, closed mouth; original clothes tagged with the name of the doll; all in excellent condition.

Maggie, 1948—1953:
  14in (36cm)   **$250**
  17in (43cm)   **275—300**
Polly Pigtails, 1949:
  14in (36cm)   **300—325**
Kathy, 1951:
  14in (36cm)   **350**
Alice in Wonderland, 1950—1951:
  14in (36cm)   **275—300**
  17in (43cm)   **325—350**
Annabelle, 1952:
  17in (43cm)   **325—350**
Peter Pan, 1953: **450**

17in (43cm) *Alice in Wonderland*, all original. *H&J Foulke, Inc.*

Madame Alexander continued

Winnie and Binnie: 1953—1955. All-hard plastic, walking body, later with jointed knees and vinyl arms; lovely wig, sleep eyes, closed mouth; original clothes; all in excellent condition.

15in (38cm)	**$225—250**
18in (46cm)	**250—275**
24in (61cm)	**325—350**

Cissy: 1955—1959. Head, torso and jointed legs of hard plastic, jointed vinyl arms; synthetic wig, sleep eyes, closed mouth, pierced ears; original clothes; all in excellent condition.
MARK: On head: "ALEXANDER"
On dress tag: "Cissy"

21in (53cm)	**$225 up***
Queen Elizabeth II	**400**

*Depending upon costume.

Lissy: 1956—1958. All-hard plastic, jointed at neck, shoulders, hips, elbows and knees; synthetic wig, sleep eyes, closed mouth; original clothes; all in excellent condition.
MARK: None on doll
On dress tag: "Lissy" or name of character

12in (31cm)	**$350**

Kelly: 1959. Same doll as **Lissy** but does not have jointed elbows and knees; original clothes; all in excellent condition.

12in (31cm)	**$350—400**
Little Women, 1957—1967	**250—300**
Katie and Tommy, 1962	**1000—1200**
McGuffey Ana, 1963	**1000—1200**
Laurie, 1967	**500**

21in (53cm) **Cissy**, all original. *H&J Foulke, Inc.*

12in (31cm) **Kelly**, all original. *H&J Foulke, Inc.*

Madame Alexander continued

Little Genius: 1956—1962. Hard plastic head with short curly wig, sleep eyes, drinks and wets; vinyl torso, arms and legs; original clothes; all in good condition.
8in (20cm) **$185**

Cissette: 1957—1963. All-hard plastic, jointed at neck, shoulders, hips and knees; synthetic wig, sleep eyes, closed mouth, pierced ears; original clothes; all in excellent condition.

MARK: None on doll
On dress tag: "Cissette"

10in (25cm)	**$185 up***
Margot, 1961	350—400
Sleeping Beauty, 1960s	350—400
Jacqueline, 1962	550—600
Gibson Girl, 1963	1000
Gold Rush, 1963	1250

*Depending upon costume.

Portrettes

Southern Belle, 1968	**$400**
Melinda (turquoise), 1968	**500**
Renoir (navy), 1968	**500**
Agatha, 1968	**500**
Godey, 1968—1970	**500**
Melinda (pink lace), 1969	**400**
Melanie (yellow lace), 1970	**400**
Jenny Lind, 1969—1970	**550**
Renoir (aqua), 1970	**500**
Scarlett, 1968—1973	**450**
Queen, 1972—1973	**400**
Southern Belle, 1969—1973	**400**

8in (20cm) *Little Genius*, all original. *H&J Foulke, Inc.*

Madame Alexander continued

Elise: 1957—1964. All-hard plastic with vinyl arms, completely jointed; lovely wig, sleep eyes, closed mouth; original clothes; all in excellent condition.
16½—17in (42—43cm) **$225 up***
*Depending upon costume

See color photo on page 254.

Sleeping Beauty: 1959. All-hard plastic with vinyl arms, completely jointed; blonde wig, sleep eyes, closed mouth; original clothes; all in excellent condition.
16½in (42cm) **$400—450**

10in (25cm) *Sleeping Beauty*, all original; made with straight legs and flat feet. *H&J Foulke, Inc.*

Shari Lewis: 1959. All-hard plastic with slim fashion body; auburn hair, brown eyes, closed mouth; original clothes; all in excellent condition.
14in (36cm) **$350**
21in (53cm) **450—475**

Maggie Mixup: 1960—1961. All-hard plastic, fully-jointed; red straight hair, green eyes, closed mouth, freckles; original clothes; all in excellent condition.
16½—17in (42—43cm) **$325—375**

16½in (42cm) *Sleeping Beauty*, all original. *Private Collection.*

Madame Alexander continued

Alexander-Kins: All-hard plastic, jointed at neck, shoulders and hips; synthetic wig, sleep eyes, closed mouth; original clothes; all in excellent condition.

7½—8in (19—20cm)
1953, straight leg non-walker
1954—1955, straight leg walker
1956—1964, bent-knee walker
1965—1972, bent knee
1973—current, straight leg
1978, face change
1981, white face

MARK: On back of torso: "ALEX"
After 1978:
"MADAME ALEXANDER"
On dress tag:
"Madame Alexander"
"Alexander-Kins" or specific name of doll

Wendy in dresses	$250 up
Wendy Ballerina	250 up
Quizkin	650 up
Little Lady	400
Special Outfits:	
Scarlett O'Hara, print dress	400
Enchanted Doll	350—375
Korea, Africa, Hawaii, Vietnam, Spanish Boy, Greek Boy, Morocco, Equador, Bolivia	400
Amish Boy and Girl, Cowboy, Cowgirl, English Guard, Pocahontas, Hiawatha	500
Bent-knee	
Internationals	75
Storybooks	85
Little Women	100
Maggie Mixup	425

Little Boy Blue: Ca. 1950. Vinyl head, molded and painted hair and eyes; stuffed "magic skin" body; original clothes; all in very good condition.
9—10in (23—25cm) **$150—175**

Sonja Henie: 1951. Vinyl character face with open smiling mouth and dimples, rooted hair; body of hard plastic; original clothes; all in excellent condition.
18in (46cm) **$500**

Madelaine: 1952, 1953, 1961. Vinyl character face with rooted hair; ball-jointed hard plastic body; original clothes; all in excellent condition.
18in (46cm) **$300—325**

8in (20cm) basic *Wendy*, all original.
H&J Foulke, Inc.

Madame Alexander continued

Kelly Face: 1958—on. Vinyl character face with rooted hair, vinyl arms, hard plastic torso and legs, jointed waist; original clothes; all in excellent condition.
MARK: On head:

Kelly, 1958—1959:
15in (38cm) **$225—250**
Pollyana, 1960—1961:
15in (38cm) **225—250**
Marybel, 1959—1965:
15in (38cm), in case **275**
Edith, 1958—1959:
15in (38cm) **225—250**

Jacqueline: 1961—1962. Vinyl and hard plastic; rooted dark hair, sleep eyes, closed mouth; original clothes; all in excellent condition.
21in (53cm) **$700—750**

Caroline: 1961—1962. Hard plastic and vinyl; rooted blonde hair, smiling character face; original clothes; in excellent condition.
15in (38cm) **$300—350**

Smarty: 1962—1963. Hard plastic and vinyl, smiling character face with rooted hair, knock-kneed and pigeon-toed; original clothes; in excellent condition.
12in (31cm) **$250**
Katie (black), 1965 **400**

Littlest Kitten: 1963—1964. All-vinyl with rooted hair, jointed at neck, shoulders and hips; original tagged clothes; all in excellent condition.
8in (20cm) **$185**

12in (31cm) **Rozy**, all original. *H&J Foulke, Inc.*

Janie: 1964—1966. Vinyl and hard plastic with rooted hair, impish face, pigeon-toed and knock-kneed; original tagged clothes; all in excellent condition.
12in (31cm) **$275**
Lucinda, 1969—1970 **350**
Rozy, 1969 **400**
Suzy, 1970 **400**

15in (38cm) **Edith, the Lonely Doll**, all original. *Private Collection.*

Madame Alexander continued

Patty: 1965. Vinyl head with laughing face, rooted blonde or brown shoulder length hair with top bow, sleeping eyes; hard plastic toddler body with jointed neck, shoulders and hips; original clothes; excellent condition.
18in (46cm) **$250**

Polly Face: All-vinyl with rooted hair, jointed at neck, shoulders and hips; original tagged clothes; all in excellent condition.
17in (43cm):

Polly, 1965	**$250—275**
Leslie (black),	
1965—1971	**300—350**

18in (46cm) Alexander ***Patty***, all original.
H&J Foulke, Inc.

17in (43cm) ***Leslie***, all original. *H&J Foulke, Inc.*

Madame Alexander continued

Sound of Music: Large set 1965-1970; small set 1971—1973. All dolls of hard plastic and vinyl with appropriate synthetic wigs and sleep eyes; original clothes; all in excellent condition.
MARK: Each doll tagged as to character.

Small set

8in (20cm) *Friedrich*	$225
8in (20cm) *Gretl*	200
8in (20cm) *Marta*	200
10in (25cm) *Brigitta*	225
12in (31cm) *Maria*	300
10in (25cm) *Louisa*	375
10in (25cm) *Liesl*	300

Large set*

11in (28cm) *Friedrich*	275
11in (28cm) *Gretl*	225
11in (28cm) *Marta*	225
14in (36cm) *Brigitta*	225
17in (43cm) *Maria*	350
14in (36cm) *Louisa*	300
14in (36cm) *Liesl*	250

*Allow considerably more for sailor outfits.

Nancy Drew Face: Introduced in 1967 and used widely to present a variety of dolls. Only discontinued dolls are listed here. Vinyl head and arms, hard plastic torso and legs; appropriate synthetic wig, sleep eyes; original clothes; all in excellent condition.
12in (31cm) only:

Nancy Drew, 1967	$200—225
Renoir Child, 1967	250
Blue Boy, 1972—1983	110
Lord Fauntleroy, 1981—1983	125

Peter Pan Set: 1969. Vinyl and hard plastic with appropriate wigs and sleep eyes; original clothes; all in excellent condition.

14in (36cm) **Peter Pan** ("Mary Ann" face)	$250—275
14in (36cm) **Wendy** ("Mary Ann" face)	250—275
12in (31cm) **Michael** ("Jamie" face)	350
11in (28cm) **Tinker Bell** ("Cissette")	350

17in (43cm) *Maria*, all original. *Private Collection.*

Madame Alexander continued

14in (36cm) *Julia Tyler*, all original. *H&J Foulke, Inc.*

First Ladies: Hard plastic and vinyl with rooted synthetic hair individually styled and sleep eyes; original tagged clothes; in mint condition. "Martha" and "Mary Ann" faces.

14in (36cm)

Series I: 1976—1978
Martha Washington, Abigail Adams, Martha Randolph, Dolley Madison, Elizabeth Monroe and *Louisa Adams.*

Set:	**$950**
Individual:	**150**
Martha Washington:	**250**

Series II: 1979—1981
Sarah Jackson, Angelica Van Buren, Jane Findlay, Julia Tyler, Sarah Polk and *Betty Taylor Bliss.*

Set:	**$650**
Individual:	**110**

Series III: 1982—1984
Jane Pierce, Abigail Fillmore, Mary Todd Lincoln, Martha Johnson Patterson, Harriet Lane and *Julia Grant.*

Set:	**$550**
Individual:	**90**
Mary Todd Lincoln:	**125**

Mary Ann Face: Introduced in 1965 and used widely to present a variety of dolls. Only discontinued dolls are listed here. Vinyl head and arms, hard plastic torso and legs; appropriate synthetic wig, sleep eyes; original clothes; all in excellent condition.

MARK: On head: "ALEXANDER
                                            19©65"

14in (35cm) only:

Madame, 1967—1975	$ 300	*Easter Girl*, 1968	1500	
Mary Ann, 1965	250	*Scarlett #1495*, 1968	450—500	
Orphant Annie, 1965—1966	300	*Jenny Lind & Cat*, 1969—1971	350	
Gidget, 1966	250	*Jenny Lind*, 1970	450	
Little Granny, 1966	200	*Grandma Jane*, 1970—1972	200	
Riley's Little Annie, 1967	300	*Disney Snow White*, to 1977	500	
Renoir Girl, 1967—1971	250	*Goldilocks*, 1978—1982	100	

Madame Alexander continued

14in (35cm) Disney *Snow White*, all original. *H&J Foulke, Inc.*

21in (53cm) *Madame Pompadour*, 1970, all original. *Private Collection.*

Portrait Dolls: Jacqueline face. 1965 to present. Vinyl and hard plastic; rooted hair with elaborate hair styles; lovely original clothes; all in excellent condition.
21in (53cm) **$350 up***
*Depending upon individual doll.

Coco: 1966. Vinyl and hard plastic, rooted blonde hair, jointed waist, right leg bent slightly at knee; original clothes; all in excellent condition. This face was also used for the 1966 portrait dolls.
21in (53cm) **$1800 up**

See color photo on page 252.

Elise: 1966 to present. Vinyl face, rooted hair; original tagged clothes; all in excellent condition.
17in (43cm)   **$150***
 Portrait Elise, 1973   **300**
 Marlo, 1967   **500**
 Maggie, 1972—1973   **300**
*Discontinued styles only.

All-Bisque Dolls
(French)

Maker: Various French firms
Date: Ca. 1880—on
Material: All-bisque
Size: Various small sizes, under 12in (31cm)
Mark: None, sometimes numbers

All-Bisque French Doll: Jointed at shoulders and hips, swivel neck, slender arms and legs; good wig, glass eyes, closed mouth; molded shoes or boots and stockings; appropriately dressed; all in good condition, with proper parts.

4½—5in (12—13cm) **$600—650**
5½—6in (14—15cm) **650—700**
With bare feet,
5—6in (13—15cm) **700—800**
With jointed elbows and knees,
5—6in (13—15cm) **2200****
With jointed elbows,
5—6in (13—15cm) **1600****

**Not enough price samples to compute a reliable range.

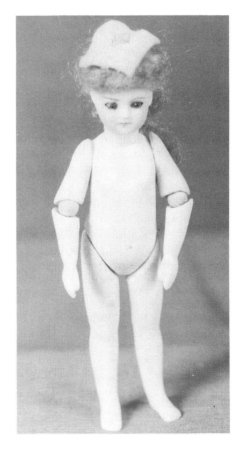

5½in (14cm) French all-bisque with ball-jointed elbows. *Jan Foulke Collection.*

All-Bisque Dolls
(German)

Maker: Various German firms
Date: Ca. 1880—on
Material: Bisque
Size: Various small sizes, most under 12in (31cm)
Mark: Some with "Germany" and/or numbers; some with paper labels on stomachs

All-Bisque French-type: Ca. 1880—on. Jointed usually by wire or pegging at shoulders and hips, slender arms and legs; good wig, glass eyes, closed mouth; molded shoes or boots and stockings; dressed or undressed; all in good condition, with proper parts.

3—4in (8—10cm)	**$150—175**
6—6½in (15—17cm)	**275—300**

Black or mulatto:

4in (10cm)	**225**

Swivel neck:

3½—4in (9—10cm)	**275—300**
6—6½in (15—17cm)	**375—400**

See color photo on page 66.

4¼in (11cm) French-type all-bisque. *H&J Foulke, Inc.*

All-Bisque with painted eyes: Ca. 1880—on. Jointed at shoulders and hips, stationary neck; molded and painted hair or mohair wig, painted eyes, closed mouth; molded and painted shoes and stockings; fine quality work; dressed or undressed; all in good condition, with proper parts.

1¼in (3cm)	**$50—60**
1½—2in (4—5cm)	**50—60**
4—5in (10—13cm)	**115—140**
6—7in (15—18cm)	**160—185**

Swivel neck:

2½in (9cm)	**125—150**
4—5in (10—13cm)	**160—185**

Fine early quality,

6in (15cm)	**250—300**

See color photo on page 66.

3½in (9cm) all-bisque with painted eyes. *H&J Foulke, Inc.*

All-Bisque Dolls (German) continued

All-Bisque with molded clothes: Ca. 1890—on. Many by Hertwig & Co. Jointed only at shoulders, molded and painted clothes or underwear; molded and painted hair, sometimes with molded hat, painted eyes, closed mouth; molded shoes and socks (if in underwear often barefoot); good quality work; all in good condition, with proper parts.

Children:

4—5in (10—13cm)	**$125—150**
6—7in (15—18cm)	**200—225**
Black, 5in (13cm)	**325—350**
Early-style characters, jester and clown, 4—5in (10—13cm)	**275—325**
Punch, Judy and other white bisque characters, 3—4in (8—10cm)	**85—95**

Hatted dolls, see page 169.

All-Bisque with glass eyes: Ca. 1890—on. Very good quality bisque, jointed at shoulders, stiff or jointed hips; good wig, glass eyes, closed mouth; molded and painted shoes and stockings; dressed or undressed; all in good condition, with proper parts.

3in (8cm)	**$175**
4—5in (10—13cm)	**160—185**
6—7in (15—18cm)	**235—285**
8in (20cm)	**375—400**
9in (23cm)	**550—600**
11in (28cm)	**800—850**
12in (31cm)	**900—950**

7in (18cm) all-bisque boy by Hertwig & Co. *H&J Foulke, Inc.*

4¾in (12cm) unmarked all-bisque with glass eyes, all original. *H&J Foulke, Inc.*

7½in (19cm) 237 all-bisque with glass eyes. *H&J Foulke, Inc.*

All-Bisque Dolls (German) continued

All-Bisque with swivel neck and glass eyes: Ca. 1890—on. Swivel neck, pegged shoulders and hips; good wig, glass eyes, closed mouth; molded and painted shoes and stockings; dressed or undressed; all in good condition, with proper parts.

4in (10cm)	**$ 250—275**
5—6in (13—15cm)	**325—350**
7in (18cm)	**400—425**
8in (20cm)	**550—600**
10in (25cm)	**850—900**

Early Kestner or S&H type:

6—7in (15—18cm)	**800—850**
9—10in (23—25cm)	**1250—1550**

With jointed knee:

10in (25cm)	**2000**

8in (20cm) all-bisque with swivel neck, all original. *Roberts Collection.*

All-Bisque Dolls (German) continued

All-Bisque with long black or blue stockings: Ca. 1890—on. Jointed at neck, shoulders and hips; good wig, glass sleep eyes, open mouth with teeth; molded brown shoes and molded long black or blue stockings; dressed or undressed; all in good condition, with proper parts. Sometimes marked "S & H 886" or "890."

5—6in (13—15cm) **$425—475**
7—7½in (18—19cm) **550—650**

All-Bisque Baby: 1900—on. Jointed at shoulders and hips with curved arms and legs; molded and painted hair, painted eyes; not dressed; all in good condition, with proper parts.

2½—3½in (6—9cm) **$ 60—75**
4—5in (10—13cm) **100—125**
Fine early quality,
4½in (12cm) **125—150**
Unjointed,
5in (13cm) **95**

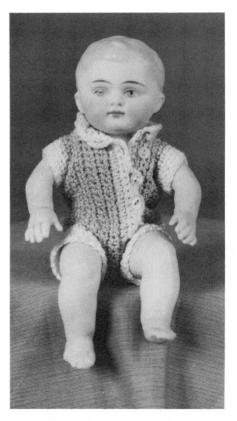

7in (18cm) 890 all-bisque with long black stockings. *H&J Foulke, Inc.*

7in (18cm) all-bisque baby, fine early quality. *H&J Foulke, Inc.*

Lady with Molded Underwear:

Ca. 1900. All-bisque lady of fine quality, beautifully molded features with painted eyes, closed mouth; original mohair wig; jointed arms only; molded white bloomers with blue trim, molded gold shoes and white stockings; dressed.

9—10in (23—25cm) **$650—750**

All-Bisque Character Baby: Ca.

1910. Jointed at shoulders and hips, curved arms and legs; molded hair, painted eyes, character face; undressed; all in good condition, with proper parts.

4in (10cm)	**$110—125**
6in (15cm)	**175—185**
With glass eyes,	
4—5in (10—13cm)	**225—250**
Swivel neck, glass eyes,	
6in (15cm)	**375—400**
Toddler, swivel neck, glass eyes,	
7½in (19cm)	**550**

10in (25cm) lady with molded underwear, wearing bridal gown. *Esther Schwartz Collection.*

8in (20cm) all-bisque toddler 177, all original. *H&J Foulke, Inc.*

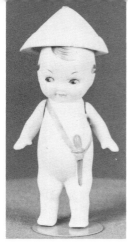

6in (15cm) boy with sword and removable hat. *H&J Foulke, Inc.*
See color photo page 67.

All-Bisque Character Dolls: 1913-on. Character faces with painted features and molded hair; usually jointed only at arms. Also see individual listings.

Chin Chin (Heubach),
  4in (10cm)   **$ 225—250**
Small pink bisque characters
  (many by Hertwig & Co.),
  up to 3in (8cm)   **30—40**
Orsini, MiMi or DiDi,
  5in (13cm)   **1000—1100**
Our Fairy (Hertel, Schwab & Co.),
  6in (15cm)   **850**
Boy with removable hat,
  6in (15cm)   **135**
*Our Fairy-type, painted eyes,
  molded hair*,
  4½in (12cm)   **110**
Kewpie,
  4—5in (10—13cm)   **100—125**
Molded clothes immobiles,
  4in (10cm)   **75—85**
Boy with clenched fists,
  5½in (14cm)   **125—150**
HEbee SHEbee,
  4½in (12cm)   **300**
Happifats boy or girl,
  4½in (12cm)   **225**

4½in (11cm) Heubach *Chin Chin. H&J Foulke, Inc.*

All-Bisque with glass eyes: Ca. 1915. Jointed at shoulders and hips; good wig, glass eyes, closed or open mouth; molded and painted black one-strap shoes and stockings; undressed or dressed; all in good condition, with proper parts.

4—5in (10—13cm)	**$125—150**
7in (18cm) m)	**225—250**
8in (20cm) m)	**275—300**
11in (28cm) ι)	**550**

See color photo page 66.

8in (20cm) all-bisque with glass eyes. *H&J Foulke, Inc.*

All-Bisque Dolls (German) continued

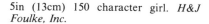
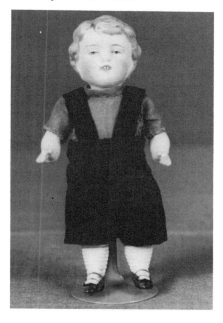

5in (13cm) 150 character girl. *H&J Foulke, Inc.*

5in (13cm) 160 character boy. *H&J Foulke, Inc.*

All-Bisque with character face: Ca. 1915. Jointed at shoulders and hips; good wig, smiling character face, closed or open mouth; molded and painted black one-strap shoes and stockings; dressed or undressed; all in good condition, with proper parts.

Painted eyes, molded hair, 5in (13cm)   **$140—165**
#150 open/closed mouth with two painted teeth,
  5½—6in (14—15cm) glass eyes   **200—250**
  5—5½in (13—14cm) painted eyes   **135—160**
Kestner type, swivel neck, glass eyes,
  4½—5½in (12—14cm)   **400—500**

All-Bisque with painted eyes: Ca. 1920. Jointed at shoulders and hips, stationary neck; mohair wig or molded hair, painted eyes, closed mouth; molded and painted one-strap shoes and white stockings; dressed or undressed; all in good condition, with proper parts.

4½—5in (12—13cm)   **$ 75—85**
6—7in (15—18cm)   **110—135**

See color photo page 66.

Flapper doll house family with molded hats, all original and in original box. *H&J Foulke, Inc.*

All-Bisque "Flapper:" Ca. 1920. Pink bisque with wire joints at shoulders and hips; molded bobbed hair and painted features; painted shoes and socks; original factory clothes; all in good condition, with proper parts.

3in (8cm) **$ 40—45**
Molded hats **125—150**

All-Bisque Nodder Characters: Ca. 1920. Many made by Hertwig & Co. Nodding heads, elastic strung, molded clothes; all in good condition. Marked Germany.

3—4in (8—10cm) **$45**
German Comic Characters, 3—4in (8—10cm) **65 up**

3½in (9cm) nodder pair. *H&J Foulke, Inc.*

2½in (6cm) immobile **Santa**. *H&J Foulke, Inc.*

All-Bisque Immobiles: Ca. 1920. All-bisque figures with molded clothes, molded hair and painted features. Decoration is not fired, so it wears and washes off very easily. Marked Germany.

Tinies: adults and children,
1½—2¼in (4—6cm) **$25—30**
Children,
3¼in (8cm) **30—35**
Bride & Groom,
4—5in (10—13cm) **50—60**
Santa,
3in (8cm) **75—85**

Bathing Beauty: 1920s. All-bisque lady, either nude or partially dressed in painted-on clothing; modeled in various sitting, lying or standing positions; painted features; molded hair; possibly with bathing cap or bald head with mohair wig; may be dressed in bits of lace.

Common type,
3—4in (8—10cm) **$ 55—75**
Fine quality,
5—6in (13—15cm) **300—400**
8—9in (20—23cm) **700—800**

All-Bisque "Flapper" (tinted bisque): Jointed at shoulders and hips; molded bobbed hair with loop for bow, painted features; long yellow stockings, one-strap shoes with heels; undressed or dressed; all in good condition, with proper parts.

5in (13cm) **$250—275**
7in (18cm) **325—375**

All-Bisque Baby: Pink bisque, jointed at shoulders and hips, curved arms and legs; painted hair, painted eyes; original factory clothes; all in good condition, with proper parts.

2½—3in (6—8cm) **$60—65**

Painted Bisque Children: Ca. 1930. Layer of flesh-colored paint over bisqué, not fired in; molded hair, painted features; jointed at shoulders and hips; molded and painted shoes and socks; dressed or undressed.

4in (10cm) boy or girl **$25—30**
7in (18cm) boy or girl **45—50**
4in (10cm) baby **30—35**

All-Bisque Dolls
(Made in Japan)

Maker: Various Japanese firms
Date: Ca. 1915—on
Material: Bisque
Size: Various small sizes
Mark: "Made in Japan" or "NIPPON"

Baby Doll with bent limbs: Jointed shoulders and hips; molded and painted hair and eyes; not dressed; all in good condition.

White, 4in (10cm)	$ 20
Black, 4in (10cm)	30
Betty Boop-type,	
4—5in (10—13cm)	15—20
6—7in (15—18cm)	25—30
Child,	
4—5in (10—13cm)	20—25
6—7in (15—18cm)	30—35
Comic Characters,	
3—4in (8—10cm)	25 up*
Stiff Characters,	
3—4in (8—10cm)	5—8
6—7in (15—18cm)	20—25
Cho-Cho San,	
4½in (12cm)	65-75
Nodders,	
4in (10cm)	25
Orientals,	
3—4in (8—10cm)	20—25
Queue San,	
4in (10cm)	65—75
Marked "Nippon" Characters,	
4—5in (10—13cm)	35—45
Three Bears boxed set,	100—125

*Depending upon rarity.

6in (15cm) girl with molded hairbow. *H&J Foulke, Inc.*

Box *Three Bears* set, 5in (13cm) *Papa*, 4¼in (11cm) *Mama*, 3in (8cm) *Baby. H&J Foulke, Inc.*

Alt, Beck & Gottschalck

Maker: Alt, Beck & Gottschalck, porcelain factory, Nauendorf near Ohrdruf, Thüringia, Germany. Made heads for many producers including Wagner & Zetzsche.

Date: 1854—on

Material: China and bisque heads for use on composition, kid or cloth bodies; all-bisque or all-china dolls.

Size: Up to 42in (107cm)

Mark: See below

China Shoulder Head: Ca. 1880. Black or blonde-haired china head; old cloth body with china limbs or kid body; dressed; all in good condition. Mold numbers, such as 1000, 1008, 1028, 1142.

MARK: *1008 X 9*

Also X or /o in place of X
14—16in (36—41cm) **$250—275**
21—23in (53—58cm) **350—400**

Bisque Shoulder Head: Ca. 1880. Molded hair, painted or glass eyes, closed mouth; cloth body with bisque lower limbs; dressed; all in good condition. Mold numbers, such as 1000, 1008, 1028, 1142, 1254.

MARK: See above
Painted eyes,
13—15in (33—38cm) **$225—275***
19—21in (48—53cm) **375—425***
Glass eyes,
16—18in (41—46cm) **500—600**

*Allow extra for unusual hairdo.

15in (38cm) 639 #6 bisque turned shoulder head child, all original. *Esther Schwartz Collection.*

Alt, Beck & Gottschalck continued

Bisque Shoulder Head: Ca. 1885—on. Turned shoulder head, mohair or human hair wig, plaster dome or bald head, glass sleeping or set eyes, closed mouth; kid body with gusseted joints and bisque lower arms, dressed; all in good condition. Mold numbers, such as 639, 698, 1123.

MARK: 6 3 9 ✕ 6   with DEP after 1888

14—16in (36—41cm)	**$625—675**
19—21in (48—53cm)	**800—850**
22—24in (56—61cm)	**900—1000**

With open mouth:

MARK: 6 9 8 ½ *Germany Dep No. 10*

16—18in (41—46cm)	**$350—400**
22—24in (56—61cm)	**450—500**
28—29in (71—74cm)	**750—850**

17in (43cm) 698½ bisque turned shoulder head child, open mouth, all original. *Dolly Valk Collection.*

Character: 1910—on. Perfect bisque head, good wig, sleep eyes, open mouth; some with open nostrils; composition body; all in good condition; suitable clothes.

MARK: See below (child doll)

#1352, 1361,

10—12in (25—31cm)	**$325—375***
16—18in (41—46cm)	**475—525***
22—23in (56—58cm)	**725—775***

#1357,

16—18in (41—46cm) toddler	**650—700****

#1322,

15—17in (38—43cm)	**450—500**

#1358 (See color photo page 180),

18—20in (46—51cm)	**2500****

*Allow extra for flirty eyes or toddler body.
**Not enough price samples to compute a reliable average.

18in (46cm) ABG 1357 toddler with molded hair *Lesley Hurford Collection.*

7in (18cm) 83/100 all-bisque girl. *H&J Foulke, Inc.*

All-Bisque Girl: 1911. Chubby body, loop strung shoulders and hips, inset glass eyes, open/closed mouth, painted eyelashes, full mohair or silky wig; molded white stockings, blue garters, black Mary Janes.

MARK: Also 100 and 150 in place of 225.

Bottom number is centimeter size.

5in (13cm)	**$150**
7in (18cm)	**225—250**
8in (20cm)	**275—300**

Child Doll: 1914—on. Mold number 1362. Perfect bisque head, good wig, sleep eyes, open mouth; ball-jointed body in good condition; appropriate clothes.

MARK:

17—19in (43—48cm)	**$375—425**
22—24in (56—61cm)	**450—550**
28in (71cm)	**750—800**
32—33in (81—84cm)	**1000—1100**
36in (91cm)	**1400—1500**

Louis Amberg & Son

Maker: Louis Amberg & Son, New York, N.Y., U.S.A.
Date: 1911—on (although Amberg had been in the doll business under other names since 1878)

Jointed Girl: 1912. Composition dolly face head, sleeping eyes, open mouth, human hair wig; jointed composition body; all in good condition with appropriate clothes.
MARK: Body:

"AMBERG
VICTORY
DOLL"

Head: "L.A. &S"
22—24in (56—61cm) **$250**

New Born Babe: 1914, reissued 1924. Designed by Jeno Juszko. Bisque head of an infant with painted hair, sleep eyes, closed mouth; soft cloth body with celluloid, rubber or composition hands; appropriate clothes; all in good condition.
MARK: "© L.A.&S. 1914, G 45520 Germany #4",
also
"Heads copyrighted by LOUIS AMBERG and Son",
also
"© L. Amberg & Son Germany 886/2"

Length:
10—11in (25—28cm) **$350—400**
12—13in (31—33cm) **450—500**

23in (58cm) Amberg *Victory Doll. Dr. Carole Stoessel Zvonar Collection.*

Louis Amberg & Son continued

Charlie Chaplin: 1915. Composition portrait head with molded and painted hair, painted eyes to the side, closed full mouth, molded mustache; straw-filled cloth body with composition hands; original clothes; all in good condition.

MARK: cloth label on sleeve:
"CHARLIE CHAPLIN DOLL
World's Greatest Comedian
Made exclusively by Louis Amberg
& Son, N.Y.
by Special Arrangement with
Essamay Film Co."
14in (36cm) **$350—450**

Composition Mibs: 1921. Composition shoulder head with wistful expression, molded and painted blonde or reddish hair, blue painted eyes, closed mouth; cloth body with composition arms and legs with painted shoes and socks; appropriate old clothes; all in good condition.

MARK: None on doll; paper label only:
"Amberg Dolls
Please Love Me
I'm Mibs"
16in (41cm) **$400—450**

Baby Peggy: 1923. Composition head, arms and legs, cloth body; molded brown bobbed hair, painted eyes, smiling closed mouth; appropriately dressed; all in good condition.
20in (51cm) **$450—550****

**Not enough price samples to compute a reliable range.

All-Bisque Mibs: 1921. Molded and painted features, jointed at shoulders and sometimes hips; painted shoes and socks; undressed; all in good condition.

MARK: Sometimes on back:
"©
LA&S 1921
Germany"
or paper label on chest:
'Please
Love Me
I'm
MIBS"
3in (8cm) **$225**
4¾in (12cm) **300—325**

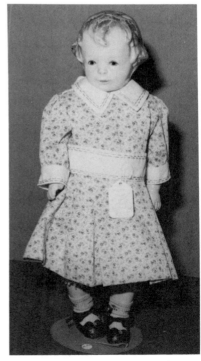

16in (41cm) ***Mibs***, redressed. *Catherine White.*

Louis Amberg & Son continued

Baby Peggy: 1924. Perfect bisque head with character face; brown bobbed mohair wig, brown sleep eyes, closed mouth; composition or kid body, fully-jointed; dressed or undressed; all in very good condition.

MARK:

> "19 © 24
> LA & S NY
> Germany
> —50—
> 982/2"

also:
973 (smiling socket head)
972 (pensive socket head)
983 (smiling shoulder head)
982 (pensive shoulder head)
18—20in (46—51cm) **$2400—2700**

All-Bisque Baby Peggy: 1924. Smiling face with painted brown bobbed hair or sometimes brown mohair wig, painted eyes, closed mouth; jointed arms and legs; brown strap shoes and socks; undressed; all in excellent condition. Unmarked, but had a paper label on stomach.
3in (8cm)   **$225**
5½in (14cm) **300—325**

20in (51cm) **Baby Peggy**. *Kay and Wayne Jensen Collection.*

Vanta Baby: 1927. A tie-in with Vanta baby garments. Composition or bisque head with molded and painted hair, sleep eyes, open mouth with two teeth (closed mouth and painted eyes in all-composition small dolls); muslin body jointed at hips and shoulders, curved composition arms and legs; suitably dressed; all in good condition.

MARK:
"VANTA BABY -- AMBERG"
20in (51cm):
Composition head   **$200—225**
Bisque head   **650—700**

14in (36cm) **Edwina.** *Catherine White.*

Sue or Edwina: 1928. All-composition with molded and painted hair, painted eyes; jointed neck, shoulders and hips, a large round ball joint at waist; dressed; all in very good condition.

MARK:
"AMBERG
PAT. PEND.
L.A. & S. © 1928"
14in (36cm)   **$300—325**

Tiny Tots Body Twists: 1928. All-composition with jointed shoulders and a large round ball joint at the waist; molded and painted hair in both boy and girl styles, painted eyes; painted shoes and socks; dressed; all in good condition.

MARK: tag on clothes:
"An Amberg Doll with
BODY TWIST
all its own
PAT. PEND. SER. NO.
32018"
8in (20cm)   **$165**

8in (20cm) **Body Twist** doll, all original with label. *Jean Mettee.*

American Character

Maker: American Character Doll Co., New York, N.Y., U.S.A.
Date: 1919—on
Mark: Various for each doll

Sally: 1927. Composition head, arms and legs, cloth torso; molded and painted hair, tin sleep eyes, closed mouth; original clothes; all in good condition.
MARK:

> "PETITE
> SALLY"

16—18in (41—46cm)	**$190—215**
All-composition, painted eyes	
12in (31cm)	**140—165**

See color photo on page 251.

12in (31cm) *Sally*, tagged and all original. *H&J Foulke, Inc.*

American Character continued

Marked Petite Girl Dolls: 1930s. Composition head, arms and legs, cloth torso or all-composition; mohair or human hair wig, sleep eyes, closed mouth; original clothes; all in good condition.

16—18in (41—46cm)   **$150—175**
24in (61cm)   **200—225**

Puggy: 1931. All-composition chubby body jointed at neck, shoulders and hips; molded and painted hair, painted eyes to the side, closed mouth, pug nose, frowning face; original clothes; all in good condition.
MARK: "A PETITE DOLL"
12in (31cm) **$400—450**

24in (61cm) ***Petite Girl***, all original. *H&J Foulke, Inc.*

12in (31cm) ***Puggy***, all original. *Kay and Wayne Jensen Collection.*

American Character continued

Tiny Tears: 1950. Hard plastic head with sleep eyes and tear ducts, molded hair, drinks, wets; rubber body; original clothes; all in good condition. (Later dolls had inset hair and vinyl body; still later dolls were all vinyl.) Various sizes.

MARK:
"Pat No. 2675644
Ame—Character"

Early model:
12in (31cm)	$ 95
21in (53cm)	150—165

Sweet Sue: 1953. Hard plastic and vinyl, some with walking mechanism, some fully-jointed including elbows, knees and ankles; original clothes; all in excellent condition.

MARKS: Various, including: "A.C.", "Amer. Char. Doll", "American Character" in a circle.
14in (36cm)	$100—125
18in (46cm)	150—165
24in (53cm)	185—210

Betsy McCall: 1957. All-hard plastic with vinyl arms, legs jointed at knees; rooted saran hair, round face with sleep eyes, plastic eyelashes; original clothes; all in good condition.

MARK:

8in (20cm) $85—95

Betsy McCall: 1960. All-vinyl with rooted hair, lashed sleep eyes, round face, turned-up mouth; slender arms and legs; original clothes; all in excellent condition.
14in (36cm)	$125—135
20in (51cm)	150—165
30—36in (76—91cm)	225—250

20in (51cm) *Betsy McCall*, all original.
H&J Foulke, Inc.

Arranbee

Maker: Arranbee Doll Co., New York, N.Y., U.S.A.
Date: 1922—1960
Mark: "ARRANBEE" or "R & B"

Baby: 1924. Perfect solid dome bisque head with molded and painted hair, sleep eyes, open mouth with teeth, dimples; cloth body with celluloid or composition hands, may have a molded celluloid bottle in hand; dressed; all in good condition.
Head circumference:
12—13in (31—33cm) **$350—425**

My Dream Baby: 1924. Perfect bisque head with solid dome and painted hair, sleep eyes, closed or open mouth; all-composition or cloth body with composition hands; dressed; all in good condition. Heads made by Armand Marseille, mold 341 or 351. Some heads incised "ARRANBEE."
Head circumference:
11—12in (28—31cm) **$300—350**
13—14in (33—36cm) **425—475**
15in (38cm) **600—650**

Bottletot: 1926—on. All-composition baby with bent arms and legs; molded and painted hair, sleep eyes, open mouth; celluloid hand with molded bottle. Doll is unmarked; bottle is marked "Arranbee/Pat Aug. 10, 26". Original clothes; all in good condition.
12—13in (31—33cm) **$125**

Storybook Dolls: 1930s. All-composition with swivel neck, jointed arms and legs; molded and painted hair, painted eyes; all original storybook costumes; all in good condition.
10in (25cm) **$150**

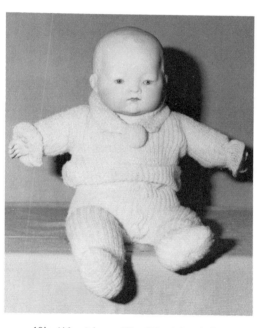

18in (46cm) long, 12in (31cm) head circumference baby incised "ARRANBEE."
Dr. Carole Stoessel Zvonar Collection.

Arranbee continued

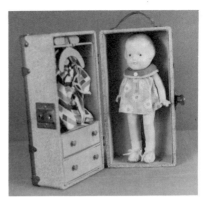

21in (53cm) **Debu' Teen**, all original except shoes. *H&J Foulke, Inc.*

12in (31cm) **Nancy**, all original with trunk and wardrobe. *H&J Foulke, Inc.*

Debu' Teen: 1938—on. All-composition or composition swivel shoulder head and limbs on cloth torso; mohair or human hair wig, sleep eyes, closed mouth, original clothes; all in good condition.
MARK: "R & B"

14in (36cm)	$150—165
18in (46cm)	185—200
21in (53cm)	225—250
Skating doll, 14in (36cm)	165—175

Nancy Lee: 1940s. All-composition with jointed neck, shoulders and hips; mohair or human hair wig, sleep eyes, closed mouth; original clothes; all in good condition. This face mold was also used for dolls which were given other names.
MARK: "R & B"

14in (36cm)	$150—165
21in (53cm)	200—225

See color photo on page 255.

Nancy: Up to 1940. All-composition or composition swivel shoulder head and limbs on cloth torso; molded hair or original mohair or human hair wig, sleep eyes and open mouth with teeth (smaller dolls have painted eyes and closed mouth); original or appropriate clothes; all in good condition.
MARK: "ARRANBEE" or "NANCY"
All composition

12in (31cm)	$140—165
16in (41cm)	190—215

See color photo on page 253.

Nanette: 1950s. All-hard plastic, jointed at neck, shoulders and hips; synthetic wig, sleep eyes, closed mouth; original clothes; all in excellent condition. This face mold was also used for dolls which were given other names.
MARK: "R & B"

17—18in (43—46cm)	$160—185

See color photo on page 251.

22in (56cm) Max Handwerck child. *Esther Schwartz. Collection. For further information see page 195.*

LEFT: 5in (13cm) French-type all-bisque girl, all original. *H&J Foulke, Inc. For further information see page 43 (under All-Bisque French-type).* **RIGHT:** 6in (15cm) early fine quality untinted all-bisque doll, bare feet, all original. *H&J Foulke, Inc. For further information see page 43 (under All-bisque with painted eyes.)*

LEFT: 6in (15cm) all-bisque girl with open mouth, all original. *H&J Foulke, Inc. For further information see page 48 (under All-bisque with glass eyes).* **RIGHT:** 6½in (15cm) all-bisque pouty boy, probably Limbach. *H&J Foulke, Inc. For further information see page 49 (under All-bisque with painted eyes).*

LEFT: 5½in (14cm) all-bisque character, jointed arms. *H&J Foulke, Inc. For further information see page 48 (under All-Bisque Character Dolls).* **RIGHT:** 5½in (14cm) A.M. child with closed mouth, all original. *H&J Foulke, Inc. For further information see page 280 (under Child Doll, closed mouth).*

LEFT: 6½in (17cm) incised "Italy" boy, all original. *H&J Foulke, Inc. For further information see page 222.* **RIGHT:** 5½in (14cm) untinted bisque ***Frozen Charlotte*** or bathing doll, fine early quality, all original. *H&J Foulke, Inc. For further information see page 162.*

68

13in (33cm) Unis 60 girl, original outfit. *Nancy Schwartz Blaisure Collection. For further information see page 366.*

23in (58cm) Kley & Hahn *Walkure* child. *Dolly Valk Collection. For further information see page 261.*

21in (53cm) Simon & Halbig 1039 flirty-eyed doll. *Dolly Valk Collection. For further information see page 350 (under Child doll with open mouth and composition body).*

19in (48cm) sleep-eyed Schoenhut girl. *Dolly Valk Collection. For further information see page 343.*

TOP LEFT: 16in (41cm) Schoenhut smiling character girl, all original. *Esther Schwartz Collection. For further information see page 340.* **ABOVE:** 16in (41cm) Gebrüder Heubach 7602 pouty toddler boy. *Private Collection. For further information see page 208 (under Heubach infants).*

ABOVE: 14in (36cm) unmarked German character baby, all original. *Esther Schwartz Collection. For further information see page 172.* **RIGHT:** 16in (41cm) Lenci child. *Nancy Schwartz Blaisure Collection. For further information see page 272.*

14in (36cm) Einco character toddler. *Esther Schwartz Collection. For further information see page 155.*

ABOVE: 18in (46cm) Munich Art doll. *Nancy Schwartz Blaisure Collection. For further information see page 294.* **BELOW:** 13in (33cm) Kling 189-1 child with glass eyes. *Nancy Schwartz Blaisure Collection. For further information see page 263 (under Bisque shoulder head).*

ABOVE: 18in (46cm) unmarked German fashion-type doll, all original. *Private Collection. For further information see page 170.* **BELOW:** 13in (33cm) F. G. Bébé. *Private Collection. For further information see page 165 (under Marked F. G. Bébé: Ca. 1887-1900).*

ABOVE LEFT: 21in (53cm) incised Jumeau Bébé. *Esther Schwartz Collection. For further information see page 228 (under Incised Jumeau Déposé Bébé).*

ABOVE RIGHT: 17in (43cm) ABG 698 1/2 child. *Dolly Valk Collection. For further information see page 54.*

LEFT: 21in (53cm) *Eden Bébé. Esther Schwartz Collection. For further information see page 142.*

Baby Bo Kaye

Maker: Composition heads by Cameo Doll Co.; bisque heads made in Germany, possibly by Alt, Beck, & Gottschalck; bodies by K & K Toy Co., New York, N.Y., U.S.A.

Date: 1925

Material: Bisque, composition or celluloid head with flange neck; composition or celluloid limbs, cloth body

Designer: J. L. Kallus

Mark: "Copr. by
J. L. Kallus
Germany
1394/30"

Baby Bo Kaye: Perfect bisque head marked as above, molded hair, glass eyes, open mouth with two lower teeth; body as above; dressed; all in good condition.
18—20in (46—51cm) **$2200—2500**
Celluloid or composition:
16in (41cm) **550—600****

**Not enough price samples to compute a reliable range

All-Bisque Baby Bo Kaye: Molded hair, glass sleep eyes, open mouth with two teeth; swivel neck, jointed shoulders and hips; molded shoes and socks; unmarked.
MARK:

6in (15cm) **$1250—1500****

**Not enough price samples to compute a reliable range.

20in (51cm) *Baby Bo Kaye. Ruth West Antiques.*

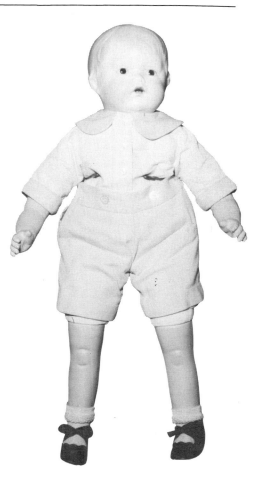

Babyland Rag

Maker: E. I. Horsman, New York, N.Y., U.S.A
Date: 1904—1920
Material: All-cloth
Size: 12—30in (31—76cm)
Mark: None

Babyland Rag: Cloth face with hand-painted features, later with printed features, sometimes mohair wig; cloth body jointed at shoulders and hips; original clothes; all in good condition.
Early hand-painted:

13—15in (33—38cm)	**$ 500—600**
30in (76cm)	**1400—1500**
Later:	
13—15in (33—38cm)	**350—400**
Topsy Turvy,	
13—15in (33—38cm)	**450—500**
Black,	
20in (51cm)	**850—900**

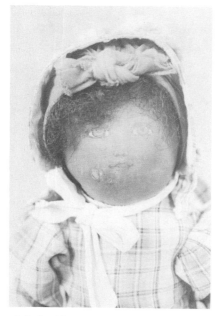 

Babyland Rag *Topsy*, early hand-painted face. *H&J Foulke, Inc.*

Babyland Rag ***Golf Boy***, life-like face of 1907. *H&J Foulke, Inc.*

Bähr & Pröschild

Maker: Bähr & Pröschild, porcelain factory, Ohrdruf, Thüringia, Germany. Made heads for Bruno Schmidt, Heinrich Stier, Kley & Hahn and others.

Date: 1871—on

Material: Bisque heads for use on composition or kid bodies, all-bisque dolls

Size: Various

Mark: See below

Marked Belton-type Child Doll:

Ca. 1880. Perfect bisque head, solid dome with flat top having 2 or 3 small holes, paperweight eyes, closed mouth with pierced ears; wood and composition jointed body with straight wrists; dressed; all in good condition. Mold numbers in 200 series.

MARK: 204

16—18in (41—46cm) **$1600—1800**

22—24in (56—61cm) **2200—2400**

Belton-type doll incised "204."
Joanna Ott Collection.

Bähr & Pröschild continued

Marked Child Doll: 1888—on. Perfect bisque shoulder or socket head, sleeping eyes, open mouth with 4 or 6 upper teeth, good human hair or mohair wig; gusseted kid or jointed composition body (many of French-type); dressed; all in good condition. Mold numbers in 200 and 300 series.

MARK: 224
　　　　 dep

#224, 239, 379 and other
socket heads:
　　14—16in (36—41cm) **$450—500**
　　22—24in (56—61cm) **650—750**
#246, 309 and other shoulder heads;
　　20—22in (51—56cm) **450—475**
　　28—29in (71—74cm) **750—850**

Black child: see page 82.

14in (36cm) 224 on French body. *H&J Foulke, Inc.*

28in (71cm) 246 shoulder head on kid body. *Emma Wedmore Collection.*

Bähr & Pröschild continued

Marked B. P. Character Child: Ca. 1910. Perfect bisque socket head, good wig, sleep or painted eyes, closed mouth; toddler or jointed composition body; dressed; all in good condition. Mold #2072, 536.

MARK:

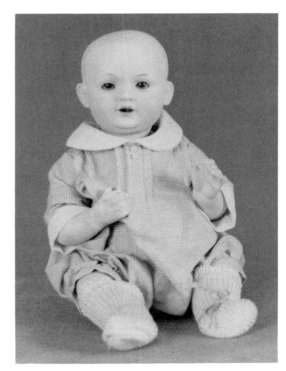

15—16in (36—38cm)   **$2500**
19—20in (48—51cm)   **3000—3500**

Marked B. P. Character Baby: Ca. 1910—on. Perfect bisque socket head, solid dome or good wig, sleep eyes, open mouth; composition bent-limb baby body; dressed; all in good condition. Mold #585, 604, 624, 678, 619, 641.

MARK: See above
10—12in (25—31cm)   **$325—375***
14—16in (36—41cm)   **425—475***
20—22in (51—56cm)   **675—725***
　　26in (66cm)   **950—1000***

*Allow extra for a toddler body.

10in (25cm) character baby, mold number not clear, possibly 526. *H&J Foulke, Inc.*

Belton-type
(So-called)

Maker: Various French and German firms, such as Bähr & Pröschild
Date: 1875—on
Material: Bisque socket head, ball-jointed wood and composition body with straight wrists
Mark: None, except sometimes numbers

Belton-type Child Doll: Perfect bisque socket head, solid but flat on top with two or three small holes, paperweight eyes, closed mouth, pierced ears; wood and composition ball-jointed body with straight wrists; dressed; all in good condition.

13—14in (33—36cm) **$ 900—1000**
17—19in (43—48cm) **1250—1550**
22—24in (56—61cm) **1750—1950**
Early, fine quality:
12—13in (31—33cm) **1150—1300**
16—18in (41—46cm) **1650—1850**
21—23in (53—58cm) **2250—2450**
Tiny with five-piece body,
8—9in (20—23cm) **550—600**

See also color photo on page 105.

15½in (39cm) Belton-type doll with skin wig. *Private Collection.*

C. M. Bergmann

Maker: C. M. Bergmann of Waltershausen, Thüringia, Germany; heads manufactured for this company by Armand Marseille, Simon & Halbig, Alt, Beck & Gottschalck and perhaps others.

Date: 1888—on

Material: Bisque head, composition ball-jointed body

Trademarks: Cinderella Baby (1897), Columbia (1904)

Mark: C.M. BERGMANN ⁴/₀   C. M. Bergmann Waltershausen Germany 1916 6½ a

---

Bergmann Child Doll: Ca. 1889-on. Marked bisque head, composition ball-jointed body, good wig, sleep or set eyes, open mouth; dressed; all in nice condition.

19—21in (48—53cm)	**$ 400—450**
24—25in (61—63cm)	**500—600**
28—30in (71—76cm)	**700—850**
34—35in (84—86cm)	**1150—1250**

Bergmann Character Baby: 1909-on. Marked bisque socket head, mohair wig, sleep eyes, open mouth; composition bent-limb baby body; dressed; all in good condition.

14—15in (36—38cm) **$425—450****

#612 (open/closed mouth)

14—16in (36—41cm) **700—800****

**Not enough price samples to compute a reliable range.

24in (61cm) C.M. Bergmann child. *H&J Foulke, Inc.*

Black Dolls

Black Bisque Doll: Ca. 1880—on. Various French and German manufacturers from their regular molds or specially designed ones with Negroid features. Perfect bisque socket head either painted dark or with dark coloring mixed in the slip, this runs from light brown to very dark; composition or sometimes kid body in a matching color, cloth bodies on some baby dolls; appropriate clothes; all in good condition.

Bru, Circle & Dot. For photo see page 87. 17in (43cm)	**$13,500**
Jules Steiner, open mouth, 14—15in (36—38cm)	**2500—2700**
Jumeau, open mouth, 13—15in (33—38cm)	**1750—1850**
HK 399 or ***458***,	
8—9in (20—23cm)	**300—350**
14—15in (36—38cm)	**450—550**
25in (63cm)	**1000**
S.F.B.J./Unis 60, 12—14in (31—36cm)	**300—350**
German, unmarked, good quality	
10—13in (25—33cm) jointed body	**350—400**
8—9in (20—23cm) five-piece body	**250—275**
5in (13cm) closed mouth	**225**
Simon & Halbig or ***Hardwerck child***	
9in (23cm)	**325—350**
18—20in (46—51cm)	**750—850**
S & H 1358, 15—16in (38—41cm)	**3500—3700**
AM 341 or ***351***, 12—13in (31—33cm) long	**400—475**
17—20in (43—51cm) long	**750—850**
Kestner 134, 12in (31cm)	**500—550**
AM 390, 14—16in (36—41cm)	**375—425**
Hanna, 8—10in (20—25cm)	**225—275**
K★R 100, 14in (36cm)	**1000**
HK 463 toddler or ***444***, 10in (25cm)	**550**
Heubach 7671, 14—16in (26—31cm)	**1800—2000**
7668, wide smiling mouth, 10in (25cm)	**1900**
S.F.B.J. 235, 12in (31cm) baby	**1600**
B.P. 277, 14in (36cm)	**650**
Paris Bébé, 14—15in (36—38cm)	**2200—2400**
JDK Hilda, 12in (31cm) toddler	**3500**
K★R 126 toddler, 8in (20cm)	**500—525**
K★R child, 13in (33cm)	**500—550**
34-18, fully-jointed 8in (20cm)	**350—400**
34-24, 14—15in (36—38cm)	**3200—3500**

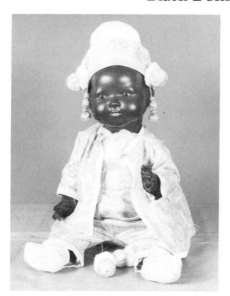

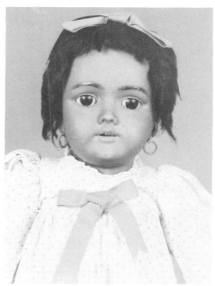

24in (61cm) A.M. 351 character baby. *Lackenby's Antiques.*

24in (61cm) H. Handwerck child, all original. *Anna May Case Collection.*

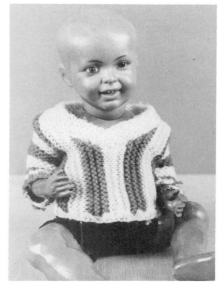

15in (38cm) S & H 1358 character child. *Private Collection.*

12in (31cm) S.F.B.J. 235 character baby. *Richard Wright Antiques.*

Black Dolls continued

13in (33cm) Ernst Heubach 458 **Abyssinian Baby**. *Lackenby's Antiques.*

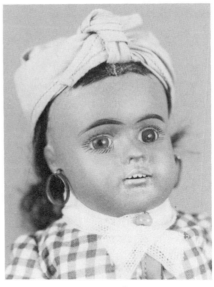

12in (31cm) Bähr & Pröschild 277 child. *India Stoessel Collection.*

14½in (37cm) Jules Steiner *Le Parisien* A-7 child. *Private Collection.*

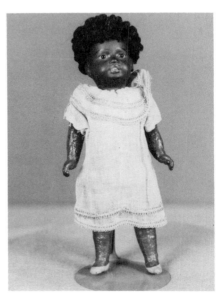

8in (20cm) 34-18 child, possibly by Gebrüder Kuhnlenz, all original. *India Stoessel Collection.*

Black Dolls continued

Papier-Mâché Black Doll: Ca.
1890. By various German manufacturers. Papier-mâché character face, arms and legs, cloth
body; glass eyes; original or
appropriate clothes; all in good
condition.
10—12in (25—31cm) **$250—275**

Tony Sarg's Mammy Doll: Composition character face with wide
smiling mouth, painted features;
large composition hands and
molded shoes; cloth body; original clothes, carrying a white
baby; all in good condition.
18in (46cm) **$450—500**

Cloth Black Doll: Ca. 1910.
American-made cloth doll with
black face, painted, printed or
embroidered features; jointed
arms and legs; original clothes;
all in good condition.

Mammy-type,	**$250 up***
Babyland Rag-type,	
13—15in (33—38cm)	**500—600**
Beecher-type,	**900**
1930s Mammy,	
14—16in (36—41cm)	**125—175***
WPA, molded cloth face,	
22in (56cm)	**450—500**

*Depending upon appeal.

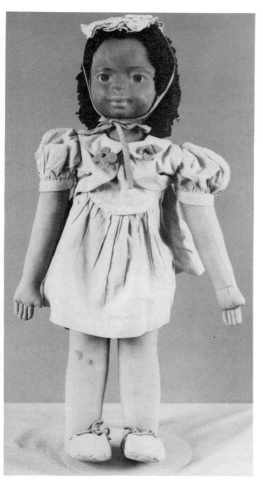

22in (56cm) W.P.A. Girl #7040, Milwaukee, Wisconsin. *Private Collection.*

15in (38cm) black Mammy. *Nancy
Schwartz Blaisure Collection.*

Black Dolls continued

Black Composition Doll: Ca. 1920 on. German made character doll, all-composition, jointed at neck, shoulders and hips; molded hair or wig, glass eyes (sometimes flirty); appropriate clothes; all in good condition.

14in (36cm)   **$500**
18—20in (46—51cm)   **625—700**

Black Composition Doll: Ca. 1930. American-made bent-limb baby or mama-type body, jointed at hips, shoulders and perhaps neck; molded hair, painted or sleep eyes; original or appropriate clothes; some have three yarn tufts of hair on either side and on top of the head; all in good condition.

Baby, 10—12in (25—31cm)   **$ 65—85**
Mama Doll, 20—22in (51—56cm)   **135—150**

Black German composition character baby. *Lackenby's Antiques.*

9in (23cm) *Topsy*, composition, all original. *H&J Foulke, Inc.*

Bonnie Babe

Maker: Bisque heads by Alt, Beck & Gottschalck of Nauendorf, Thüringia, Germany; Cloth bodies by George Borgfeldt & Co. of New York, N.Y., U.S.A. Dolls sold by K & K Toy Co. of New York, N.Y., U.S.A.
Date: 1926
Material: Bisque head with cloth body or all-bisque
Size: Various
Designer: Georgene Averill
Mark: 1005/3652 plus another number, *Copr. by Georgene Averill Germany*
such as 1402 or 1368

Marked Bonnie Babe: Perfect bisque head with molded hair, glass sleep eyes, open mouth with two lower teeth, smiling face; cloth body with composition extremities often of poor quality; all in good condition.
Head circumference:

12—13in (31—33cm)	**$750—800**
15in (38cm)	**950—1000**
Celluloid head, 16in (41cm) tall	**425—475**

All-Bisque Bonnie Babe: Molded hair, glass eyes, open mouth with two lower teeth; pink or blue molded slippers; jointed at neck, shoulders and hips; unmarked except for round paper label as shown.

4½in (12cm)	**$650—700**
7in (18cm)	**850—950**

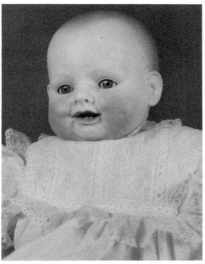

13in (33cm) h.c. *Bonnie Babe*, 1005/3652/4. *Esther Schwartz Collection.*

7in (18cm) *Bonnie Babe*, all original. *Private Collection.*

Boudoir Dolls

Maker: Various French, U.S. and Italian firms
Date: Early 1920s into the 1940s
Material: Heads of composition and other materials; bodies mostly cloth but also of composition and other substances
Size: Many 24—36in (61—91cm); some smaller
Mark: Mostly unmarked

Boudoir Doll: Head of composition, cloth or other material, painted features, composition or cloth stuffed body, unusually long extremities, usually high heeled shoes; original clothes elaborately designed and trimmed; all in good condition.

28—30in (71—76)	**$ 85—95***
1940s, 28in (71cm)	**50—60**

Jointed composition smoking doll:

25in (64cm)	**175—200**

*More depending upon costume and quality.

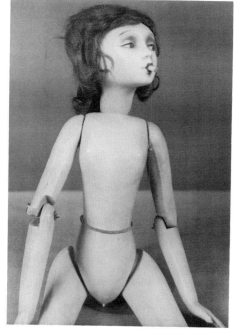

28in (71cm) boudoir doll with cloth face. *H&J Foulke, Inc.*

25in (64cm) jointed composition smoking doll. *Dolly Valk Collection.*

Bru

Maker: Bru Jne. & Cie, Paris, France
Date: 1866—1899
Material: Bisque swivel head on body as indicated below
Size: 10in (25cm) and up; size 0 is the smallest
Mark: On head, shoulder plate and body as shown below

Marked Brevete Bébé: Ca. 1870s.
Bisque swivel head on shoulder
plate, cork pate, skin wig,
paperweight eyes with shading
on upper lid, closed mouth with
white space between lips, full
cheeks, pierced ears; gusseted
kid body pulled high on shoulder
plate and straight cut with bisque
lower arms (no rivet joints);
dressed; all in good condition.
MARK: Size number only on
head.
Oval sticker on body:

> BÉBÉ
> Breveté SGDG
> PARIS

13—14in (33—36cm) **$5500—6500**
16—17in (41—43cm) **8000—8500**

*Marked Crescent or Circle Dot
Bébé:* Ca. late 1870s. Bisque
swivel head on a deep shoulder
plate with molded breasts, cork
pate, attractive wig, paperweight
eyes, closed mouth with slightly
parted lips, plump cheeks, pierced
ears; gusseted kid body with
bisque lower arms (no rivet
joints); dressed; all in good condition.
MARK: ∩ ◉
Sometimes with "BRU Jⁿᵉ"
16—17in (41—43cm) **$ 8500—9500**
16—17in (41—43cm)
Black **13,500**

See color photo on page 181.

17in (43cm) Circle Dot Bru
Jne Bébé. *Kay and Wayne
Jensen Collection.*

Bru continued

Marked Nursing Bru (Bébé Teteur): 1878—1898. Bisque head, shoulder plate and lower arms, kid body; upper arms and upper legs of metal covered with kid, lower legs of carved wood, or jointed composition body; attractive wig, lovely glass eyes, open mouth with hole for nipple, mechanism in head sucks up liquid, operates by turning key; nicely clothed; all in good condition.
13—15in (33—38cm)   **$4500—5500**

Marked Bru Jne Bébé: Ca. 1880s. Bisque swivel head on deep shoulder plate with molded breasts, cork pate, attractive wig, paperweight eyes, closed mouth, pierced ears; gusseted kid body with scalloped edge at shoulder plate, bisque lower arms with lovely hands, kid over wood upper arms, hinged elbow, wooden legs (sometimes on a jointed composition body); dressed; all in good condition.

MARK: "BRU J^ne"
Body Label:

> BÉBÉ BRU B TE   S.G.D.G.
> Tout Contrefacteur sera saisiet poursuivi
> conformement a la Loi

15—17in (38—43cm) **$ 7000—8000**
20—23in (51—58cm)   **9000—10,000**
25—26in (64—66cm)   **12,500—13,500**

13in (33cm) *Bébé Teture. Kay and Wayne Jensen Collection.*

25in (64cm) Bru Jne. *Kay and Wayne Jensen Collection.*

Bru continued

Marked Bru Jne R Bébé: Ca. Early 1890s. Bisque head on a jointed composition body; attractive wig, paperweight eyes, closed mouth, pierced ears; dressed all in good condition.

MARK: BRU Jᴺᴱ R
11

Body Stamp: "Bebe Bru" with size number

22in (56cm):

Very pretty	**$5500—6500**
Ugly	**4000—4500**

Marked Bru Bébé with open mouth: Ca. 1895. Bisque head on a jointed composition body with kiss-throwing and walking mechanism; attractive wig, sleep eyes, open mouth with upper teeth, pierced ears; dressed; all in good condition.

MARK: "BRU Jⁿᵉ"

22—24in (56—61cm):

Very pretty	**$4000—4500**
Ugly	**3000—3500**

22in (56cm) Bru Jne R. *Private Collection.*

Brückner Rag Doll

Maker: Albert Brückner, Jersey City, N.J., U.S.A.
Date: 1901—on
Material: All-cloth with stiffened mask face
Size: About 12—15in (31—38cm)
Mark: On right front shoulder: PAT'D. JULY 8ᵀᴴ 1901

Marked Brückner: Cloth head with printed features on stiffened mask face, cloth body flexible at shoulders and hips; appropriate clothes; all in good condition.

12in (31cm) White	**$150—165**
12in (31cm) Black	**175—190**
12in (31cm) *Topsy Turvy*	**300—350**

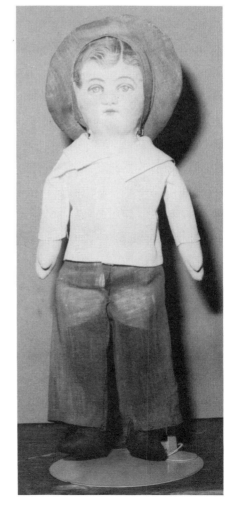

12in (31cm) Brückner rag doll, all original.
Pat Brown.

Bye-Lo Baby

Maker: Bisque heads — J. D. Kestner; Alt, Beck & Gottschalck; Kling & Co.;
Hertel Schwab & Co.; all of Thüringia, Germany.
Composition heads — Cameo Doll Co., New York, N.Y., U.S.A.
Celluloid heads — Karl Standfuss, Saxony, Germany
Wooden heads (unauthorized) — Schoenhut of Philadelphia, PA.,
U.S.A.
All-Bisque Baby — J. D. Kestner
Cloth Bodies and Assembly — K & K Toy Co., New York, N.Y.,
U.S.A.
Date: 1922—on
Size: Bisque head - seven sizes
9—20in (23—51cm)
All-bisque - up to 8in (20cm)
Designer: Grace Storey Putnam,
U.S.A.
Distributor: George Borgfeldt,
New York, N.Y., U.S.A.
Mark: See various marks below

Bisque Head Bye-Lo Baby: Ca.
1923. Perfect bisque head, cloth
body with curved legs (sometimes
with straight legs), composition
or celluloid hands; sleep eyes;
dressed. (May have purple "Bye-
Lo Baby" stamp on front of
body.) © 1923 *by*
MARK: Grace S. Putnam
MADE IN GERMANY

Large and small *Bye-Lo Babies* with
bisque heads. *Dolly Valk Collection.*

8—10in (20—25cm)	$ 350—400
12—13in (31—33cm)	475—550
14in (36cm)	650—675
15in (38cm)	800
17in (43cm)	1000—1100
18in (46cm)	1250—1500
Composition body, 13—14in (33—36cm) long	1200—1300
Smiling, very rare	4500**

**Not enough samples to compute
a reliable range.

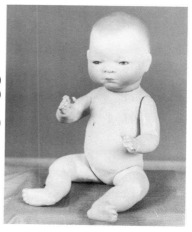

10in (25cm) h.c. *Bye-Lo* on composition
body. *Private Collection.*

13in (33cm) long *Bye-Lo* with composition head. *H&J Foulke, Inc.*

Composition Head Bye-Lo Baby: Ca. 1924. Cloth body with curved legs, composition hands; sleep eyes; nice clothes; all in excellent condition.
Head Circumference:
13in (33cm) **$350—375**

Marked All-Bisque Bye-Lo Baby:
1925—on.

MARK: Dark green paper label on front torso often missing; incised on back "20-12" (or other stock and size number)

"Copr. by
G.S. Putnam"

a. Solid head with molded hair and painted eyes, jointed shoulders and hips.

4in (10cm)	**$250—275**
5in (13cm)	**375**

With booties, 4in (10cm)

b. Solid head with swivel neck, glass eyes, jointed shoulders and hips.

5—6in (13—15cm) **550—650**

c. Head with wig, glass eyes, jointed shoulders and hips.

4—5in (10—13cm) **550—650**

d. Action *"Bye-Lo Baby,"* immobile in various positions, painted features.

3in (8cm) **325—375**

Schoenhut Bye-Lo Baby: Ca. 1925. Wooden head with sleep eyes; cloth body; nice clothes; all in good condition.

$1400—1600

Painted Bisque Head Bye-Lo Baby: Ca. late 1920s. Head has coating of flesh-colored paint, not baked in, washes and rubs off easily, sleep eyes; cloth body with composition hands; dressed; all in good condition.

Head circumference:

13in (33cm) **$325—375**

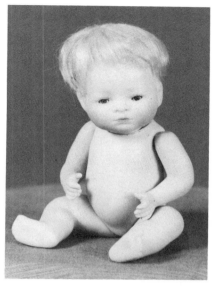

6in (15cm) *Bye-Lo* all-bisque with wig and glass eyes. *H&J Foulke, Inc.*

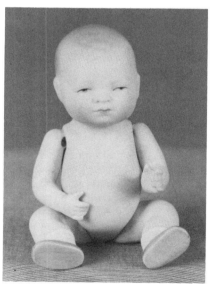

5in (13cm) *Bye-Lo* all-bisque with molded blue shoes. *H&J Foulke, Inc.*

Cameo Doll Company

Maker: Cameo Doll Company, New York, N.Y. U.S.A.; later Port Allegany, PA., U.S.A.
Date: 1922—on
Material: Wood-pulp composition and wood

(See also *Kewpie* and *Baby Bo Kaye*)

14in (36cm) black *Scootles*, all original. *H&J Foulke, Inc.*

Scootles: 1925. Designed by Rose O'Neill. All-composition, unmarked, jointed at neck, shoulders and hips; molded hair, blue or brown painted eyes looking to the side, closed smiling mouth; not dressed; all in good condition.

MARK: Wrist tag only

7—8in (18—20cm)	**$225—250**
12in (31cm)	**350—375**
16in (41cm)	**425—450**
Black, 14in (36cm)	**500—600**

All-Bisque Scootles: 1925. Jointed at shoulders only, very good detail modeling in torso and legs; molded yellow hair, blue eyes looking to the side; smiling face.

MARK: "Scootles" on red and gold chest label
"Scootles" and "Rose O'Neill" on feet

5—6in (13—15cm):

Germany	**$450—500**
Japan	**200—225**

Composition Little Annie Rooney: 1925. Designed by Jack Collins. All-composition, jointed at neck, shoulders and hips, legs as black stockings, feet with molded shoes; braided yarn wig, painted round eyes, watermelon mouth; original clothes; all in good condition.

MARK: None
16in (41cm) **$650****

**Not enough samples to compute a reliable range.

All-Bisque Little Annie Rooney: 1925. Designed by Jack Collins. Molded clothes, jointed arms: yellow yarn hair with braids, painted features with large round eyes and watermelon mouth; red felt hat; excellent condition.

MARK: Germany.
LITTLE ANNIE ROONEY
REG. U.S. PAT. OFF
CORP. BY JACK COLLINS

4in (10cm) **$200—225**

Margie: 1929. Designed by J. L. Kallus. Composition head with smiling face, molded hair, painted eyes, closed mouth with painted teeth; segmented wood body; undressed; all in good condition.

MARK:　Red triangle label on chest:

"MARGIE
Des. & Copyright
by Jos. Kallus"

10in (25cm)　**$225—250**

Pinkie: 1930. Designed by J. L. Kallus. Composition head, molded hair, painted eyes, closed mouth; segmented wood body; undressed; all in good condition.

MARK:　Triangle on chest:

"PINKIE
Des. & Copyright
by Jos. Kallus"

10in (25cm)　**$275—325**

10in (25cm)
Pinkie (left) and
Margie (right).
H&J Foulke, Inc.

Joy: 1932. Designed by J. L. Kallus. Composition head with smiling face, molded curls with loop for a bow, blue side-glancing eyes, watermelon mouth; wood segmented body; undressed; all in good condition.

MARK: Round label on chest:
"JOY
Des. & Copy't
J. L. Kallus"

10in (25cm)	**$275—325**
15in (38cm)	**375—425**

See color photo on page 250.

Betty Boop: 1932. Designed by J. L. Kallus. Composition swivel head, painted and molded black hair, large goo-goo eyes, tiny closed mouth; composition torso with molded-on and painted bathing suit, wood segmented arms and legs; all in good condition. (Also made in a rare form without the molded bathing suit and with composition legs; wearing a cotton print dress.)

MARK: Heart-shaped label on chest:
"BETTY—BOOP
Des. & Copyright
by Fleischer
Studios"

12in (31cm) **$450—500**

Giggles: 1946. Designed by Rose O'Neill. All-composition, unmarked, jointed at neck, shoulders and hips, molded hair with bun in back, large painted side-glancing eyes, closed mouth; original romper; all in good condition.

MARK: Paper wrist tag only

14in (36cm) **$425—475**

14in (36cm) *Giggles. Catherine White.*

Campbell Kid

Maker: E. I. Horsman Co., Inc., New York, N.Y., U.S.A.; American Character Doll Co., New York, N.Y., U.S.A.

Date: 1910—on

Material: Composition head and arms, cloth body and legs; or all-composition

Size: Usually 9—16in (23-41cm)

Designer: Grace G. Drayton

Campbell Kid: 1910-1914. By Horsman. Marked composition head with flange neck, molded and painted bobbed hair, painted round eyes to the side, watermelon mouth; original cloth body, composition arms, cloth legs and feet; original romper suit; all in fair condition.

MARK: On head:

E.I.H. © 1910

Cloth label on sleeve:

> The Campbell Kids
> Trademark by
> Joseph Campbell
> Mfg. by E. I. HORSMAN Co.

10—13in (25—33cm) **$150**

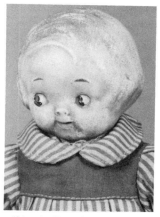

12in (31cm) *Campbell Kid*, 1910, all original. *H&J Foulke, Inc.*

Campbell Kid: 1923. By American Character, sometimes called "Dolly Dingle". All-composition with swivel head, jointed shoulders and hips; molded and painted hair, eyes to the side, watermelon mouth; original clothes; all in good condition.

MARK: On back:
"A PETITE DOLL"

12in (31cm) **$425—475**

Campbell Kid: 1948. By Horsman. Unmarked all-composition, molded painted hair, painted eyes to the side, watermelon mouth; painted white socks and black slippers; original clothes; all in good condition.

12in (31cm) **$250-275**

12in (31cm) *Campbell Kid*, 1948, all original. *Private Collection.*

Catterfelder Puppenfabrik

Maker: Catterfelder Puppenfabrik, Catterfeld, Thüringia, Germany
Heads by J. D. Kestner and other porcelain makers

Date: 1902—on
Material: Bisque head; composition body
Trademark: My Sunshine
Mark:

C. P.
2 0 8
45
N

C.P. Child Doll: Ca. 1902—on.
Perfect bisque head, good wig,
sleep eyes, open mouth with teeth;
composition jointed body; dressed; all in good condition.
17—19in (43—48cm) **$375—425**
#264 (made by Kestner)
22—24in (56—61cm) **650—750****

**Not enough price samples to
compute a reliable range.

C.P. Character Baby: Ca. 1910—
on. Perfect bisque character face
with wig or molded hair, painted
or glass eyes; jointed baby body;
dressed; all in good condition.
#263, 208, 209, 201, 262, 200
15—18in (38—46cm) **$450—500**
23—25in (59—64cm) **750—850**

C.P. Character Child: Ca. 1910-
on. Perfect bisque character
face with wig, painted eyes;
composition jointed body;
dressed; all in good condition.
Sometimes mold 207.
15in (38cm) **$2650****

**Not enough price samples to
compute a reliable range.

20in (51cm) 262 character baby made by
J.D. Kestner for Catterfelder Puppenfabrik. *Dr. Carole Stoessel Zvonar Collection.*

Celluloid Dolls

Makers: Germany:

Rheinische Gummi und Celluloid Fabrik Co. (Turtle symbol)
Buschow & Beck. *Minerva* trademark. (Helmet symbol)
E. Maar & Sohn. *Emasco* trademark. (3 M symbol)
Cellba. (Mermaid symbol)

Poland:

P.R. Zask. (ASK in triangle)

France:

Petitçolin. (Eagle symbol)
Société Nobel Francaise. (SNF in diamond)
Neumann & Marx. (Dragon symbol)

United States:

Parsons-Jackson Co., Cleveland, Ohio and other companies

Date: 1895—1940s

Material: All-celluloid or celluloid head with jointed kid, cloth or composition body.

Size: up to 25in (64cm)

Marks: Various as indicated above: sometimes also in combination with the marks of J. D. Kestner, Kämmer & Reinhardt, Bruno Schmidt, Käthe Kruse and König & Wernicke

---

Celluloid shoulder head Child doll: Ca. 1900—on. Molded hair or wig, painted or glass eyes, open or closed mouth; cloth or kid body, celluloid or composition arms; dressed; all in good condition.

Painted eyes:
14—15in (36—38cm) **$110—125**
Glass eyes:
14—16in (36—41cm) **150—175**
20—22in (51—56cm) **200—225**

13in (33cm) celluloid shoulder head. *H&J Foulke, Inc.*

Celluloid Dolls continued

All-Celluloid Child Doll: Ca. 1900—on. Jointed at neck, shoulders, and hips; molded hair or wig, painted eyes; dressed; all in good condition.

6—7in (13—15cm)	**$ 30—40**
9—10in (23—25cm)	**75—85**
13—14in (33—36cm)	**110—135**

Glass eyes:

12—13in (31—33cm)	**150—165**
15—16in (38—41cm)	**200—250**
18in (46cm)	**275—325**

Molded clothes:

8in (20cm)	**60—65**

8in (20cm) Dutch children with molded clothing. Turtle Mark. *Dolly Valk Collection.*

17in (43cm) all-celluloid boy with glass eyes. *H&J Foulke, Inc.*

Celluloid Dolls continued

Celluloid socket head Child Doll: Ca. 1910—on. Wig, glass eyes, sometimes flirty, open mouth with teeth; ball-jointed or bent-limb composition body; dressed; all in good condition.

15—18in (38—46cm)	$225—275
22—24in (56—61cm)	325—375

Characters:

K★R 701, 12—13in (31—33cm)	650—750
K★R 717, 24in (61cm) flirty	450—500
K★R 728, 12—13in (31—33cm) baby	300—325
K★R 700 baby, 14in (36cm)	450—500
K&W toddler, 14in (36cm)	300

See color photo on page 107.

All-Celluloid Baby: Ca. 1910—on. Bent-limb baby, molded hair, painted eyes, closed mouth; jointed arms and/or legs; no clothes; all in good condition.

8—10in (20—25cm)	$ 75—85
14—15in (36—38cm)	110—125
Glass eyes,	
10—11in (25—28cm)	125
14—15in (36—38)	150—175
Japanese, 20in (51cm)	150—200
Parsons-Jackson with Stork trademark, 12in (31cm)	125—150

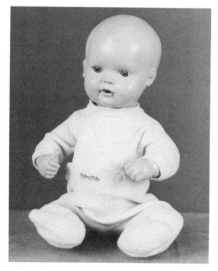

14in (36cm) all-celluloid baby with Turtle Mark. *H&J Foulke, Inc.*

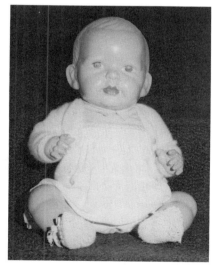

19in (48cm) all-celluloid baby "Made in Japan." *Lesley Hurford Collection.*

Century Doll Co.

Maker: Century Doll Co., New York, N.Y., U.S.A.; bisque heads by J.D. Kestner, Germany

Date: 1909—on

Material: Bisque head, cloth body, composition arms (and legs)

Mark: "Century Doll Co." Sometimes 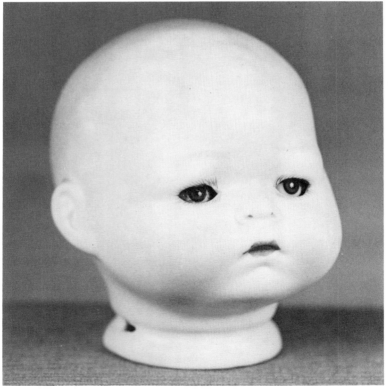(for Kestner). "Germany"

Marked Century Infant: Ca. 1925. Perfect bisque solid-dome head, molded and painted hair, sleep eyes, open/closed mouth; cloth body, composition hands or limbs; dressed; all in good condition.

14—15in (36—38cm) long **$550—650**

Mama doll shoulder head #281,
    21in (53cm)   **550—650****

**Not enough price samples to compute a reliable average.

8½in (22cm) head circumference *Century Baby. Emma Wedmore Collection.*

Chad Valley

Maker: Chad Valley Co. (formerly Johnson Bros., Ltd.), Birmingham, England
Date: 1923—on
Material: All-cloth
Mark: Cloth label usually on foot:

"HYGENIC TOYS
Made in England by
CHAD VALLEY CO. LTD."

Cardboard tag:

"The
'Mabel Lucie Attwell"
Doll
Regd & Patented   or
Sole Makers
Chad Valley
Co. Ltd."

"THE
CHAD VALLEY
HYGENIC
TEXTILE
TOYS
Made in England"

Chad Valley Doll: All-cloth, usually felt face and velvet body, jointed neck, shoulders and hips; mohair wig, glass or painted eyes; original clothes; all in excellent condition.

Characters, painted eyes,
  10in (25cm)   **$ 55—65**
  11—12in (26—28cm)   **65—85**
Children, painted eyes,
  13—14in (33—36cm)   **160—195**
  16—18in (41—46cm)   **300—400**
Children, glass eyes,
  16—18in (41—46cm)   **400—500**
Royal Children, glass eyes
  16—18in (41—46cm) **1000—1200**
Mabel Lucie Attwell, glass inset side-glandinc eyes, smiling watermelon mouth,
    14in (36cm)   **400—450**

Scots Girl, all original. *Jean Mettee.*

Martha Chase

Maker: Martha Jenks Chase, Pawtucket, R.I., U.S.A.

Date: 1893 to present

Material: Stockinette and cloth, painted in oils; some fully painted washable models; some designed for hospital training use.

Size: 9in (23cm) to life-size

Designer: Martha Jenks Chase

Mark: "Chase Stockinet Doll" stamp on left leg or under left arm, paper label on back (usually gone)

PAWTUCKET, R.I
MADE IN U.S.A.

Chase Doll: Pre-1930. Head and limbs of stockinette, treated and painted with oils, rough-stroked hair to provide texture, cloth bodies jointed at shoulders, hips, elbows and knees, later ones only at shoulders and hips; some bodies completely treated; not in perfect condition.

Baby,

12—13in (31—33cm)	$ 350—375
16—20in (41—51cm)	525—600
Child, molded bobbed hair, 15—17in (38—43cm)	750—850
Lady, 15in (38cm)	1200—1300
Black, 27in (69cm)	3600

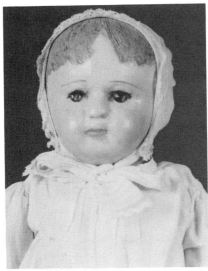

16in (41cm) Chase baby. *H&J Foulke, Inc.*

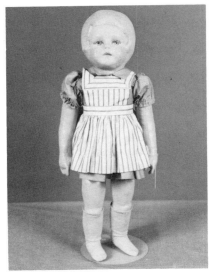

16in (41cm) Chase girl with side-parted hair. *Private Collection.*

14in (36cm) SFBJ 226 toddler. *Nancy Schwartz Blaisure Collection. For further information see page 331.*

20in (51cm) Belton-type child. *Nancy Schwartz Blaisure Collection. For further information see page 78.*

Peter Scherf 1899 (right) and A.M. 4008 (middle) and 3500 dolls. *Dolly Valk Collection. For further information see pages 333 and 280.*

ABOVE: 15½in (39cm) Belton-type doll with skin wig. *Private Collection. For further information see page 78.* **BELOW:** 17in (43cm) German fashion-type doll with swivel neck and open mouth. *Esther Schwartz Collection. For further information see page 171 (under Child Doll: 1880s–1900).*

ABOVE: 20in (51cm) wax-over-composition socket head on shoulder plate, all original. *Dolly Valk Collection. For further information see page 377.* **BELOW:** 17in (43cm) Lenci child. *Nancy Schwartz Blaisure Collection. For further information see page 272.*

RIGHT: 10½in (23cm) and 12in (31cm) A.M. *Florodora* dolls, all original. *Private Collection. For further information see page 280.*

BOTTOM LEFT: 12in (31cm) Kämmer & Reinhardt 701 celluloid *Marie*, and 8in (20cm) all-celluloid pair with turtle mark. *Dolly Valk Collection. For further information see page 101.*

BOTTOM RIGHT: 14in (36cm) Schoenhut toddler, all original. *Esther Schwartz Collection. For further information see page 342 (under Baby Face Toddler).*

21in (53cm) Schoenau & Hoffmeister **Princess Elizabeth**. *Esther Schwartz Collection. For further information see page 339.*

TOP LEFT: 34in (87cm) J. D. Kestner 241 character child. *Esther Schwartz Collection. For further information see page 245.*

TOP RIGHT: 10in (25cm) Japanese papier-mâché baby girl, all original. *H&J Foulke, Inc. For further information see page 299 (under Japanese Traditional Baby Doll).*

LEFT: 20in (51cm) SFBJ 235 character child. *Private Collection. For further information see page 330.*

TOP LEFT: 25in (63cm) E 10 D Bébé, open mouth. *Esther Schwartz Collection. For further information see page 141 (under Open mouth).*

TOP RIGHT: 18in (46cm) unmarked German fashion-type doll, all original. *Private Collection. For further information see page 170 (under kid body).*

LEFT: 10½in (29cm) J. D. Kestner *Gibson Girl. Private Collection. For further information see page 247.*

24in (61cm) Parian-type lady. *Esther Schwartz Collection. For further information see page 305 (under Very fancy hairdo).*

17in (43cm) Parian lady. *Esther Schwartz Collection. For further information see page 305.*

21in (53cm) Ludwig Greiner, '58 label, all original. *Esther Schwartz Collection. For further information see page 193 (under '58 label).*

19in (48cm) china head doll. *Dolly Valk Collection. For further information see page 116 (under High-Brow, so-called).*

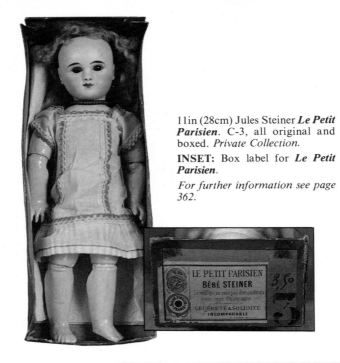

11in (28cm) Jules Steiner *Le Petit Parisien*. C-3, all original and boxed. *Private Collection.*

INSET: Box label for *Le Petit Parisien*.

For further information see page 362.

23in (59cm) Jumeau fashion lady, cloth body with kid arms. *Esther Schwartz Collection. For further information see page 226.*

China Heads
(German)

Maker: Firms such as Kling & Co., Alt, Beck & Gottschalck, Kestner & Co., Hertwig & Co. and others
Material: China head, cloth or kid body, china or leather arms
Mark: Often unmarked, sometimes marked with numbers and/or "Germany"

Bald (so-called Biedermeier): Ca. 1840. China shoulder head with bald head, some with black areas on top of head, proper wig, blue painted eyes; cloth body, bisque, china or leather arms; nicely dressed; all in good condition.
Fine quality,

16—18in (41—46cm)	**$ 850—950**
22—24in (56—61cm)	**1100**

Ordinary,

16—18in (41—46cm)	**375—475**

16in (41cm) Biedermeier china head with wig. *Joe Jackson and Joel Pearson.*

Wood-Body: Ca. 1840. Head with early hair style mounted on a peg-wooden body; usually with china lower limbs; undressed; in good condition.
Covered Wagon,

6—7in (15—18cm)	**$ 800—1000**
15—17in (38—43cm)	**1800—2000**

Unusual hairdo,

15—17in (38—43cm)	**2500—2800**

Bun: Ca. 1840s. Black-haired china shoulder head with pink tint, hair pulled back into braided bun, ears sometimes exposed; old cloth body; dressed; all in good condition.
18—21in (46—53cm) **$950—3500***

*Depending upon quality, hairdo and rarity.

Fine black-haired china head with braided bun and brush strokes framing face. *Private Collection.*

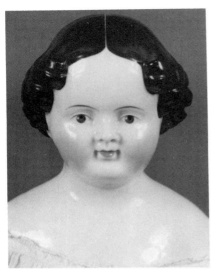

29in (74cm) brown-eyed china with smooth-top hairdo. *Esther Schwartz Collection.*

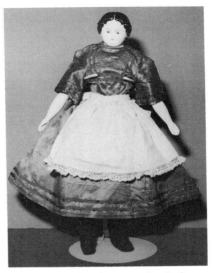

China head with glass eyes. *Joe Jackson and Joel Pearson.*

Brown Eyes: Ca. 1850. Black hair parted in center, smooth to the head, pulled behind the ears; cloth body with leather arms; dressed; all in good condition.
MARK: None
Greiner-style,

14—15in (36—38cm)	**$600—700**
19—22in (41—53cm)	**850—950**

Smooth-top, waves framing face,

18—21in (41—53cm)	**450—550**

Child, Motschmann-type with swivel neck: Ca. 1850. China head and flange neck with shoulder plate, midsection and lower limbs of china; black painted hair, blue painted eyes; with or without clothes; all in good condition.
MARK: None
10—12in (25—31cm) **$1550—1650**

Glass Eyes: Ca. 1850. Black-haired china shoulder head with hair parted in middle and styled very close to head, dark glass eyes; cloth body with leather arms; appropriate clothes; all in good condition.
MARK: None
19—21in (48—53cm) **$2500—2700**

Man: Ca. 1850. Black-haired china shoulder head with short hair, brush marks around face, blue painted eyes, cloth body; appropriate clothes; all in good condition.
MARK: None
18—22in (46—56cm) **$ 500—600**
Early fine quality,
21in (53cm) **1200—1400**

21in (53cm) black-haired china head with covered wagon hairdo, pink tinted complexion. *Esther Schwartz Collection.*

15in (38cm) china head lady with curly-top hairdo. *Joe Jackson and Joel Pearson.*

Fancy Hairdo: Ca. 1860. China shoulder head with black hair, brush marks, elaborate style with braids, wings, ornaments, blue painted eyes; old cloth body; appropriate clothes; all in good condition.

18—21in (46—53cm)   **$650 up***

*Depending upon quality, hairdo and rarity.

Covered Wagon (so-called): 1850—1870. Black-haired china shoulder head with pink tint, hair parted in middle and close to head with vertical sausage curls; old cloth body with varied extremities; well dressed; all in good condition.

MARK: None

10—12in (25—31cm)	**$300—325**
16—18in (41—46cm)	**450—500**
22—24in (56—61cm)	**600—700**

Curly Top (so-called): Ca. 1860. Black- or blonde-haired shoulder head with distinctive large horizontal curls around forehead and face; old cloth body with leather arms or china arms and legs; nicely dressed; all in good condition.

MARK: None

15—17in (38—43cm)	**$450—500**
20—22in (51—56cm)	**550—600**

China shoulder head with fancy hair style. *Catherine Magann.*

China Heads (German) continued

13in (33cm) china head with pierced ears, ordinary hair style. *Sheila Needle.*

11½in (29cm) blonde-haired china head with light blue snood. *Private Collection.*

10½in (26cm) black-haired china with flat-top hairdo, all original. *H&J Foulke, Inc.*

Pierced Ears: Ca. 1860. China shoulder head with black hair styled with curls on forehead and pulled back to curls on lower back of head, blue painted eyes, pierced ears; original cloth body with leather arms or china arms and legs; appropriate clothes; all in good condition.

MARK: None
18—22in (46—56cm)   **$650 up***
Common style,
   13—15in (33—38cm) **475—500**

*Depending upon quality, hairdo and rarity.

Snood: Ca. 1860. China shoulder head with black painted hair, slender features, blue painted eyes, molded eyelids, gold-colored snood on hair; cloth body with leather arms or china limbs; appropriate clothes; all in good condition.

MARK: None
18—22in (46—56cm) **$ 650 up***
Grape Lady,
   20in (51cm)   **1350**

*Depending upon rarity, quality and hairdo.

Flat Top (so-called): Ca. 1860-1870. China shoulder head with black hair parted in middle, smooth on top with short curls, blue painted eyes; old cloth body, extremities of leather or china; appropriate clothes; all in good condition.

MARK: None
14—16in (36—41cm) **$150—175**
20—22in (51—56cm)   **200—225**
24—26in (61—66cm)   **275—325**

High Brow (so-called): Ca. 1860-1870. China shoulder head with black painted hair, high forehead, center part, smooth top, curls clustered above ears; cloth body, china arms; dressed; all in good condition.

15—17in (38—43cm) **$200—225**
22—24in (56—61cm)   **300—325**
28in (71cm)   **350—375**

See color photo on page 111.

Adelina Patti (so-called): Ca. 1870. Black-haired china shoulder head with high forehead, white center part with wings on each side, short overall curls, brush marks at temple; cloth body with leather arms or china arms and legs.

MARK: None

11—13in (28—33cm)	**$225—250**
20—24in (51—61cm)	**450—550**

Dolley Madison (so-called): 1875-1895. Black-haired china shoulder head with molded ribbon bow in front and molded band on back of head, blue painted eyes; old cloth body with leather arms; nicely dressed; in good condition.

MARK: None

18—20in (46—51cm)	**$375—400**
24in (61cm)	**450—475**

10in (25cm) Adelina Patti china head. *H&J Foulke, Inc.*

16in (41cm) blonde-haired china with curly bangs. *H&J Foulke, Inc.*

Spill Curl: Ca. 1870. China shoulder head with café-au-lait or black painted hair, massed curls on top spilling down back and sides onto shoulders, brush marks around the forehead and temples, exposed ears; cloth body with china arms and legs; appropriate clothes; all in good condition.

MARK: None

18—20in (46—51cm)   **$500—600**

Bangs: Ca. 1880. Black- or blonde-haired china shoulder head with bangs on forehead; cloth body with china arms and legs to kid body; dressed; all in good condition.

MARK: Some marked "Germany" or Kling & Co:

14—16in (36—41cm)	**$250—275**
21—23in (53—58cm)	**350—400**

China Heads (German) continued

16in (41cm) blonde-haired china with short wavy hair and exposed ears. *H&J Foulke, Inc.*

25in (63cm) black-haired china head with common hairdo. *H&J Foulke, Inc.*

16in (41cm) black-haired china with wavy 1890s hair-do. *H&J Foulke, Inc.*

Blonde-haired pet name china head. *H&J Foulke, Inc.*

Boy or Child: Ca. 1880s. Black-or blonde-haired china shoulder head with short wavy hair and exposed ears; cloth body with china limbs; dressed; all in good condition.

15—17in (38—43cm)	**$225—250**
21—24in (48—61cm)	**325—375**

Common or Low Brow: Ca. 1890s—on. Black or blonde wavy hair style on china shoulder head, blue painted eyes; old cloth or kid body with stub, leather, bisque or china limbs; appropriate clothes; all in good condition.

7—8in (18—20cm)	**$ 65—75**
12—13in (31—33cm)	**100—125**
15—17in (39—43cm)	**150—175**
21—24in (53—61cm)	**200—250**

1890s Style: Black- or blonde-haired china shoulder head with center part and distinctly molded waves showing ear lobes, pale blue eyes with black and red eyelines, small mouth; cloth body with china limbs or kid body with bisque arms; dressed; all in good condition.

16in (41cm)   **$165—175**

Pet Name: Ca. 1905. Made by Hertwig & Co. for Butler Bros., N.Y. China shoulder head, molded yoke with name in gold; black or blonde painted hair (one-third were blonde), blue painted eyes; old cloth body (some with alphabet or other figures printed on cotton material), china limbs; properly dressed; all in good condition. Used names such as ***Agnes, Bertha, Daisy, Dorothy, Edith, Esther, Ethel, Florence, Helen, Mabel, Marion*** and ***Pauline***.

9—10in (23—25cm)	**$125—135**
16—18in (41—46cm)	**200—225**
21—24in (53—61cm)	**275—325**

Cloth, Printed

Maker: Various American companies, such as Cocheco Mfg Co., Lawrence & Co., Arnold Print Works, Art Fabric Mills and Selchow & Righter.

Date: 1896—on

Material: All-cloth

Size: 6—30in (15—76cm)

Mark: Mark could be found on fabric part which was discarded after cutting, Art Fabric Mills marked on foot.

Cloth, Printed Doll: Face, hair, underclothes, shoes and socks printed on cloth; all in good condition, some soil acceptable. Dolls in printed underwear are sometimes found dressed in old petticoats and frocks. Names such as *Dolly Dear, Merry Marie*, and so on.

6—7in (15—18cm)	**$ 75**
16—18in (41—46cm)	**135—150**
24—26in (61—66cm)	**175—200**

Brownies: 1892. Designed by Palmer Cox; marked on foot.

8in (20cm)	**85—95**

Boys and Girls with printed outer clothes, Ca. 1903,

12in (31cm)	**150—175**

Darkey Doll, uncut **150**

Aunt Jemima Family
(four dolls)	**75—85 each**

Punch & Judy **150—175**

Santa **150**

George and Martha Washington Art Fabric, 1901,
Pair	**450**

Black Child, Art Fabric,
18in (46cm)	**450**

Photograph face,
18in (46cm)	**300**

25in (64cm) 1918 *Standish No Break Life Size Doll. H&J Foulke, Inc.*

18in (46cm) Photographic face child. *H&J Foulke, Inc.*

Cloth, Russian

Maker: Unknown craftsmen
Date: Ca. 1930
Material: All-cloth
Size: 13—15in (33—38cm)
Mark: "Made in Soviet Union" sometimes with identification of doll, such as "Ukranian Woman", "Village Boy", "Smolensk Districk Woman"

Russian Cloth Doll: All-cloth with stockinette head and hands, molded face with hand-painted features; authentic regional clothes; all in very good condition.

10—11in (25—28cm)	**$50—60**
13—15in (33—38cm)	**85—95**

11in (28cm) Russian stockinette child. *H&J Foulke, Inc.*

Cloth Shoulder Head

Maker: Unknown
Date: Ca. 1850
Material: All-cloth
Size: 22in (56cm)

Cloth Shoulder Head: Cloth shoulder head with molded features, painted black hair, glass or painted eyes, closed mouth; cloth body; appropriate old clothes. Very rare.
22in (56cm)　**$1200—1500 up****

**Not enough price samples to compute a reliable range.

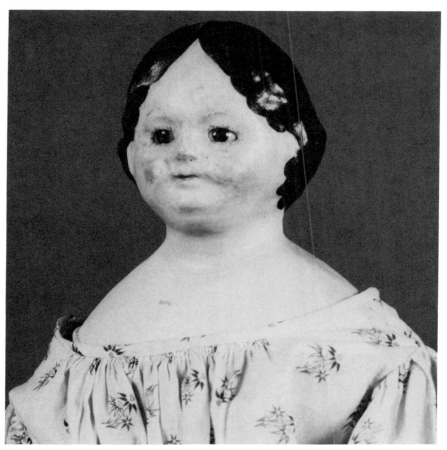

22in (56cm) cloth shoulder head doll with glass eyes.

Clowns

Maker: Various French and German firms
Date: 1890—on
Material: Bisque or papier-mâché head, composition body or wooden limbs with squeeze mechanism in torso
Mark: Various

13in (33cm) clown with bisque head incised "157;" eyes move and hands clap when stomach is pressed. *Private Collection.*

Molded Bisque: Clown with molded bisque smiling face, molded hair or wig, painted or glass eyes, clown paint on face; composition body; clown costume.
12—14in (31—36cm) **$600—650**

Standard Bisque: Clown having standard bisque head painted with clown make-up, wig, glass eyes, open mouth; composition body or wooden limbs and clapping mechanism; clown costume.
12—14in (31—36cm) **$350—400**

Papier-mâché: Molded papier-mâché character face with painted features, wooden limbs; squeeze stomach and hands clap; original clothes.
12—14in (31-36cm) **$250—300**
Composition body, original clothes, glass eyes,
14in (36cm) **400—450**

Polichinelle: French bisque head, (F.G. in scroll), jointed limbs controlled by strings, long feet, humped back, protruding stomach. Original jester costume not faded.
18—20in (46—51cm) **$1200—1600**

Dewees Cochran

Maker: Dewees Cochran, Fenton, CA., U.S.A.
Date: 1940—on
Material: Latex
Size: 9—18in (23—46cm)
Designer: Dewees Cochran
Mark: Signed under arm or behind right ear

Dewees Cochran Doll: Latex with jointed neck, shoulders and hips; human hair wig, painted eyes, character face; dressed; all in good condition.

15—16in (38—41cm) *Cindy,* 1947-1948.　　**$ 600—700**

Grow-up Dolls: Stormy, Angel, Bunnie, J.J. and *Peter Ponsett* each at ages 5, 7, 11, 16 and 20, 1952-1956.　　**1000—1200**

Look-Alike Dolls (6 different faces) **1000—1100**

Baby, 9in (23cm)　　**900—1000****

Individual Portrait Children　　**1200 up**

Composition American Children (See Effanbee)

**Not enough price samples to compute a reliable average.

See color photos on page 255.

16in (41cm) *Look-Alike* doll, all original.
Nancy Schwartz Blaisure Collection.

Columbian Doll

Maker: Emma and Marietta Adams
Date: 1891—1910 or later
Material: All-cloth
Size: 15—29in (38—74cm)
Mark: Stamped on back of body

Before 1900:	After 1906:
"COLUMBIAN DOLL	"THE COLUMBIAN DOLL
EMMA E. ADAMS	MANUFACTURED BY
OSWEGO CENTRE	MARIETTA ADAMS RUTTAN
N.Y."	OSWEGO, N.Y."

Columbian Doll: All-cloth with hair and features hand-painted; treated limbs; appropriate clothes; all in good condition, showing wear.

17—22in (43—56cm)   **$1200—1600**
Columbian type, 15—16in (38—41cm)   **450—550**

*One auction price of $3100 suggests an imminent rise for this doll.

19in (48cm) *Colum-bian* doll. *Private Collection.*

Composition
(American)

Maker: Various United States firms, many unidentified
Date: 1912—on
Material: All-composition or composition head and cloth body, some with composition limbs
Size: 6in (15cm) up
Mark: Various according to company; most unmarked

All-Composition Child Doll: 1912—1920. Various firms, such as Bester Doll Co., New Era Novelty Co., New Toy Mfg. Co., Superior Doll Mfg. Co., Colonial Toy Mfg. Co. Composition with mohair wig, sleep eyes, open mouth; ball-jointed composition body; appropriate clothes; all in good condition. These are patterned after German bisque head dolls.
22—24in (56-61cm) **$250**

See photos on pages 56 and 144.

All-Composition Character Baby:
1912—1920. Composition with good wig, sleep eyes, open mouth with teeth; bent-limb baby body; appropriate clothes; all in good condition. Patterned after German bisque head babies.

13—14in (33—36cm)	**$125—150**
18—20in (46—51cm)	**200—250**
24—25in (61—64cm)	**275—325**

12in (31cm) early composition character baby. *H&J Foulke, Inc.*

Early Composition Character Head: Ca. 1912. Composition head with molded hair and painted features; hard cloth body with composition hands; appropriate clothes; all in good condition.
12—13in (31—33cm) **$150**

16in (41cm) Mama doll, all original. *H&J Foulke, Inc.*

Girl-type Mama Dolls: Ca. 1920—on. Made by various American companies. Composition head with lovely hair wig, sleep eyes, open mouth with teeth; composition shoulder plate, arms and legs, cloth body; original clothes; all in good condition, of good quality.

16—18in (41—46cm)	**$125—150**
22—25in (56—64cm)	**175—225**

Composition (Miscellaneous) continued

Orphan Annie: Ca. 1920s. All-composition with yellow molded hair, large painted eyes; red cotton dress with white collar; all in good condition.

12in (31cm) **$140—165**

12in (31cm) **Orphan Annie**, replaced clothing. *Dolly Valk Collection.*

Patsy-type Girl: Ca. 1930s. All-composition with molded bobbed hair, sleep or painted eyes, closed mouth; jointed at neck, shoulders and hips; original clothes; all in very good condition, of good quality.

9—10in (23—25cm) **$ 90—100**
14—15in (36—38cm) **150—175**

Composition Baby: Ca. 1930. All-composition with molded and painted hair, painted or sleep eyes, closed mouth; jointed at neck, shoulders and hips with curved limbs; original clothes; all in very good condition, of good quality.

10—12in (25—31cm) **$ 65—85**
16—18in (41—46cm) **125—150**

Dionne-type Doll: Ca. 1935. All-composition with molded hair or wig, sleep eyes (painted in small dolls), closed or open mouth; jointed at neck, shoulders and hips; original clothes; all in very good condition, of good quality.

7in (18cm) baby **$ 50—60**
18in (46cm) toddler **160—185**

14in (36cm) **Patsy**-type doll, all original. *H&J Foulke, Inc.*

20in (51cm) toddler with caracul wig, all original. *H&J Foulke, Inc.*

19in (48cm) **Shirley**-type, all original. *H&J Foulke, Inc.*

Shirley Temple-type Girl: Ca. 1935—on. All-composition, jointed at neck, shoulders and hips; blonde curly mohair wig, sleep eyes, open smiling mouth with teeth; original clothes; all in excellent condition, of good quality.

16—18in (41—46cm) **$160—185**

Bride: Ca. 1940. **Juliette** bride by Eugenia Doll Co., N.Y., all-composition with lashed sleeping eyes, closed mouth, curly mohair wig; original clothing; all in very good condition.

13in (33cm) **$125—135**

Jackie Robinson, all original. *Private Collection.*

13in (33cm) Eugenia **Juliette** bride, all original. *H&J Foulke, Inc.*

Jackie Robinson Doll: Allied-Grand Doll Mfg. Co., Inc., Brooklyn, N.Y. All-composition doll with brown complexion, painted eyes to side, molded black hair; original Dodgers baseball outfit. All in good condition.

13½in (34cm) **$375—425**

Composition
(German)

Maker: Various German firms, such as König & Wernicke, Kämmer & Reinhardt and others
Date: Ca. 1925
Material: All-composition or composition head and cloth body
Size: Various

All-Composition Child Doll:

Socket head with good wig, sleep (sometimes flirty) eyes, open mouth with teeth; jointed composition body; appropriate clothes; all in good condition, of excellent quality.

13—15in (33—38cm)	**$175—200**
20—22in (51—56cm)	**250—275**

Character face,

20—22in (51—56cm)	**350—400**

All-Composition Character:

Composition socket head with good wig, sleep eyes, open mouth with teeth; bent-limb baby body; appropriate clothes; all in good condition, of excellent quality.

18—20in (46—51cm)	**$250—300**
24—26in (61—66cm)	**450—475**

Toddler,

18in (46cm)	**275—300**

Painted eyes,

10—12in (25—31cm)	**75—85**

22in (56cm) character boy 455 with flirty eyes. *Betty Harms Collection.*

Composition Shoulder Head
(Patent Washable Dolls)

Maker: Various German firms
Date: 1890—1915
Material: Composition shoulder head, cloth body, composition lower limbs
Size: 10—42in (25—107cm)
Mark: None

Composition Shoulder Head: Good quality composition with mohair or skin wig, glass eyes, closed or open mouth; cloth body with composition arms and lower legs, sometimes with molded boots; appropriately dressed; all in good condition.

Excellent Quality:

12—14in (31—36cm)	**$225—275**
16—18in (41—46cm)	**300—350**
22—24in (56—61cm)	**375—425**

Lesser Quality:

10—11in (25—28cm)	**110—125**
14—16in (36—41cm)	**150—175**
22—24in (56—61cm)	**225—275**
30in (76cm)	**350—400**

15in (38cm) composition shoulder head, excellent quality, all original. *Kay and Wayne Jensen Collection.*

Creche Figures

Maker: Various European craftsmen, primarily Italian
Date: 18th and 19th centuries
Material: Wood and terra-cotta on a wire frame
Size: Various
Mark: None

Creche Figures of various people in a Christmas scene: 18th century. Gesso over wood head and limbs, fabric-covered wire frame body; beautifully detailed features with carved hair and glass inset eyes, lovely hands; original or appropriate replacement clothes; all in good condition.

13—14in (33—35cm) **$350—450***
18—20in (46—51cm)   **750—850***

*Allow more for wood-jointed body.

Mid 19th Century: Later doll with terra-cotta head and limbs, painted eyes; fabric-covered wire frame body; workmanship not as detailed; original or appropriate clothes; all in good condition.

11—13in (28—33cm)   **$150—200**

*Price would be higher on "art" and "antiques" market.

16in (41cm) 18th century creche lady. *Private Collection.*

DEP
(Closed Mouth)

Maker: Unknown German porcelain factory
Date: 1885—1890
Material: Bisque head, jointed wood and composition French body
Mark: DEP

Marked DEP Child: Perfect bisque head, closed mouth, paperweight eyes, heavy eyebrows, painted upper and lower lashes, human hair wig; jointed French composition and wood body; dressed; all in good condition.
24in (61cm) **$2500—2750**

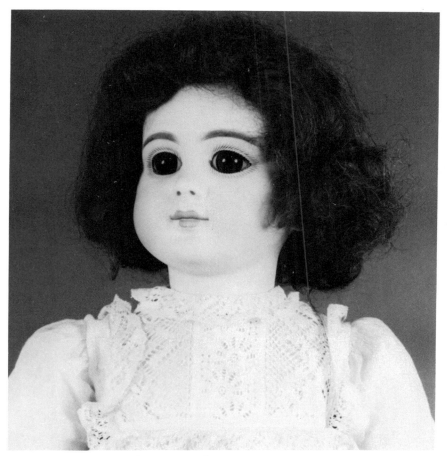

28in (71cm) DEP child. *Carol Green Collection.*

D E P*
(Open Mouth)

Maker: Maison Jumeau, Paris, France; (heads possibly by Simon & Halbig, Gräfenhain, Thüringia, Germany)

Date: Late 1890s

Material: Bisque socket head, French jointed composition body (sometimes marked Jumeau)

Size: About 12—33in (31—84cm)

Mark: "DEP" and size number (up to 16 or so); sometimes stamped in red "Tete Jumeau;" body sometimes with Jumeau stamp or sticker

DEP: Perfect bisque socket head, human hair wig, sleep eyes, painted lower eyelashes only, upper hair eyelashes (sometimes gone), deeply molded eye sockets, open mouth, pierced ears; jointed French composition body; lovely clothes; all in good condition.

14—16in (36—41cm) $ 675—775
19—21in (48—53cm)   900—1000
25—26in (64—66cm) 1200—1300
33—35in (84—89cm) 1800—2000

*The letters DEP appear in the mark of many dolls, but the particular dolls priced here have only "DEP" and a size number (unless they happen to have the red stamp "Tete Jumeau"). The face is characterized by deeply molded eye sockets and no painted upper eyelashes.

20in (51cm) DEP with French body. *H&J Foulke, Inc.*

Doll House Dolls

Maker: Various German firms
Date: Ca. 1890—1920
Material: Bisque shoulder head, cloth body, bisque arms and legs
Size: Under 7in (18cm)
Mark: Sometimes "Germany"

Doll House Doll: Man or lady 5½—7in (14—18cm), as above with molded
 hair, painted eyes; original clothes or suitably dressed; all in nice condition.
Man or lady **$150—165***
With molded hair and painted eyes, ca. 1920 **100—125**
Lady with glass eyes and wig **300—325**

*Allow more for molded hats, grandfathers and unusual characters.

6in (16cm) doll house lady with glass eyes. *H&J Foulke, Inc.*

Door of Hope

Maker: Door of Hope Mission, China; heads by carvers from Ning-Po
Date: 1917—on
Material: Wooden heads; cloth bodies, sometimes with carved wooden hands
Size: Usually under 13in (33cm)
Mark: Sometimes "Made in China" label

Door of Hope: Carved wooden head with painted and/or carved hair, carved features; cloth body, sometimes carved hands; original handmade clothes, exact costuming for different classes of Chinese people; all in good condition. 25 dolls in the series.

11—13in (28—33cm)

Adult

11—13in (28—33cm)	**$250—350**

Child

6—7in (15—18cm)	**375—425**

Mother and Baby

11in (28cm)	**450—475**

Door of Hope child with molded braid.
H&J Foulke, Inc.

Grace G. Drayton

Maker: Various companies
Date: 1909—on
Material: All-cloth, or composition and cloth combination, or all-composition
Size: Various
Designer: Grace G. Drayton
Mark: Usually a cloth label or a stamp

(See also *Campbell Kids*)

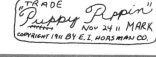

Puppy Pippin: 1911. Horsman Co., New York, N.Y., U.S.A. Composition
   head with puppy dog face, plush body with jointed legs; all in good condition.
   Cloth label.
8in (20cm) sitting   **$350**

Puppy Pippin and ***Dolly Dingle***. *Jan Foulke Collection.*

Grace G. Drayton continued

Peek-a-Boo: 1913—1915. Horsman Co., New York, N.Y., U.S.A. Composition head, arms, legs and lower torso, cloth upper torso; character face with molded hair, painted eyes to the side, watermelon mouth; dressed in striped bathing suit, polka dot dress or ribbons only; cloth label on outfit; all in good condition.

7½in (19cm) **$125—150**

Hug-Me-Tight: 1916. Colonial Toy Mfg. Co., New York, N.Y., U.S.A. Mother Goose characters and others in one piece, printed on cloth; all in good condition.

11in (28cm) **$225—250**

Chocolate Drop: 1923. Averill Manufacturing Co., New York, N.Y., U.S.A. Brown cloth doll with movable arms and legs; painted features, three yarn pigtails; appropriate clothes; all in good condition. Stamped on front torso and paper label.

11in (28cm) **$300—350**

Dolly Dingle: 1923. Averill Manufacturing Co., New York, N.Y., U.S.A. Cloth doll with painted features and movable arms and legs; appropriate clothes; all in good condition. Stamped on front torso and paper label.

DOLLY DINGLE
COPYRIGHT BY
G.G. DRAYTON

11in (28cm) **$300—350**

7½in (19cm) *Peek-a-Boo*, replaced clothing. *Private Collection.*

Dressel

Maker: Cuno & Otto Dressel verlager & doll factory of Sonneberg, Thüringia, Germany. Heads by Armand Marseille, Simon & Halbig, Ernst Heubach, Gebrüder Heubach.

Date: 1700

Material: Composition, wax over or bisque head, kid, cloth body or ball-jointed composition body

Trademarks: Fifth Ave. Dolls (1903), Jutta (1907), Bambina (1909), Poppy Dolls (1912), Holz-Masse (1875)

Mark:

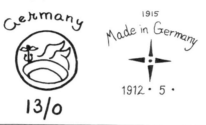

Marked Holz-Masse Heads: 1875 —on. Composition shoulder head, molded hair or sometimes mohair wig, usually painted eyes, sometimes pierced ears; cloth body with composition arms and legs with molded boots; old clothes; all in good condition.

MARK:

Molded hair:
18—21in (46—53)	**$275—300**
26in (66cm)	**375—400**

Wigged with glass eyes:
(Patent Washable)
14—16in (36—41cm)	**275—300**
19—22in (48—56cm)	**350—375**

22in (56cm) *Holz-Masse* doll with molded black curly hair. *Private Collection.*

Dressel continued

Child Doll: 1895—on. Perfect bisque head, original jointed kid or composition body; good wig, glass eyes, open mouth; suitable clothes; all in good condition.

MARK: Various including those above and

COD 93-3 DEP

Composition body:

16—18in (41—46cm)	$275—325
23—24in (58—61cm)	375—425
32in (81cm)	700—800

Kid body:

14—16in (36—41cm)	225—250*
20—22in (51—56cm)	300—350*

*Allow extra for fine, early bisque.

Portrait Series: 1896. *Admiral Dewey* and his men, *Uncle Sam* and perhaps others. Perfect bisque heads with portrait faces, glass eyes, some with molded mustaches and goatees; composition body; original clothes; all in good condition. Sometimes marked with "S" or "D" and a number. Heads by Simon & Halbig.

Admiral Dewey & Men,
15in (38cm) **$1800—2000**
Uncle Sam,
14—15in (36—38cm) **1500—1800**

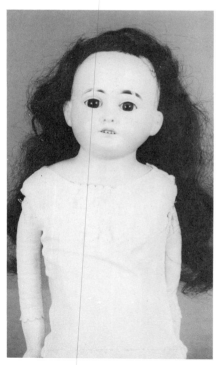

22in (56cm) COD 93-3 child, kid body. *H&J Foulke, Inc.*

10in (25cm) *Uncle Sam. Private Collection.*

Dressel continued

14½in (38cm) Dressel 1349 child. *Dolly Valk Collection.*

Marked Jutta Child: Ca. 1906—1921. Perfect bisque socket head, good wig, sleep eyes, open mouth, pierced ears; ball-jointed composition body; dressed; all in good condition. Head made by Simon & Halbig.
Mold 1348 or 1349
MARK:

1349
Jutta
S & H
11

13—14in (33—36cm)	$ 375—425
17—19in (43—48cm)	475—500
24—26in (61—66cm)	700—800
32in (81cm)	1100

Character Child: 1909—on. Perfect bisque socket head, ball-jointed composition body; mohair wig, painted eyes, closed mouth; suitable clothes; all in good condition. Glazed inside of head.

14—16in (36—41cm)	$2000—2500**

**Not enough price samples to compute a reliable average.

C.O.D. Character Baby: Ca. 1910—on. Perfect bisque character face with wig or molded hair, painted or glass eyes; jointed baby body; dressed; all in good condition.

12—13in (31—33cm)	**$325—350**
16—18in (41—46cm)	**400—425**
22—24in (56—61cm)	**575—675**

Marked Jutta Character Baby: Ca. 1910—1922. Perfect bisque socket head, good wig, sleep eyes, open mouth; bent-limb composition baby body; dressed; all in good condition.
MARK:

Heubach 6½ Koppelsdorf
Jutta - Baby
Dressel
Germany
1922
10½

Jutta
1914
8

16—18in (41—46cm)	$ 525—600
22—24in (56—61cm)	800—1000
Toddler,	
21in (53cm)	1000

Lady Doll: Ca. 1920s. Mold #1469. Bisque socket head with young lady face, good wig, sleep eyes, closed mouth; jointed composition body in adult form with molded bust, slim waist and long arms and legs, feet modeled to wear high-heeled shoes; appropriate clothes; all in good condition.
MARK:

1469
C.O. Dressel
Germany
2.

14in (36cm)	**$1250—1450**

Dressel, Kister & Co.

Maker: Dressel, Kister & Co., near Rudolstadt, Thüringia, Germany
Date: 1837
Material: China
Mark:

Marked D.K. Pincushion or Half Doll: Ca. 1915. Perfect china half figure, usually of a lady with molded hair and painted features, sometimes with molded clothes, hats or accessories; lovely modeling and painting. Most desirable have fancy clothing or hair ornamentation and extended arms. Special D.K. characteristics are highlighted brush-stroked hair and a narrow base.

$150 and up*

*Depending upon rarity.

2½in (6cm) young girl half figure with large extended hands. *H&J Foulke, Inc.*

Lady half doll with extended arms holding flower on original shell base. *H&J Foulke, Inc.*

E. D. Bébé

Maker: Unknown as yet but *possibly* by E. Denamur of Paris, France
Date: Ca. 1885 into 1890s
Material: Bisque head, wood and composition jointed body
Mark:

E 8D

――――――― DEPOSÉ ―――――――――――――

Marked E. D. Bébé: Perfect bisque head, wood and composition jointed
body; good wig, beautiful blown glass eyes, pierced ears; nicely dressed; good
condition. Often found on a marked Jumeau body.
Closed mouth:

16—18in (41—46cm)	$2400—2500
23—25in (58—64cm)	3100—3300

Open mouth:

14—15in (36—38cm)	1100—1300
23—25in (58—64cm)	2100—2500

See color photo on page 110.

29in (74cm) E.D. *Kay and Wayne Jensen Collection.*

Eden Bébé

Maker: Fleischmann & Bloedel, doll factory, of Fürth, Bavaria, and Paris, France

Date: Founded in Bavaria in 1873. Also in Paris by 1890, then on into S.F.B.J. in 1899, closed 1926.

Material: Bisque head, composition jointed body

Trademark: Eden Bébé (1890), Bébé Triomphe (1898)

Mark: "EDEN BÉBÉ, PARIS"

Marked Eden Bébé: Ca. 1890. Perfect bisque head, fully-jointed or five-piece composition jointed body; beautiful wig, large set paperweight eyes, closed or open/closed mouth, pierced ears; lovely clothes; all in nice condition.

Closed mouth, 19—21in (48—53cm)   **$2500—2600**

Open mouth, 21—24in (53—61cm)   **2000**

Kissing, Walking, Flirting Doll: 1892. Head from mold 1039 by Simon & Halbig, ball-jointed composition body with mechanism for walking, throwing kisses and flirting eyes.

20—22in (51—56cm)   **$850—950**

See color photo on page 72.

14in (36cm) ***Eden Bébé*** with open mouth. *Betty Harms Collection.*

23in (58cm) Fleischman & Bloedel walking, kissing and flirting doll with Simon & Halbig 1039 head. *Elsa McCallum Collection.*

EFFanBEE

Maker: EFFanBEE Doll Co., New York, N.Y., U.S.A.
Date: 1912—on
Marks: Various, but nearly always marked "EFFanBEE" on torso or head. Wore a metal heart-shaped bracelet; later a gold paper heart label.

EFFANBEE
DURABLE
DOLLS

Metal Heart Bracelet: **$45**

Baby Dainty: 1912—1922. Composition shoulder head, painted molded hair, painted facial features (sometimes with tin sleep eyes); cloth stuffed body jointed at shoulders and hips, with curved arms and straight legs of composition; original or appropriate old clothes; all in good condition. Came with metal heart bracelet.
MARK: First Mold:

Effanbee

Second Mold:

EFFANBEE
BABY DAINTY

15in (38cm)   **$150—175**

Baby Grumpy: 1912—1939. Composition shoulder head with frowning face, molded and painted hair, painted eyes, closed mouth; composition arms and legs, cloth body; original or appropriate old clothes; all in good condition. Came with metal heart bracelet.
MARK:

EFFANBEE
DOLLS
WALK-TALK-SLEEP

12in (31cm),
White   **$165—185**
Black   **225—250**

15in (41cm) *Baby Grumpy*, brown composition. *Private Collection.*

EFFanBEE continued

Mary Jane: 1917—1920. Composition "dolly face" head with metal sleeping eyes, painted eyebrows and eyelashes, open mouth with teeth, original human hair or mohair wig; jointed composition body with wood arms; dressed; all in very good condition.

MARK: *Effanbee* back of head and torso in raised letters

20—24in (51—61cm) **$250**

Marilee: 1924. Composition shoulder head, arms and legs, cloth torso; human hair wig, sleep eyes, open mouth with teeth; original clothes; all in good condition. Various sizes. Came with metal heart bracelet.

MARK:
```
  EFFANBEE
   MARILEE
    COPYR.
     DOLL
```

22in (56cm) **$200—225**

Bubbles: 1924—on. Composition head with blonde molded and painted hair, sleep eyes, open mouth with teeth, smiling face; cloth body, curved composition arms and legs; original or appropriate old clothes; all in good condition. Came with metal heart bracelet or necklace.

MARK:
```
    19 © 24
  EFFANBEE            EFFANBEE
    DOLLS             BUBBLES
WALK-TALK-SLEEP      COPYR. 1924
 MADE IN U.S.A.    MADE IN U.S.A.
```

16—18in (41—46cm) **$200—225**   22—24in (56—61cm) **275—325**

24in (61cm) *Mary Jane* with original wig; old clothes. *H&J Foulke, Inc.*

18in (46cm) *Bubbles*, all original. *H&J Foulke, Inc.*

13in (33cm) *Pat-O-Pat*, replaced clothes. *H&J Foulke, Inc.*

Pat-O-Pat: 1925. Infant composition head, painted molded hair, painted eyes, closed mouth; composition hands, cloth body and legs; appropriate old clothes. Contains a mechanism so that the baby claps her hands when her stomach is pressed. All in good condition.

13—15in (33—38cm)   **$95—125**

Rosemary: 1925. Composition shoulder head, human hair wig, open mouth, tin sleep eyes; cloth torso, composition arms and legs; original or appropriate old clothes; all in good condition. Various sizes. Came with metal heart bracelet.

MARK:

EFFanBEE
ROSEMARY
WALK-TALK-SLEEP

14in (36cm)   **$165—175**
22in (56cm)   **200—225**

Mae Starr: 1928. Composition shoulder head with human hair wig, sleep eyes, open/closed mouth; cloth body, composition limbs; talking device in center of torso with records.

MARK: MAE
            STARR
             DOLL

29—30in (74—76cm)   **$400—450**

EFFanBEE continued

Mary Ann and Mary Lee: 1928-on. Composition head on *Lovums* shoulder plate, composition arms and legs, cloth torso; human hair wig, sleep eyes, open smiling mouth; appropriate clothes; in good condition. Later version came on an all-composition body marked "Patsy-Ann" for *Mary Ann* and "Patsy-Joan" for *Mary Lee*. Came with metal heart bracelet. ©

MARK: MARY-ANN

16in (41cm) *Mary Lee* $175—200
19in (48cm) *Mary Ann* 200—225

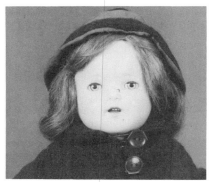

16in (41cm) *Mary Lee*. *H&J Foulke, Inc.*

22in (56cm) *Patsy Lou*, all original. *H&J Foulke, Inc.*

Lovums: 1928—1939. Composition swivel head on shoulder plate, arms and legs; molded painted hair or wig, pretty face, sleep eyes, smiling open mouth with teeth; cloth body; original or appropriate clothes; all in good condition. Various sizes. Came with metal heart bracelet. Note: The "Lovums" shoulder plate was used for many other dolls as well.

MARK: EFF AN BEE
LOVUMS
©
PAT. N°. 1,283,558

16—18in (41—46cm) **$200—225**
22—24in (56—61cm) **275—300**

Patsy Family: 1928—on. All-composition, jointed at neck, shoulders and hips; molded hair (sometimes covered with wig), bent right arm on some members, painted or sleep eyes; original or appropriate old clothes; may have some crazing. Came with metal heart bracelet.

MARK: Bracelet
EFFanBEE
PATSY
BABY KIN

EFFanBEE
PATSY
DOLL

EFFANBEE
PATSY JR.
DOLL

6in (15cm) **Wee Patsy**,
all original **$300**
7in (18cm)
Baby Tinyette 165—175
9in (23cm)
Patsy Babyette 175—185
Patsyette 190—210
11in (28cm)
Patsy Baby 200—215
Patsy Jr. 235—265
Patricia Kin 235—265

14in (36cm)	
Patsy	250—300
Patricia	250—300
16in (41cm)	
Patsy Joan	300—325
19in (48cm)	
Patsy Ann	300—350
22in (56cm)	
Patsy Lou	375—425
26in (66cm)	
Patsy Ruth	500 up
30in (76cm)	
Patsy Mae	500 up

9in (23cm) *Patsyette*, all original. *H&J Foulke, Inc.*

11in (28cm) *Patsy Baby*, all original. *H&J Foulke, Inc.*

9in (23cm) *Patsy Babyette*, all original. *H&J Foulke, Inc.*

6in (15cm) *Wee Patsy*, all original. *H&J Foulke, Inc.*

Skippy: 1929. All-composition, jointed at neck, hips and shoulders, (later a cloth torso, still later a cloth torso and upper legs with composition molded boots for lower legs); molded hair, painted eyes to the side; original or appropriate clothes; all in good condition. Came with metal heart bracelet.

MARK: EFFANBEE
SKIPPY
©
P. L. Crosby

14in (36cm)   **$300—350**

Composition Girl with Molded Hair: Ca. 1930. All-composition, jointed at neck, shoulders and hips; molded hair painted brown, large painted eyes looking left, closed mouth; original clothes; all in good condition.

MARK:
EFFANBEE
MADE IN U.S.A.
9in (23cm)   **$150**

14in (36cm) *Skippy*, all original. *Kay and Wayne Jensen Collection.*

9in (23cm) girl with molded hair, unnamed, original costume, missing headwear. *H&J Foulke, Inc.*

Lamkin: 1930s. Composition head, arms and legs with very deep and detailed molding, cloth body; molded hair, sleep eyes, bow mouth; original or appropriate clothes; all in good condition.

MARK: On head:
"LAMBKINS"
(note spelling)
Paper heart tag: "Lamkin"
16in (41cm)   **$250—300**

Betty Brite: 1933. All-composition, jointed at neck, shoulders and hips;   caracul wig, sleep eyes, open mouth with teeth; original or appropriate clothes; all in good condition.

MARK: On torso:
"EFFANBEE
BETTY BRITE"
16½in (42cm)   **$225**

EFFanBEE continued

Dy-Dee Baby: 1933—on. First dolls had hard rubber head with soft rubber body, caracul wig or molded hair, open mouth for drinking, soft ears (after 1940). Later dolls had hard plastic heads with rubber bodies. Still later dolls had hard plastic heads with vinyl bodies. Came with paper heart label. Various sizes from 9—20in (23—51cm).

MARK:
"EFF-AN-BEE
DY-DEE BABY
US PAT.-1-857-485
ENGLAND-880-060
FRANCE-723-980
GERMANY-585-647
OTHER PAT PENDING"
Rubber body:
   14—16in (36—41cm) **$100—110**

15in (38cm) **Dy-Dee Baby**, hard plastic head, rubber body. *H&J Foulke, Inc.*

15in (38cm) **Anne Shirley**, all original. *H&J Foulke, Inc.*

Anne Shirley: 1935—1940. All-composition, jointed at neck, shoulders and hips; human hair wig, sleep eyes, closed mouth; original clothes; all in good condition. Various sizes. Came with metal heart bracelet. "Anne Shirley" body used on other dolls as well.

MARK: On back:
"EFFanBEE/ANNE SHIRLEY."
15—16in (38—41cm)   **$200—225**
20—21in (51—53cm)   **275—300**
27in (69cm)   **400—450**

Sugar Baby: 1936. Composition head, curved arms and toddler legs, cloth body; molded hair or caracul wig, sleep eyes, closed mouth; appropriately dressed; all in good condition.

MARK:
"EFFanBEE
SUGAR BABY"
16—18in (41—46cm) **$200—225**

150

American Children: 1936-1939. Composition swivel head on composition *Anne Shirley* body, jointed at shoulders and hips. Four different faces designed by Dewees Cochran with either open or closed mouths, human hair wigs, painted or sleep eyes; original clothes; all in good condition. Came with metal heart bracelet and paper heart label. Sizes: 15in (38cm), 17in (43cm), 19in (48cm) and 21in (53cm).

MARK: On head:
"EFFANBEE//
AMERICAN//CHILDREN"
On body:
"EFFANBEE//ANNE SHIRLEY"
The boy and the open-mouth girl are not marked.

Open mouth:
15in (38cm)
Barbara Joan   **$ 600—650**
17½in (45cm)
Barbara Ann   **650—700**
21in (53cm)
Barbara Lou   **750—800**
Closed mouth:
19—21in (48—53cm)**1000—1200**
17in (43cm) boy   **1000—1200**

Pennsylvania Dutch Dolls: 1936-1940s. Used **Baby Grumpy** shoulder head, cloth torso, composition arms and legs; dressed in costumes to represent "Amish", "Mennonite" or "Brethren". Green wrist tag with black stamp indicated sect.

MARK:

12—13in (31—33cm)   **$165—185**

17½in (45cm) *American Child*, all original. *Nancy Schwartz Blaisure Collection.*

12in (31cm) *Amish Father*, all original. *H&J Foulke, Inc.*

Charlie McCarthy: 1937. Composition head, hands and feet, cloth body; painted hair and eyes; strings at back of head to operate mouth; original clothes; all in good condition.

MARK:
"EDGAR BERGEN'S CHARLIE McCARTHY,
AN EFFanBEE PRODUCT"
17—20in (43—51cm)   **$250—300**

EFFanBEE continued

Historical Dolls: 1939. All-composition, jointed at neck, shoulders and hips. Three each of 30 dolls portraying the history of American fashion, 1492—1939. "American Children" heads used with elaborate human hair wigs and painted eyes; elaborate original costumes using velvets, satins, silks, brocades, and so forth; all in good condition. Came with metal heart bracelet.

MARKS: On head:
"EFFANBEE
AMERICAN CHILDREN"
On body:
"EFFANBEE
ANNE SHIRLEY"
21in (53cm) **$1200—1500**

Historical Doll Replicas: 1939. All-composition, jointed at neck, shoulders and hips. Series of 30 dolls, popular copies of the original historical models (see above). Human hair wigs, painted eyes; original costumes all in cotton, copies of those on the original models. Came with metal heart bracelet.

MARK: On torso:
"EFFanBEE
ANNE SHIRLEY"
14in (36cm) **$375—425**

Button Nose: Ca. 1939. All-composition with swivel head, joints at shoulders and hips; brown molded hair, painted eyes, closed mouth; appropriately dressed; all in good condition.

MARK: "EFFANBEE"
9in (23cm) **$175—200**

14in (36cm) ***Suzanne***, all original. *H&J Foulke, Inc.*

Suzette: 1939. All-composition, jointed at neck, shoulders and hips; mohair wig, eyes painted to the side, closed mouth; original clothes; all in good condition. Came with metal heart bracelet.

MARK: SUZETTE
EFF an BEE
MADE IN
U.S.A.
11½in (29cm) **$160—185**

Tommy Tucker: 1939—1949. Composition head with painted hair or mohair wig, flirting eyes, closed mouth, chubby cheeks; composition hands, stuffed body; original clothes; all in good condition. Also called ***Mickey*** and ***Baby Bright Eyes.*** Came with paper heart tag. Sizes: 15—24in (38—61cm).

MARK: On head:
"EFFANBEE
U.S.A."
16—18in (41—46cm) **$200—225**
22—24in (56—61cm) **275—300**

EFFanBEE continued

Suzanne: 1940. All-composition jointed at neck, shoulders and hips; mohair wig, sleep eyes, closed mouth; original clothes; all in good condition. Came with metal heart bracelet.

MARK: SUZANNE
EFFANBEE
MADE IN U.S.A

14in (36cm) **$200—225**

11in (28cm) Portrait *Colonial. H&J Foulke, Inc.*

Portrait Dolls: 1940. All-composition, jointed at neck, shoulders and hips; mohair wigs, sleep eyes; in costumes, such as ballerina, **Bo-Peep, Gibson Girl**, bride and groom, dancing couple, all original, in good condition.

MARK: None

11in (28cm) **$175—225**

Storybook-type or Sewing Doll: Ca. 1940. All-composition, jointed at shoulders and hips; the same doll as **Wee Patsy** sometimes with added mohair wig, painted eyes, molded shoes and socks; all original; in good condition. Sewing doll comes with fabric and patterns for making clothes.

6in (15cm) **$300**

Little Lady: 1940—1949. All-composition, jointed at neck, shoulders and hips, separated fingers; mohair or human hair wig, sleep eyes, closed mouth; same face as *Anne Shirley*; original clothes; all in good condition. (During "war years" some had yarn wigs and/or painted eyes.) Various sizes.

MARK: On back:
"EFFanBEE
U.S.A.
Paper heart:
'I am Little Lady' "

14—15in (36—38cm) **$175—200**
20—21in (51—53cm) **275—300**

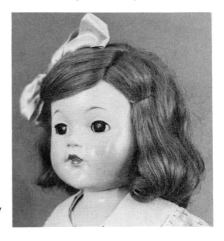

21in (53cm) *Little Lady*, all original. *H&J Foulke, Inc.*

EFFanBEE continued

Brother and Sister: 1942. Composition swivel heads and hands, stuffed cloth body, arms and legs; yarn wig, painted eyes. Original pink (sister) and blue (brother) outfits.

MARK: "EFFANBEE"

12in (31cm) *Sister*   **$150—160**

16in (41cm) *Brother*   **175—185**

Sweetie Pie: 1942. Composition head and limbs, cloth torso; caracul wig, flirty eyes, closed mouth; original clothes; all in good condition. Available in 16in (41cm), 20in (51cm) and 24in (61cm).

MARK: "EFFANBEE © 1942"

16—18in (41—46cm)   **$200—225**

22—24in (56—61cm)   **275—300**

Candy Kid: 1946. All-composition toddler, jointed at neck, shoulders and hips; molded hair, sleep eyes; original clothes; all in good condition. Came with paper heart tag.

MARK: "EFFanBEE"

12in (31cm)   **$225—250**

12in (31cm) *Sister*, all original. *H&J Foulke, Inc.*

12in (31cm) *Candy Kid*, all original. *H&J Foulke, Inc.*

EFFanBEE continued

Honey: 1949—1955. All-hard plastic, jointed at neck, shoulders and hips; synthetic, mohair or human hair, sleep eyes; original clothes; all in good condition.

MARK: EFFANBEE

14in (36cm)	**$140—160**
18in (46cm)	**175—195**
24in (61cm)	**250—275**

15in (38cm) *Patsy Ann* as Official Girl Scout, all original. *H&J Foulke, Inc.*

Official Girl Scout: 1960—61. All vinyl, jointed at neck, shoulders and hips, using *Patsy Ann* face, lashed sleeping eyes, freckles, closed mouth, rooted saran hair; original Girl Scout uniform. All in excellent condition. Also came dressed as Official Brownie.

MARK:
> EFFANBEE
> PATSY ANN
> 1959

15in (38cm) **$90—100**

18in (46cm) *Honey*, all original. *H&J Foulke, Inc.*

Effanbee Limited Edition Dolls:
1975—on. All-vinyl jointed doll; original clothes; excellent condition.

1975 *Precious Baby*	**$350**	
1976 *Patsy*	**350**	
1977 *Dewees Cochran*	**175—200**	
1978 *Crowning Glory*	**150—175**	
1979 *Skippy*	**300—325**	
1980 *Susan B. Anthony*	**150**	
1981 *Girl with Watering Can*	**150**	
1982 *Princess Diana*	**150**	
1983 *Sherlock Holmes*	**125**	

1976 *Patsy* Limited Edition, all original. *H&J Foulke, Inc.*

Eisenmann & Co.

Maker: Eisenmann & Co., exporter of dolls and toys, Fürth, Germany, and London, England

Date: 1881 on

Material: Bisque head, composition body

Mark:

$$Einco$$
$$Germany$$

Einco Character Baby: Perfect bisque head with solid dome; painted eyes, open/closed mouth; bent limb baby body; dressed; all in good condition.

12—14in (31—36cm)   **$ 400—500**

Glass eyed toddler, 14in (36cm)   **2000—2500****

**Not enough price samples to compute a reliable range.

14in(36cm)Einco toddler. *Esther Schwartz Collection.*

Maude Tousey Fangel

Maker: Averill Manufacturing Co. and Georgene Novelties, New York, N.Y.,
U.S.A.
Date: 1938
Material: All-cloth
Size: 10in (25cm) and up
Designer: Maude Tousey Fangel
Mark: "M.T.F.©" at side of face on hair, but often inside the seam

---

Maude Tousey Fangel Doll: All-cloth with printed face in several variations
which came dressed as a baby or child; some bodies are of printed cloth, some
plain; soft stuffed, flexible arms and legs; original or appropriate clothes; all
in good condition.
12—16in (31—41cm) **$450—475**
Baby with removable clothes,
16—17in (41—43cm) **600—700**

Marked M.T.F. © girl,
all original. *H&J Foulke,
Inc.*

Farnell's Alpha Toys

Maker: J. K. Farnell Co., Ltd., Acton, London, England
Date: 1930s
Material: Felt and cloth
Mark: Cloth label on foot:

> FARNELL'S
> ALPHA TOYS
> MADE IN ENGLAND

Alpha Toys Child: All-cloth with felt face, painted features, mohair wig; cloth body jointed at neck, shoulders and hips; original clothes; all in good condition.

Child, 14in (36cm)   **$250—300**

Alpha Toys Coronation Doll of King George VI, 16in (41cm)   **350**

16in (41cm) Farnell's *King George VI*.
Private Collection.

French Bébé
(Unmarked)

Maker: Numerous French firms
Date: Ca. 1880—1925
Material: Bisque head, jointed composition body
Size: Various
Mark: None, except perhaps numbers, Paris, or France

Unmarked French Bébé: Perfect bisque head, swivel neck, lovely wig, set paperweight eyes, closed mouth, pierced ears; jointed French body; pretty costume; all in good condition, excellent quality.

14—16in (36—41cm)	**$1900—2200**
22—24in (56—61cm)	**2600—2900**

Mediocre quality:

18—20in (46—51cm)	**1800—2000**

Very early face:

13—15in (33—38cm)	**3000—3500**
19—21in (48—53cm)	**4500—4800**

Open Mouth:
1890s:

14—16in (36—41cm)	**1200—1400**
21—23in (53—59cm)	**1700—1900**

1920s:

16—18in (41—46cm)	**625—675***
22—23in (56—58cm)	**750—850***

*Very pretty only.

26in (66cm) *French Bébé* incised "Paris." *Kay and Wayne Jensen Collection.*

French Fashion-Type
(Unmarked)

Maker: Various French firms
Date: Ca. 1860—1930
Material: Bisque shoulder head, jointed kid body, some with bisque lower limbs.
Mark: None, except possibly numbers or letters

French Fashion: Perfect unmarked bisque shoulder head, swivel or stationary neck, kid body, kid arms -- some with wired fingers or old bisque arms; original or good wig, lovely blown glass eyes, closed mouth, earrings; appropriate clothes; all in good condition.

Early fine quality:

10—12in (25—31cm)	**$1100—1300 and up***
14—15in (36—38cm)	**1500—1600 and up***
17—18in (43—46cm)	**1800—2100 and up***
21—22in (53—56cm)	**2300—2600 and up***

Blown kid body, 17in (43cm) **4000***
Kid over wood upper arms, bisque lower,
15in (38cm) **1800—1900***
Later models:

12in (31cm)	**900—950**
14in (36cm)	**1000—1100**
20in (51cm)	**1350—1550**

*Greatly depending upon the appeal of the face.
*Allow extra for original clothes.

Shoulder head French Fashion lady, all original. *Private Collection.*

19in (48cm) French Fashion lady with skin wig. *Elizabeth McIntyre.*

French Fashion-Type
(Wood Body)

Maker: Unknown
Date: Ca. 1860—on
Material: Bisque head, fully-jointed wood body
Mark: Size numbers only

Wood Body Lady: Perfect bisque swivel head on shoulder plate, good wig, paperweight eyes, closed mouth, pierced ears; wood body, fully-jointed at shoulders, elbows, wrists, hips and knees; dressed; all in good condition. Rare with ball-joint at waist and ankle joints.

16—19in (41—48cm) **$3500 and up**

Wood-bodied French fashion lady, fully-jointed, including waist and ankle. *Grace Dyar.*

Freundlich

Maker: Freundlich Novelty Corp., New York, N.Y., U.S.A.
Date: 1923—on
Material: All-composition

Baby Sandy: 1939—1942. All-composition with swivel head, jointed shoulders and hips, chubby toddler body; molded hair, smiling face, larger sizes have sleep eyes, smaller ones painted eyes; appropriate clothes; all in good condition.

MARK: On head:
"Baby Sandy"
On pin:
"The Wonder Baby
Genuine Baby Sandy Doll"

8in (20cm)	**$110—125**
12in (31cm)	**140—165**
14—15in (36—38cm)	**200—250**

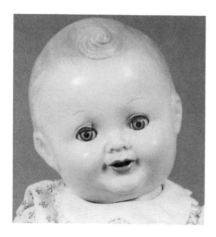

15in (38cm) ***Baby Sandy***, original pin. *H&J Foulke, Inc.*

General Douglas MacArthur: Ca. 1942. All-composition portrait doll, molded hat, painted features, one arm to salute if desired; jointed shoulders and hips; original khaki uniform; all in good condition.

MARK: Cardboard tag:
"General MacArthur"
18in (46cm) **$200—225**

18in (46cm) ***General Douglas MacArthur*** with ***WAVE*** and ***WAAC***. *Private Collection.*

Military Dolls: Ca. 1942. All-composition with molded hats, jointed shoulders and hips, character face, painted features; original clothes. ***Soldier, Sailor, WAAC***, and ***WAVE***, all in good condition.

MARK: Cardboard tag
15in (38cm) **$125—150**

Frozen Charlotte
(Bathing Doll)

Maker: Various German firms
Date: Ca. 1850s—early 1900s
Material: Glazed china; sometimes untinted bisque
Size: 1—18in (3—46cm)
Mark: None, except for "Germany," or numbers or both

Frozen Charlotte: All-china doll, black or blonde molded hair parted down the middle, painted features; hands extended, legs separated but not jointed; no clothes; perfect condition.

2—3in (5—8cm)	**$ 30—40**
4—5in (10—13cm)	**70—85**
6—7in (15—18cm)	**100—125**
10—11in (25—28cm)	**225—250**
14—15in (36—38cm)	**325—375**
Pink tint,	
5in (13cm)	**150—165**
Pink tint with bonnet,	
5in (13cm)	**275—300**
Parian-type (untinted bisque),	
5in (13cm)	**125—150**
Alice style with pink boots,	
5in (13cm)	**225—250**
Tinted bisque, molded blonde hair,	
3½in (9cm)	**85**

*Allow extra for pink tint, fine decoration and modeling and unusual hairdos.

5in (13cm) Parian-type Frozen Charlotte with *Alice* hairdo, pink luster boots, all original. *H&J Foulke, Inc.*

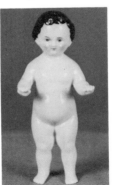

5½in (14cm) china Frozen Charlotte, faint pink tint. *H&J Foulke, Inc.*

Fulper

Maker: Heads by Fulper Pottery Co. of Flemington, N.J., U.S.A.
for other companies, often Amberg or Horsman
Date: 1918—1921
Material: Bisque heads; composition ball-jointed or jointed
kid bodies
Mark: "Fulper—Made in U.S.A."

*Made in
USA
13*

Fulper Child Doll: Perfect bisque head, good wig; kid jointed or composition
ball-jointed body; set or sleep eyes, open mouth; suitably dressed; all in good
condition.
Kid body, 16—19in (41—48cm)   **$350—400***
Composition body, 18—20in (46—51cm)   **475—525***

Fulper Baby or Toddler: Same as
above, but with bent-limb or
jointed toddler body.
15—16in (36—41cm) **$450—500***
19—21in (48—53cm)   **600—700***
24in (61cm)   **800—850***

*Do not pay as much for an ugly
doll or one with poor bisque.

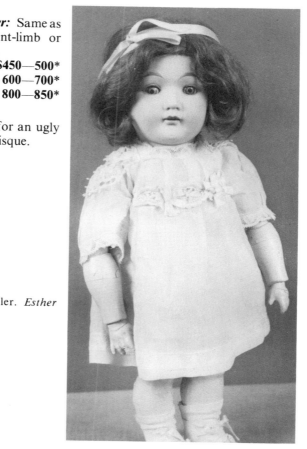

17in (43cm) Fulper toddler. *Esther
Schwartz Collection.*

Gaultier

Maker: François Gauthier name changed to Gaultier in the early 1870s; St. Maurice, Charenton, Seine, Paris, France (This company made only porcelain parts, not bodies.)
Date: Late 1860s—on
Material: Bisque head; kid or composition body

Marked F. G. Fashion Lady: Late 1860s to 1930. Bisque swivel head on bisque shoulder plate, original kid body, kid arms with wired fingers or bisque lower arms and hands; original or good French wig, lovely large stationary eyes, closed mouth, ears pierced; dressed; all in good condition.
MARK: "F.G." on side of shoulder
12—13in (31—33cm) **$1000—1100***
16—18in (41—46cm) **1400—1650***
21—22in (53—56cm) **2000—2200***
Late doll in ethnic costume:
11—12in (28—31cm) **750—850**

*Greatly depending upon the appeal of the face.

21in (53cm) F.G. fashion lady. *Esther Schwartz Collection.*

Gaultier continued

Marked F. G. Bébé: Ca. 1879—1887. Bisque swivel head on shoulder plate and gusseted kid body with bisque lower arms or chunky jointed composition body; good wig, large bulgy paperweight eyes, closed mouth, pierced ears; dressed; all in good condition.

MARK: "F. 7 G." (or other size number)

14—16in (38—41cm)	**$2500—2800**
19—22in (48—56cm)	**3000—3300**
25—26in (64—66cm)	**3750—4250**

Marked F. G. Bébé: Ca. 1887—1900 and probably later. Bisque head, composition jointed body; good French wig, beautiful large set eyes, closed mouth, pierced ears; well dressed; all in good condition.

MARK:

15—17in (38—43cm)	**$1800—2100***
22—24in (56—61cm)	**2400—2800***
27—28in (69—71cm)	**3000—3500***
Open mouth:	
15—17in (38—43cm)	**1200—1500**
20—22in (51—56cm)	**1600—1900**

*And up, depending upon appeal of face.

See color photo on page 71.

28in (71cm) F 12 G child. *Kay and Wayne Jensen Collection.*

Georgene Novelties

Maker: Georgene Novelties, Inc., (Georgene Averill, Madame Hendren), New York, N.Y., U.S.A.
Date: 1930s—on
Material: All-cloth or composition and cloth
Designer: Many dolls by Georgene Averill; also see Maude Tousey Fangel, Grace Drayton and Madame Hendren
Mark: Usually a paper tag

Internationals and Children: Mask face with painted features, yarn hair, some with real eyelashes; cloth body with movable arms and legs; attractive original clothes; all in excellent condition.

International:

12in (31cm)	**$ 50—60**
Mint-in-box with wrist tag,	
12in (31cm)	**70—80**
24—26in (61—66cm)	**125—150**

Children:

12—14in (31—36cm)	**100—125**
10in (25cm) *Topsy & Eva*	**100—125**
14in (36cm) *Little Lulu*, 1944	**300****
14in (36cm) *Nancy*, 1944	**350****
14in (36cm) *Sluggo*, 1944	**350****
14in (36cm) *Tubby Tom*, 1951	**350****

**Not enough price samples to compute a reliable range.

12in (31cm) *England* International doll, all original. *Private Collection.*

14in (36cm) *Sluggo*, all original. *Kay and Wayne Jensen Collection.*

Georgene Novelties continued

Harriet Flanders: 1937. All-composition with jointed neck, shoulders and hips; chubby toddler body; solid dome head with tufts of molded blonde hair, lashed sleeping eyes, closed mouth; original clothes. Very good condition. Designed by Harriet Flanders.

MARK: HARRIET © FLANDERS

16in (41cm)   **$250**

Painted eyes, 12in (31cm)   **150**

Harriet Flanders, all original.
H&J Foulke, Inc.

German Bisque
(Unmarked or Unidentified Marks)

Maker: Various German firms
Date: 1860s—on
Material: Bisque head, composition, kid or cloth body
Mark: Some numbered, some "Germany," some both

Molded Hair Doll: Ca. 1880. Tinted bisque shoulder head with beautifully molded hair (usually blonde), painted eyes (sometimes glass), closed mouth; original kid or cloth body; appropriate clothes; all in good condition.

13—15in (33—38cm)	**$225—275***
19—21in (48—53cm)	**375—425***
24in (61cm)	**475—500***
Unusual style, 16in (41cm)	**500—600**
Glass eyes, 16—18in (41—46cm)	**500—600**
Tiny doll, 5—7in (13—18cm)	**90—110**

*Allow extra for glass eyes and elaborate or unusual hairdo.

16in (41cm) molded hair child with black hair band. *Joe Jackson and Joel Pearson.*

American School Boy (so-called): Ca. 1880s. Perfect bisque head, molded blonde hair (sometimes brown hair), glass eyes, closed mouth; composition, kid or cloth body; nicely dressed; all in good condition.

Shoulder head,	
12in (31cm)	**$350**
16—17in (41—43cm)	**475—550**
Socket head,	
9—10in (23—25cm)	**400—425**

17in (43cm) so-called ***American School Boy***. *Roberts Collection.*

German Bisque continued

Hatted or Bonnet Doll: Ca. 1880—1920. Bisque head with painted molded hair and molded fancy bonnet with bows, ribbons, flowers, feathers, and so forth; painted eyes and facial features; original cloth body with bisque arms and legs; good old clothes or nicely dressed; all in good condition.

12—15in (31—38cm) "Marqueritas" (stone bisque)	$ 200—250
12—15in (31—38cm) fine quality	350—400
18in (46cm) bonnet with scarf, glass eyes	2300**
17in (43cm) bonnet with molded flowers, pierced ears	4800**
All-bisque, 5in (13cm)	
Common-type	75—95
More unusual style	185—225
All-bisque flappers, 3—4in (8—10cm)	125—150

**Not enough price samples to compute a reliable range.

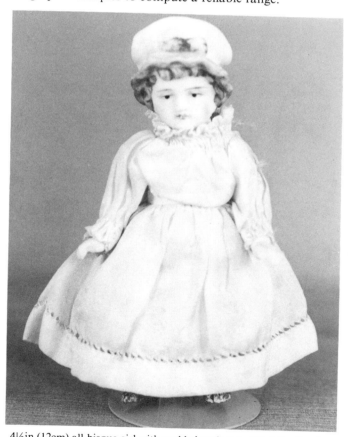

4½in (12cm) all-bisque girl with molded mob cap. *H&J Foulke, Inc.*

German Bisque continued

Child Doll with closed mouth: Ca. 1880—1890. Perfect bisque head; kid or cloth body, gusseted at hips and knees with good bisque hands or jointed composition body; good wig; nicely dressed; all in good condition.

Kid or cloth body,

12—13in (31—33cm)	**$ 500—600***
17—19in (38—48cm)	**750—850***
21—23in (53—58cm)	**900—1000***

Composition body:

11—13in (28—33cm)	**1100—1200**
16—19in (41—48cm)	**1450—1750**
23—25in (58—64cm)	**1850—2100**

*Allow extra for swivel neck or unusual face.

39in (99cm) unmarked child with open/closed mouth and molded teeth, composition body. *Wayne and Kay Jensen Collection.*

18in (46cm) closed mouth child, swivel neck, kid body, all original. *Private Collection.*

15in (38cm) closed mouth lady, swivel neck, kid body. *Edna Black Collection.*

German Bisque continued

Child Doll with open mouth: Late 1880s—1900. Perfect fine, pale bisque head, ball-jointed composition body or kid body with bisque lower arms; good wig, glass eyes, open mouth; dressed; all in good condition.

16—18in (41—46cm) **$375—425***
22—24in (56—61cm) **500—550***
28—30in (71—76cm) **850—950***

*Allow extra for swivel neck or unusual face.

14in (36cm) 51/4 child with open mouth, swivel neck, kid body, all original. *Esther Schwartz Collection.*

17in (43cm) child with open mouth, swivel neck, kid body, all original. *Esther Schwartz Collection.*

Child Doll with open mouth: 1900—1940. Perfect bisque head, ball-jointed composition, kid or cloth body with bisque lower arms; good wig, glass sleep eyes, open mouth; pretty clothes; all in good condition.

12—14in (31—36cm) **$200—250**
16—18in (41—46cm) **275—325**
22—24in (56—61cm) **375—425**
28—30in (71—76cm) **500—600**

7½in (19cm) tiny child doll. *H&J Foulke, Inc.*

Tiny child doll: 1890 to World War I. Perfect bisque socket head of good quality, five-piece composition body of good quality with molded and painted shoes and stockings; good wig, set or sleep eyes, open mouth; cute clothes; all in good condition.

5—6in (13—15cm) **$150—200**
8—10in (20—25cm) **200—250**
Fully-jointed body,
7—8in (18—20cm) **275—300**
Closed mouth:
4½—5½in (12—14cm) **225—250**
8in (20cm) **325—375**

German Bisque continued

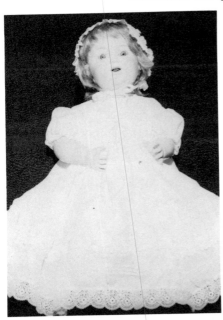

26in (66cm) character baby with unidentified fancy mark. *Hurford Collection.*

Character Baby: 1910—on. Perfect bisque head, good wig or solid dome with painted hair, sleep eyes, open mouth; composition bent-limb baby body; suitably dressed; all in good condition.

7—8in (18—20cm) painted eyes	**$200—225**
13—15in (33—38cm)	**425—475***
18—20in (46—51cm)	**550—600***
22—24in (56—61cm)	**700—800***

*Allow more for open/closed mouth, closed mouth or unusual face.

See color photo on page 69.

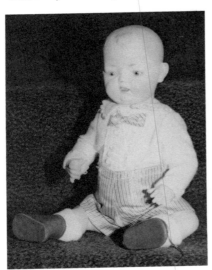

13½in (34cm) character baby 596-4. *Hurford Collection.*

18in (46cm) character baby 614. *Esther Schwartz Collection.*

German Bisque continued

Character Child: 1910—on. Bisque head with good wig or solid dome head with painted hair, sleep or painted eyes, open or closed mouth, expressive character face; jointed composition body; dressed; all in good condition.

15—18in (38—46cm) **$1200 up***

#111, 128

18—20in (46—51cm)   **8000 up****

*Depending upon individual face.

**Not enough price samples to compute a reliable average.

Infant, unmarked or unidentified maker: 1924—on. Perfect bisque head with molded and painted hair, glass sleep eyes; cloth body, celluloid or composition hands; dressed; all in good condition.

10—12in (25—31cm) long   **$300—350***

15—18in (38—46cm) long   **500—600***

*More depending upon appeal and rarity of face.

13in (33cm) long 134 infant with open nostrils. *H&J Foulke, Inc.*

Rare character child incised "111." *Old Curiosity Shop.*

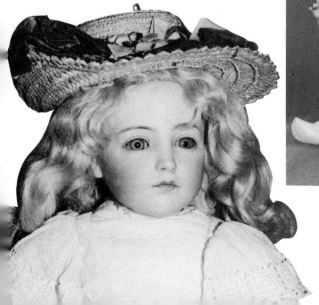

German Bisque "Dolly" Faces

Numerous companies produced girl dolls with open mouths, sleep eyes, mohair wigs and ball-jointed composition or kid bodies between 1900—1930. These all run approximately the same price for a perfect good-quality bisque head and appropriate body with nice clothes. Do not pay as much for the very late bisques and the cheaply-made bodies.

Trade Names	Makers
My Girlie	G & S
My Sweetheart	MOA Welsch
Viola	E. U. Steiner
Daisy	G. B.
Ruth	L H B
Dollar Princess	L H K
Majestic	Gebrüder Knoch
Pansy	

Very good quality:

16—18in (41—46cm)	$375—425
21—23in (53—58cm)	475—525
28—30in (71—76cm)	750—850

Mediocre quality socket or shoulder head:

12—13in (31—33cm)	175—200
15—16in (38—41cm)	225—250
18—20in (46—51cm)	300—325
23—24in (58—61cm)	350—400
27—28in (69—71cm)	500—550

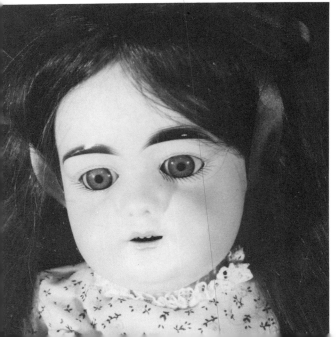

20in (51cm) LHK child, unidentified maker. *H&J Foulke, Inc.*

Gesland

Maker: Heads: François Gaultier, Paris, France
Bodies: E., F. & A. Gesland, Paris, France
Date: Late 1860s—on
Material: Bisque head, stockinette stuffed body on wire frame, bisque or composition lower arms and legs
Mark: Head: **F. G** Body: Sometimes stamped E. Gesland

Gesland Bodied: Fashion lady: bisque swivel head, good wig, paperweight eyes, closed mouth, pierced ears; stockinette body with bisque hands and legs; dressed; all in good condition.
16—19in (41—48cm) **$3000—3500**

Bébé-type bisque swivel head: Good wig, paperweight eyes, closed mouth, pierced ears; stockinette body with composition lower arms and legs; dressed; all in good condition.
14—16in (36—41cm) **$2400—2600***
22—24in (56—61cm) **3700—4200***

*For beautiful early face. Do not pay as much for later face.

17½in (45cm) Gesland fashion lady, all original. *Private Collection.*

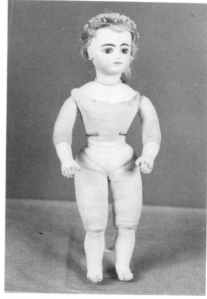

13½in (34cm) Gesland bébé with F. G. head. *Private Collection.*

Giebeler-Falk

Maker: Giebeler-Falk Doll Corporation, New York, N.Y., U.S.A.
Date: 1918—1921
Material: Aluminum head, sometimes aluminum hands and feet, wood or composition torso, arms and legs
Size: 16, 18, 20, 22 and 25in (41, 46, 51, 56 and 64cm)
Mark:

U. S. PAT.

Marked Giebeler-Falk Doll: Aluminum head with smiling face, open/closed mouth with painted upper teeth, metal sleeping eyes, chin dimple, mohair wig; jointed wood or composition body, sometimes with metal hands and feet with jointed ankles; appropriate clothing; all in good condition.
16—18in (46—51cm) **$250****

**Not enough price samples to compute a reliable average.

Giebeler-Falk doll with metal head, hands and feet; jointed wood torso and upper limbs. *Dolly Valk Collection.*

LEFT: 15in (38cm) Heinrich Handwerck child, all original. *Esther Schwartz Collection. For further information see page 194.* **ABOVE:** 23in (59cm) A.M. 1894 child. *H&J Foulke, Inc. For further information see page 280.*

24in (61cm) A.M. 400 character girl. *Esther Schwartz Collection. For further information see page 282.*

14½in (37cm) Jules Steiner *Le Parisien* Bébé, A-7. *Private Collection. For further information see pages 80 and 362.*

21in (53cm) Chase boy. *Dolly Valk Collection. For further information see page 104.*

18in (46cm) German character baby 614. *Esther Schwartz Collection. For further information see page 172.*

ABOVE: 17in (43cm) Fulper toddler, all original. *Esther Schwartz Collection. For further information see page 163.* **BELOW:** 15in (38cm) A.M. pouty character girl. *Esther Schwartz Collection. For further information see page 282 (under Character Children).*

13½in (34cm) Kämmer & Reinhardt 101 character boy with glass eyes, all original. *Esther Schwartz Collection. For further information see page 237.*

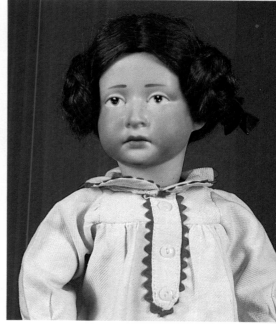

10in (25cm) Simon & Halbig *Uncle Sam*, S3. *Private Collection. For further information see page 138.*

17½in (45cm) Gesland fashion lady, all original. *Private Collection. For further information see page 175.*

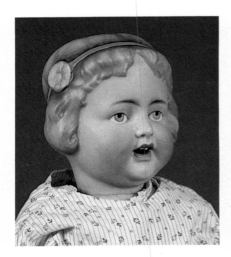

20in (51cm) ABG 1358 character. *Esther Schwartz Collection. For further information see page 55.*

23in (59cm) Ernst Heubach 300 character baby. *Esther Schwartz Collection. For further information see page 205.*

18in (46cm) Jules Steiner *Le Parisien* A-11 Bébé, all original. *Esther Schwartz Collection. For further informations ee page 362.*

13in (33cm) Bébé Bru with circle dot mark. *Esther Schwartz Collection. For further information see page 87 (under Marked Crescent or Circle Dot Bébé).*

21in (53cm) F. G. fashion lady. *Esther Schwartz Collection. For further information see page 164.*

TOP LEFT: 16in (41cm) Käthe Kruse, Doll I, all original. *Private Collection. For further information see page 267.*

TOP RIGHT: 15in (38cm) Kämmer & Reinhardt 115A toddler. *Esther Schwartz Collection. For further information see page 237.*

LEFT: 13in (33cm) Kämmer & Reinhardt 101 child, all original. *Private Collection. For further information see page 237.*

TOP LEFT: 10in (25cm) A.M. 210 and 6½in (16cm) A.M. 320 googlies. *Private Collection. For further information see page 189.*

TOP RIGHT: 9in (23cm) googly with composition face, all original. *H&J Foulke, Inc. For further information see page 192 (under Composition face).*

LEFT: 17in (43cm) Simon & Halbig 949 child, all original. *Private Collection. For further information see page 348.*

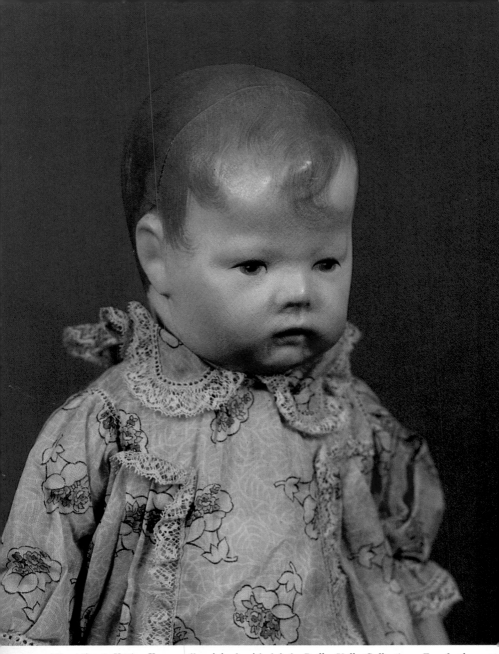

17in (43cm) Käthe Kruse, all original with label. *Dolly Valk Collection. For further information see page 267.*

Gladdie

Maker: Made in Germany for George Borgfeldt, New York, N.Y., U.S.A.
Date: 1929
Material: Ceramic head, cloth torso, composition arms and legs
Size: 17—22in (43—56cm)
Designer: Helen W. Jensen
Mark:

[sic] *Gladdie
Copyriht By
Helen W. Jensen*

Marked Gladdie: Ceramic head, molded and painted hair, glass eyes, open/closed mouth with molded teeth, laughing face; cloth torso, composition arms and legs; dressed; all in good condition.
18—19in (46—48cm) **$ 850—950**
Bisque head,
   13in (33cm)   **2800****

**Not enough price samples to compute a reliable range.

18in (46cm)
Gladdie, all
original.
*Private
Collection.*

Godey's Little Lady Dolls

Maker: Ruth Gibbs, Flemington, N.J., U.S.A.
Date: 1946
Material: China head and limbs, cloth body
Size: Most 7in (18cm); a few 12 or 13in (31 or 33cm)
Designer: Herbert Johnson
Mark: Paper label inside skirt "Godey's Little Lady Dolls;" "R. G." incised on
back plate.

Ruth Gibbs Doll: China head with painted black, brown, blonde or auburn
hair and features; pink cloth body with china limbs and painted slippers
which often matched the hair color; original clothes, usually in an old-
fashioned style.

7in (18cm)	**$ 50—60**
13in (33cm) undressed	**100—110**

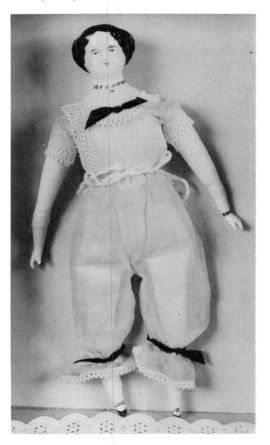

13in (33cm) *Mrs. Mary Ruth* in
camisole and long panties with
molded necklace and bracelet.
H&J Foulke, Inc.

Goebel

Maker: F. & W. Goebel porcelain factory, near Coburg, Thüringia, Germany
Date: 1879—on
Material: Bisque heads, composition bodies; also all-bisque
Mark: ~~[logo]~~ or ~~[logo]~~   "B" + number; "Germany"

sometimes A, C, G, H, K, S, SA & T

Goebel Child Doll: 1895—on. Perfect bisque socket head, good wig, sleep
  eyes, open mouth; composition jointed body; dressed; all in good condition.

4½—5in (12—13cm)	**$150**
16—18in (41—46cm)	**275—325**
22—24in (56—61cm)	**375—450**

Goebel Character Doll: Ca. 1910. Perfect bisque head with molded hair in
  various styles, some with hats, character face smiling or somber with painted
  features; papier-mâché five-piece body; all in excellent condition.
6½in (17cm) **$300—350**

4½in (12cm) child doll 120. *H&J Foulke, Inc.*

6½in (17cm) unmarked girl with molded flowers in her hair, typical of small character heads produced by Goebel. *H&J Foulke, Inc.*

Goebel continued

Goebel Character Baby: Ca. 1910. Perfect bisque socket head, good wig, sleep eyes, open mouth with teeth; composition jointed baby body; dressed; all in good condition.

18—20in (46—51cm)   **$450—550**

Pincushion Half Doll: Ca. 1915. Perfect china half figure usually of a lady with molded hair and painted features, sometimes with molded clothing, hats or accessories; lovely modeling and painting. Most desirable have fancy clothing or hair ornamentation and extended arms.

MARK:

4in (10cm)   **$150 and up***

*Depending upon rarity.

6½in (17cm) marked Goebel lady with fancy hairdo and extended arms. *Nancy Schwartz Blaisure Collection.*

Googly-Eyed Dolls

Maker: J. D. Kestner, Armand Marseille, Hertel, Schwab & Co., Heubach, H. Steiner, Goebel and other German and French firms

Date: Ca. 1911—on

Material: Bisque heads and composition or papier-mâché bodies or all-bisque

---

All-Bisque Googly: Jointed at shoulders and hips, molded shoes and socks; mohair wig, glass eyes, impish mouth; undressed; in perfect condition.

5in (13cm)	**$ 450—500**
Swivel neck, 5in (13cm)	**600—650**
Jointed elbows and knees (Kestner), 5in (13cm)	**1600—1750**
Painted eyes, 4—4½in (10—12cm)	**300—350**
Baby, 4½in (12cm)	**400—425**

Painted eyes, composition body: Perfect bisque swivel head with molded hair, painted eyes to the side, impish mouth; composition body jointed at shoulders and hips with molded and painted shoes and socks; cute clothes; all in good condition. By A.M., Heubach, Goebel and others.

6—7in (15—18cm)	**$325—350**
10in (25cm)	**450—500**

See color photo on page 183.

5in (13cm) all-bisque Kestner 189 googlies, all original. *Jane Alton Collection.*

Googly-Eyed Dolls continued

Glass eyes, composition body: Perfect bisque head, mohair wig or molded hair, sleep or set large googly eyes, impish mouth closed; original composition body jointed at neck, shoulders and hips, sometimes with molded and painted shoes and socks; cute clothes; all in nice condition.

JDK 221:

12—13in (31—33cm) Toddler	**$3500—4500**
17—18in (43—46cm) Toddler	**5500—6000**

AM #323 and other similar models by H. Steiner, Heubach and Goebel:

6½—7½in (17—19cm)	**550—650**
9—10in (23—25cm)	**800—900**
12—14in (31—36cm)	**700—800**
Baby body, 10—11in (25—28cm)	**1350—1400**

AM #253: Watermelon mouth:

6½—7½in (17—19cm)	**650—750**

SFBJ #245:

8in (20cm)	**1000—1200**
15in (38cm)	**4500—5000**

K ★ R 131:

15—16in (38—41cm)	**6500—7500**

AM #240, 241, 200:

11—12in (28—31cm)	**2000—2500**

Heubach Einco:

14—15in (36—38cm)	**6000—7000**

Oscar Hitt:

15in (38cm)	**6500—7500**

Hertel, Schwab & Co. #165:

11in (28cm) Baby	**2500—2800**
15in (38cm) Toddler	**3500—4000**

Hertel, Schwab & Co. #172, 173:

15—16in (38—41cm)	**4500—5500****

Demalcol (Dennis, Malley, & Co., London, England)

Head only, no eyes	**150—225**
Complete doll, 9—11in (23—28cm)	**500—650**

**Not enough price samples to compute a reliable range.

OPPOSITE PAGE: CLOCKWISE:

7in (18cm) Goebel googly, all original. *H&J Foulke, Inc.*

11in (28cm) A.M. 323 googly baby. *Private Collection.*

5½in (14cm) googly 393/10. *H&J Foulke, Inc.*

18in (46cm) JDK 221 googly. *Jackie's Dolls of the Valley.*

Googly-Eyed Dolls continued

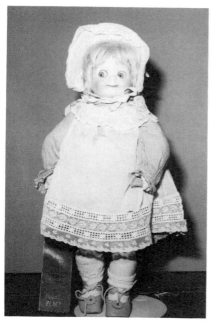

Googly-Eyed Dolls continued

Composition face: 1911—1914.
Made by various companies in
9½—14in (24—36cm) sizes;
marked with paper label on
clothing. Called "Hug Me Kid-
dies," "Little Bright Eyes," as
well as other trade names. Round
all-composition or composition
mask face, wig, round glass eyes
looking to the side, watermelon
mouth; felt body; original clothes;
all in very good condition.

9—10in (23—25cm)   **$500—600**
12in (31cm)   **700—800**

Googly with molded hat: 1915.
Perfect bisque head with glass
side-glancing eyes, watermelon
mouth, molded hat; jointed
composition body. Made for
Max Handwerck, possibly by
Hertel, Schwab & Co. All were
soldiers: "U.S." (Uncle Sam hat);
"E," (English Bellhop-type hat);
"D," German; "T," Austrian/
Turk (two faces).

MARK:
"Dep
Elite"

12—13in (31—33cm) **$2000—2500**
Two faces:
13in (33cm)   **2800—3200**

Composition face googly, all original.
H&J Foulke, Inc.

13in (33cm) googly with English hat.
Esther Schwartz Collection.

Greiner

Maker: Ludwig Greiner of Philadelphia, PA., U.S.A.
Date: 1858—1883
Material: Heads of papier-mâché, cloth bodies, homemade in most cases, but later some Lacmann bodies were used.
Size: Various, 13—over 35in (33—over 89cm)
Mark: Paper label on back shoulder:

GREINER'S
IMPROVED
PATENTHEADS
Pat. March 30TH '58

or

GREINER'S
PATENT DOLL HEADS
No 7
Pat. Mar. 30 '58. Ext.' 72

Greiner: Blonde or black molded hair, painted features; homemade cloth body, leather arms; nice old clothes; entire doll in good condition.

'58 label:

20—23in (51—58cm)	$ 900—1100
28—30in (71—76cm)	1500—1700

Much worn:

20—23in (51—56cm)	500—600
28—30in (71—76cm)	700—800

Glass eyes,

20—23in (51—58cm)	1700—1900

'72 label:

19—22in (48—56cm)	450—500
29—31in (71—79cm)	700—800

31in (78cm) Greiner with '58 label. *Private Collection.*

Heinrich Handwerck

Maker: Heinrich Handwerck, doll factory, Waltershausen, Thüringia, Germany. Heads by Simon & Halbig.

Date: 1855—on

Material: Bisque head, composition ball-jointed body or kid body

Trademarks: Bébé Cosmopolite, Bébé de Réclame, Bébé Superior

Mark: "Germany—Handwerck" sometimes with "S & H" and numbers 69, 79, 89, 99, 109, 119 and others

Hch 6/0 H.

HANDWERCK— *Germany*

Marked Handwerck Child Doll: Ca. 1885—on. Perfect bisque socket head, original or good wig, sleep or set eyes, open mouth, pierced ears; ball-jointed body; dressed; entire doll in good condition.

#89 Closed mouth:

22—24in (56—61cm)	**$1600—1800**

Open mouth:

17—19in (43—48cm)	**375—425**
22—24in (56—61cm)	**450—550**
27—28in (69—71cm)	**725—800**
30in (76cm)	**850—900**
32—33in (81—84cm)	**1000—1100**
35—36in (89—91cm)	**1400—1500**
39—42in (99—107cm)	**2500 up**

See color photo on page 177.

24in (61cm) Heinrich Handwerck/ Simon Halbig child. *H&J Foulke, Inc.*

Max Handwerck

Maker: Max Handwerck, doll factory, Waltershausen, Thüringia, Germany. Some heads by Goebel.

Date: 1900—on

Material: Bisque head, ball-jointed composition or kid body

Trademarks: Bébé Elite, Triumph-Bébé

Mark: also "Bébé Elite"

Marked Max Handwerck Child Doll: Perfect bisque socket head, original or good wig, set or sleep eyes, open mouth, pierced ears; original ball-jointed body; well dressed; all in good condition.

16—18in (41—46cm)	**$350—400**
22—24in (56—61cm)	**450—500**

Marked Bébé Elite Character: Perfect bisque socket head with sleep eyes, open mouth with upper teeth, smiling character face; bent-limb composition baby body; appropriate clothes; all in good condition.

16—18in (41—46cm)	**$425—525**
22—24in (56—61cm)	**600—650**

Googlies. (See page 192.)

22in (56cm) Max Handwerck child.
Esther Schwartz Collection.

Karl Hartmann

Maker: Karl Hartmann, doll factory, Stockheim/Upper Franconia, Germany
Date: 1911—1926
Material: Bisque head, jointed composition body
Mark:

Marked Karl Hartmann Doll: Perfect bisque head, good wig, glass eyes, open mouth; jointed composition body; suitable clothing; all in good condition.
22—24in (56—61cm) **$550—650**

23in (58cm) *Baby Clare* with Hartmann mark, all original. *Esther Schwartz Collection.*

Mme. Hendren

Maker: Averill Manufacturing Co., New York, N.Y., U.S.A.
Date: 1915—on
Material: Composition heads, cloth and composition bodies
Designer: Many by Georgene Averill
Mark: Cloth tag attached to clothes

Tagged Mme. Hendren Character: Ca. 1915—on. Composition character face, usually with painted features, molded hair or wig (sometimes yarn); hard-stuffed cloth body with composition hands; original clothes often of felt, included Dutch children, Indians, sailors, cowboys, blacks; all in good condition.

10—14in (25—36cm) **$100—125**

Marked Mama Dolls: Ca. 1920-on. Composition shoulder head, lower arms and legs, cloth torso with cry box; mohair wig or molded hair, sleep eyes, open mouth with teeth or closed mouth; appropriately dressed; all in good condition. Names such as *Baby Hendren, Baby Georgene* and others.

16—18in (41—46cm) **$125—150**
22—24in (56—61cm)   **175—225**

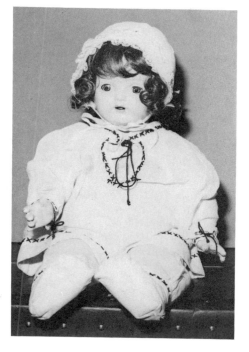

Madame Hendren mama doll. *Miriam Blankman Collection.*

Mme. Hendren continued

Dolly Reckord: 1922. Composition shoulder head, lower arms and legs, cloth torso with record player; nice human hair wig, sleep eyes, open mouth with upper teeth; appropriate clothes; all in good condition with records.
26in (66cm) **$425—475**

Whistling Doll: 1925—1929. Composition head with molded hair, side-glancing eyes, mouth pursed to whistle through round opening; composition arms, cloth torso; legs are coiled spring bellows covered with cloth; when head is pushed down or feet are pushed up, the doll whistles. Original or appropriate clothes; all in good condition.
MARK: None
Original Cardboard Tag:
"I whistle when you dance me on one foot and then the other.
      Patented Feb. 2, 1926
Genuine Madame Hendren Doll."
14—15in (36—38cm)
  sailor, cowboy, cop or boy
(Dan)   **$150—165**
14—15in (36—38cm)
  black **Rufus** or
  Dolly Dingle   **250**

Snookums: 1927. Composition shoulder head, molded and painted hair with hole for one tuft of hair, painted eyes, smiling face with open/closed mouth; composition yoke and arms, cloth body and legs; dressed; all in good condition. From the comic strip "The Newlyweds" by George McManus.
14in (36cm) **$275—325**

14in (36cm) **Whistling Cowboy**, all original. *Dolly Valk Collection.*

Body Twists: 1928. All-composition, jointed at neck, shoulders, hips, at waist with a large round ball joint; molded and painted hair, painted eyes, closed mouth; dressed; all in good condition. Advertised as **Dimmie** and **Jimmie**.
14½in (37cm) **$275—300**

Sunny Boy and Girl: Ca. 1929. Marked on head. Celluloid head with glass eyes; stuffed body with composition arms and legs; original clothes; all in good condition.
15in (38cm) **$250****

**Not enough price samples to compute a reliable range.

Hertel, Schwab & Co.

Maker: Stutzhauser Porzellanfabrik, Hertel Schwab & Co., Stutzhaus, near Ohrdruf, Thüringia, Germany

Date: 1910

Material: Bisque heads to be used on composition, cloth or leather bodies, all-bisque dolls, pincushion dolls

Mark:

*Moda
in
Germany
757/2*

*152
4*

Marked Character Baby: Perfect bisque head, molded and painted hair or good wig, sleep or painted eyes, open or open/closed mouth with molded tongue; bent limb baby body; dressed; all in good condition. Mold numbers 130, 150, 151, 152, 142.

10—12in (25—31cm)	**$275—325**
15—17in (38—43cm)	**425—475**
23—24in (58—61cm)	**700—750**

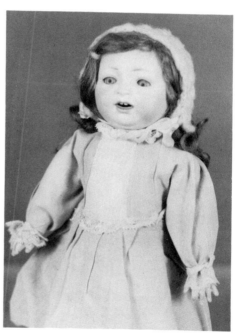

13½in (34cm) 152 character on toddler body. *Private Collection.*

11in (28cm) 151 character baby. *H&J Foulke, Inc.*

Hertel, Schwab & Co. continued

Marked Character Child: Perfect bisque head, painted or sleeping eyes,
closed mouth; jointed composition body; dressed; all in good condition.
#134, 149, 141:
    19—21in (48-53cm)   **$4500—5500**
#154 (closed mouth):
    14—16in (36-41cm)   **1500—2000**

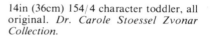

22in (56cm) character child 141. *Esther Schwartz Collection.*

14in (36cm) 154/4 character toddler, all original. *Dr. Carole Stoessel Zvonar Collection.*

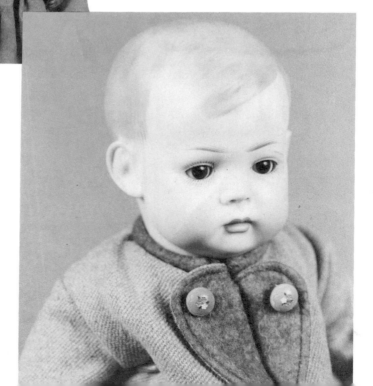

Hertel, Schwab & Co. continued

All-Bisque Doll: Jointed shoulders and hips; good wig, glass eyes, closed or open mouth; molded and painted shoes and stockings; undressed; all in good condition. Mold #208.

4—5in (10—13cm)	**$160—185**
6—7in (15—18cm)	**250—300***
8in (20cm)	**375—425***
Swivel neck,	
6—7in (15—18cm)	**350—425***

*This is for fine quality bisque, lovely tinting. Do not pay these prices for mediocre dolls.

Marked Googly: Perfect bisque head, large glass side-glancing sleeping eyes, wig or molded hair, impish closed mouth; composition body; cute clothes; all in good condition. Molds #163, 165, 172, 173.

#165:

11in (28cm) baby	**$2500—2800**
15in (38cm) toddler	**3500—4000**

#163:

17in (43cm) baby	**5500****

#172, 173:

15—16in (38—41cm)	
	4500—5500**

**Not enough price samples to compute a reliable range.

5½in (14cm) all-bisque 208 child. *H&J Foulke, Inc.*

Hertwig & Co.

Maker: Hertwig & Co., porcelain factory, Katzhutte, Thüringia, Germany
Date: 1864—on
Material: China and bisque shoulder heads, all-bisque dolls, half-bisque dolls
Mark: Germany

Bisque Shoulder Heads with Molded Bonnets: Ca. 1880—1920. (See German Bisque Section.)

Pet Name China Heads: Ca. 1905. China shoulder head, molded yoke with name in gold; black or blonde painted hair (one-third were blonde), blue painted eyes; old cloth body (some with alphabet or other figures printed on cotton material), china limbs; properly dressed: all in good condition. Names such as ***Agnes, Bertha, Daisy, Dorothy, Edith, Esther, Ethel, Florence, Helen, Mabel, Marian*** and ***Pauline***. Made for Butler Brothers, New York.

9—10in (23—25cm)   **$125—135**
16—18in (41—46cm)   **200—225**
24in (61cm)   **275—325**

19in (48cm) *Dorothy* china head. *H&J Foulke, Inc.*

Hertwig & Co. continued

Half-Bisque Dolls: 1911. Head and body to waist of one-piece bisque, molded hair, painted features, bisque hands, lower legs with white stockings and molded shoes with heels and bows, other parts of body are cloth. Appropriate clothes; all in good condition.

4½in (12cm)   **$200**
6½in (17cm)   **250**

All-Bisque Children with Molded Clothes: 1900—1910. (See All-Bisque Section.)
Pink Bisque Characters: 1920. (See All-Bisque Section.)
All-Bisque Nodders: 1920. (See All-Bisque Section.)
Snow Babies: After 1910. (See Snow Babies Section.)

4½in (12cm) half-bisque girl, all original. *H&J Foulke, Inc.*

3¼in (8cm) Hertwig nodder. *H&J Foulke, Inc.*

7in (18cm) all-bisque Hertwig boy with molded clothing. *H&J Foulke, Inc.*

Ernst Heubach

Maker: Ernst Heubach, porcelain factory, Köppelsdorf, Thüringia, Germany
Date: 1887—on
Material: Bisque head; kid, cloth or composition bodies
Mark: Heubach-Köppelsdorf
250 - 15/o
Germany

D.E.P. 1902

2/o

Heubach Child Doll: Ca. 1888—on. Perfect bisque head, good wig, sleep eyes, open mouth; kid, cloth or jointed composition body; dressed; all in good condition.

Kid or cloth body, often mold 275; 1900 or 1902:

13—15in (33—38cm)	**$150—185**
19—21in (48—53cm)	**250—300**

Composition body, often mold 250:

8—9in (20—23cm)	**$125—150**
16—18in (41—46cm)	**275—325**
23—24in (58—61cm)	**375—425**
29—30in (74—76cm)	**550—650**

13½in (34cm) mold 250 child, all original.
H&J Foulke, Inc.

23in (58cm) mold 300 character baby. *Esther Schwartz Collection.*

Character Baby: 1910—on. Often mold numbers 300, 320 and 342. Perfect bisque head, good wig, sleep eyes, open mouth (sometimes also wobbly tongue and pierced nostrils); composition bent-limb baby or toddler body; dressed; all in good condition.

9—11in (23—28cm)	**$250—300**
14—16in (36—41cm)	**400—425**
19—21in (48—53cm)	**500—550**
25—27in (64—69cm)	**700—800**

#320, jointed composition body, 28in (71cm)

Toddler:
9in (23cm) 5 pc. body

	$275—325
15—17in (38—43cm)	**550—600**
23—25in (58—64cm)	**750—850**

Character Children: 1910—on. Perfect bisque shoulder head with molded hair in various styles, some with hair bows, painted eyes, open/closed mouth; cloth body with composition lower arms.

#262 and others:
12in (31cm) **$375—425****

**Not enough price samples to compute a reliable range.

Infant: Ca. 1925. Perfect bisque head, molded and painted hair, sleep eyes, closed mouth; cloth body, composition or celluloid hands, appropriate clothes; all in good condition.

#349, 339, 350:
10—12in (25—31cm)
$450—500**
#338, 340:
14—16in (36—41cm)
700—800**

**Not enough price samples to compute a reliable range.

Gypsy: Ca. late 1920s. Tan bisque head, matching toddler body; mohair wig, sleep eyes, open mouth with teeth, brass earrings; appropriate costume; all in good condition.

#452:

9in (23cm)	**$250—300**
12in (31cm)	**375—425**

Gebrüder Heubach

Maker: Gebrüder Heubach, porcelain factory, Licht and Sonneberg,
Thüringia, Germany
Date: 1820—on; doll heads 1910—on
Material: Bisque head, kid, cloth or jointed composition body or composition
bent-limb body, all bisque
Mark:

Heubach Character Child: Ca. 1910. Perfect bisque head, molded hair, glass
or intaglio eyes, closed or open/closed mouth, character face; jointed
composition or kid body ; dressed; all in good condition.

#1907 for Jumeau, 23in (58cm)	$1250—1500
#5636 laughing child, glass eyes, JCB, 12—14in (31—36cm)	1200—1400
#5689 smiling child, large glass eyes, open mouth. See *6th Blue Book of Dolls &*	
Values, page 197.	
18—20in (46—51cm)	1600—1800
#5730 Santa child, JCB, 20—22in (51—56cm)	2500—2600
#5777 Dolly Dimple, JCB, 24in (61cm)	2500—3000
#6692 and other pouty or smiling shoulder heads, intaglio	
eyes, 14—15in (36—38cm)	375—425
#6896 pouty, JCB, 19in (48cm)	750
#6969, 6970, 7246, 7407, 8017, 8420, pouty child, glass eyes, JCB:	
12—13in (31—33cm)	1600—1800
17—18in (43—46cm)	2500—2600
23in (58cm) Baby	3000
#7604 laughing child, intaglio eyes, composition body,	
13in (33cm) Baby	500
14—15in (36—38cm)	450—500
#7622 pouty with molded hair, JCB, 16in (41cm)	900—1000
#7634, crying, 15in (38cm)	850—950
#7644 shoulder head, laughing child, 14—15in (36—38cm)	400—450
#7711, 10532 open mouth child, JCB, 22—24in (56—61cm)	800—850
#7877, 7977, Baby Stuart: 11—12in (28—31cm), JCB	1000—1100
11in (28cm) shoulder head	550—650
#7911, 8191 grinning JCB, 12—13in (31—33cm)	750—850
#7925, 7926 lady, 17—19in (43—48cm)	2500—3000
#7975, Baby Stuart: glass eyes, removable bonnet,	1650
12in (31cm) JCB	
#8192 open mouth child:	
8—9in (20—23cm) five-piece body	325—375
14—15in (36—38cm)	500—550
Smiling, open/closed mouth with tongue showing (photograph on page 207.)	
15—16in (38—41cm)	850—950

#8774 *Whistling Jim*, 13in (33cm)
#9355 smiling shoulder head, 22in (56cm)
#10586, 10633 open mouth child, JCB, 19—20in (48—51cm)
#10731 *Mirette*, 26in (66cm)

12½in (32cm) shoulder head body with laughing face. *H&J Foulke, Inc.*

16in (41cm) character with open/closed mouth and tongue between teeth. *Private Collection.*

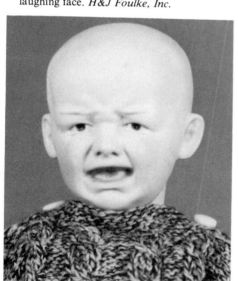

15in (38cm) character 7634 with crying face. *Private Collection.*

16in (41cm) character 7602 with pouty face. *Private Collection.*

Gebrüder Heubach continued

11in (28cm) character 6970 with pouty face. *Private Collection.*

BOTTOM RIGHT: 18in (46cm) character 5777 ***Dolly Dimple.*** *Hurford Collection.*

All-Bisque:
Position Babies,
  4—5in (10—13cm) **$250—300**
Girl with bows or hair band,
  7in (18cm) **750—850**
Bunny Boy or ***Girl,***
  5½in (14cm)
All-bisque boy or girl,
  4in (10cm)
Chin-Chin character,
  4in (10cm)
Action figures:
  6in (15cm)
  4in (10cm)
Pat-a-Cake Baby, 11in (28cm)
  smiling face with glass eyes,
  walking **600—650**

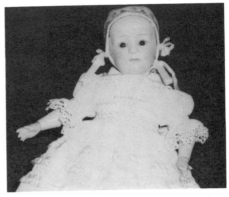

12in (31cm) character 7975 with molded removable cap and glass eyes. *Hurford Collection.*

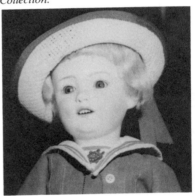

Heubach Infants: Ca. 1910. Perfect bisque head, molded hair or good wig, intaglio eyes, open or closed mouth, character face; composition bent-limb body; dressed; all in nice condition.
Pouty Babies ***#7602, 6898*** and others:
  6in (15cm) **$200**
  10in (25cm) **325—350**
  14in (36cm) **475**
  18in (46cm) **675—725**
Shoulder head on kid body,
  12—14in (31—36cm) **300—375**

Horsman

Maker: E. I. Horsman Co., New York, N.Y., U.S.A.
Date: 1901—on

Billiken: 1909. Composition head with peak of hair at top of head, slanted slits for eyes, watermelon mouth; velvet or plush body; in good condition only.
MARK: Cloth label on body; "Billiken" on right foot
12in (31cm)   **$300—350**

See color photo on page 252.

Baby Bumps: 1910. Composition head with molded hair and painted features; stuffed cloth body. Head looks like Kämmer & Reinhardt's "Baby" mold number 100.
MARK: None
10—12in (25—31cm)   **$135—165**
Black, 10in (25cm)   **165—185**

Can't Break 'Em Characters: Ca. 1910. Heads and hands of "Can't Break 'Em" composition, hard stuffed cloth bodies with swivel joints at shoulders and hips; molded hair, painted eyes, character faces; appropriate clothes; all in good condition.
MARK: "E.I.H.1911"
12in (31cm)   **$125—150**

Campbell Kid: 1910.
See page 97.

Early Babies: Ca. 1915. Head of strong composition, hard stuffed cloth body, composition hands; good wig, glass eyes; appropriate clothes, all in good condition.
MARK: "E.I.H. 1915"
10—12in (25—31cm)   **$100—125**

12in (31cm) *Can't Break 'Em* - type character with pouty face. *H&J Foulke, Inc.*

16in (41cm) all-composition toddler with glass eyes. *Nancy Schwartz Blaisure Collection.*

Early All-Composition Dolls:

Composition socket head, glass or painted eyes, wig or molded hair, closed mouth; composition toddler body; appropriate clothing; all in good condition.

Glass-eyed toddler,
16in (41cm) **$300****

Walking toddler,
20in (51cm) **$150—200****

**Not enough price samples to compute a reliable range.

Gene Carr Character: 1916. Composition head with molded and painted hair, eyes painted open or closed, wide smiling mouth with teeth; cloth body with composition hands; original or appropriate clothes; all in good condition. Names such as: *"Snowball"* (Black Boy); *"Mike"* and *"Jane"* (eyes open); *"Blink"* and *"Skinney"*(eyes closed). Designed by Bernard Lipfert from Gene Carr's cartoon characters.

MARK: None

13—14in (33—36cm) **$225—250**

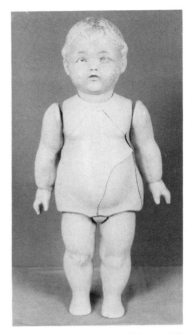

20in (51cm) Horsman walking toddler. *H&J Foulke, Inc.*

13in (33cm) Gene Carr *Blink*, all original. *H&J Foulke, Inc.*

Horsman continued

Rosebud: 1920s. Composition swivel head, mohair wig, tin sleep eyes, open mouth with teeth, smiling face with dimples; cloth torso, composition arms and legs; original clothes; all in good condition. Various sizes.

MARK: "ROSEBUD"

18—22in (46—56cm) **$175—225**

Mama Dolls: Ca. 1920—1940. Composition head, cloth body, composition arms and lower legs; mohair wig or molded hair, sleep eyes; original clothes; all in very good condition.

MARK: "E. I. H. Co." or "HORSMAN"

12—14in (31—36cm) **$ 90—100**
20—22in (51—56cm) **125—150**

12in (31cm) mama doll, all original, boxed. *H&J Foulke, Inc.*

Jackie Coogan: 1921. Composition head with molded hair, painted eyes, closed mouth; cloth torso with composition hands; appropriate clothes; all in good condition.

MARK: "E. I. H. Co. 19 © 21"

14in (36cm) **$400—450****

**Not enough price samples to compute a reliable range.

Marked Tynie Baby: 1924. Solid dome infant head with sleep eyes, closed mouth, slightly frowning face; cloth body with composition arms; appropriate clothes; all in good condition. Designed by Bernard Lipfert.

MARK: © 1924 E.I. Horsman Inc. Made in Germany

Bisque head,
12in (31cm) **$ 600—650**

Composition head,
15in (38cm) **250—275**

All-bisque with swivel neck, glass eyes, wigged or solid dome head,
9—10in (23—25cm) **1000—1200****

**Not enough price samples to compute a reliable range.

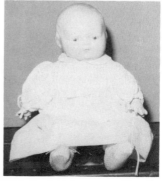

Horsman *Tynie Baby,* composition head. *Miriam Blankman Collection.*

Horsman continued

HEbee-SHEbee: 1925. All-composition, jointed at shoulders and hips, painted eyes, molded white chemise and real ribbon or wool ties in molded shoes; all in good condition. Blue shoes indicate a **HEbee**, pink ones a **SHEbee**.
11in (28cm)   **$400—450**

Ella Cinders: 1925. Composition head with molded hair, painted eyes; cloth body with composition arms and lower legs; original clothes; all in fair condition. From the comic strip by Bill Conselman and Charlie Plumb, for the Metropolitan Newspaper Service.
  MARK: "1925 © MNS"
18in (46cm)   **$500**

Baby Dimples: 1928. Composition head with molded and painted hair, tin sleep eyes, open mouth, smiling face; soft cloth body with composition arms and legs; original or appropriate old clothes; all in good condition. Various sizes.
  MARK: " ©
   E. I. H. CO. INC."
16—18in (41—46cm)   **$150—175**
22—24in (56—61cm)   **200—225**

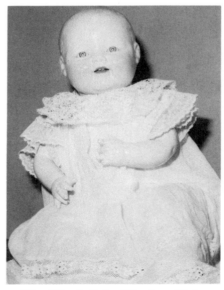

11in (28cm) all-composition **HEbee-SHE-bee,** repainted. *H&J Foulke, Inc.*

22in (56cm) **Baby Dimples**. *Miriam Blankman Collection.*

Horsman continued

Child Dolls: Ca. 1930s and 1940s. All-composition with swivel neck, shoulders and hips; mohair wig, sleep eyes; original clothes; all in good condition.

MARK: "HORSMAN"

13—14in (33—36cm) **$100—125**
16—18in (41—46cm) **150—165**
Chubby Toddler,
   16—18in (41—46cm) **150—175**

Jeanie: Ca. 1937. All-composition with swivel neck, shoulders and hips; molded and painted hair with peak on top, sleep eyes, closed mouth; appropriate old clothes; all in good condition.

MARK:
   "JEANIE
   HORSMAN"
14in (36cm) **$125—150**

Jo-Jo: 1937. All-composition toddler with swivel neck, shoulders and hips; mohair wig with braids, sleep eyes, closed mouth; appropriate old clothing; all in good condition.

MARK:
   © JO-JO
   1937 HORSMAN
12½in (32cm) **$150**

JO-JO, all original. *H&J Foulke, Inc.*

Mary Hoyer

Maker: The Mary Hoyer Doll Mfg. Co., Reading, PA., U.S.A.
Date: Ca. 1925—on
Material: First all-composition, later all-hard plastic
Size: 14 and 18in (36 and 46cm)
Mark: Embossed on torso: or in a circle:
        "The   "ORIGINAL
    Mary Hoyer   Mary Hoyer
      Doll"   Doll"

Marked Mary Hoyer: Material as above; swivel neck; jointed shoulders and hips, original wig, sleep eyes with eyelashes, closed mouth; all in good condition. Original tagged factory clothes or garments made at home from Mary Hoyer patterns.

Composition, 14in (36cm)   **$225—250**
Hard plastic, 14in (36cm)   **275—325**

14in (36cm) Mary Hoyer, all original.
Virginia Ann Heyerdahl Collection.

Huret

Maker: Maison Huret, Paris, France

Date: 1850—on

Material: China or bisque heads; kid or wood jointed bodies, sometimes with pewter hands and feet

Size: Various

Mark: "Huret" or "Maison Huret" stamped on body

Marked Huret Doll: China or bisque shoulder head, good wig, painted or glass eyes, closed mouth; kid or wood jointed body; beautifully dressed; all in good condition.

16—20in (41—51cm)   **$4000—4500 up**

Huret-type china head with painted eyes. *Grace Dyar.*

Ideal

Maker: Ideal Novelty and Toy Co., Brooklyn, N.Y., U.S.A.
Date: 1907—on
Mark: Various, usually including "IDEAL"

Uneeda Kid: 1914—1919. Composition head with molded brown hair, blue painted eyes, closed mouth; cloth body with composition arms and legs with molded black boots; original bloomer suit, yellow slicker and rain hat; carrying a box of Uneeda Biscuits; all in good condition, showing some wear.

16in (41cm)	**$200—250**
Molded hat	**275—300**

Mama Doll: Ca. 1920—1940. Composition head, cloth body, composition arms and lower legs; mohair wig or molded hair, sleep eyes; appropriate old clothes; all in very good condition.
MARK: IDEAL DOLL
14—16in (36—41cm) **$100—125**

Snoozie: 1933. Composition head, character expression with yawning mouth, sleeping eyes, molded hair, composition arms and legs or rubber arms, cloth body; baby clothes; all in good condition. 13, 16 and 20in (33, 41 and 51cm).
MARK:

©

By B. LIPFERT
16in (41cm) **$125—150**

20in (51cm) *Snoozie,* replaced clothing. *Betty Harms Collection.*

Shirley Temple: 1935. For detailed information see pages 345, 346 and 347.

Betsy Wetsy: 1937—on. Composition head with molded hair, sleep eyes; soft rubber body jointed at neck, shoulders and hips; drinks, wets; appropriate clothes; all in good condition. This doll went through many changes including hard plastic head on rubber body, later vinyl body, later completely vinyl. Various sizes.
MARK: "IDEAL"
12—14in (31—36cm)

Rubber body	**$90—100**

Ideal continued

Snow White: 1937. All-composition, jointed at neck, shoulders and hips; black mohair wig, lashed sleep eyes, open mouth; original dress with velvet bodice and cape, and rayon skirt with figures of seven dwarfs; in good condition. 11in (28cm), 13in (33cm) and 18in (46cm) sizes.

MARK: On body:
"SHIRLEY TEMPLE/18"
On dress:
"An Ideal Doll"

11—13in (28—33cm)	**$400—450**
18in (46cm)	**375—425**

Molded black hair, painted blue bow, painted eyes,

13—14in (33—36cm)	**125—175**

14in (36cm) *Snow White* with molded black hair and blue bow. *H&J Foulke, Inc.*

18in (46cm) flirty-eyed baby, replaced clothing. *H&J Foulke, Inc.*

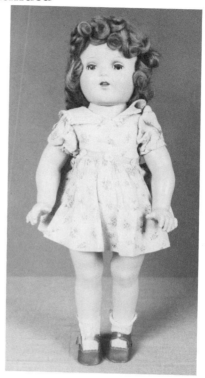

Betty Jane, all original. *H&J Foulke, Inc.*

Betty Jane: All-composition *Shirley Temple*-type doll with jointed neck, shoulders and hips; lashed sleeping eyes (sometimes flirty), open mouth with teeth; all original; very good condition.

MARK: IDEAL
18

18in (46cm)	**$175—200**

Flirty-eyed Baby: 1938. Composition head, lower arms and legs, cloth body; flirty eyes, closed mouth, molded hair; original clothing; all in good condition.

18in (46cm)	**$125—150**

Ideal continued

Fanny Brice, all original. *Dolly Valk Collection.*

Baby Snooks (Fanny Brice): 1938. Head, torso, hands and feet of composition, arms and legs made of flexible metal cable; molded hair, smiling mouth; original clothes; all in good condition.

MARK: On head: "IDEAL" Round paper tag:

"FLEXY — an Ideal Doll Fanny Brice's Baby Snooks"

12in (31cm)   **$225—250**

Mortimer Snerd: 1938—1939. Head, hands and feet of composition, arms and legs of flexible metal cable, torso of wire mesh; in original clothes; all in good condition.

MARK: Head embossed: "Ideal Doll"

13in (33cm)   **$225—250**

Deanna Durbin: 1938. All-composition, jointed at neck, shoulders and hips; original human hair or mohair wig, sleep eyes, smiling mouth with teeth; original clothing; all in good condition. Various sizes.

MARK: Metal button with picture: "DEANNA DURBIN, IDEAL DOLL, U.S.A."

14in (36cm)   **$300—400**
20—21in (51—53cm)   **500—550**

Judy Garland as Dorothy of the Wizard of Oz: 1939. All-composition, jointed at neck, shoulders and hips; dark human hair wig, dark sleep eyes, open mouth with teeth; original dress; all in good condition.

MARK: On head and body: "IDEAL DOLL"

16in (41cm)   **$900—1000 up**

Composition and wood segmented characters: 1940. Molded composition heads with painted features, wood segmented bodies. Label on front torso gives name of character.

Pinocchio,
10½in (27cm)   **$200—225**
King-Little,
14in (36cm)   **175—225**
Jiminy Cricket,
9in (23cm)   **175—225**

Ideal continued

Magic Skin Baby: 1940. Composition head with molded hair (later babies had hard plastic heads), sleep eyes, closed mouth; stuffed latex rubber body, jointed shoulders and hips; appropriate clothes; all in good condition. Various sizes.

MARK: On head: "IDEAL"

14—15in (36—38cm)   **$65—85**

12in (31cm) **Flexy Soldier,** all original. *H&J Foulke, Inc.*

14in (36cm) **Magic Skin Baby,** all original. *H&J Foulke, Inc.*

Flexy Dolls: Ca. 1942. Head, hands and feet of composition, arms and legs of flexible metal cable, torso of wire mesh; in original clothes; all in good condition.

MARK: On head: "Ideal Doll"

12in (31cm)   **$150—200**

Brother Coos: 1948—1952. Hard plastic head with dark molded hair, sleep eyes, closed mouth; composition arms and legs, cloth body; dressed; all in good condition. Sounds like a baby when squeezed.

MARK: Ideal Doll
Made in U.S.A.

25—30in (64—77cm)   **$125—150**

Baby Coos in sizes
14—30in (36—77cm) with
Magic Skin body,
14—18in (36—46cm)   **65—85**

25in (64cm) **Brother Coos,** replaced clothing. *Betty Harms Collection.*

Ideal continued

Toni and P-90 and P-91 Family:
1948—on. Series of girl dolls. Most were completely of hard plastic with jointed neck, shoulders and hips, nylon wig, sleep eyes, closed mouth; original clothes; all in excellent condition. Various sizes, but most are 14in (36cm).

MARK: On head:
"IDEAL DOLL"
On body:
"IDEAL DOLL
P-90
Made in USA"

Toni,
14—15in (36—38cm) **$100—125**
21in (53cm) **n)** **200—225**
Mary Hartline,
14in (36cm) **125—150**
22in (56cm) **225—250**
Betsy McCall, vinyl head,
14in (36cm) **125—150**
Harriet Hubbard Ayer, vinyl head,
14in (36cm) **125—150**
Miss Curity,
14in (36cm) **125—150**
Sara Ann, 14in (36cm) **125—150**

LEFT: 14in (36cm) *Mary Hartline*, all original. *Dolly Valk Collection.*

OPPOSITE PAGE: 35in (89cm) *Patty Playpal,* all original. *Dr. Carole Stoessel Zvonar Collection.*

Saucy Walker: 1951. All-hard plastic, jointed at neck, shoulders and hips with walking mechanism; synthetic wig, flirty eyes, open mouth with tongue and teeth; original clothes; all in excellent condition.
MARK: "IDEAL DOLL"
17in (43cm) **$65—85**
20in (51cm) **90—100**

Miss Revlon: 1955. Vinyl head with rooted hair, sleep eyes, closed mouth, earrings; hard plastic body with jointed waist and knees, high-heeled feet, vinyl arms with polished nails; original clothes; all in good condition.
MARK: On head and body:
"IDEAL DOLL"
Miss Revlon,
17—19in (43—48cm) **$85—110**
Little Miss Revlon,
10½in (27cm) **65—75**

Peter and Patty Playpal: 1960. Vinyl heads with rooted hair, sleep eyes; hard vinyl body, jointed at shoulders and hips; appropriate clothes; all in excellent condition.
MARK: Peter:
"IDEAL TOY CORP.
BE—35—38"
Patty:
"IDEAL DOLL
G-35"
35—36in (89—91cm) **$225**

Italian Bisque

Maker: Ceramica Furga of Canneto sull'Oglio, Mantua, Italy, and others
Date: Ca. 1910—on for those shown here
Material: Bisque head, composition body sometimes with cardboard torso
Mark:

"Furga   or $Italy$
Canneto & Oglio" $I/6$

Marked Italian Bisque Doll: Perfect bisque dolly-face head with suitable wig, painted eyebrows and eyelashes, glass eyes, closed or open mouth with teeth; composition body (some quite crude); dressed; all in good condition.

Closed mouth,
7—8in (18—20cm) **$200—250******
Open mouth,
14—16in (36—41cm)
275—325****

**Not enough price samples to compute a reliable range.

6½in (17cm) marked "Italy" boy, all original. *H&J Foulke, Inc.*

Italian Hard Plastic

Maker: Bonomi, Ottolini, Ratti, Furga and other Italian firms
Date: Later 1940s and 1950s
Material: Heavy hard plastic, sometimes painted, or plastic coated papier-mâché
Mark: Usually a wrist tag; company name on head

Italian Hard Plastic: Heavy, fine quality material jointed at shoulders and hips; human hair wig, sleep eyes, sometimes flirty, often a character face; original clothes; all in excellent condition.

15—17in (38—43cm)   **$ 85—100**
19—21in (48—53cm)   **110—135**
Black,
14—15in (36—38cm)   **100—125**

Rare black girl tagged "Fata." *H&J Foulke, Inc.*

Japanese Bisque Caucasian Dolls

Maker: Various Japanese firms; heads were imported by New York importers, such as Morimura Brothers, Yamato Importing Co. and others.

Date: 1915—on

Material: Bisque head, composition body

Mark: Morimura Brothers
Various other marks with Japan or Nippon, such as J. W., F. Y., and others

---

Character Baby: Perfect bisque socket head with solid dome or wig, glass eyes, open mouth with teeth, dimples; composition bent-limb baby body; dressed; all in good condition.

9—10in (23—25cm) painted eyes	$100—125
14—15in (36—38cm)	200—250*
20—22in (51—56cm)	400—450*

Child Doll: Perfect bisque head, mohair wig, glass sleep eyes, open mouth; jointed composition or kid body; dressed; all in good condition.

14—16in (36—41cm)	$200—250*
20—22in (51—56cm)	275—325*

*Do not pay as much for doll with inferior bisque heads.

17in (43cm) Nippon character baby. *Dr. Carole Stoessel Zvonar Collection.*

Jullien

Maker: Jullien, Jeune of Paris, France
Date: 1875—1904 when joined with S.F.B.J.
Material: Bisque head, composition and wood body
Mark: "JULLIEN" with size number

JuLLieN
1

Marked Jullien Bébé: Bisque head, lovely wig, paperweight eyes, closed mouth, pierced ears; jointed wood and composition body; pretty old clothes; all in good condition.

16—18in (41—46cm)	$2800—3100
23—25in (59—64cm)	3600—3800
Open mouth, 22—24in (56—61cm)	2000—2400

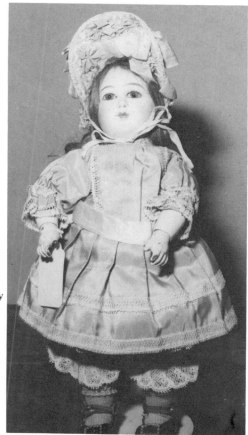

10in (25cm), unmarked but possibly *Jullien. Elizabeth McIntyre.*

Jumeau

Maker: Maison Jumeau, Paris, France
Date: 1842—on
Material: Bisque head, kid or composition body
Trademark: Bébé Jumeau (1886)
          Bébé Prodige (1886)
          Bébé Français (1896)
Mark: Body stamped in blue after 1878. Later an oval sticker "Bébé Jumeau."
Various head marks (see individual dolls listed below).

Fashion Lady: Late 1860s—on. Usually marked with number only on head, blue stamp on body. Perfect bisque swivel head on shoulder plate, good wig, paperweight eyes, closed mouth, pierced ears; all-kid body or kid with bisque lower arms and legs or cloth Lacmann body with leather arms; appropriate clothes; all in good condition.

14—15in (36—38cm) **$2100—2500**
20—22in (51—56cm) **3000—3400**
27in (69cm)   **4800**

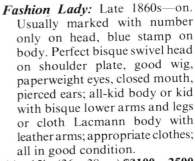

23in (59cm) Jumeau lady on Lacmann body. *Esther Schwartz Collection.*

Long-Face Triste Bébé: Ca. 1870s.
Usually marked with number
only on head, blue stamp on
body. Perfect bisque socket head
with beautiful wig, blown glass
eyes, closed mouth, applied
pierced ears; jointed composition
body with straight wrists; lovely
clothes; all in good condition.
20—22in (51—56cm) **$10,000**
30in (76cm) **13,000 up**

23in (59cm) early almond-eyed Portrait
Jumeau. *Kay and Wayne Jensen Collection.*

E. J. Bébé: Ca. 1880. Head incised
as below, blue stamp on body.
Perfect bisque socket head with
good wig, paperweight eyes,
closed mouth, pierced ears;
jointed composition body with
straight wrists; lovely clothes;
all in good condition.
MARK: On head: **DÉPOSÉ E. 7 J.**

12—14in (31—36cm) **$4400—4900***
19—22in (48—56cm) **5600—6400***
26—28in (66—71cm) **7500—8500***

*EJA slightly higher; Tête-style face
slightly lower.

29in (74cm) long-face Triste Bébé. *Kay and Wayne Jensen Collection.*

Early Almond—Eyed Bébé (so-called Portrait Jumeau): Ca.
1870s. Usually marked with size
number only on head with skin
or other good wig; unusually
large paperweight eyes, closed
mouth, pierced ears; jointed
composition body with straight
wrists; nicely dressed; all in
good condition.
14—16in (36—41cm) **$4500—5000**
20—23in (51—58cm) **5600—6100**

28in (71cm) E. J. bébé. *Kay and Wayne Jensen Collection.*

Jumeau continued

Incised Jumeau Déposé Bébé: Ca.
1880. Head incised as below, blue
stamp on body. Perfect bisque
socket head with good wig, paperweight eyes, closed mouth, pierced
ears; jointed composition body
with straight wrists; lovely clothes;
all in good condition.

MARK: Incised on head:
"JUMEAU
DEPOSE"

16—18in (41—46cm)	**$3900—4300**
23—25in (59—64cm)	**5500—6000**

14in (36cm) incised Jumeau. *Private Collection.*

Tête Jumeau Bébé: 1879—1899, then through S.F.B.J. Red stamp on head as
indicated below, blue stamp or "Bebe Jumeau" oval sticker on body.
Perfect bisque head, original or good French wig, beautiful stationary eyes,
closed mouth, pierced ears; jointed composition body with jointed or
straight wrists; original or lovely clothes; all in good condition.

MARK:

DÉPOSÉ
TETE JUMEAU
Bᵀᴱ SGDG
6

11—13in (28—33cm)	**$2000—2400***
14—16in (36—41cm)	**2300—2600***
18—20in (46—51cm)	**2700—3100***
21—23in (53—58cm)	**3200—3500***
25—27in (64—69cm)	**3600—4200***
31—33in (79—84cm)	**5200—6200***
Composition lady body, 20in (51cm)	**5000—5500**
Open mouth:	
14—16in (36—41cm)	**1400—1600**
20—22in (51—56cm)	**2000—2200**
24—25in (61—64cm)	**2400—2500**
32—34in (81—86cm)	**3200—3400**

*Allow more for an especially fine example.

Jumeau continued

25in (64cm) Tête Jumeau, all orignial. *Private Collection.*

22½in (57cm) Tête Jumeau, lady body. *Kay and Wayne Jensen Collection.*

1907 Jumeau Child: Ca. 1900. Sometimes red-stamped "Tete Jumeau." Perfect bisque head, good quality wig, set or sleep eyes, open mouth, pierced ears; jointed composition body; nicely dressed; all in good condition.

16—18in (41—46cm) **$1400—1600***
24—25in(61—64cm) **2000—2200***
33—34in (84—87cm) **3000—3300***

*Allow more for an especially pretty example.

Jumeau Great Ladies: Ca. 1930s. Perfect bisque socket head with adult features, fancy mohair wig, fixed eyes, closed mouth; five-piece composition body with painted black slippers, metal stand attached to foot; a series of ladies dressed in fancy costumes; all original; in excellent condition.

MARK: "221" on head
10—11in (25—28cm) **$500—550**

Princess Elizabeth Jumeau: 1938 through S.F.B.J. Perfect bisque socket head highly colored, good wig, glass flirty eyes, closed mouth; jointed composition body; dressed; all in good condition.

MARK:

71 UNIS FRANCE 149
306
JUMEAU
1938
PARIS

Body Incised:

JUMEAU
PARIS
Princess

19in (48cm) **$1000—1200**

K & K

Maker: K & K Toy Co., New York, N.Y., U.S.A.
Date: 1915—1925
Material: Bisque head, cloth and composition body
Mark: Used mold numbers 45, 56 and 60

*Germany
K & K
60
Thuringia*

K & K Character Child: Perfect bisque shoulder head, mohair wig, sleep eyes, open mouth with teeth; cloth body with composition arms and legs; appropriate clothes; all in good condition.

18—20in (46—51cm)   **$375—425**
Composition head, 18—20in (46—51cm), all original   **150—200**

19in (48cm) K & K character child with bisque head. *Private Collection.*

Kamkins

Maker: Louise R. Kampes Studios, Atlantic City, N.J., U.S.A.
Date: Ca. 1920
Material: Molded mask face, cloth stuffed torso and limbs
Size: About 16—19in (41—48cm)
Mark: Red paper heart on left side of chest:
Also sometimes stamped with
black on foot or back of head:

KAMKINS

A DOLLY MADE TO LOVE
PATENTED BY L.R. KAMPES
ATLANTIC CITY,   N.J.

KAMKINS
A DOLLY MADE TO LOVE
PATENTED
FROM
L.R. KAMPES
ATLANTIC CITY
N.J.

Marked Kamkins: Molded mask face with painted features, wig; cloth body and limbs; dressed; all in excellent condition.
18—20in (46—51cm)   **$825—925**
Fair to good condition   **550—650**

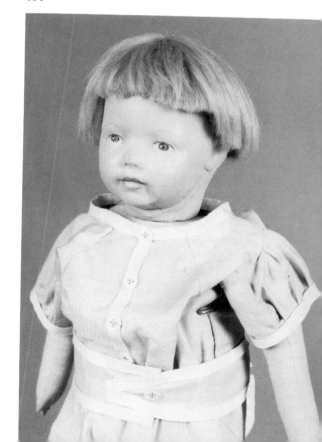

18in (46cm) *Kamkins*.
Private Collection.

Kämmer & Reinhardt

Maker: Kämmer & Reinhardt of Waltershausen, Thüringia, Germany
Heads often by Simon & Halbig
Date: 1886—on
Material: Bisque socket head, composition body, later papier-mâché, rubber
or celluloid heads, composition bodies
Size: 5½ to 42in (14 to 107cm)
Trademarks: Magestic Doll, Mein Liebling (My Darling), Der Schelm (The
Flirt), Die Kokette (The Coquette)
Mark: In 1895 began using K(star)R, sometimes with "S & H." Mold number
for bisque socket head begins with a 1; for
papier-mâché, 9; for celluloid, 7.
Size number is height in centimeters.

$$K \quad \bigstar \quad R$$

$$SIMON\ \&\ HALBIG$$
$$116/A$$
$$50$$

Child Doll: 1886—1895. Perfect
bisque head, original or good
wig, sleep or set eyes, closed
mouth, pierced ears; ball-jointed
composition body; dressed; all in
good condition. Mold 192.
16—18in (41—46cm) **$1200—1500**
22—24in (56—61cm) **1700—1800**
Open mouth,
6—7in (15—18cm) **300—350**
16—18in (41—46cm) **575—675**
25—27in (64—69) **1000—1250**

Child Doll: 1895—1930s. Often
mold number 403. Perfect bisque
head, original or good wig, sleep
eyes, open mouth, pierced ears;
dressed; ball-jointed composition
body; all in good condition.
14—16in (36—41cm) **$ 400—500**
19—21in (48—53cm) **600—700**
23—25in (58—64cm) **700—800**
28—29in (71—74cm) **900—950**
32—33in (81—84cm) **1200—1500**
35—36in (89—91cm) **1700—1900**
39—42in (99—107cm) **2500 up**
Walker,
20—22in (51—56cm) **650—700**

Tiny Child Doll: Perfect bisque
head, mohair wig, sleep eyes,
open mouth; five-piece composition body with molded and
painted shoes and socks.
6—7in (15—18cm) **$250—300**
8—9in (20—23cm) **300—350**
Walker,
6—7in (15—18cm) **350—375**
Closed mouth,
6in (15cm) **350—375**

32in (81cm) K★R child. *Dr. Carole
Stoessel Zvonar Collection.*

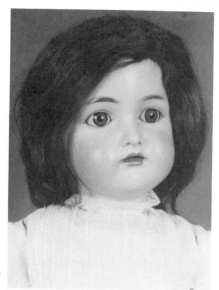

26½in (67cm) K★R child. *Elba Buehler Collection.*

24in (61cm) K★R child, all original. *Esther Schwartz Collection.*

7in (18cm) K★R 192 child. *H&J Foulke, Inc.*

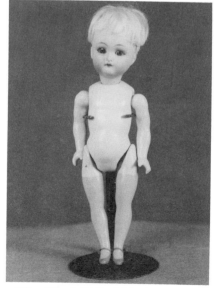

8½in (22cm) K★R child. *H&J Foulke, Inc.*

Kämmer & Reinhardt continued

Baby #100 (so-called Kaiser Baby): 1909. Perfect bisque solid-dome head, original composition bent-limb body; intaglio eyes, open/closed mouth; dressed; all in good condition.

14—16in (36—41cm)	**$ 600—675**
20—21in (51—53cm)	**900—1000**
Child, jointed body,	
18in (46cm)	**1250**
Glass eyes (unmarked),	
13—15in (33—38cm)	**1500—1800**
All-bisque, 8in (20cm)	**550—650****

**Not enough price samples to compute a reliable range.

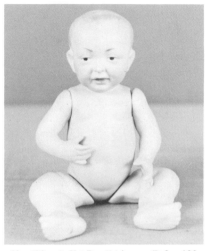

20in (51cm) K★R *Baby* with glass eyes. *Esther Schwartz Collection.*

8in (20cm) K★R all-bisque *Baby* 100. *Richard Wright Antiques.*

Character Babies or Toddlers:

1909—on. Usually mold number 126, less often mold numbers 121, 122 and 128. Perfect bisque head, original or good wig, sleep eyes, open mouth; composition bent-limb or jointed toddler body; nicely dressed; may have voice box or spring tongue; all in good condition.

#126, #22, #26 Baby:

10—12in (25—31cm)	$ 375—425
15—18in (38—46cm)	500—600*
22—25in (56—64cm)	800—900*
31—33in (76—84cm)	1800—2000

#126 Toddler:

6—7in (15—18cm)	350—400
10—12in (25—31cm)	550—600*
15—17in (38—43cm)	650—750*
22—24in (56—61cm)	1000—1200*
28—30in (71—76cm)	1600—1800

#126 Child:

36—38in (91—97cm)	2500—3000

#121 Baby:

14—15in (36—38cm)	550—650
22—24in (56—61cm)	900—1000

#122, 128 Baby:

16—18in (41—46cm)	750—850
22—25in (56—64cm)	1000—1350

#122, 128 Toddler:

16—18in (41—46cm)	1000—1200
28in (71cm)	2000

#118A Baby:

18—20in (46—51cm)	1600—1800**

#119 Baby:

24in (61cm)	3500**

#135 Baby:

20in (51cm)	1600—1800**

*Allow $50 extra for flirty eyes.
**Not enough price samples to compute a reliable range.

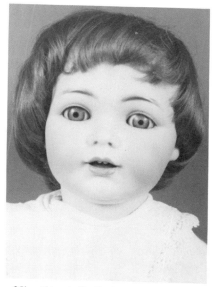

25in (64cm) K★R 22 character baby. *Esther Schwartz Collection.*

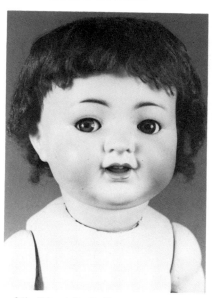

26in (66cm) K★R 126 character toddler. *Dr. Carole Stoessel Zvonar Collection.*

25in (64cm) K★R 122 character toddler.
Dr. Carole Stoessel Zvonar Collection.

Character Children: 1910—on. Perfect bisque socket head, good wig, painted or glass eyes, closed mouth; composition ball-jointed body; nicely dressed; all in good condition.

#101:

7in (18cm) five-piece body	$ 950
7—8in (18—20cm) jointed body	1100
16—18in (41—46cm)	2300—2600
Glass eyes, 16in (41cm)	4000**

#102:

12in (31cm)	8500**

#103, 104:

18—20in (46—51cm)	15,000**

#107:

20in (51cm)	8500—9500**

#109:

20in (51cm)	7500—8500

#112, 112x:

16in (41cm)	6500—7500**
Glass eyes, 12in (31cm)	5000**

#114:

7in (18cm) five-piece body	1100
7—8in (18—20cm)	1200—1300
17—19in (43—48cm)	3700—4200
25in (64cm)	5500—6000
Glass eyes, 14in (36cm)	3700—4000**

#115, 115A:

Baby, 18—20in (46—51cm)	3500—4000
Toddler, 16—18in (41—46cm)	3500—4000*
27in (69cm)	6500*

#116, 116A, open/closed mouth:

Baby, 17—19in (43—48cm)	2000—2200
Toddler, 19—21in (48—53cm)	2600—3200*

#116A, open mouth:

Baby, 14—16in (36—41cm)	1400—1500
Toddler, 16—18in (41—46cm)	2000—2200

#117, 117A:

12—14in (31—36cm)	2500—3000
18—20in (46—51cm)	4000—4500
23—25in (59—64cm)	5000—6000
28—30in (71—76cm)	6500—7000

#117, open mouth:

26—27in (66—69cm)	3200—3700

#117x, open mouth:

15—16in (38—41cm)	1500—1700**

*Allow more for molded hair.

**Not enough price samples to compute a reliable range.

Kämmer & Reinhardt continued

#117n, flirty eyes:
18—20in (46—51cm)	**1300—1600**
25—26in (64—66cm)	**2000—2200**
31—34in (79—86cm)	**2800—2900**

#123, 124:
17in (43cm)	**8500—10,000**

#127:
Baby, 11—12in (28—31cm)	**800—850**
18—20in (46—51cm)	**1100—1300**
Toddler, 20—23in (51—58cm)	**1700—1900**

*Allow more for molded hair.
**Not enough price samples to compute a reliable range.

Infant: 1924—on. Perfect bisque head, molded and painted hair, glass eyes, open mouth; pink cloth body, composition hands; nicely dressed; all in good condition.
14in (36cm)   **$1100—1200**

13in (33cm) K★R 101 character *Marie*, all original. *Private Collection.*

13in (33cm) K★R 101 *Peter* with glass eyes, all original. *Esther Schwartz Collection.*

OPPOSITE PAGE: 17in (43cm) K★R 112 character, all original. *Richard Wright Collection.*

240

23in (58cm) K★R 114 *Hans*. *Roberts Collection.*

17in (43cm) K★R 116A character. *Kay and Wayne Jensen Collection.*

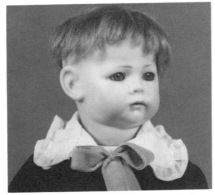

15in (38cm) K★R 115A character. *Esther Schwartz Colleciton.*

23in (58cm) K★R 117 character child. *Esther Schwartz Collection.*

20in (51cm) K★R 117n character girl with flirty eyes. *Claire Dworkin Collection.*

Kestner

Maker: J. D. Kestner, Jr., doll factory, Waltershausen, Thüringia, Germany.
Kestner & Co., porcelain factory, Ohrdruf.

Date: 1816—on

Material: Bisque heads, kid or composition bodies, bodies on tiny dolls are
jointed at the knee, but not the elbow, all bisque

Size: Up to 42in (107cm)

Mark: Socket Head — Numbers such as "171," "146," "164," "192" (pierced
ears), "195" (see Mark A)
Shoulder Head — Numbers such as "154," "148" (see Mark A)
Both — "A5," "B6," "C7" and "Made in Germany"
Composition Body — See Mark B
Kid Body — Sometimes Mark C

Mark A: D *made in Germany. 8.* 162.   Mark B: Excelsior DRP N. 70686 Germany   Mark C:

*Child doll, closed mouth, marked
with size number only:* Ca.
1880. Perfect bisque head, plaster
dome, good wig, paperweight or
sleep eyes, closed mouth; composition ball-jointed body with
straight wrists; well dressed; all
in good condition.

169, 128, X:

15—17in (38—43cm)	$1600—1900
24—25in (61—64cm)	2300—2400
28—29in (71—74cm)	2650—2850

XI and pouty:

16—17in (41—43cm)	2000—2200
20—22in (51—56cm)	2400—2500
25—27in (64—69cm)	3000

Kid body:

19—21in (48—53cm)	1400—1600

A.T.-type:

18in (46cm) composition body	3500
18in (46cm) kid body, swivel neck	2500

17in (43cm) 128 Kestner child. *Esther
Schwartz Collection.*

Kestner continued

Closed Mouth Shoulder Head Child: Ca. 1880s. Perfect bisque head, plaster dome, good wig, set or sleep eyes, closed mouth; sometimes head is slightly turned; kid body with bisque lower arms; marked with size letters or numbers.

14—16in (36—41cm) **$ 650—750***
18—21in (46—53cm)   **850—950***
25—26in (64—66cm) **1200—1400***
Open/closed mouth,
  17—19in (42—48cm) **650—750**
Open mouth
 (often with square cut teeth),
    16—18in (41—46cm) **450—500***
    22—24in (56—61cm) **600—700***

*Allow more for a very pouty face or swivel neck.

20in (51cm) A.T.-type Kestner. *Kay and Wayne Jensen Collection.*

25—26in (64—66cm) closed mouth child. *H&J Foulke, Inc.*

Bisque shoulder head on jointed kid body: Late 1880s to late 1930s. Mold numbers such as 154, 147, 148, 149, 166, 195 and heads with letter sizing only. Plaster dome, good wig, sleep eyes, open mouth; dressed, all in good condition.

14—16in (36—41cm)   **$325—375**
19—22in (48—56cm)   **450—500**
25—26in (64—66cm)   **675—725**
28—30in (71—76cm)   **850—950**

18in (46cm) 148 Kestner child. *Dolly Valk Collection.*

14in (36cm) 154 Kestner child. *H&J Foulke, Inc.*

Kestner continued

7in (18cm) tiny Kestner child, all original.
Kay and Wayne Jensen Collection.

Child doll, open mouth: Late 1880s to late 1930s. Mold numbers such as 129, 142, 144, 146, 152, 156, 160, 164, 167, 168, 171, 174, 196, 214. Bisque socket head on ball-jointed body; plaster dome, good wig, sleep eyes, open mouth; dressed; all in good condition.

MARK: *made in* D *Germany.* 8. *162.*

12—14in (31—36cm)	**$ 400—450**
16—17in (41—43cm)	**425—450**
19—22in (48—56cm)	**450—550**
24—26in (61—66cm)	**600—700**
28—30in (71—76cm)	**800—900**
33—36in (84—91cm)	**1200—1600**
42in (107cm)	**2500**

#155:
7—9in (18—23cm)	**375—425**

#171 Daisy,
blonde mohair wig,
18in (46cm)	**550**

19in (48cm) Kestner 161 child. *H&J Foulke, Inc.*

23in (58cm) Kestner 152 child. *H&J Foulke, Inc.*

ABOVE AND RIGHT: Kestner "character doll" set with heads 174, 178, 180 and 185. *Esther Schwartz Collection.*

Character Child: 1910—on. Perfect bisque head character face, plaster pate, wig, painted or glass eyes, closed or open/closed mouth; good jointed composition body; dressed; all in good condition.

#143:

7—8in (18—20cm)	**$ 400—450**
12—14in (31—36cm)	**550—700**
19—20in (48—51cm)	**850—950**

#178-190, 212:

Painted Eyes:

12in (31cm)	**1600—1700**
15in (38cm)	**2300**
18in (46cm)	**3000**

Glass Eyes:

12in (31cm)	**2000—2200**
15in (38cm)	**2800**
18in (46cm)	**3500**

Boxed Set, one body, four heads:

12in (31cm)	**6500**

#241: (See color photo on page 109).

18—22in (46—56)	**3500—4500**

#249:

20—22in (51—56cm)	**1000—1300**

#260 Toddler:

8in (20cm)	**425—450**
12—14in (31—36cm)	**650—700**
18in (46cm)	**750—800**

16in (41cm) Kestner 143 child. *Private Collection.*

Kestner continued

20in (51cm) JDK character baby. *Esther Schwartz Collection.*

20in (51cm) JDK 257 character baby. *H&J Foulke, Inc.*

Character Baby: 1910—on. Perfect bisque head, molded and/or painted hair or good wig, sleep or set eyes, open mouth; bent-limb body; well dressed; nice condition.

MARK:

made in F. Germany. 10 211 J.D.K.

#211, 226, JDK (solid dome):

12—15in (31—38cm)	$ 400—500
17in (43cm)	600—650
19—21in (48—53cm)	750—850
24—25in (61—64cm)	1100—1250

#220:

18in (46cm) toddler	3000

#234, 235, 238:

16in (41cm)	550—650**

#245, 237 and solid dome (Hilda):

14—16in (36—41cm)	2300—2700
19—21in (48—53cm)	3200—3500
24in (61cm)	4500—5000

#247:

14—16in (36—41cm)	1200—1300

#257:

15—17in (38—43cm)	600—700
20—22in (53—56cm)	800—900

Solid dome, fat-faced:

14—15in (36—38cm)	650—750
18—20in (46—51cm)	900—1000
24in (61cm)	1600—1800

**Not enough price samples to compute a reliable range.

LEFT: TOP TO BOTTOM:
18in (46cm) JDK *Hilda* 245 character baby. *Wayne and Kay Jensen Collection.*

JDK 234 character baby. *Gail Hiatt Collection.*

24in (61cm) JDK 226 character baby. *H&J Foulke, Inc.*

10½in (27cm) Kestner 172 *Gibson Girl.* *Private Collection.*

Gibson Girl: Ca. 1910. Sometimes mold number 172; sometimes marked "Gibson Girl" on body. Perfect bisque shoulder head with good wig, glass eyes, closed mouth, up-lifted chin; kid body with bisque lower arms; beautifully dressed; all in good condition.

10—12in (26—31cm) **$1200—1400**
20—21in (51—53cm) **3500—3900**

16in (41cm) Kestner lady 162. *Dolly Valk Collection.*

Lady Doll: Mold number 162. Perfect bisque socket head, plaster dome, wig in ***Gibson Girl*** style, sleep eyes, open mouth with upper teeth; jointed composition body with molded breasts, nipped-in waist, slender arms and legs; appropriate lady clothes; all in good condition.

16—18in (41—46cm) **$1000—1200**
21—23in (53—59cm) **1400—1800**

O.I.C. Baby: Perfect bisque solid dome head with screaming features, tiny glass eyes, wide open mouth with molded tongue; cloth body; dressed; all in good condition.

MARK: "255
            3
            O.I.C."

13in (33cm) **$1500—1600**

Siegfried: Perfect bisque solid dome head with molded hair and flange neck, sleep eyes, closed mouth, side nose, pronounced philtrum; cloth body with composition hands; dressed; all in good condition. Mold #272.

MARK: Siegfried
        made in Germany
            9

Head circumference: 12—13in (31—33cm) **$1800—2000**

Life-size Swaine & Co. **Lori** baby. *Dolly Valk Collection. For further information see page 363.*

13in (33cm) composition shoulder head with molded loop for bow. *H&J Foulke, Inc. For further information see page 125 (under Girl-type Mama Dolls).*

15in (38cm) *Joy* by Joseph Kallus. *H&J Foulke, Inc. For further information see page 96.*

8in (20cm) Alexander composition **Dionne Quintuplets**, all original. *Private Collection. For further information see page 20.*

17in (43cm) Effanbee *American Child*, all original. *Nancy Schwartz Blaisure Collection. For further information see page 150.*

10½in (27cm) carved wood Swiss girl, all original. *Dolly Valk Collection. For further information see page 381.*

17in (43cm) Arranbee hard plastic *Nanette*, all original. *H&J Foulke, Inc. For further information see page 64.*

12in (31cm) American Character *Sally* twins, all original. *H&J Foulke, Inc. For further information see page 60.*

21in (53cm) 1966 Alexander Portrait doll with **Coco** face, all original. *Private Collection. For further information see page 41.*

12in (31cm) Horsman **Billiken**, all original. *Private Collection. For further information see page 209.*

ABOVE: 11in (28cm) Effanbee Portrait **Colonial**, all original. *H&J Foulke, Inc. For further information see page 152.* **RIGHT:** 15in (38cm) Molly's **Sabu**, all original. *Dolly Valk Collection. For further information see page 291.*

TOP LEFT: 7in (18cm) Alexander composition *Scots*, all original. *Private Collection. For further information see page 23.* **ABOVE:** 17in (43cm) Ideal composition *Shirley Temple*, all original. *Private Collection. For further information see page 345.* **BOTTOM LEFT:** 13in (33cm) Arranbee composition *Nancy*, all original. *Private Collection. For further information see page 64.* **BELOW:** 14in (36cm) Effanbee 1948 *Patsy*, all original. *H&J Foulke, Inc. For further information see page 147.*

14in (36cm) Alexander hard plastic ***Poor Cinderella***, all original. *Private Collection. For further information see page 31.*

13in (33cm) composition ***Juliette*** by Eugenia. *H&J Foulke, Inc. For further information see page 127.*

16in (41cm) Alexander hard plastic ***Elise*** ballerina, all original. *Private Collection. For further information see page 34.*

13in (33cm) Madame Hendren ***Whistling Cowboy*** and 13in (33cm) Ideal ***Fanny Brice***; both all original. *Dolly Valk Collection. For further information see pages 198 and 218.*

LEFT: Dewees Cochran Grow-up Doll *Angela Appleseed* (Angel), at 5, 11 and 20 years. *Nancy Schwartz Blaisure Collection. For further information see page 123 (under Grow-up Dolls).*

BELOW: Dewees Cochran Grow-up Doll *Jeff Jones* (J.J.) at 5, 11 and 20 years. *Nancy Schwartz Blaisure Collection. For further information see page 123 (under Grow-up Dolls).*

21in (53cm) Arranbee composition *Nancy Lee*, all original. *Private Collection. For further information see page 64.*

15in (38cm) Norah Wellings boy and 16in (41cm) Lenci-type girl, both all original. *Dolly Valk Collection. For further information see pages 274 and 378.*

ABOVE: 19in (48cm) Poir, all original. *H&J Foulke, Inc. For further information see page 315.*

BELOW: Large Ravca-type character man, all original. *Dolly Valk Collection. For further information see page 322.*

12in (31cm) *Girl Scout*, all original. *H&J Foulke, Inc. For further information see page 166 (under Children).*

Kewpie

Maker: Various
Date: 1913—on
Size: 2in (5.1cm) up
Designer: Rose O'Neill, U.S.A. U.S. Agent: George Borgfeldt & Co., New York, N.Y., U.S.A.
Mark: Red and gold paper heart or shield on chest and round label on back

---

All-Bisque: Made by J. D. Kestner and other German firms. Often have imperfections in making. Sometimes signed on foot "O'Neiſſ." Standing, legs together, arms jointed, blue wings, painted features, eyes to side.

2—2½in (5—6cm)	$ 85—95
4—5in (10—13cm)	100—125
6in (15cm)	150
7in (18cm)	200—250
8—9in (20—23cm)	350—400
13in (33cm)	1500
Jointed hips, 4in (10cm)	400—450
Shoulder head, 2½in (6cm)	200—250
Black Hottentot, 5in (13cm)	350
Button hole,	150—165
Pincushion, 2—3in (5—8cm)	200—250
Painted shoes and socks, 11in (28cm)	950

3in (8cm) ***Kewpie in Basket.*** *Richard Wright Collection.*

6½in (17cm) ***Kewpie*** with original label. *H&J Foulke, Inc.*

Kewpie continued

Action Kewpies (sometimes stamped ©):

Thinker, 4in (10cm)	250—275
Kewpie with cat, 3½in (9cm)	350
Confederate Soldier, 3½in (9cm)	275—300
Kewpie holding pen, 3in (8cm)	350
Lying on stomach, 4in (10cm)	350
Gardener, Sweeper, Soldier, Farmer, 4in (10cm)	400
Kewpie with rabbit, 2in (5cm)	250
Doodledog:	
3in (9cm)	600 up
1½in (4cm)	350
Huggers, 3½in (9cm)	150—175
Guitar player, 3½in (9cm)	250
Traveler, 3½in (9cm)	275
Governor, 3½in (9cm)	350
Kewpie with teddy, 4in (10cm)	600
Kewpie with turkey, 2in (5cm)	350
Kewpie and *Doodledog* on beach, 3½in (9cm)	1400 up
Perfume bottle, 3½in (9cm)	450
Kewpie with rose, 2in (5cm)	250
Kewpie with outhouse, 2½in (6cm)	825
Kewpie with umbrella and *Doodledog*, 3½in (9cm)	750
Kewpie with Prussian helmet, 6in (15cm)	550
Kewpie with drawstring bag, 4½in (12cm)	450
Kewpie in basket, 3in (8cm)	350

5in (13cm) *Kewpie Traveler*. *H&J Foulke, Inc.*

4in (10cm) *Kewpie Thinker*. *H&J Foulke, Inc.*

Kewpie continued

Bisque head on chubby jointed composition toddler body, glass eyes: Made by J. D. Kestner.
MARK:

> "Ges. gesch.
> O'Neill J.D.K."

10in (25cm)
    five-piece body   **$2500**
12—14in (31—36cm)   **3500—4500****

**Not enough price samples to compute a reliable range.

Bisque head on cloth body:
12in (31cm)
    Glass eyes
    (mold #1377),   **$2000—2500****
    Painted eyes   **1600—2000****

**Not enough price samples to compute a reliable range.

Celluloid: Made by Karl Standfuss, Deuben near Dresden, Saxony, Germany. Straight standing, arms jointed, blue wings; very good condition.
2½in (6cm)   **$ 30—35**
5in (13cm)   **50—60**
8in (20cm)   **100—110**
Black, 2½in (6cm)   **60—65**

All-Composition: Made by Cameo Doll Co., Rex Doll Co., and Mutual Doll Co., all of New York, N.Y., U.S.A. All-composition, jointed at shoulders, some at hips; good condition.
8in (20cm)   **$100—115**
11—13in (28—33cm)   **150—165**
Black,
12—13in (31—33cm)   **225—250**
Talcum container,
7in (18cm)   **150—175**

9in (23cm) celluloid *Kewpie* with heart sticker. *H&J Foulke, Inc.*

11in (28cm) composition *Kewpie* with label. *H&J Foulke, Inc.*

260

All-Cloth: Made by Richard G. Kreuger, Inc., New York, N.Y., U.S.A. Patent number 1785800. Mask face with fat-shaped cloth body, including tiny wings and peak on head. Cloth label sewn in side seam.

10—12in (25—31cm)   **$110—135**

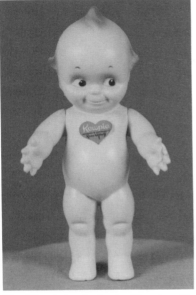

8in (20cm) hard plastic *Kewpie* with label. *H&J Foulke, Inc.*

Vinyl: Ca. 1960s made by Cameo Doll Co.

Ragsy Kewpie,
  Molded suit and cap,
    8in (20cm)   **$ 40—50**
  Fully-jointed,
    12in (31cm)   **90—100**
  Mint-in-box,
    27in (69cm)   **225—250**
  Kewpie baby,
  hinged body
    16in (41cm)   **150—175**

16in (41cm) vinyl *Kewpie* baby with hinged body. *H&J Foulke, Inc.*

12in (31cm) cuddle *Kewpie. H&J Foulke, Inc.*

Hard Plastic: Ca. 1950s.
Standing Kewpie, one piece
  with jointed arms,
    8in (20cm)   **$ 55—65**
Fully-jointed with
  sleep eyes; all original clothes,
    13in (33cm)   **250—300****

**Not enough price samples to compute a reliable range.

Kley & Hahn

Maker: Kley & Hahn, doll factory, Ohrdruf, Thüringia, Germany. Heads by Hertel, Schwab & Co. (100 series), Bähr & Pröschild (500 series) and J. D. Kestner (250, 680 and Wälkure).

Date: 1902—on

Material: Bisque head, composition body

Trademarks: Wälkure, Meine Einzige, Special, Dollar Princess

Mark:

> K&H <
Germany

K H
Walküre

Child Doll: Mold #250 or Wälkure mark. Perfect bisque head, wig, glass eyes, open mouth; jointed composition child body; fully dressed; all in good condition.

17—19in (43—48cm)	**$ 375—425**
24—26in (61—66cm)	**525—575**
32—33in (81—84)	**1000—1100**

See color photo on page 68.

Kley & Hahn 536 character child with glass eyes. *Esther Schwartz Collection.*

Kley & Hahn continued

Kley & Hahn 536 character child with painted eyes. *Lesley Hurford Collection.*

Character Child: Perfect bisque head, wig, glass or painted eyes, closed mouth; jointed composition child or toddler body; fully dressed; all in good condition.

#520, 526, 536, 546, 549:
19—21in (48—53cm) **$3500—4200**

#154, 166 (molded hair):
Open mouth,
18—19in (46—48cm) **900—1100**
Closed mouth,
16—17in (41—43cm) **2200**

#157, 169:
16—17in (41—43cm) **2200—2500**

Character Baby: Perfect bisque head with molded hair or good wig, sleep or painted eyes, open or closed mouth; bent-limb baby body; nicely dressed; all in good condition.

#138, 158, 160, 167, 176, 525, 531:
10—12in (25—31cm) **$350—400***
15—17in (38—43cm) **500—550***
22—25in (56—64cm) **750—850***

#680, Toddler:
16—18in (41—46cm) **750—850**

#568, Toddler:
20—22in (51—56cm) **900—1000**

#159, two-faced Baby,
12in (31cm) **750—850**

*Allow extra for toddler or jointed body.

16in (41cm) 167-4 character. *Dolly Valk Collection.*

Kling

Maker: Kling & Co., porcelain factory, Ohrdruf, Thüringia, Germany
Date: 1836—on (1870—on for dolls)
Material: Bisque or china shoulder head, cloth body, bisque lower limbs; bisque socket head, composition body, all-bisque.
Mark:  and numbers, such as 167, 176, 189, 190, 203, 377, 372

China shoulder head: Ca. 1880. Black- or blonde-haired china head with bangs, sometimes with a pink tint; cloth body with china limbs or kid body; dressed; all in good condition.

14—16in (36—41cm)	**$250—275**
21—23in (53—58cm)	**350—400**

Bisque shoulder head: Ca. 1880. Molded hair or mohair wig, painted eyes, closed mouth; cloth body with bisque lower limbs; dressed; all in good condition.

13—15in (33—38cm)	**$250—350**
19—21in (48—53cm)	**400—450**
24in (61cm)	**500—550**

Molded hair, glass eyes,

14—16in (36—41cm)	**450—500**

See color photo on page 71.

Bisque head: Ca. 1890. Mohair or human hair wig, glass sleep eyes, open mouth; kid or cloth body with bisque lower arms or jointed composition body; dressed; all in good condition.

Shoulder head:

16—18in (41—46cm)	**$350—400**
22—23in (56—58cm)	**425—475**

Socket head:

13—15in (33—38cm)	**300—325**
19—21in (48—53cm)	**425—475**

All-bisque Child: Jointed shoulders and hips; wig, glass eyes, closed mouth; molded footwear.
MARK: Kling bell
and/or
"36-10n"

4in (10cm)	**$160—185**

4½in (11cm) all-bisque child 36 10/11.
H&J Foulke, Inc.

14in (36cm) Kling
child, all original.
*Esther Schwartz Col-
lection.*

König & Wernicke

Maker: König & Wernicke, doll factory, Waltershausen, Thüringia, Germany.
Heads by Hertel, Schwab & Co. and Bähr & Pröschild
Date: 1912—on
Material: Bisque heads, composition bodies or all-composition
Trademarks: Meine Stolz, My Playmate
Mark: *K & W* Also mold numbers 98, 99, 100

1070

Body Mark:

K & W Character: Bisque head with good wig, sleep eyes, open mouth; composition baby or toddler body; appropriate clothes; all in good condition.

15—17in (38—43cm) **$500—550***
22—25in (56—64cm) 750—850***
Slim, teenage body,
21—22in (53—56cm) 600—700

*Allow $50 extra for flirty eyes.
  Allow $100—150 extra for toddler body.

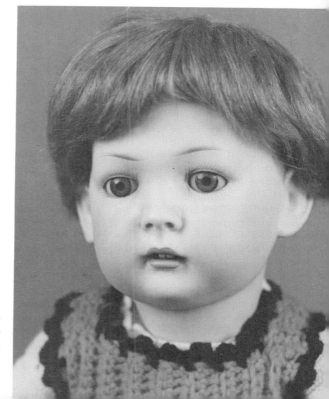

17in (43cm) K & W
1070 baby. *Dr. Carole Stoessel Zvonar Collection.*

Richard G. Krueger, Inc.

Maker: Richard G. Krueger, Inc.,
New York, N.Y., U.S.A.
Date: 1917—on
Material: All-cloth, mask face
Mark: Cloth tag or label

All-Cloth Doll: Ca. 1930. Mask
face with painted features, rosy
cheeks, painted eyes with large
black pupil and two highlights
each eye, curly thick painted
upper lashes, curly mohair wig
on cloth cap; oil cloth body with
hinged shoulders and hips.
Simple dotted swiss dress with
attached undie, pink taffeta coat
and hat with lace trim. All in
excellent condition.
LABEL:
Krueger, N.Y.
Reg. U.S. Pat Off.
Made in U.S.A.
16in (41cm) **$90—100**

16in (41cm) Krueger cloth doll, all original. *H&J Foulke, Inc.*

Pinocchio: Ca. 1940. Mask character face with black yarn hair,
attached ears, round nose, large
oval eyes, curved mouth; wood
jointed body; original clothes.
All in very good condition.
LABEL: Richard G. Krueger,
Inc., N.Y.
15in (38cm) **$250****

**Not enough price samples to
compute a reliable range.

15in (38cm) *Pinocchio* by Krueger.
Richard Wright Antiques.

Käthe Kruse

Maker: Käthe Kruse, Berlin, Germany

Date: 1910—on

Material: Molded muslin head (hand-painted), jointed cloth body, later of hard plastic material.

Mark: On cloth: "Käthe Kruse" on sole of foot, sometimes also "Germany" and a number

Hard plastic on back: Turtle mark and "Käthe Kruse"

Käthe Kruse
81971

Made in Germany

Cloth Käthe Kruse: Molded muslin head, hand-painted; jointed at shoulders and hips:

Doll I (1910—1929), painted hair, wide hips, 16—17in (41—43cm):
Mint, all original	**$1200—1500 up**
Good condition, suitably dressed	**750—850**

Doll IH (after 1929), wigged, 16—17in (41—43cm):
Mint, all original	**1100—1300**
Good condition, suitably dressed	**700—800**

Doll II (1922) ***"Schlenkerchen"*** Smiling Baby, 13in (33cm)   **850—950**

Doll V (1925) Babies ***"Traumerchen"*** (closed eyes) and ***"Du Mein"*** (open eyes), 19½—23½in (50—60cm)   **2000—2400**

Doll VIII (1929) wigged "German Child" 20½in (52cm):
Mint, all original	**1200—1400**
Good condition, suitably dressed	**750—850**
U. S. Zone Germany (1945—1951), 14in (36cm)	**600—650**

See color photos on pages 182 and 184.

14in (36cm) Käthe Kruse **Piete**, all original. *Private Collection.*

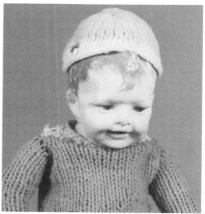

13in (33cm) Käthe Kruse Doll II. *Private Collection.*

Käthe Kruse continued

All-Hard Plastic Käthe Kruse: Wig or molded hair and sleep or painted eyes; jointed neck, shoulders and hips; original clothes; all in excellent condition. Turtle mark. (1955—1961).
16in (41cm) **$325—375**

Hard Plastic Head: Ca. 1950s—on. Hard plastic head with lovely wig, painted eyes; pink muslin body; original clothes; all in excellent condition.
U.S. Zone Germany,
14in (36cm) **$500—550**
Ca. 1952—1975:
10in (25cm) **250—275**
14in (36cm) **425—475**
1975—on:
10in (25cm) **150—200**
14in (36cm) **325—375**
18—20in (46—51cm) **400—450**

16in (41cm) hard plastic Käthe Kruse child, all original. *H&J Foulke, Inc.*

10in (25cm) Käthe Kruse ***Robertchen***, U.S. Zone Germany. *H&J Foulke, Inc.*

Gebrüder Kuhnlenz

Maker: Gebrüder Kuhnlenz, porcelain factory, Kronach, Bavaria
Date: 1884—on
Material: Bisque head, composition or kid body
Size: Various
Mark: " G.K. "
with numbers, such as:
41-28   56-18   44-15

G^{br} 165 K
9
Germany

G. K. doll with closed mouth: Ca. 1890. Perfect bisque socket head, inset glass eyes, closed mouth, round cheeks; jointed composition body; dressed; all in good condition.

Mold *#32,*
    14—16in (36—41cm)   **$ 850—950**
    20—22in (51—56cm)   **1250—1450**
Mold *#34,* Bru-type,
  French JCB, Gosset label,
    16—18in (41—46cm)   **2500**
Kid body, Mold *#38* shoulder head:
    14—16in (36—41cm)   **625—675**
    20—22in (51—56cm)   **800—850**

16in (41cm) G.K. 34-26. *Kay and Wayne Jensen Collection.*

Gebrüder Kuhnlenz continued

G. K. child doll: Ca. 1890—on. Perfect bisque socket head with distinctive face, almost a character look, long cheeks, sleep eyes, open mouth, molded teeth; jointed composition body; dressed; all in good condition.

Mold **#41, 44, 56**

    16—18in (41—46cm) **$450—550**

    22—24in (56—61cm) **700—800**

Mold **#165**

    17—19in (43—48cm) **300—350**

    23—24in (58—61cm) **400—450**

G. K. Tiny Dolls: Perfect bisque socket head, wig, stationary glass eyes, open mouth with molded teeth; five-piece composition body with molded shoes and socks; all in good condition. Usually mold #44.

8—8½in (20—22cm)   **$140—165**

Closed mouth, Belton-type head, 8in (20cm)   **450—500**

24in (61cm) G.K. 56-30 child. *Richard Wright Antiques.*

8in (20cm) G. K. 44-16½ child, all original. *H&J Foulke, Inc.*

Lanternier

Maker: A Lanternier & Cie. of Limoges, France
Date: 1855—on
Material: Bisque head, papier-mâché body
Mark:

FABRICATION
FRANÇAISE

AL ε Cⁱᵉ
LIMOGES
A   1

Marked Lanternier Child: Ca. 1915. Perfect bisque head, good or original wig, large stationary eyes, open mouth, pierced ears; papier-mâché jointed body; pretty clothes; all in good condition.

Cherie, Favorite or ***La Georgienne***
16—18in (41—46cm) **$625—675***
22—23in (56—58cm)   **800—900***

*Do not pay as much for an ugly doll of poor quality.

Marked Toto: Ca. 1915. Perfect bisque smiling character face, good wig, glass eyes, open/closed mouth with molded teeth, pierced ears; jointed French composition body; dressed; all in good condition.
18in (46cm)   **$850—900**

Lanternier Lady: Ca. 1915. Perfect bisque head with adult look, good wig, stationary glass eyes, open/closed mouth with molded teeth; composition lady body; dressed; all in good condition.
Lorraine
16—18in (41—46cm) **$650—750**

18in (46cm) ***Lorraine*** lady. *Nancy Schwartz Blaisure Collection.*

20in (51cm) ***Cherie***. *Esther Schwartz Collection.*

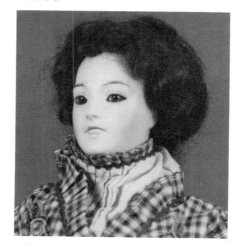

Lenci

Maker: Enrico & Elenadi Scavini, Turin, Italy
Date: 1920—on
Material: Pressed felt head with painted features, jointed felt bodies
Size: 5—45in (13—114cm)
Mark: "LENCI" on cloth and various paper tags; sometimes stamped on bottom of foot

Lenci: All-felt (sometimes cloth torso) with swivel head, jointed shoulders and hips; painted features, eyes usually side-glancing; original clothes, often of felt or organdy; in excellent condition.

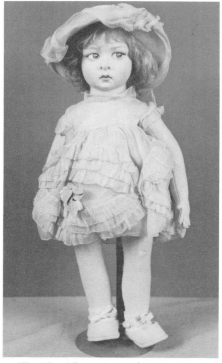

17in (43cm) Pouty Lenci girl, all original. *Esther Schwartz Collection.*

Miniatures and Mascottes:

8—9in (20—23cm) Regionals	**$ 200—225**
Children or unusual costumes	**250 up**

Children #300, 109, 149, 159, 111:

13in (33cm)	**650 up**
16—18in (41—46cm)	**850 up**
20—22in (51—56cm)	**1000 up**

"Lucia" face,

14in (36cm)	**400 up**

Ladies and long-limbed novelty dolls,

24—28in (61—71cm)	**1200 up**

Glass eyes,

20in (51cm)	**2800—3000**

Celluloid-type,

6in (15cm)	**40—50**

"Surprised Eye" (round painted eyes)

20in (51cm)	**1500—1800**

Collector's Note: Mint examples of rare dolls will bring higher prices. To bring the prices quoted, Lenci dolls must be clean and have good color. Faded and dirty dolls bring only about one-third to one-half these prices.

See color photos on pages 70 and 106.

Lenci continued

19in (48cm) Lenci boy, all original. *Betty Harms Collection.*

9in (23cm) Lenci Mascotte, all original. *H&J Foulke, Inc.*

Lenci-Type

Maker: Various Italian, French and English firms such as Marguerin, Alma and others.
Date: 1920—1940
Material: Felt and cloth
Size: 6in (15cm) up
Mark: Various paper labels, if any

Felt or Cloth Doll: Mohair wig, painted features; original clothes or costume.
Child dolls,
    16—18in (41—46cm)
                    up to **$400**
        depending upon quality
Foreign costume,
    7½in—8½in (19—22cm) **30—40**
    12in (31cm)   **60—65**

16in (41cm) Lenci-type girl, all original. *Dolly Valk Collection.*

Liberty of London

Maker: Liberty & Co. of London, England
Date: 1906—on
Material: All-fabric
Size: 5½—10in (14—25cm)
Mark: Cloth label or paper tag "Liberty of London"

British Coronation Dolls: 1939. All-cloth with painted and needle-sculpted faces; original clothes; excellent condition. The Royal Family and Coronation Participants.
5½—9½in (14—24cm)   **$75—85**

Other English Historical and Ceremonial Characters: All-cloth with painted and needle-sculpted faces, original clothes; excellent condition.
9—10in (23—25cm)   **80—90**

King George VI in coronation robes. *H&J Foulke, Inc.*

Limbach

Maker: Limbach Porzellanfabrik, Limbach, Thüringia, Germany (porcelain factory)
Date: Factory started in 1772
Material: Bisque head, composition body; all bisque
Mark:

MADE IN GERMANY

All-Bisque Child: Ca. 1900. Child all of bisque (sometimes pink bisque) with wire jointed shoulders and hips; molded hair (often with a blue molded bow) or bald head with mohair wig, painted eyes, closed mouth, white stockings, blue garters, brown slippers or strap shoes.

MARK: P23

GERMANY

4—5in (10—13cm)	$ 65—75
Glass eyes,	
5in (13cm)	150
Character, jointed arms only,	
4—5in (10—13cm)	65—75

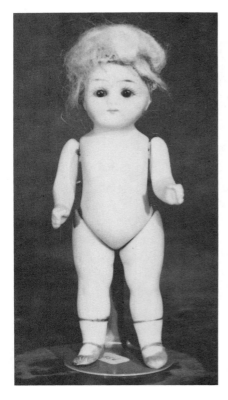

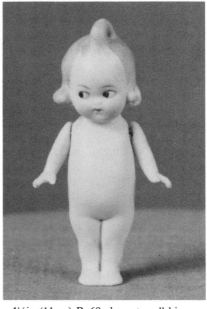

4¼in (11cm) P. 69 character all-bisque. *H&J Foulke, Inc.*

5in (13cm) P. 607/II Limbach all-bisque. *H&J Foulke, Inc.*

Limbach continued

17in (43cm) *Norma*.
Courtesy of Jane Walker.

Limbach Character Baby: Ca. 1910. Bisque head with molded hair, glass or painted eyes, open/closed mouth; composition baby body; dressed; all in good condition.

Mold *#8682,* 15in (38cm)   **$900—1000****

**Not enough price samples to compute a reliable range.

All-Bisque Baby: Ca. 1910. Baby with painted hair and facial features; wire jointed shoulders and hips, bent arms and legs; bare feet.

MARK: Clover and number with P.

4—5in (10—13cm)   **$65—85**

Limbach Child Doll: Ca. 1919. Perfect bisque head, good wig, glass eyes, open mouth with teeth; composition jointed body; dressed; all in good condition. Sometimes *Wally, Rita* or *Norma.*

16—18in (41—46cm) **$425—475****
23—24in (58—61cm)   575—**625****

**Not enough price samples to compute a reliable range.

London Rag Baby

Maker: Unknown English firm or firms
Date: Ca. 1870—on
Material: Muslin covered wax mask face, cloth body
Size: 14—22in (36—56cm)
Mark: None

London Rag Baby: Wax mask face covered with muslin, painted features, some with hair; original cap tied tightly around face; cloth body; all in fair condition.

14—17in (36—43cm)   **$675—775****

**Not enough price samples to compute a reliable range.

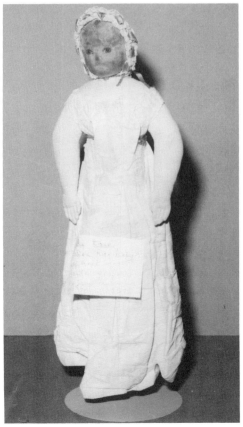

London Rag Baby. *Joe Jackson and Joel Pearson.*

Albert Marque

Maker: Unknown, possibly artist produced
Date: 1916
Material: Bisque head, jointed composition body with bisque lower arms
Size: 21—22in (53—56cm) one size only
Designer: Albert Marque, French sculptor
Mark:

A. Marque Doll: Bisque head with wistful character face, mohair wig, paperweight eyes, closed mouth; jointed composition body of special design with bisque lower arms and hands, fixed wrists; appropriate clothes (some original ones from Paris designer Margaines-Lacroix).
21—22in (53—56cm) **$35,000—38,000**

Signed A. Marque doll. *Elizabeth McIntyre.*

Armand Marseille
(A.M.)

Maker: Armand Marseille of Köppelsdorf, Thüringia, Germany (porcelain factory)

Date: 1865—on

Material: Bisque socket and shoulder head, composition, cloth or kid body

Size: Various

Mark: *Armand Marseille Germany 990 A ⁹/₀ M*

Child Doll: Ca. 1890—on. Mold numbers such as 390, 1894, 370, 3200, also sometimes horseshoe mark. Perfect bisque head, nice wig, set or sleep eyes, open mouth; composition ball-jointed body or jointed kid body with bisque lower arms; pretty clothes; all in good condition.

19in (48cm) A.M. 4008 child. *Dolly Valk Collection.*

#390, (larger sizes marked only "A M" with size number):

12—14in (31—36cm)	**$ 175—225**
Stick-type body	**125—175**
16—18in (41—46cm)	**275—325**
23—24in (58—61cm)	**375—425**
28—30in (71—76cm)	**500—600**
32in (81cm)	**700—800**
35—36in (89—91cm)	**1100—1200***
40—42in (102—107cm)	**1800—2000***

Five-piece composition body,

5—6in (13—15cm)	**125—135**
8—9in (20—23cm)	**125—150**

Closed mouth, 5½in (14cm) **200**

#1894 (composition body):

15—16in (38—41cm)	**350—400**
19—20in (48—51cm)	**425—475**
23—24in (58—61cm)	**500—550**

#370, 3200, 1894 (kid body) and ***Florodora*** (kid body):

16—18in (41—46cm)	**225—275**
22—24in (56—61cm)	**300—350**

Florodora (composition body):

15—17in (38—43cm)	**250—300**
22—24in (56—61cm)	**375—425**

Queen Louise:

23—25in (58—64cm)	**425—475**
32—33in (81—84cm)	**800—900**

Baby Betty:

15—16in (38—41cm)	**300—350**

*Less if not very pretty with fine bisque.

Armand Marseille (A.M.) continued

Name shoulder head child: 1898 to World War I. Perfect bisque shoulder head marked with doll's name, jointed kid or cloth body, bisque lower arms; good wig, glass eyes, open mouth; well dressed; all in good condition. Names include ***Rosebud, Lilly, Alma, Mabel, Darling, Beauty*** and ***Princess.***

16—18in (41—46cm) **$200—250**
21—22in (53—56cm)   **275—325**

23in (59cm) A.M. 1894 child. *H&J Foulke, Inc.*

8½in (21cm) A.M. 390 child, all original. *H&J Foulke, Inc.*

Armand Marseille (A.M.) continued

Character Children: 1910—on.
Mold numbers such as 500, 550,
590, 600 and others. Bisque head,
molded hair or wig, glass or
painted eyes, open or closed
mouth; composition body;
dressed; all in good condition.

#500, 600:
15in (38cm) $ 450—550
#550:
18—20in (46—51cm) **2800—3200**
#230, Fany (molded hair):
16—17in (41—43cm) **4500—5500**
#231, Fany (wigged):
16—17in (41—43cm) **4000—5000**
#400 (child body):
13—15in (33—38cm) **2500—3000**
A.M. (intaglio eyes, closed mouth):
16—17in (41—43cm) **3000****

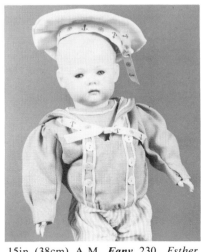

15in (38cm) A.M. *Fany* 230. *Esther Schwartz Collection.*

Character Baby: 1910—on. Mold numbers such as 990, 992, 985, 971, 996
and others. Bisque head, good wig, sleep eyes, open mouth some with teeth;
composition bent-limb body; suitably dressed; all in nice condition.

Mold #990, 985, 971, 996, 1330, 326 (solid dome),
  327, 329 and other common numbers:
    13—15in (33—38cm) $ **350—400***
    18—20in (46—51cm)   **450—525***
    24in (61cm)   **675—725***
#233: 13—15in (33—38cm)   **425—475**
#518: 16—18in (41—46cm)   **450—550**
#560A:
    15—17in (38—43)   **475—525***
    20—22in (51—56cm)   **675—725***
#580, 590 (open/closed mouth):
    16—18in (41—46cm)   **1250—1350***
#590 (open mouth):
    16—18in (41—46cm)   **850—950**
#248, 251 (open/closed mouth):
    12—14in (31—36cm)   **1200—1400***
#248, 251 (open mouth):
    12—14in (31—36cm)   **600—800**
Melitta (toddler): 20in (51cm)   **850—900**
#410, 2 rows teeth,
    15in (38cm) toddler: **900****

  *Allow extra for a toddler body.
  **Not enough price samples to compute a reliable range.

Armand Marseille (A.M.) continued

19½in (49cm) A.M. *Fany* 231. *Kay and Wayne Jensen Collection.*

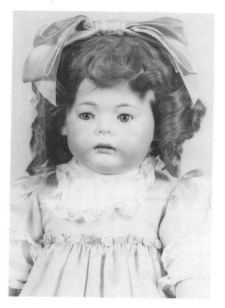

14in (36cm) A.M. 985 character baby. *H&J Foulke, Inc.*

Lady: 1910—1930. Bisque head with mature face, mohair wig, sleep eyes, open or closed mouth; composition lady body with molded bust, long slender arms and legs; appropriate clothes; all in good condition.

#401 and **400** (slim body):
14in (36cm)

Open mouth,	**$ 750—800**
Closed mouth,	**1200—1400**
Painted bisque, closed mouth,	**700—750**

12in (31cm) A.M. 580 character baby. *H&J Foulke, Inc.*

Armand Marseille (A.M.) continued

17in (41cm) long, 13in (33cm) head circumference A.M. 341 baby, all original. *H&J Foulke, Inc.*

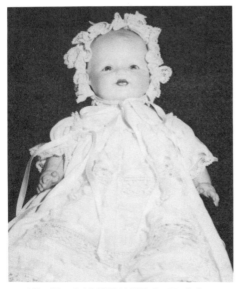

15in (38cm) AM 382/242 *Baby Hushabye.* *Lesley Hurford Collection.*

Infant: 1924—on. Mold numbers 351 (open mouth) or 341 (closed mouth). Solid-dome bisque head with molded and/or painted hair, sleep eyes; composition body or hard-stuffed jointed cloth body or soft-stuffed cloth body; dressed; all in good condition.

#351, 341 Kiddiejoy and Our Pet:
Head circumference:

9—10in (20—25cm)	**$225—275**
13—14in (33—36cm)	**425—475**
15in (38cm)	**600—650**
18in (46cm)	**850**

#352:

13in (33cm) long	**300**
20in (51cm) long	**500**

#347
Head circumference:

8in (20cm)	**250**
13—14in (33—36cm)	**475—525**

Marked Just Me Character: Ca. 1925. Perfect bisque socket head, curly wig, glass eyes to side, closed mouth; composition body; dressed; all in good condition. Some of these dolls, particularly the painted bisque ones, were used by Vogue Doll Company in the 1930s and will be found with original Vogue labeled clothes.

MARK:

Just ME
Registered
Germany
A 310/5/0 M

9in (23cm)	**$1000—1100**
11in (28cm)	**1200—1400**
Painted bisque:	
7—8in (18—20cm)	**500—550**

10in (25cm) *Just Me* character. *Richard Wright Antiques.*

Marked Baby Phyllis: Baby Phyllis Doll Co., Brooklyn, N.Y., U.S.A. Heads by Armand Marseille. Perfect solid dome bisque head with painted hair, sleep eyes, closed mouth; cloth body with composition hands; appropriate clothes; all in good condition.

MARK: BABY PHYLLIS
Made in Germany   Head circumference:
2 4014   12—13in (31—33cm) **$400—450**

Marked Baby Gloria: Perfect solid dome head with molded and painted hair, sleep eyes, smiling face with open mouth and two upper teeth, dimples; cloth mama doll body with composition limbs; appropriately dressed; all in good condition.

MARK: Baby Gloria
Germany   15—16in (38—41cm) long   **$600—700****

**Not enough price samples to compute a reliable range.

Mascotte

Maker: May Freres Cie, 1890—1897; Jules Nicholas Steiner, 1898—on. Paris,
France
Date: 1890—1902
Material: Bisque head, composition and wood jointed body
Mark: "BÉBÉ MASCOTTE
PARIS"

Bébé Mascotte: Bisque socket head, good wig, closed mouth, paperweight
eyes, pierced ears; jointed composition and wood body; appropriate clothes;
all in good condition.
18—20in (46—51cm) **$3200—3500**
24—26in (61—66cm) **4000—4400**

31in (78cm) *Bébé Mas-
cotte. Kay and Wayne
Jensen Collection.*

Mengersgereuth

Maker: Porcellanfabrik Mengersgereuth, porcelain factory, Mengersgereuth, Sonneberg, Thüringia, Germany
Date: 1908—on
Material: Bisque head, composition or kid body
Mark:

Marked Shoulder Head Child:
Perfect bisque socket head, wig, sleep eyes, open mouth; kid body with bisque hands; appropriate clothing; all in good condition.
MARK: Triangle as above
24—26in (61—66cm) **$550—650****

**Not enough price samples to compute a reliable range.

Marked "Trebor" Child:
Perfect bisque socket head, wig, sleep eyes, open mouth; jointed composition body; appropriate clothing; all in good condition.
16—18in (41—46cm) **$425—475****

**Not enough price samples to compute a reliable range.

Marked Character Baby:
Ca. 1910—on. Perfect bisque socket head, good wig, sleep eyes, open mouth; five-piece composition bent-limb baby body; dressed; all in good condition. Molds 914, 23, **Grete** or **Herzi**.

10—12in (25—31cm)	**$275—325**
18—20in (46—51cm)	**450—500**
24in (61cm)	**675—725**

26in (66cm) Mengersgereuth child with sunrise in triangle. *Dr. Carole Stoessel Zvonar Collection.*

Metal Heads

Maker: Buschow & Beck, Germany (Minerva); Karl Standfuss, Germany (Juno); Alfred Heller, Germany (Diana)

Date: Ca. 1888—on

Material: Metal shoulder head, kid or cloth body

Mark:

Marked Metal Head: Metal shoulder head on cloth or kid body, bisque or composition hands; dressed; very good condition, not repainted.

With molded hair, painted eyes, 12—14in (31—36cm)	$ 90—110
With molded hair, glass eyes, 16—18in (41—46cm)	135—165
With wig and glass eyes, 18—20in (46—51cm)	175—200

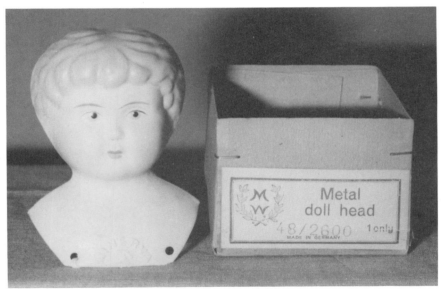

Minerva metal head with original box. *Private Collection.*

Metal, Swiss

Maker: A. Bucherer, Amriswil, Switzerland
Date: 1921
Material: Composition head, hands and feet, metal ball-jointed body
Size: 8in (20cm) average
Mark:

"MADE IN
SWITZERLAND
PATENTS
APPLIED FOR"

Bucherer Doll: Composition character head often with molded hat; metal ball-jointed body; original clothes, often felt; all in good condition.
Comic characters: ***Mutt, Jeff, Maggie, Jiggs,*** and others   **$250 up**
Regular People: lady, man, fireman and others   **135—160**

8in (20cm) Swiss metal man and lady. *Howard Foulke Collection.*

Missionary Ragbabies

Maker: Julia Beecher, Elmira, N.Y., U.S.A.
Date: 1893—1910
Material: All-cloth
Size: 16—23in (41—58cm)
Designer: Julia Jones Beecher
Mark: None

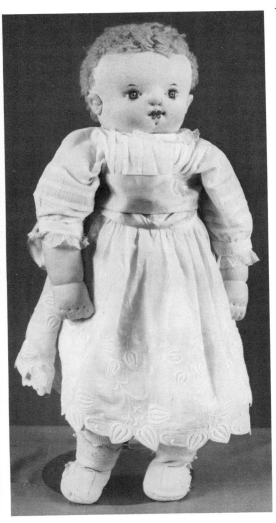

Beecher Baby: Handmade stuffed stockinette doll with looped wool hair, painted eyes and mouth, needle-sculpted face; appropriately dressed; all in good condition.
20—23in (51—59cm)   **$1000****

**Not enough price samples to compute a reliable range.

One auction price of $4300 indicates this doll may experience an imminent rise.

20in (51cm) Beecher ***Missionary Ragbaby***. *Pearl D. Morley Collection.*

Molly-'es

Maker: International Doll Co., Philadelphia, PA., U.S.A. Made clothing only. Purchased undressed dolls from various manufacturers.
Date: 1920s—on
Material: All-cloth or all-composition, later hard plastic and vinyl
Clothes Designer: Mollye Goldman
Mark: Usually a cardboard tag, dolls unmarked except for vinyl

Babies: All-composition, jointed at neck, shoulders and hips; molded hair or wigs, sleep eyes; beautiful original outfits; all in good condition.
12—15in (31—38cm) **$100—125**

Internationals: All-cloth with mask faces, mohair wigs (sometimes yarn), painted features; variety of costumes, all original clothes; in excellent condition with wrist tag.
13in (33cm) **$55—75**

Sabu: All-brown composition; very elaborate costume based on the character in *The Thief of Baghdad*; original clothes; all in good condition.
15in (38cm) **$400—425**

Toddlers: All-composition, jointed at neck, shoulders and hips; mohair wig, sleep eyes; original clothes; all in good condition.
14—16in (36—41cm) **$135—160**

22in (56cm) "Molly-'es" all-composition brown toddler, all original. *H&J Foulke, Inc.*

Leo Moss

Maker: Leo Moss, black doll maker from southern United States
Date: Early 1900s
Material: Papier-mâché head, arms and legs; cloth body
Mark: Sometimes "L.M."

Leo Moss Doll: Individually sculpted black papier-mâché head with character face, molded hair, inset eyes, some with tears; cloth body with papier-mâché arms and legs; dressed; all in good condition.
20in (51cm) **$5000—6000 up**

20in (51cm) Leo Moss black child. *Ralph's Antique Dolls & Museum.*

Mothereau

Maker: Alexandre Mothereau, Paris, France
Date: 1880—1895
Material: Bisque head, wood and composition body
Trademark: Bébé Mothereau
Mark: B.M.

Bébé Mothereau: Perfect bisque head, beautiful blown glass eyes, closed mouth, good wig, pierced ears; wood and composition jointed body; beautifully dressed; all in good condition.
26—28in (66—71cm) **$15,000—16,000**

27½in (70cm) B 11 M Child. *Wayne and Kay Jensen Collection.*

Munich Art Dolls

Maker: Marion Kaulitz
Date: 1908—1912
Material: All-composition, fully-jointed bodies
Size: Various
Designer: Paul Vogelsanger, and others
Mark: Sometimes signed on doll's neck

Munich Art Dolls: Molded composition character heads with hand-painted features; fully-jointed composition bodies; dressed; all in good condition. 18—19in (46—48cm) **$1750—1950**

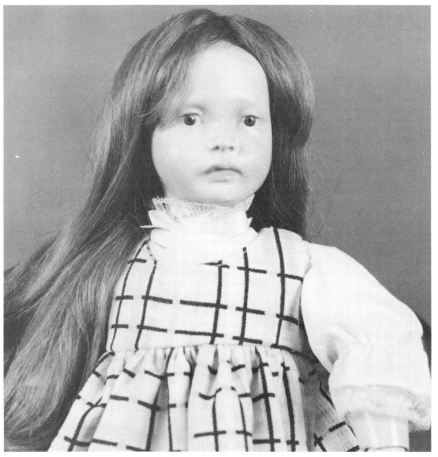

18in (46cm) Munich Art Doll. *Nancy Schwartz Blaisure Collection.*

Nancy Ann Storybook

Maker: Nancy Ann Storybook Dolls Co., South San Francisco, CA., U.S.A.
Date: Mid 1930s
Material: Painted bisque, later plastic
Size: About 5½in (14cm)
Mark: Painted Bisque:

<table>
<tr><td>"Story
Book
Doll
U.S.A."</td><td>Hard Plastic:
"STORYBOOK
DOLLS
U.S.A.
TRADEMARK
REG."</td></tr>
</table>

Also a wrist tag identifying particular model

Marked Storybook Doll: Painted bisque, mohair wig, painted eyes; one-piece body, head and legs, jointed arms; original clothes; excellent condition.

Painted Bisque,	**$ 40 up**
Hard Plastic,	**35 up**
Bent-limb baby:	
Painted bisque,	**75—85**
Hard plastic,	**60—65**
Nancy Ann Style Show,	
hard plastic,	
17in (43cm)	**325**

Hard plastic storybook doll, ***Pussy Cat,***
Pussy Cat, all original. *Private Collection.*

Ohlhaver

Maker: Gebrüder Ohlhaver, doll factory, Sonneberg, Thüringia, Germany. Heads made by Gebrüder Heubach, Ernst Heubach and Porzellanfabrik Mengersgereuth.

Date: 1912—on

Material: Bisque socket head, ball-jointed composition body

Trademarks: Revalo

Mark:

Revalo
Germany
3

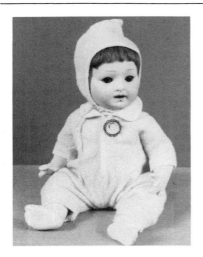

Revalo Character Baby or Toddler: Perfect bisque socket head, good wig, sleep eyes, hair eyelashes, painted lower eyelashes, open mouth; ball-jointed toddler or baby bent-limb body; dressed; all in good condition. Mold #22.
Baby,
14—16in (36—41cm) **$450—550***

*Allow $150 extra for toddler body.

Revalo Character Doll: Bisque head with molded hair, painted eyes, open/closed mouth; composition body; dressed; all in good condition.
Coquette,
10—12in (25—31cm) **$600—650**

Revalo Child Doll: Bisque socket head, good wig, sleep eyes, hair eyelashes, painted lower eyelashes, open mouth; ball-jointed composition body; dressed; all in good condition. Sometimes marked only 150.
16—18in (41—46cm)   **$450—500**
22—24in (56—61cm)   **600—650**

LEFT: TOP: 14in (36cm) *Revalo* 22.5 character baby. *Esther Schwartz Collection.*

18in (46cm) child incised 150. *H&J Foulke, Inc.*

Old Cottage Dolls

Maker: Old Cottage Toys, Allargate, Rustington, Littlehampton, Sussex, Great Britain

Date: 1948

Designers: Greta Fleischmann and her daughter Susi

Material: Composition or hard plastic heads, stuffed cloth bodies

Size: 8—9in (20—23cm) usually

Mark: Paper label — Old Cottage Toys, handmade in Great Britain

---

Old Cottage Doll: Hard plastic face with hand painted features, wig, stuffed cloth body; original clothing; excellent condition.

8—9in (20—23cm)	**$125 and up***
12—13in (31—33cm), mint in box	275—300**

*Depending upon rarity.
**Not enough price samples to compute a reliable range.

Group of Old Cottage dolls, including rare large girl and character nanny with baby. *Esther Schwartz Collection.*

Oriental Dolls

Japanese Traditional Girl or Boy Doll: 1850—on. Papier-mâché swivel head on shoulder plate, hips, lower legs and feet (early ones have jointed wrists and ankles); cloth midsection, cloth (floating) upper arms and legs; hair wig, dark glass eyes, pierced ears and nostrils; original or appropriate clothes; all in good condition.

Ca. 1890

13—15in (33—38cm)	**$225—250**
18—20in (46—51cm)	**325—350**
Boy, 18—20in (46—51cm)	**350—400**
Ca. 1930—1940, 13—15in (33—38cm)	**65—85**
Lady, 1920—1930, 10—12in (25—31cm)	**150**

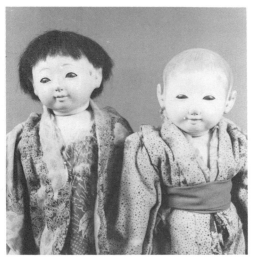

16in (41cm) sexed Oriental boy and girl, ca. 1900, all original. *Dr. Carole Stoessel Zvonar Collection.*

10in (25cm) fine Oriental lady, all original. *H&J Foulke, Inc.*

Oriental continued

Japanese Traditional Baby Doll: Ca. 1920—on. Papier-mâché with bent arms and legs; hair wig, dark glass eyes; original or appropriate clothes; all in good condition.

7—8in (18—20cm)	$ 50—55
11—12in (28—31cm)	80—90
18in (46cm)	150—160

Japanese Baby with Bisque Head: Ca. 1926—on. White bisque head, sleep eyes, closed mouth; five-piece papier-mâché body; original clothes; excellent condition.

7—8in (18—20cm)	$ 45—55
11—12in (28—31cm)	110—135
18in (46cm)	250

Oriental Bisque Dolls: Ca. 1900-on. Made by German firms such as Simon & Halbig, Armand Marseille, J. D. Kestner and others. Bisque head tinted yellow; matching ball-jointed or baby body.

S&H 1329 girl,
14—16in (36—41cm)	$1800—2000
19—20in (48—51cm)	2400

A.M. 353 baby,
14—16in (36—41cm)	1250—1450

J.D.K. 243 baby,
13—15in (33—38cm)	4000—5000 up

S&H 1099, 1129, and 1199 girl,
14—16in (36—41cm)	2200—2400

#220,
16—17in (41—43cm)	2800—3200

A.M. girl,
8—9in (20—23cm)	600—700

#164,
16—17in (41—43cm)	2000—2200

JDK molded hair baby,
17in (43cm)	5000 up**

All-bisque S&H,
7in (18cm)	850—900

BSW #500,
14—15in (36—38cm)	1600—1700

S P B H #4900,
16—17in (41—43cm)	1100—1200

**Not enough price samples to compute a reliable range.

7in (18cm) S&H all-bisque Oriental. *Roberts Collection.*

See additional photos on page 300.

Oriental continued

Baby Butterfly: 1911—1913. Made by E. I. Horsman. Composition head and hands, cloth body; painted black hair, painted features. See photo in *6th Blue Book of Dolls & Values*, page 286.
13in (33cm) **$150—175****

**Not enough price samples to compute a reliable range.

Ming Ming Baby: Quan-Quan Co., Los Angeles and San Francisco, CA., U.S.A. Ca. 1930. All-composition baby, jointed at shoulders and hips; painted facial features; sometimes with black yarn hair, original costume of colorful taffeta with braid trim; feet painted black or white for shoes.
10—12in (25—31cm) **$90—100**

Ming Ming all-composition baby showing queue and original box. *Courtesy of Beverly Schrader.*

LEFT: 13in (33cm) Oriental 21/164. *Private Collection. (See information on page 299.)*

16in (41cm) S&H 1329 Oriental. *Esther Schwartz Collection. (See information on page 299.)*

Papier-mâché
(So-Called French-Type)

Maker: Heads by German firms such as Johann Müller of Sonneberg and Andreas Voit of Hildburghausen, were sold to French and other doll makers

Date: 1816—1860

Material: Papier-mâché shoulder head, pink kid body

Mark: None

French-type Papier-mâché: Shoulder head with painted black pate, brush marks around face, nailed on wig (often missing), set-in glass eyes, closed or open mouth with bamboo teeth, pierced nose; pink kid body with stiff arms and legs; appropriate old clothes; all in good condition, showing some wear.

11½in (29cm) painted eyes **$ 625—675**

18—22in (46—56cm) **1000—1250**

26—28in (66—71cm) **1600—1800**

9½in (24cm) painted eyes, all original
and boxed with original wardrobe **3600**

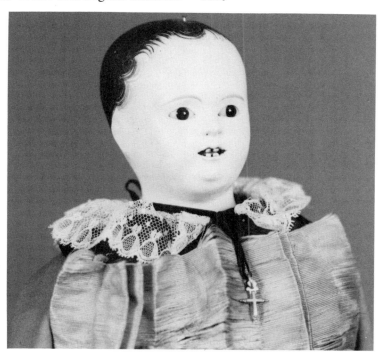

So-called French-type papier-mâché, 20in (51cm). *Private Collection.*

Papier-mâché
(German)

Maker: Various German firms of Sonneberg such as Johann Müller, Müller & Strasburger, F. M. Schilling, Heinrich Steir, A. Wislizenus, and Cuno & Otto Dressel

Date: 1816—on

Material: Papier-mâché shoulder head, cloth body, sometimes leather arms or kid body with wood limbs

Mark: Usually unmarked; some marked

A.W. Serial3 △ or

M & S Superior 2015

Papier-mâché Shoulder Head: Ca. 1820s to 1850s. Unretouched shoulder head, molded hair, painted eyes; cloth body; original or appropriate old clothing; entire doll in good condition.

23—25in (58—64cm)	**$ 800—900**
Glass eyes:	
24in (61cm) flirty	**1200—1300**
16in (41cm) slit for holding wig	**1000**
16in (41cm) outstanding example, rare hairdo, all original, mint condition	**3000**

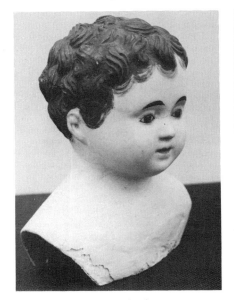

7½in (19cm) papier-mâché shoulder head with short molded curls and glass eyes. *Richard Wright Antiques.*

17½in (45cm) papier-mâché shoulder head with long molded curls. *Private Collection.*

Molded Hair Papier-mâché: (so-called Milliners' models.) 1820s-1860s. Unretouched shoulder head, various molded hairdos, eyes blue, black or brown, painted features; original kid body, wooden arms and legs; original or very old handmade clothing; entire doll in fair condition.

8—9in (20—23cm) **$ 300—350 up***
14—15in (36—38cm) **500 up***
19—20in (48—51cm) **850 up***
20in (51cm) rare hairdo with high beehive and curls, all original and fine
condition **2800**

Fully wigged model or partially molded with real curls framing face,
12in (31cm) **1200****
Males,
18—22in (46—56cm) **950****

*Depending upon condition and rarity of hairdo.
**Not enough price samples to compute a reliable range.

12in (31cm) molded hair papier-mâché lady, all original. *Private Collection.*

German Papier-mâché: Ca. 1880-1910. Shoulder head with molded and painted black or blonde hair, painted eyes, closed mouth; cloth body sometimes with leather arms; old or appropriate clothes; all in good condition, showing some wear.

17—19in (43—48cm) **$200—250**
22—24in (56—61cm) **325—375**
With wig and glass eyes:
22—24in (56—61cm) **375—425**

19in (48cm) papier-mâché shoulder head with molded short curls. *H&J Foulke, Inc.*

Papier-Mâché (German) continued

17in (43cm) Patent Washable-type papier-mâché boy. *Private Collection.*

Patent Washable-type: 1880s to 1914. Shoulder head with mohair wig, glass inset eyes, closed mouth; cloth body with papier-mâché lower arms and legs, some with fancy molded boots; old or appropriate clothing; all in good condition, showing some wear.

Standard quality:

10—11in (25—27cm)	**$110—125**
14—16in (36—41cm)	**150—175**
22—24in (56—61cm)	**225—275**
30in (76cm)	**350—400**

Superior quality:

12—14in (31—36cm)	**225—275**
22—24in (56—61cm)	**375—425**

German Papier-mâché: Ca. 1920-on. Papier-mâché head and hands or arms, hard stuffed cloth body; good hair wig, painted eyes, original child clothes; all in good condition of excellent quality.

8in (20cm)	**$60—65**
12in (31cm)	**85—95**

9in (23cm) late papier-mâché child, all original in box. *H&J Foulke, Inc.*

Parian-Type
(Untinted Bisque)

Maker: Various German firms
Date: Ca. 1860s through 1870s
Material: Untinted bisque shoulder head, cloth or kid body, leather, wood, china or combination extremities
Mark: Usually none, sometimes numbers

Unmarked Parian: Pale or untinted shoulder head, sometimes with molded blouse, beautifully molded hairdo, (may have ribbons, beads, comb or other decoration), painted eyes, closed mouth; cloth body; lovely clothes; entire doll in fine condition.

16—18in (41—46cm)	**$ 425—475**
22—24in (56—61cm)	**625—675**
Very fancy hairdo and/or elaborately decorated blouse	**700 up**
Very fancy with glass eyes	**1250 up**
Common, plain style, 16—18in (41—46cm)	**275—325**
Alice hairdo with swivel neck,	
Motschmann-type body, 14in (36cm)	**1500—1600**

19in (49cm) Parian-type child. *Esther Schwartz Collection.*

17in (43cm) Parian-type lady with fancy hairdo and pierced ears. *Esther Schwartz Collection.*

Paris Bébé

Maker: Danel & Cie., Paris, France, (later possibly Jumeau)
Date: 1889—1895
Material: Bisque socket head, jointed composition body
Mark: On head: On body:

TÊTE DÉPOSÉ
PARIS BEBE

PARIS-BEBE
Bréveté

Marked Paris Bébé: Bisque socket head, good wig, paperweight eyes, closed
  mouth; pierced ears; composition jointed body; dressed; all in good
  condition.
24—26in (61—66cm)   **$3800—4300**

24½in (62cm) *Paris Bébé. Kay and Wayne Jensen Collection.*

Peg-Wooden or Dutch Dolls

Maker: Craftsmen of the Grödner Tal, Austria, and Sonneberg, Thüringia, Germany
Date: Late 18th—20th century
Material: All-wood, ball-jointed (larger ones) or pegged
Mark: None

Early to Mid 19th Century: Delicately carved head, varnished, carved and painted hair and features, sometimes with a yellow tuck comb in hair, painted spit curls, sometimes earrings; mortise and tenon peg joints; old clothes; all in good condition.

4—5in (10—13cm)	$ 300—400*	
7—8in (18—20cm)	600—700*	
10—12in (25—31cm)	800—900*	
14in (36cm)	1100—1200*	

Rare examples at auction:

28in (71cm) Ca. 1805	7800	
28in (71cm) Ca. 1800	16,000	

*Depending upon rarity and desirability.

Late 19th Century: Wooden head with painted hair, carving not so elaborate as previously, sometimes earrings, spit curls; dressed; all in good condition.

8—10in (20—25cm)	**$175—225**	
12in (31cm)	**225—250**	

Early 20th century:

11—12in (28—31cm)	**50—75**	

12in (31cm) early 20th century peg-wooden doll, replaced clothes. *H&J Foulke, Inc.*

LEFT: Small late 19th century peg-wooden doll, replaced clothes. *H&J Foulke, Inc.*

Dora Petzold

Maker: Dora Petzold, Berlin, Germany
Date: 1920—on
Material: Composition or cloth head, cloth body
Mark: "DORA PETZOLD
      Registered
      Trade Mark
      Doll
      Germany"

Dora Petzold Doll: Molded composition or cloth head with closed mouth, hair wig, pensive character face, painted features; cloth body sometimes with especially long arms and legs; dressed; all in good condition. Many unmarked.

20—24in (51—61cm)   **$700—800**

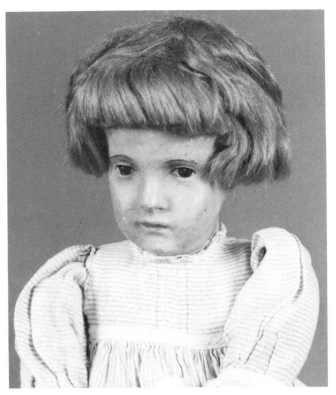

20in (51cm) Dora Petzold child. *Private Collection.*

Phénix Bébé

Maker: Henri Alexandre, Paris, France; Torrel; Jules Steiner; Jules Mettais
Date: 1889—1900
Material: Bisque head, jointed composition body (sometimes one-piece arms and legs)
Designer: Henri Alexandre
Mark:

PHÉNIX
★ 95

Marked Bébé Phénix: 1889—1900. Perfect bisque head, French jointed body, sometimes with one-piece arms and legs; lovely old wig, bulbous set eyes, closed mouth, pierced ears; well dressed; all in good condition.

★ *92, 94, 95,*
16—18in (41—46cm) $2600—2900
24in (61cm)   3500—3800
Open mouth,
20—22in (51—56cm)   2100—2300

24in (61cm) ★ 94, *Phénix Bébé. Betty Harms Collection.*

Philadelphia Baby

Maker: J. B. Sheppard & Co., Philadelphia, PA., U.S.A.
Date: Ca. 1900
Material: All-cloth
Size: 18—22in (46—56cm)
Mark: None

Philadelphia Baby: All-cloth with treated shoulder-type head, lower arms and
legs; painted hair, well-molded facial features, ears; stocking body; good
condition.

20—22in (51—56cm)	**$1200—1400**
Fair condition, showing wear	**800**
At auction, all original and mint condition	
from original owner's family	**2300**

22in (56cm) ***Philadelphia Baby.*** *Private Collection.*

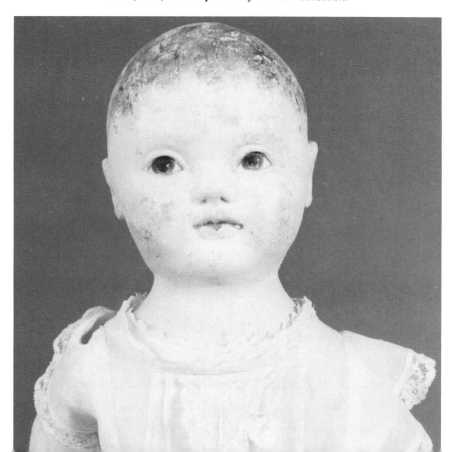

Piano Baby

Maker: Gebrüder Heubach, Kestner and other German makers
Date: 1880—on
Material: All-bisque
Size: Usually under 12in (31cm), some larger
Mark: Many unsigned; some with maker's particular mark

Piano Baby: All-bisque immobile with molded clothes and painted features; made in various sitting and lying positions. Heubach quality.

3—4in (8—10cm)	**$110—135**
7—8in (18—20cm)	**275—325**
11—12in (28—31cm)	**500—600**
4—5in (10—13cm) wigged	**225—250**

8½in (21cm) piano baby with pig. *H&J Foulke, Inc.*

Pincushion Dolls*

Maker: Various German firms, such as William Goebel, Dressel, Kister & Co.,
J. D. Kestner, Simon & Halbig, Limbach, Hertwig & Co., Gebrüder
Heubach

Date: 1900—on

Material: China, sometimes bisque

Size: Up to about 7in (18cm)

Mark: "Germany" and numbers

Pincushions: China half figures with molded hair and painted features; usually
with molded clothes, hats, lovely modeling and painting.

Arms close	$ 25—35
Arms extending but hands coming back to figure	**40 up**
Hands extended	**75 up**
Bisque child, glass eyes, 2in (5cm)	**165—175**

*Also called half-dolls.

3in (8cm) Gebrüder Heubach, child. *H&J Foulke, Inc.*

5½in (14cm) lady with arms extended, fancy initial mark. *Esther Schwartz Collection.*

3½in (9cm) flapper lady. *H&J Foulke, Inc.*

4in (10cm) flapper lady. *H&J Foulke, Inc.*

3½in (9cm) court lady holding fan and rose. *H&J Foulke, Inc.*

Pintel & Godchaux

Maker: Pintel & Godchaux, Montreuil, France
Date: 1890—1899
Material: Bisque head, jointed composition body
Trademark: Bébé Charmant
Mark: B

 P 9 G

Marked P.G. Doll: Perfect bisque head, paperweight eyes, closed mouth, good wig; jointed composition and wood body; appropriate clothing; all in good condition.
20—22in (48—53cm) **$2500—2800**

19in (48cm) P. G. Child. Private Collection.

Poir

Maker: Eugenie Poir, Paris, France; also Gre-Poir (French doll makers)
Date: 1920s
Material: All-cloth, felt face and limbs or all-felt
Mark: None on doll; paper label on clothes

Poir Child: All-fabric movable arms and legs; mohair wig; painted facial
features; original clothes, all in good condition.
17—21in (43—53cm) **$400—450**

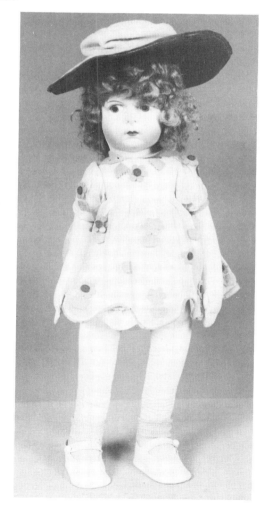

20in (51cm) Poir, all original. *H&J Foulke, Inc.*

Pre-Greiner
(So-called)

Maker: Unknown and various
Date: First half of 1880s
Material: Papier-mâché shoulder head, stuffed cloth body, mostly homemade, wood, leather or cloth extremities
Mark: None

Unmarked Pre-Greiner: Papier-mâché shoulder head; molded and painted black hair, pupil-less black glass eyes; cloth stuffed body, leather extremities; dressed in good old or original clothes; all in good condition.

20—23in (51—59cm)	**$ 900—1000**
28—31in (71—79cm)	**1500—1700**
Fair condition with much wear, 20—23in (51—59cm)	**450—550**
Painted eyes, 22in (56cm)	**750—800**
Fair condition	**350**

27in (69cm) pre-Greiner with glass eyes and open mouth with teeth. *Richard Wright Antiques.*

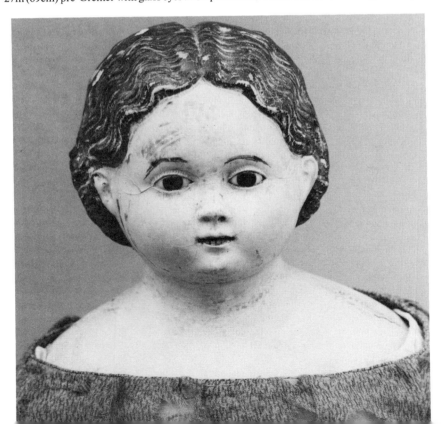

Queen Anne-Type

Maker: English Craftsmen
Date: Late 17th—mid 19th century
Material: All-wood or wooden head and torso with leather or cloth limbs
Mark: None

Early to Mid 18th Century: Carved wooden face, flax or hair wig, pupil-less glass eyes (sometimes painted), dotted eyebrows and eyelashes; jointed wooden body; old clothes, all in fair condition.

16—18in (41—46cm)	$ 6000—7500
24in (61cm)	**11,000—13,000**
Fine original example, excellent condition,	
24in (61cm)	**20,000**

Late 18th Century: Wooden head, gessoed, dotted eyelashes and eyebrows, glass eyes (later sometimes blue); pointed torso; old clothes; all in fair condition.

15—16in (38—41cm) **3500—4000**
22—24in (56—61cm) **5000—6000**

Early 19th Century: Wooden head, gessoed, painted eyes, pointed torso, flax or hair wig; old clothes (dress usually longer than legs); all in fair condition.

18—19in (46—48cm) **$2800—3000**

26in (66cm) 18th century Queen Anne-type. *Elizabeth McIntyre.*

18in (46cm) late 18th century Queen Anne-type. *Elizabeth McIntyre.*

Rabery & Delphieu

Maker: Rabery & Delphieu of Paris, France
Date: 1856 (founded)—1899—then with S. F. B. J.
Material: Bisque head, composition body
Mark: "R. D." (from 1890)
On back of head:
Body mark:
(Please note last two lines illegible)

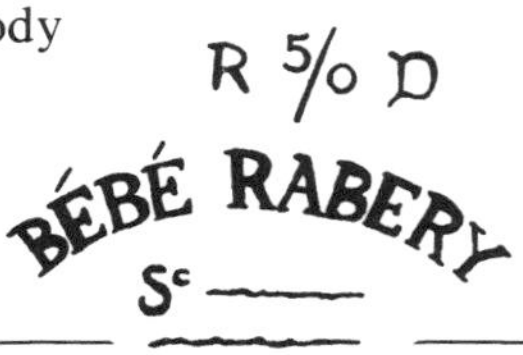

Marked R. D. Bébé: Ca. 1880s. Bisque head, lovely wig, paperweight eyes, closed mouth; jointed composition body; beautifully dressed; entire doll in nice condition.

20—22in (51—56cm) **$2650—2850***
26—28in (66—71cm) **3000—3400***
Open mouth,
17—21in (43—53cm) **1600—1800***

*Allow more for an especially pretty face.

24in (61cm) R. D. bébé. *Kay and Wayne Jensen Collection.*

Raggedy Ann and Andy

Maker: Various
Date: 1915 to present
Material: All-cloth
Size: 4½—39in (12—99cm)
Creator: Johnny B. Gruelle

Early Raggedy Ann or Andy: All-cloth with movable arms and legs; brown yarn hair, button eyes, painted features; legs or striped fabric for hose and black for shoes; original clothes; all in fair condition.
MARK: "PATENTED SEPT. 7, 1915"
(black stamp on front torso)
16in (41cm) **$550—650**

Molly-'es Raggedy Ann or Andy: 1935—1938, manufactured by Molly-'es Doll Outfitters. Same as above, but with red hair and printed features; original clothes; all in good condition.
MARK:
"Raggedy Ann and Raggedy Andy Dolls
Manufactured by Molly'es Doll Outfitters"
(printed writing in black on front torso)
16in (41cm) **$150—175**

Georgene Raggedy Ann or Andy: 1938-1963, manufactured by Georgene Novelties. Same as above, but with red hair and printed features; original clothes; all in good condition.
MARK: Cloth label sewn in side seam of body.
15—18in (38—46cm) **$ 45—55**
Beloved Belindy **250****

Knickerbocker Toy Co. Raggedy Ann or Andy: 1963 to 1982.
12in (31cm) **$12—15**
24in (61cm) **60—65**
36in (91cm) **85**

Applause Raggedy Ann and Andy, embroidered features. Available in toy stores.

**Not enough price samples to compute a reliable range.

See photos on page 320.

Raggedy Ann & Andy continued

ABOVE LEFT: Georgene *Raggedy Ann* and *Andy*, all original. *Esther Schwartz Collection.*

ABOVE RIGHT: Unmarked *Raggedy Ann* and *Andy*, all original. *Esther Schwartz Collection.*

Georgene *Beloved Belindy*, missing white apron. *Jan Foulke Collection.*

Raleigh

Maker: Jessie McCutcheon Raleigh, Chicago, IL., U.S.A.
Date: 1916—1920
Material: All-composition or composition heads and cloth bodies
Designer: Jessie McCutcheon Raleigh
Mark: None

Raleigh Doll: Composition head, molded hair or wig, sleep or painted eyes; composition or cloth body; appropriate clothes; all in good condition.
13in (33cm)   **$325—350**
18in (46cm)   **475—500**

12in (31cm) Raleigh girl with original wrist tag: "I AM A RALEIGH DOLL. My name is Mary Had a Lamb. No. 24." *Esther Schwartz Collection.*

Ravca

Maker: Bernard Ravca, Paris, France. After 1939, New York, N.Y., U.S.A.
Date: 1924—on
Material: Cloth with stockinette faces
Size: Various
Mark: Paper label: "Original Ravca Fabrication Francaise"

Ravca Doll: Stockinette face individually needle sculpted; cloth body and
limbs; original clothes; all in excellent condition.
10in (25cm)   **$ 75**
23in (58cm)   **200—225**

For color photo, see page 256.

10in (25cm) French peasant
woman. *H&J Foulke, Inc.*

Raynal

Maker: Raynal, France
Date: 1925
Material: Felt and cloth, sometimes celluloid hands
Size: 17—18in (43—46cm)
Mark: "Raynal" on necklace or shoe soles

Raynal Doll: Molded felt mask face with mohair wig, beautifully painted eyes, closed lips, rosy cheeks; stuffed cloth body (may have celluloid hands); original clothes often of felt; all in good condition.
17—18in (43—46cm) **$400—500**

20in (51cm) Raynal girl, all original with necklace. *Esther Schwartz Collection.*

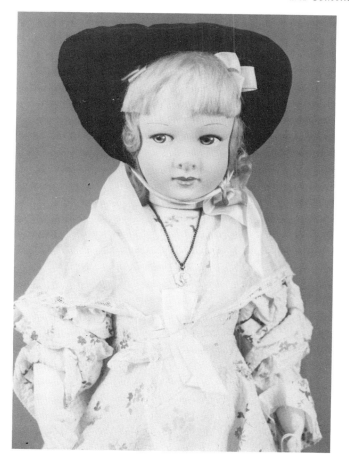

Recknagel

Maker: Th. Recknagel, porcelain factory, Alexandrienthal, Thüringia, Germany
Date: 1886—on
Material: Bisque head, composition or wood-jointed body
Size: Usually small
Mark: "R.A." with numbers, sometimes "Germany"

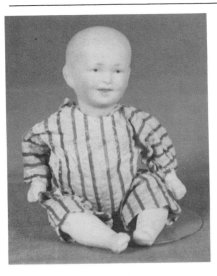

R. A. Child: Ca. 1890s-World War I. Perfect marked bisque head, jointed composition or wooden body; good wig, set or sleep eyes, open mouth; some dolls with molded painted shoes and socks; all in good condition. Mold #s 1909, 1914, 1924:

8—10in (20—25cm) **$125—150**
18—20in (46—51cm) 325—375*

*Fine quality bisque only.

R. A. Character Baby: 1909-World War I. Perfect bisque socket head; composition bent-limb baby or straight-leg curved-arm toddler body; sleep or set eyes; nicely dressed; all in good condition. Mold #127 and others.

8—10in (20—25cm) **$175—225**
Bonnet Baby with painted eyes, mold #22 & 28,
8—9in (20—23cm) 325—350
Pouty with glass eyes, closed mouth, composition body,
7—8in (18—20cm) 225—250
Molded hair, smiling face, mold #23,
7—8in (18—20cm) 225—250

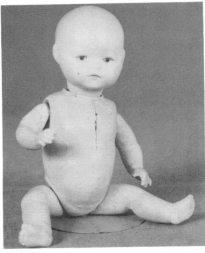

ABOVE LEFT: 7in (18cm) R.A. 23 baby. *H&J Foulke, Inc.*

8½in (21cm) R.A. 127 baby. *H&J Foulke, Inc.*

Grace Corry Rockwell

Maker: Unknown
Date: 1920s
Material: Bisque head, cloth and composition body
Size: About 20in (51cm)
Mark:

Copr. by
Grace C. Rockwell
Germany

Grace Corry Child: Composition smiling face, molded hair, sometimes with wig, painted eyes, closed mouth; cloth and composition body; appropriate clothes; all in good condition. Some dolls with tagged Madame Hendren clothing have heads by Grace Corry. See *3rd Blue Book of Dolls & Values™*, page 153.

14in (36cm)   **$400—425**

Grace Corry Rockwell Child: Bisque head with molded hair or wig, sleep eyes, closed mouth; cloth and composition body; appropriate clothes; all in good condition.

20in (51cm)   **$3200—3500****

**Not enough price samples to compute a reliable range.

20in (51cm) Grace Corry Rockwell child.
Pearl Church Collection.

Rohmer Fashion

Maker: Mademoiselle Marie Rohmer, Paris, France
Date: 1866—1880
Material: China or bisque shoulder head, jointed kid body
Mark:

Rohmer Fashion: China or bisque swivel shoulder head, jointed kid body, bisque or china arms, kid or china legs; lovely wig, set glass eyes, closed mouth, some ears pierced; fine costuming; entire doll in good condition.
16—20in (41—51cm) **$3600—4000 up**

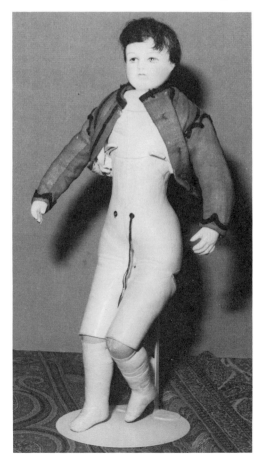

Rohmer with marked body, swivel neck, ribbon pulls up jointed knee. *Grace Dyar.*

Rollinson Doll

Maker: Utley Doll Co., Holyoke, MA., U.S.A.
Date: 1916—1919
Material: All-cloth
Size: 14—28in (36—71cm)
Designer: Gertrude F. Rollinson
Mark: Stamp in shape of a diamond with a doll in center, around border
"Rollinson Doll Holyoke, Mass."

Marked Rollinson doll: All molded cloth with painted head and limbs;
painted hair or human hair wig, painted features (sometimes teeth also);
dressed; all in good condition.
18—21in (46—53cm) $ 650—750**
26in (66cm) wigged child, excellent
original, condition at auction   **2300**

****Not enough price samples to compute a reliable range.

Rollinson doll with molded hair. *Catherine White.*

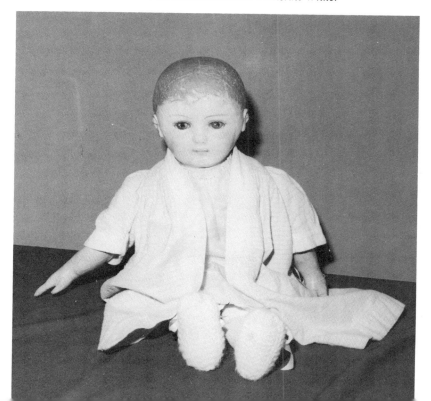

Roullet & Decamps

Maker: J. Roullet & E. Decamps, Paris, France
Date: Ca. 1895
Material: Usually bisque head, mechanical body
Mark: L'Intrêpide Bébé
      R.D.

R. D. Mechanical Doll: Bisque head, closed mouth, paperweight eyes, good wig; appropriate clothes; mechanical key-wind walking body; all in good condition.
20in (51cm)   **$3200—3500**

17in (43cm) L'Intrê-pide Bébé. *Private Collection.*

Rubber Head Dolls

Maker: Goodyear Rubber Co., New Haven, CT., U.S.A.; New York Rubber Co., B. F. Lee, India Rubber Comb Co., and others, all of New York, N.Y., U.S.A.

Date: 1851—on

Material: Rubber head, cloth body

Size: Various

Mark: Various depending upon company, but most are not marked

---

Rubber Head Doll: Rubber shoulder head with molded hair and painted features; cloth body, sometimes with leather arms; appropriate clothes; usually found in poor condition as the paint chips easily and the hardened rubber is often misshapen.

Plain hairdo, good condition:

14in (36cm)	**$ 400—425**
18—19in (46—48cm)	**500—550**

Fancy hairdo with molded braid
and flowers, excellent condition,

18—19in (46—48cm)	**1300****

**Not enough price samples to compute a reliable range.

19in (48cm) rubber head doll. *Private Collection.*

S.F.B.J.

Maker: Société Francaise de Fabrication de Bébés & Jouets, Paris, France
Date: 1899—
Material: Bisque head, composition body
Mark:

DÉPOSÉ
S.F.B.J.

29in (74cm) S.F.B.J. child, Jumeau mold.
Elizabeth McIntyre.

Child Doll: 1899—on. Perfect bisque head, good French wig, sleep eyes, open mouth, pierced ears; jointed composition body; nicely dressed; all in good condition.

Jumeau-type (no mold number):

16—18in (41—46cm)	$ 900—1100
21—23in (53—58cm)	1250—1500
26—27in (66—69cm)	1900—2000

#301:

15—16in (38—41cm)	625—675
20—22in (51—56cm)	825—875
25—27in (64—69cm)	1000—1200
31—32in (79—81cm)	1600—1800

#60:

17—18in (43—46cm)	550—600
24—25in (61—64cm)	750—800

Walking & Kiss-Throwing: 1905-on. Perfect bisque head, composition body with straight legs, walking mechanism at top, hand raises to throw a kiss, head moves from side to side, eyes flirt; good wig, glass eyes, open mouth, pierced ears; nicely dressed; all in working order.

22in (56cm)   **$1550—1650**

Character Dolls: 1910—on. Perfect bisque head, wig, molded, sometimes flocked hair on mold numbers 237, 266, 227 and 235, sleep eyes, composition body; nicely dressed; all in good condition.

S.F.B.J. continued

#226, 235:
  15—17in (38—43cm)
  $1650—1850
#227, 237:
  17—19in (43—48cm)
  1900—2200
#230
  Child, 22—24in (56—61cm)
  1800—2000**
#234
  Baby, 15in (38cm)   **1800****
#236:
  Baby, 17—18in (43—46cm)
  1200—1400
  25in (64cm)   **2000**
  Toddler,
    14—15in (36—38cm)
    1500—1600
    27—28in (69—71cm)
    2300—2500
#238:
  Child, 15—16in (38—41cm)
  2600—2800
  Lady, 23—26in (58—66cm)
  3600—4000
#247:
  Toddler,
    16—18in (41—46cm)
    2300—2500
    27in (69cm)   **3200—3400**
#251:
  Baby, 8—9in (20—23cm)
  750—850
  Toddler,
    14—15in (36—38cm)
    1150—1250
    27in (69cm)   **2300—2500**
#252:
  Toddler,
    18—20in (48—53cm)
    5000—5500
  24in (61cm)   **8000**

**Not enough price samples to compute a reliable range.

14in (36cm) S.F.B.J. 226 character child.
Nancy Schwartz Blaisure Collection.

14in (36cm) S.F.B.J. 248 character child.
Private Collection.

332

S.F.B.J. continued

16in (41cm) S.F.B.J. 236 character baby. *Private Collection.*

13in (33cm) S.F.B.J. 252 character child. *Private Collection.*

10in (25cm) S.F.B.J. 235 character child in original box with layette. *Lesley Hurford Collection.*

15in (38cm) S.F.B.J. 227 character child. *Esther Schwartz Collection.*

Peter Scherf

Maker: Peter Scherf, doll factory, Sonneberg, Thüringia, Germany. Some heads by Armand Marseille.

Date: 1879—on

Material: Bisque head, kid body

Size: Various

Mark:

Germany.

——————— *P. Sch. 1899-5/0* ———————————————

Marked Scherf Doll: 1899 on. Perfect bisque shoulder head, set glass eyes, open mouth with teeth; kid body; dressed; all in good condition. Mold numbers 1899, 1901, 1902.

16—18in (41—46cm)   **$250—275**

17in (43cm) Scherf, mold 1899. *Dolly Valk Collection.*

Bruno Schmidt

Maker: Bruno Schmidt, doll factory, Waltershausen, Thuringia, Germany.
Heads made by Bähr & Pröschild, Ohrdruf, Thüringia, Germany.
Date: 1898—on.
Material: Bisque head, composition body
Mark:

2096-4

Marked B. S. W. Character Baby: Ca. 1910. Perfect bisque head, good wig,
sleep eyes, open mouth; composition bent-limb baby body; dressed; all in
good condition.
12—15in (31—38cm)   **$400—500**
18—19in (46—48cm)   **600—650**
Toddler,
15—16in (38—41cm)   **650—750**

Marked B. S. W. Child Doll:
Bisque head, good wig, sleep
eyes, open mouth; jointed composition child body; dressed; all
in good condition.
20—22in (51—56cm)   **$450—500**
30in (76cm)   **900—950**

*Marked B. S. W. Character
Dolls:* Bisque socket head, glass
eyes; jointed composition body;
dressed; all in good condition.
#2048, 2094, 2096, Tommy Tucker,
molded hair, open mouth,
18—19in (46—48cm)
$ 900—1100
22—24in (56—61cm)
1250—1500 ·
#2097 Toddler, 12in (31cm)
550—600
#2033, Wendy, closed mouth, glass
eyes, 18in (46cm)   **5000 up**
#2048, closed mouth, molded hair,
20—22in (51—56cm)
2500—2600
#2072, closed mouth, wigged,
16—17in (41—43cm)
2200—2300
17—19in (43—48cm)
2500—2800

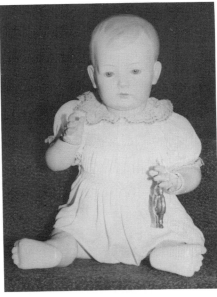

19in (48cm) B. S. W. 2048 character
baby. *Lesley Hurford Collection.*

OPPOSITE PAGE: 18in (46cm) 2072
character child made by Bähr & Pröschild
for Bruno Schmidt. *Richard Wright
Antiques.*

Franz Schmidt

Maker: Franz Schmidt & Co., doll factory, Georgenthal near Waltershausen, Thüringia, Germany. Heads by Simon & Halbig, Grafenhain, Thüringia, Germany.

Date: 1890—on

Material: Bisque socket head, jointed bent-limb or toddler body of composition

Mark:

1295
F. S. & Co.
Made in
Germany
30

S & C
SIMON & HALBIG
28

18in (46cm) F.S. & Co. 1310 toddler. *Dr. Carole Stoessel Zvonar Collection.*

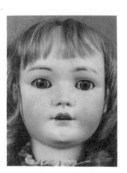

42in (107cm) S & C child doll with pierced nose. *Dr. Carole Stoessel Zvonar Collection.*

Marked F. Schmidt Doll: Ca. 1910. Perfect bisque character head, good wig, sleep eyes, open mouth, may have open nostrils; jointed bent-limb body; suitably dressed; all in good condition.

#1272, 1297:
14—16in (36—41cm) **$450—500**
22in (56cm) **700—725**

#1295, 1296, 1310:
Baby,
15—17in (38—43cm) **450—500**
22—24in (56—61cm) **700—800**
Toddler,
9—10in (23—25cm) **375—425**
16in (41cm) **600—650**

#1266, 1267:
24in (61cm) jointed body **1400****
**Not enough price samples to compute a reliable range.

Marked S & C Child Doll: Ca. 1890 on. Perfect bisque socket head, good wig, sleep eyes, open mouth; jointed composition child body; dressed; all in good condition.
12—14in (31—36cm) **$300—350**
22—24in (56—61cm) **450—550**

Imhoff Walking Doll: 1901. Bisque socket head, jointed composition body with clockwork mechanism to move legs on specially manufactured shoe soles.
17in (43cm) **$900—1100****
**Not enough price samples to compute a reliable range.

Schmitt

Maker: Schmitt & Fils, Paris, France
Date: 1863—1891
Material: Bisque socket head, composition jointed body
Size: Various
Mark: On both head and body:

Marked Schmitt Bébé: Ca. 1879. Perfect bisque socket head with skin or good wig, large paperweight eyes, closed mouth, pierced ears; Schmitt-jointed composition body; appropriate clothes; all in good condition.

16—18in (41—46cm)   **$5500—6200 up**
24in (61cm)   **8500—9500 up**

23½in (60cm) Schmitt bébé with shield mark. *Kay and Wayne Jensen Collection.*

Schoenau & Hoffmeister

Maker: Schoenau & Hoffmeister, porzellanfabrik Burggrub, Burggrub, Bavaria, Germany. Arthur Schoenau also owned a doll factory.

Date: 1901—on

Material: Bisque head, composition body

Trademarks: Hanna, Burggrub Baby, Bébé Carmencita, Viola, Kunstlerkopf, Das Lachencle Baby.

Mark:

Child Doll: 1901—on. Mold numbers such as 1909, 5500, 5800, 5700. Perfect bisque head; original or good wig, sleep eyes, open mouth; ball-jointed body; original or good clothes; all in nice condition.

16—18in (41—46cm)	**$325—375**
24—26in (61—66cm)	**475—525**
30in (76cm)	**700—750**
12in (31cm)	**200—225**

12in (31cm) S PB H 1909 child *My Darling*, all original and boxed. *Maurine Popp Collection.*

Schoenau & Hoffmeister continued

Character Baby: 1910—on. Mold numbers 169, 769, "Burggrub Baby" or "Porzellanfabrik Burggrub." Perfect bisque socket head, good wig, sleep eyes, open mouth; composition bent-limb baby body; all in good condition.

16—18in (41—46cm) **$400—450**
24in (61cm) **600—650**

Das Lachencle Baby; 1930.
For photograph see *6th Blue Book of Dolls & Values,* page 331.
18—20in (46—51cm) **500—600****

Hanna:
Baby,
12—13in (31—33cm) **400—450**
26in (66cm) **1000**
Toddler,
14in (36cm) **550—600**

22in (56cm) *Hanna* toddler. *Dolly Valk Collection.*

Pouty Baby: Ca. 1925. Perfect bisque solid dome head with painted hair, tiny sleep eyes, closed pouty mouth; cloth body with composition arms and legs; dressed; all in good condition. For photograph see *6th Blue Book of Dolls & Values,* page 331.

12—14in (31—36cm) **$700—750****

**Not enough price samples to compute a reliable range.

Princess Elizabeth: 1932. Perfect bisque head with good wig, glass sleep eyes, smiling mouth with teeth; chubby five-piece composition body; appropriate clothes; all in good condition.
MARK:
"Porzellanfabrik Burggrub/ Princess Elizabeth."
21—23in (53—58cm) **$2500—3000**

21in (53cm) *Princess Elizabeth. Esther Schwartz Collection.*

Schoenhut

Maker: Albert Schoenhut & Co., Philadephia, PA., U.S.A.
Date: 1872—on
Material: Wood, spring-jointed, holes in bottom of feet to fit metal stand
Size: Various models 11—21in (28—53cm)
Designer: Early: Adolph Graziana and Mr. Leslie
          Later: Harry E. Schoenhut
Mark: Paper label: Incised:

SCHOENHUT DOLL
PAT. JAN. 17, '11, U.S.A.
& FOREIGN COUNTRIES

Character: 1911—1930. Wooden head and spring-jointed wooden body, marked head and/or body; original or appropriate wig, brown or blue intaglio eyes, open/closed mouth with painted teeth or closed mouth; original or suitable clothing; nothing repainted. Pouty or smiling.
16—19in (41—48cm):
  Excellent condition   **$1200—1500***
  Good condition, some wear **700—800***

*More depending upon rarity of face.

16in (41cm) smiling Schoenhut girl. *Esther Schwartz Collection.*

16in (41cm) pouty Schoenhut girl. *Dolly Valk Collection.*

Schoenhut continued

Character with carved hair: Ca. 1911—1930. Wooden head with carved hair, comb marks, possibly a ribbon or bow, intaglio eyes, mouth usually closed; spring-jointed wooden body; original or suitable clothes.

14—16in (36—41cm):

Excellent condition,	**$1400—1600**
Good, some wear,	**900—1000**
Early style,	**1800**
Molded cap,	**2000 up****

** Not enough price samples to compute a reliable range.

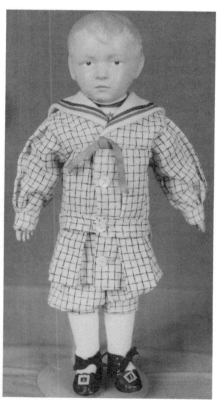

16in (41cm) girl with carved hair. *Private Collection.*

16in (41cm) boy with carved hair. *Private Collection.*

Schoenhut continued

Baby Face: Ca. 1913—1930. Wooden head and fully-jointed toddler or bent-limb baby body, marked head and/or body; painted hair or mohair wig, painted eyes, open mouth; suitably dressed; nothing repainted; all in good condition.

MARK:

Baby body, 15in (38cm) **$550—650**
Toddler,

14in (36cm)	**550—650**
11in (28cm)	**650—700**

13in (33cm) Schoenhut baby. *Dolly Valk Collection.*

12in (31cm) Schoenhut toddlers. *Dolly Valk Collection.*

Schoenhut continued

17in (43cm) *Dolly*-face Schoenhut. *Dolly Valk Collection.*

19in (48cm) Schoenhut girl with sleep eyes. *Dolly Valk Collection.*

Dolly Face: Ca. 1915—1930. Wooden head and spring-jointed wooden body; original or appropriate mohair wig, decal eyes, open/closed mouth with painted teeth; original or suitable clothes; all in excellent condition.

14—16in (36—41cm) **$500—600**
19—21in (48—53cm) **600—700**
Good condition, some wear,
14—16in (36—41cm) **325—375**

Walker: Ca. 1919—1930. All-wood with "baby face," mohair wig, painted eyes; curved arms, straight legs with "walker" joint at hip; original or appropriate clothes; all in good condition. No holes in bottom of feet.
13in (33cm) **$550—650**

Sleep Eyes: Ca. 1920—1930. Used with "baby face" or "dolly face" heads. Mouths on this type were open with teeth or barely open with carved teeth. Excellent condition.
17—19in (43—48cm) **$800—900**

Schoenhut Soft Body Mamma [sic] Doll: Ca. 1925. Wood socket head fitting into a papier-mâché yoke attached to a cloth body with wooden hands and cry box; original mohair wig, painted eyes, closed mouth; original or appropriate clothes; all in excellent condition. For photograph, see *5th Blue Book of Dolls & Values,* page 334.

MARK:

15—17in (38—43cm) **$800**

Schuetzmeister & Quendt

Maker: Schuetzmeister & Quendt, porcelain factory, Boilstadt, Thüringia, Germany, made heads for Welsch, Kämmer & Reinhardt, Wolf & Co.

Date: 1889

Material: Bisque head, composition body

Distributor: John Bing Co., New York, N.Y., U.S.A.

Mark:

301

S&

Germany

S & Q Child Doll: Ca. 1900. Mold number 101 ***Jeanette***. Perfect bisque head with mohair wig, sleep eyes, open mouth with teeth; jointed composition body; nicely dressed.

22—24in (56—61cm)   **$375—425**

S & Q Character Baby: Ca. 1910. Mold numbers 201 and 301. Perfect bisque head with mohair wig, sleep eyes, open mouth with tongue and teeth, slightly smiling; composition baby body; nicely dressed; all in good condition.

10—12in (25—31cm)   **$250—300**
17—20in (43—51cm)   **450—550**
24in (61cm)   **675—725**

10in (25cm) character baby 201. *H&J Foulke, Inc.*

Shirley Temple

Maker: Ideal Toy Corp., New York, N.Y., U.S.A.
Date: 1934 to present
Size: 7½—36in (19—91cm)
Designer: Bernard Lipfert
Mark: See individual doll listings below. (Ideal used marked Shirley Temple bodies for other dolls).

All-Composition Child: 1934 through late 1930s. Marked head and body, jointed composition body; all original including wig and clothes; entire doll in very good condition. Came in sizes 11—27in (28—69cm)

MARK:

On body: SHIRLEY TEMPLE
                        13

On head: 13
           SHIRLEY TEMPLE

On cloth label:

Genuine SHIRLEY TEMPLE DOLL REGISTERED U.S. PAT OFF	MADE IN USA
IDEAL NOVELTY & TOY CO	

11in (28cm)	$600—625*
13in (33cm)	475—500*
15—16in (38—41cm)	500—600*
18in (46cm)	500—600*
20—22in (51—56cm)	600—700*
25in (64cm)	750—800*
27in (69cm)	850—950*
Button	75—85*
Dress and button	150

*Allow more for a mint-in-box doll or one with unusual dress.

17in (43cm) composition *Shirley Temple*, all original. *Private Collection.*

Boxed rare dress with button. *H&J Foulke, Inc.*

25in (64cm) **Shirley Temple** baby, all original with tag and button. *Jimmy and Faye Rodolfus Collection.*

Baby: 1934 through late 1930s. Composition swivel head with molded hair or blonde mohair wig, sleep eyes, open smiling mouth, dimples; cloth body, composition arms and legs; appropriate clothes; all in good condition. Came in six sizes, 16—25in (41—64cm).
MARK: "Shirley Temple" on head
16—18in (41—46cm) **$600—650***

*Allow more for mint condition.

Unusual Japanese-made Shirley with molded hair: From late 1930s. All-composition.
7½in (19cm)   **$200—250**

Hawaiian Shirley: Brown composition with black yarn hair, painted eyes; original grass skirt and ornaments; all in good condition.

18in (46cm)   **$650****

**Not enough price samples to compute a reliable range.

Vinyl and Plastic: 1957. Vinyl and plastic, rooted hair, sleep eyes; jointed at shoulders and hips; original clothes; all in excellent condition. Came in sizes 12in (31cm), 15in (38cm), 17in (43cm), 19in (48cm) and 36in (91cm)

MARK: "Ideal Doll ST—12"
(number denotes size)

12in (31cm)	**$ 150**
15in (38cm)	**225**
17in (43cm)	**275—325**
19in (48cm)	**350—375**
36in (91cm)	**1100—1400**

Vinyl and Plastic: 1973. Vinyl and plastic, rooted hair, painted eyes, smiling mouth; jointed shoulders and hips; original clothes; all in mint condition.

16in (41cm) size only	**$ 75—85**
Boxed	**100—125**
Boxed dresses	**25—30**

17in (43cm) vinyl *Shirley Temple*, all original. *H&J Foulke, Inc.*

Simon & Halbig

Maker: Simon & Halbig, porcelain factory, Gräfenhain, Thüringia, Germany; purchased by Kämmer & Reinhardt in 1920

Date: 1869—on

Material: Bisque head, kid (sometimes cloth) or composition body

Mark:

S 13 H
949

1079-2
DEP
S H
Germany

13½in (34cm) S&H 908. *Kay and Wayne Jensen Collection.*

14in (36cm) S&H swivel neck, kid body, all original. *Private Collection.*

Child doll with closed mouth:
Ca. 1879. Mold numbers such as 719, 939, 949 and others. Perfect bisque socket head on ball-jointed wood and composition body; good wig, glass set or sleep eyes, closed mouth, pierced ears; dressed; all in good condition. See *Simon & Halbig Dolls - The Artful Aspect* for photographs of mold numbers not shown here.

#719, 749, 939, 949:
15—17in (38—43cm)
$1550—1850
23—25in (58—64cm)
2500—2700
27—28in (69—71cm)
2900—3100

#905, 908:
16—18in (41—46cm)
2200—2500

720, 740, 950 (kid body):
9—10in (23—25cm)
425—450
18in (46cm)
1200—1300

#939, 949 (kid body):
20—22in (51—56cm)
1450—1650

Early closed mouth shoulder head:
17—19in (43—48cm)
1200—1500**

**Not enough price samples to compute a reliable range.

Simon & Halbig continued

15in (38cm) S&H 739 child. *H&J Foulke, Inc.*

25in (64cm) S&H 1249 child. *Roberts Collection.*

24in (61cm) S&H 550 child. *H&J Foulke, Inc.*

22in (56cm) S&H 1079 child, all original. *H&J Foulke, Inc.*

Simon & Halbig continued

Child doll with open mouth and composition body: Ca. 1889 to 1930s. Perfect bisque head, good wig, sleep eyes, open mouth, pierced ears; original ball-jointed composition body; very pretty clothes; all in nice condition. See *Simon & Halbig Dolls - The Artful Aspect* for photographs of mold numbers not shown here.

#719, 739, 939, 949:

14—15in (36—38cm)	$ 600—700
18—20in (46—51cm)	850—1000
24—25in (61—63cm)	1350—1550
30—31in (76—79cm)	2200—2400

#540, 550, 1009, 1039, 1078, 1079:

12—14in (31—36cm)	350—450
17—19in (43—48cm)	450—500
22—24in (56—61cm)	550—650
28—30in (71—76cm)	900—975
32—33in (81—83cm)	1150—1250
35—36in (89—91cm)	1500—1600
39—42in (99—107cm)	2500 up

#1009, 1248:

22—24in (56—61cm)	650—750

#1249, Santa:

15—16in (38—41cm)	650—725
21—24in (53—61cm)	850—950
28in (71cm)	1300—1400

#1039 key-wind walking body:

18in (46cm)	1100—1250
Boxed, all original	1950

#1039 walking, kissing:

20—22in (51—56cm)	850—950

Baby Blanche:

23in (59cm)	550—600

#600:

21in (53cm)	675—725

11in (28cm) S&H 1009, swivel neck, kid body, all original. *H&J Foulke, Inc.*

Child doll with open mouth and kid body: Ca. 1889 to 1930s. Mold numbers such as 1010, 1040, 1080, 1250 and others. Shoulder head with stationary neck, sleep eyes, open mouth, pierced ears; kid body, bisque arms, cloth lower legs; well costumed; all in good condition.

#1010, 1040, 1080:

16—18in (41—46cm)	$450—500
23—24in (58—61cm)	575—675
29—30in (74—76cm)	850—950

#1009 fashion-type body:

18—20in (51—56cm)	600—700

#1250, 1260:

16—18in (41—46cm)	475—525
24in (61cm)	700—750

Simon & Halbig continued

8½in (22cm) S&H 1078 child, all original.
H&J Foulke, Inc.

6½in (16cm) S&H 1160 so-called *Little Women*. H&J Foulke, Inc.

Tiny Child doll: Ca. 1889 to 1930s. Usually mold number 1079 or 1078. Perfect bisque head, nice wig, sleep eyes, open mouth; composition body with molded shoes and socks; appropriate clothes; all in good condition.

7—8in (18—20cm)	**$250—300**
Fully-jointed:	
8in (20cm)	**350—375**
10in (25cm)	**400—425**

So-called Little Women type: Ca. 1900. Mold number 1160. Shoulder head with fancy mohair wig, glass set eyes, closed mouth; cloth body with bisque limbs, molded boots; dressed; all in good condition.

5½—7in (14—18cm)	**$275—325**
10—11in (25—28cm)	**375—425**

Simon & Halbig continued

20in (51cm) S&H 1294 toddler. *Dr. Carole Stoessel Zvonar Collection.*

Character Baby: Ca. 1909 to 1930s. Perfect bisque head, molded hair or wig, sleep or painted eyes, open or open/closed mouth; composition bent-limb baby or toddler body; nicely dressed; all in good condition. See *Simon & Halbig Dolls - The Artful Aspect* for photographs of mold numbers not shown here.

17in (43cm) S&H 1498 character. *Kay and Wayne Jensen Collection.*

#1294:
  Baby,
    18-20in (46—51cm)   **$ 600—700**
  Toddler,
    17in (43cm)   **750**
  Clockwork,
    24in (61cm)   **1800—2000****
#1428:
  Baby,
    12in (31cm)   **850**
  Toddler,
    12in (31cm)   **1250**
#1488:
  Baby,
    22—23in (56—58cm)   **2500—3000**
    16—18in (41—46cm)   **2000—2200**
#1489, Erika:
    21—22in (53—56cm)   **3000—3200**
#1498:
  Toddler,
    18—20in (46—51cm)   **3000—3500**

**Not enough price samples to compute a reliable range.

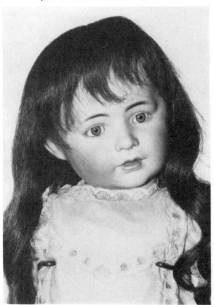

26in (69cm) S&H 1488. *Courtesy of Rhoda Shoemaker.*

Simon & Halbig continued

Character Child: Ca. 1910. Perfect bisque socket head with wig or molded hair, painted or glass eyes, open or closed mouth, character face, jointed composition body; dressed; all in good condition. See *Simon & Halbig Dolls - The Artful Aspect* for photographs of mold numbers not shown here.

#120:
20—22in (51—56cm) $ **2200—2500**
#150:
14—16in (36—41cm) **5200—6200**
20in (51cm) **9000**
#151:
16in (41cm) **5000****
#153:
16in (41cm) **6000 up****
#1279:
14—16in (36—41cm) **1000—1200**
24in (61cm) **2400**
30in (76cm) **3250**
#1299:
16—19in (41—48cm) **800—1000**
#1388:
27in (69cm)
lady with flirty eyes **14,000****
#1398:
18—20in (46—51cm) **8000****
#1478:
16—18in (41—46cm) **5000 up****
IV:
18in (46cm) **6000 up****
#1339:
18in (46cm) **1050****

**Not enough price samples to compute a reliable range.

31in (79cm) S&H 1339 child. *Roberts Collection.*

23in (58cm) S&H 151 character child. *Richard Wright Collection.*

Simon & Halbig continued

19in (48cm) S&H 1159 lady doll. *Elsa McCallum Collection.*

Lady doll: Ca. 1910. Mold number 1159. Perfect bisque socket head, good wig, sleep eyes, open mouth, pierced ears; lady body, molded bust, slim arms and legs; elegantly dressed; all in good condition.

#1159:

16in (41cm)	**$ 950—1050**
20—21in (51—53cm)	**1650—1950**
26—28in (66—71cm)	**2400—2600**

Lady doll: Ca. 1910. With closed mouth. Perfect bisque head with good wig, set glass eyes; composition lady body, molded bust, slim arms and legs; nicely dressed; all in good condition.

#1469, 14—15in (36—38cm)   **$1250—1450**
#1303, 15—16in (38—41cm)   **4500 up****

**Not enough price samples to compute a reliable range.

Simonne

Maker: F. Simonne, Paris, France
Date: 1848—1878?
Material: Bisque head, kid or composition body
Mark: Sticker or stamped on body:

Simonne Lady Doll: Late 1860s—on. Perfect bisque turning head on shoulder plate, wig, paperweight eyes, closed mouth, pierced ears; kid body, bisque arms; dressed; all in good condition.

17—18in (43—46cm) **$2700—3200****

Simonne Bébé: 1870s. Perfect bisque head, composition and wood jointed body; wig, paperweight eyes, closed mouth; pierced ears; dressed; all in good condition. Rare.

15—16in (38—41cm) **$4500****
22—24in (56—61cm)   **7000—8000****

**Not enough price samples to compute a reliable range.

18in (45.7cm) Simonne lady doll, all original. *Sheila Needle Collection. Photograph by Morton Needle.*

Snow Babies

Maker: Various German firms including Hertwig & Co. after 1910.
Date: Ca. 1890 until World War II
Material: All-bisque
Size: 1—3in (3—8cm) usually
Mark: Sometimes "Germany"

Snow Babies: All-bisque with snowsuits and caps of pebbly-textured bisque; painted features; various standing, lying or sitting positions.

1½in (4cm)	$ 30—35
1½in (4cm) snow bear	30—35
1½in (4cm) snowman	65
3in (8cm) baby riding snow bear	150—160
2½in (6cm) tumbling snow baby	100
2in (5cm) musical snow baby	40—45
2in (5cm) baby on sled	65—70
3in (8cm) baby on sled	125—135
2in (5cm) reindeer pulling snow baby	150—160
2in (5cm) early fine quality babies with high hoods	75—85

3in (8cm) snow baby riding polar bear.
H&J Foulke, Inc.

Sonneberg Täufling
(So-called Motschmann Baby)

Maker: Various Sonneberg factories such as Henrich Stier; many handled by exporter Louis Lindner & Söhn, Sonneberg, Thüringia, Germany
Date: 1851—1880s
Material: Papier-mâché, wood and cloth
Size: 8in (20cm) to about 28in (71cm)
Mark: None

Sonneberg Täufling: Papier-mâché or wax-over-composition head with painted hair or wig, glass eyes, closed mouth or open mouth with bamboo teeth; composition lower torso; composition arms and legs jointed at ankles and wrists, cloth covered midsection with voice box, upper arms and legs cloth covered, called floating joints; dressed in shirt and bonnet; wear acceptable, fair condition.

12—14in (31—36cm)	**$250—350**
18—20in (46—51cm)	**450—500**
24in (61cm)	**550—600**

NOTE: For many years it was thought that these dolls were made by Ch. Motschmann, since some were found stamped with his name; hence, they were called *Motschmann Babies* by collectors. However, research has shown that they were made by various factories and that Motschmann was the holder of the patent for the voice boxes, not the manufacturer of the dolls.

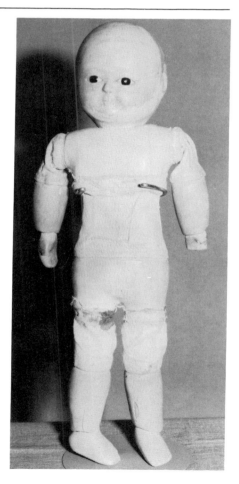

12in (31cm) Sonneberg Täufling. *Private Collection.*

Steiff

Maker: Fraulein Margarete Steiff, Würtemberg, Germany
Date: 1894—on
Material: Felt, plush or velvet
Size: Various
Mark: Metal button in ear

Steiff Doll: Felt, plush or velvet, jointed; seam down middle of face, button eyes, painted features; original clothes; most are character dolls, many have large shoes to enable them to stand; all in good condition.

Children,
  12—15in (31—38cm) **$ 550—650**
Adults,
  19in (48cm)   **750—850**
Characters,
  15—21in (38—53cm) **1000—3000**
U.S. Zone, Germany,
  12in (31cm)
    glass eyes   **675—775**

*Depending upon rarity.

18½in (47cm) Steiff character man, all original. *Kay and Wayne Jensen Collection.*

Herm Steiner

Maker: Hermann Steiner of Sonneberg, Thüringia, Germany
Date: 1921—on
Material: Bisque head, cloth or composition body
Size: Various, usually small
Mark:

15
ʜˢⱵ
Germany
240

Herm Steiner
ʜˢⱵ
Germany

Herm Steiner Child: Perfect bisque head, wig, sleep eyes, open mouth; jointed composition body; dressed; in good condition.

7—8in (18—20cm)	**$125—150**
12—14in (31—36cm)	**200—250**

Herm Steiner Infant: Perfect bisque head, molded hair, sleep eyes, closed mouth; cloth or composition bent-limb body; dressed; in good condition.

Head circumference:

8in (20cm)	**$200—225***
10—11in (25—28cm)	**250—300***

*Allow more for open mouth.

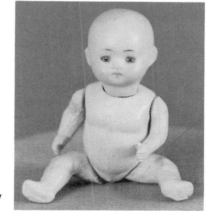

7½in (19cm) H. S. 133 googly. See page 190 for price. *H&J Foulke, Inc.*

Herm Steiner Character Baby: Ca. 1910. Perfect bisque socket head, good wig, sleep eyes, open mouth with teeth; composition jointed baby body; dressed; all in good condition.

8—9in (20—23cm)	**$175—200**
10—12in (25—31cm)	**225—300**
12in (31cm) toddler, all original	**400**

7in (18cm) long H. S. 426 infant. *H&J Foulke, Inc.*

Jules Steiner

Maker: Jules Nicholas Steiner and Successors, Paris, France
Date: 1855—1908
Material: Bisque head, jointed papier-mâché body
Size: Various
Mark: Various as shown below

Marked Bourgoin Steiner Bébé: Ca. late 1870s. Perfect socket head, cardboard pate, appropriate wig, bulgy paperweight eyes with tinting on upper eyelids, closed mouth, round face, pierced ears with tinted tips; jointed composition body; dressed; all in good condition. Sometimes with wire-operated sleep eyes.

MARK: (incised)

$$S^{TE} \ A \ O$$

(red script)

J Steiner. Bte S.g. Bg. J Bourgoin Sie

15—17in (38—43cm) $3200—3600
22—24in (56—61cm)   4200—4600

22½in (57cm) Bourgoin Steiner A-4. *Wayne and Kay Jensen Collection.*

Jules Steiner continued

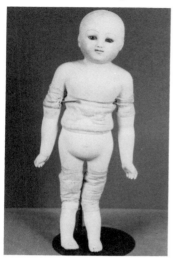

20in (51cm) Steiner with Motschmann-type body. *Private Collection.*

22in (56cm) Steiner C-4 with wire eyes. *Private Collection.*

Round face with open mouth: Ca. 1870s. Perfect very pale bisque socket head, appropriate wig, bulgy paperweight eyes, open mouth with pointed teeth, round face, pierced ears; jointed composition body; dressed; all in good condition.

MARK: None, but sometimes body has a label

Two rows of teeth, 18—20in (46—51cm)   **$2500—2700**

Kicking, crying bébé, mechanical key-wind body with composition
   arms and lower legs, 20—22in (51—56cm)   **1700—1900**

Motschmann-type body with bisque shoulders, hips and lower
   arms and legs, 18—21in (46—53cm)   **3600—4000**

"C" Series Bébé: Ca. 1880. Perfect bisque socket head, cardboard pate, appropriate wig, sleep eyes with wire mechanism, closed mouth, full cheeks, pierced ears; jointed composition body; dressed; all in good condition.

MARK:

S^{TE} C 4   (incised)

J. STEINER B. S.G. D.G.   (red stamp)

15—17in (38—43cm) **$3200—3600**

23—24in (58—61cm)   **4200—4700**

29in (74cm)   **6000—7000**

29in (74cm) Steiner fire A-19. *Wayne and Kay Jensen Collection.*

"A" Series Bébé: Ca. 1885. Perfect bisque socket head, cardboard pate, appropriate wig, paperweight eyes, closed mouth, pierced ears; jointed composition body; dressed; all in good condition.

MARK: (incised)

> J. STEINER
> Bᵀᴱ S.G.D.G.
> PARIS
> Fɪᴿᴱ A 15

11—12in (28—31cm) **$2000—2300**
17—18in (43—46cm) **3200—3500**
22—24in (56—61cm) **4000—4500**

Le Petit Parisien Bébé: Ca. 1889. Perfect bisque socket head, cardboard pate, appropriate wig, paperweight eyes, closed mouth, pierced ears; jointed composition body; dressed; all in good condition.

MARK: Stamp on head or body:

> "Le Petit Parisien
> BEBE STEINER
> MEDAILLE d'OR
> PARIS 1889"

or paper label of doll carrying flag

10—12in (25—31cm) **$1700—2000**
16—18in (36—43cm) **2800—3300**
24—25in (61—64cm) **4200—4600**
See color photo, page 112.

Bébé Le Parisien: Ca. 1892. Perfect bisque socket head, cardboard pate, appropriate wig, paperweight eyes, closed or open mouth, pierced ears; jointed composition body; dressed; all in good condition.

MARK: head (incised):

> A -19
> PARIS

(red stamp):
> "LE PARISIEN"

body (purple stamp):
> "BEBE 'LE PARISIEN'
> MEDAILLE D'OR
> PARIS"

Closed mouth:
20in (46—51cm)
    $3200—3600
24—26in (61—66cm)
    4300—4800
Open mouth:
20—22in (51—56cm)
    2200—2500

See color photos on pages 181 and 178.

Swaine & Co.

Maker: Swaine & Co., porcelain factory, Hüttensteinach, Sonneberg, Thüringia, Germany

Date: Ca. 1910—on for doll heads

Material: Bisque socket head, composition baby body

Mark: Stamped in green:

Incised Lori: Perfect bisque solid dome head, painted hair, sleep eyes, closed mouth; composition baby body with bent limbs; dressed; all in good condition.

22—25in (56—64cm)   **$2600—3000**

Mold #232,
(open-mouth *Lori*):
19—23in (48—58cm)   **1400—1700**

DIP, F.P.,
(wig, glass eyes, closed mouth):
10—11in (25—28cm)   **550—650**
16—18in (41—46cm)   **1050—1250**

DV,
(molded hair, glass eyes open/closed mouth):
14—16in (36—41cm)   **900—1000**

DI, F O, A,
(molded hair, intaglio eyes, open/closed mouth):
14—16in (36—41cm)   **800—900**

B.P., B.O.
(smiling character):
16—18in (41—46cm)   **2800—3200****

**Not enough price samples to compute a reliable range

Large *Lori* baby. *Dolly Valk Collection.*

18in (46cm) B.P. character girl. *Richard Wright Antiques.*

J. Terréne

Maker: J. Terréne, Paris, France
Date: 1863—1890
Material: Bisque head and lower arms, kid-covered wooden torso, metal upper arms
Mark: On body:

J. Terréne, 10 rue de Marché-St. Honoré
9 Medailles aux Expositions 1867-68-72-73-74

15½in (39cm) marked J. Terréne fashion lady. *Wayne and Kay Jensen Collection.*

Marked Terréne Fashion Lady:
Perfect bisque swivel neck, on bisque shoulder plate, stationary glass eyes, closed mouth, pierced ears, good wig; kid-covered wood torso, metal upper arms, bisque lower arms, wooden lower legs, kid-covered metal knee joints; beautifully dressed; all in good condition.
16—17in (41—43cm) **$4000—4500**

Terri Lee

Maker: TERRI LEE Sales Corp., V. Gradwohl, Pres., U.S.A.
Date: 1946-Lincoln, NE; then Apple Valley, CA. from 1951-Ca. 1962
Material: First dolls, rubbery plastic composition; later, hard plastic
Size: 16in (41cm) and 10in (25cm)
Mark: embossed across shoulders
First dolls:

"TERRI LEE
PAT. PENDING"

raised letters
Later dolls: "TERRI LEE"

16in (41cm) *Terri Lee. H&J Foulke, Inc.*

Terri Lee Child Doll: Original wig, painted eyes; jointed at neck, shoulders and hips; all original clothing and accessories; very good condition.

16in (41cm):

Early model	**$200—225**
Hard plastic	**150—175**
	MIB **225—250**
Black	**300—350**
Jerri Lee, 16in (41cm)	**185**
Tiny Terri Lee, inset eyes, 10in (25cm)	**110—125**
Tiny Jerri Lee, inset eyes, 10in (25cm)	**175**
Connie Lynn	**300—350**
Linda Baby	**140—165**
Gene Autry	**450 up****

**Not enough price samples to compute a reliable range.

18in (46cm) *Connie Lynn. Nancy Schwartz Blaisure Collection.*

Unis

Maker: Société Française de Fabrication de Bébés et Jouets.
(S. F. B. J.) of Paris and Montruil-sous-Bois, France
Date: 1922—on
Material: Bisque head, composition body
Size: 5in (13cm) up
Mark:

71   UNIS   FRANCE   149
301

5½in (14cm) Unis child, all original. *H&J Foulke, Inc.*

Costume Doll: Mold 301 or 60.
Perfect bisque head, mohair wig, glass eyes (painted eyes on tiny dolls), open or closed mouth; five-piece papier-mâché body; original costume; all in good condition.

5in (13cm)	**$150—175**
11—13in (28—33cm)	**250—300**
11—13in (28—33cm), dark skinned	**275—325**
8—10in (20—25cm) fully-jointed	**300—350**

Princess: See page 229.

Unis Child Doll: Perfect bisque head, papier-mâché body or wood and composition jointed body; good wig, sleep eyes, open mouth; pretty clothes; all in nice condition.

#301 or 60:

14—16in (36—41cm)	**$450—500**
21—23in (53—58cm)	**600—700**

13in (33cm) Unis 60 child, all original. *Esther Schwartz Collection.*

Verlingue

Maker: J. Verlingue of Boulogne-sur-Mer, France
Date: 1914—1921
Material: Bisque head, composition body
Size: Various
Mark:

PETITE FRANÇAISE
FRANCE
J V
3/0 D
LIANE

Marked J. V. Child: Perfect bisque head, good wig, glass eyes, open mouth; jointed papier-mâché body; nicely dressed.
16—18in (41—46cm)   **$475—525**
22—23in (56—58cm)   **650—700**

Verlingue All-bisque Doll: Head with wig, swivel neck, sleep eyes, closed mouth; jointed shoulders and hips; long painted hose, garters, black boots; undressed; mediocre quality.
7in (18cm)   **$250—275**

17in (43cm) *Liane* child. *Dr. Carole Stoessel Zvonar Collection.*

Vogue-Ginny

Maker: Vogue Dolls, Inc.
Date: 1937—on
Material: 1937—1948 composition, 1948—1962 hard plastic
Size: 7—8in (18—20cm)
Creator: Jennie Graves
Clothes Designer: Virginia Graves Carlson
Clothes Label: "Vogue," "Vogue Dolls," or

> VOGUE DOLLS, INC.
> MEDFORD, MASS. USA
> ® REG U.S. PAT OFF

All-composition Toddles: Jointed neck, shoulders and hips; molded hair or mohair wig, painted eyes looking to side; original clothes; all in good condition.

MARK: "VOGUE" on head
"DOLL CO." on back
"TODDLES" stamped
on sole of shoe

7—8in (18—20cm) **$175—225**

Vogue *Toddles*, all original. *H&J Foulke, Inc.*

Hard Plastic Ginny: All-hard plastic, jointed at neck, shoulders and hips (some have jointed knees and some walk); nice wig, sleep eyes (early ones have painted eyes, later dolls have molded eyelashes); original clothes; all in excellent condition with perfect hair and pretty coloring.

MARK: On strung dolls:
"VOGUE DOLLS"
On walking dolls:
"GINNY//VOGUE DOLLS"

7—8in (18—20cm):

Painted eyes,	
1948—1949	**$200—250***
Separate outfits	**50—65**
Painted eyelashes, strung,	
1950—1953	**200—250***
Separate outfits	**50—65**
Caracul wig,	**275—325**
Painted eyelashes, walks,	
1954	**150—200***
Separate outfits	**45—55**
Molded eyelashes, walks,	
1955—1957	**125—165***
Separate outfits	**40—50**
Molded eyelashes, walks, jointed knees,	
1957—1962	**110—135***
Separate outfits	**30—40**
Ginny's Pup	**150**
Ginny's Gym Set,	**250**
Coronation Ginny,	**1000 up**
Wee Imp,	**150—200**

*Allow extra for special outfits.

Ginny Coronation, all original. *Private Collection.*

Ginny, strung with painted eyelashes, all original. *Beth Foulke Collection.*

Two hard plastic **Ginny** babies with caracul wigs and **Wee Willie**, strung with caracul wig, all original. *Beth Foulke Collection.*

Hard Plastic Ginny Baby: Bent limbs, jointed at neck, shoulders and hips; caracul wig, painted or sleep eyes; original clothes; all in good condition. 8in (20cm) **Crib Crowd**, **$400 up**

WPA

Maker: Various artists under the sponsorship of the Works Projects Administration
Date: 1935—1943
Mark: Usually a number and location, such as "#7040, Milwaukee, Wis."

WPA Cloth doll: Stockinette head doll with yarn hair, molded face, painted features; cloth body; appropriate clothes; all in very good condition. See photo *6th Blue Book of Dolls & Values,* page 361.
22—23in (56—59cm)   **$450—550****

**Not enough price samples to compute a reliable range.

Molded composition-type doll: Finely molded individual faces, unjointed adult bodies; lovely authentic clothing representing various nationalities.
16in (41cm)   **$650 pair****

**Not enough price samples to compute a reliable range.

Plaster composition heads: Molded heads with little original detail, cloth bodies; original regional costumes.
12in (31cm)   **$25—35 each**

Group of 12in (31cm) **WPA** dolls, all original clothing. *Esther Schwartz Collection.*

OPPOSITE PAGE: 16in (41cm) **WPA** dolls with finely modeled features, authentic clothing. *Esther Schwartz Collection.*

ARAGON SPAIN
HUESCA

WSK

Maker: Wiesenthal, Schindel & Kallenberg, doll factory, Waltershausen, Thüringia, Germany (Heads made for them by porcelain factories including Simon & Halbig, Alt, Beck & Gottschalck #1321, and Bähr & Pröschild #541)

Date: 1858—on

Material: Bisque heads, composition bodies, all-bisque dolls

Mark: Character baby: $W \int \mathcal{K}$ 541 Child doll: $SIMON \ \& \ HALBIG$ $WSK \ 4^{1}/2$

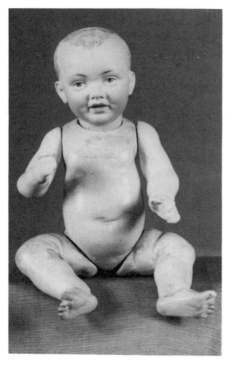

Marked Child Doll: Ca. 1890—on. Perfect bisque head with good wig, sleep eyes, stroked eyebrows, open mouth, pierced ears; ball-jointed composition body; appropriate clothes; all in good condition.

22—24in (56—61cm) **$450—500**

Marked Character Baby: Ca. 1910. Perfect bisque head with solid dome, painted hair, painted eyes, smiling open/closed mouth; composition bent-limb body; appropriate clothes; all in good condition. Mold 541 or 1321.

14—16in (36—41cm) **$475—525**

12in (31cm) character baby from mold 541. *Dr. Carole Stoessel Zvonar Collection.*

Wagner & Zetzsche

Maker: Wagner & Zetzsche, doll factory, Ilmenau, Thüringia, Germany. Bisque heads by porcelain factories including Gebrüder Heubach and Alt, Beck & Gottschalck

Date: 1875—on

Material: Bisque head, cloth, kid or composition body, celluloid-type heads

---

Closed-mouth Child: Ca. 1880s. Perfect turned bisque shoulder head with solid dome (mold 639) or open crown (mold 698), sometimes with plaster dome, mohair wig, paperweight eyes (a few with sleep eyes), flat eyebrows, closed mouth, small ears; kid or cloth body with bisque hands; appropriate clothes; all in good condition.

MARK: Blue paper body label with "W Z" initials entwined in fancy scroll.

14—16in (36—41cm) **$625—675**
19—21in (48—53cm) **800—850**
22—24in (56—61cm) **900—1000**

Character Baby or Child: Ca. 1910. Perfect bisque socket head, wig, sleep eyes, open mouth with upper teeth; dressed; all in good condition. Mold #10586 made by Gebrüder Heubach.

MARK: 10586

Germany

Baby body,
16—18in (41—46cm) **$500—550**
Composition and leather body,
16—18in (41—46cm) **450—500**

Shoulder head doll of the type used by Wagner & Zetzsche. *Esther Schwartz Collection.*

17½in (45cm) Gebruder Heubach 10586 for Wagner and Zetzsche. *H&J Foulke, Inc.*

Harald: 1915. Celluloid-type head with molded hair, painted eyes, closed mouth, pouty expression; jointed oilcloth body with jointed composition arms; appropriately dressed, head in fair condition, body in good condition.

MARK: "Harald
        W.Z."

14in (36cm) **$175—225**
8in (20cm) *Hansi,*
all original **95**

Izannah Walker

Maker: Izannah Walker, Central Falls, R.I., U.S.A.
Date: 1873, but probably made as early as 1840s
Material: All-cloth
Size: 15—30in (38—76cm)
Mark: Later dolls are marked: "*Patented Nov. 4ᵗʰ 1873* "

Izannah Walker Doll: Stockinette, pressed head, features and hair painted
with oils, applied ears, treated limbs; muslin body; appropriate clothes; in
good condition.

17—19in (43—48cm)   **$11,000—13,000**
Fair condition, quite a lot of wear,   **4000—6000**

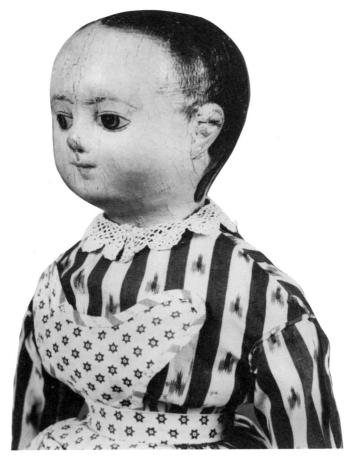

18in (46cm)
Izannah Walker.
*Private
Collection.*

Wax Doll, Poured

Maker: Various firms in England, such as Montanari, Pierotti and Lucy Peck
Date: Mid 19th century through the early 1900s
Material: Wax head, arms and legs, cloth body
Size: Various
Mark: Sometimes stamped on body with maker or store

Poured Wax Child: Head, lower arms and legs of wax; cloth body; set-in hair, glass eyes; original clothes or very well dressed; all in good condition.

16—17in (41—43cm)	**$ 900—1000***
22—24in (56—61cm)	**1200—1400***
with much wear,	**600—700**
Lady: 20in (51cm)	
unsigned	**675—775**

*Signed "Lucy Peck" could be higher.

25in (64cm) Pierotti-type poured wax. *Private Collection.*

Wax-Over-Composition

Maker: Numerous firms in England, Germany or France
Date: During the 1800s
Material: Wax-over-shoulder head of some type of composition or papier-mâché, cloth body, wax-over-composition or wooden limbs
Mark: None

English Slit-head Wax: Ca. 1830—1860. Wax-over-shoulder head, not rewaxed; human hair wig, glass eyes (may open and close by a wire), faintly smiling; original cloth body with leather arms; original or suitable old clothing; all in good condition, but showing wear.

14in (36cm)	**$275—300**
20—24in (51—61cm)	**450—500**

Molded Hair Doll: Ca. 1850—on. Wax-over-shoulder head, not rewaxed; molded hair sometimes with bow, glass sleep or set eyes; original cloth body; wax-over or wooden extremities with molded boots or bare feet; nice old clothes; all in good condition.

20—23in (51—58cm) **$400—450***
Pumpkin head with molded pompadour and hair band,
16—18in (41—46cm) **260—285**

*More or less depending upon quality.

19in (48cm) wax-over with molded hair. *H&J Foulke, Inc.*

Wax Over Composition continued

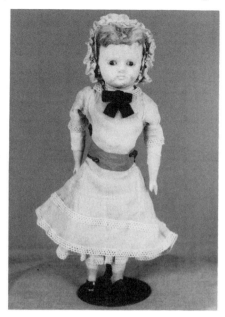

11in (28cm) wax-over with wig, all original. *H&J Foulke, Inc.*

20in (51cm) wax-over lady with wig and swivel neck. *Dolly Valk Collection.*

Wax Doll With Wig: Ca. mid 19th century into early 20th century. Wax-over-shoulder head, not rewaxed; blonde or brown human hair or mohair wig, blue, brown or black glass eyes, sleep or set, open or closed mouth; original cloth body, any combination of extremities mentioned above, also arms may be made of china; original clothing or suitably dressed; entire doll in nice condition.

11—12in (28—31cm)	**$125—150**
16—18in (41—46cm)	**300—325**
22—24in (56—61cm)	**375—425**
Lady with swivel neck, 20in (51cm)	**600—650**

Bonnet Wax Doll: Ca. 1860 to 1880. Wax-over-shoulder head, with molded bonnet; molded hair may have some mohair or human hair attached, blue, brown or black set eyes; original cloth body and wooden extremities; nice old clothes; all in good condition.

16—17in (41—43cm)   **$1750****

**Not enough price samples to compute a reliable range.

Norah Wellings

Maker: Victoria Toy Works, Wellington, Shropshire, England, for Norah Wellings
Date: 1926—Ca. 1960
Material: Fabric: Felt, velvet and velour, and other material, stuffed
Size: Various
Designer: Norah Wellings
Mark: On tag on foot: "Made in England by Norah Wellings"

Wellings Doll: All-fabric, stitch-jointed shoulders and hips; molded fabric face (also of papier-mâché, sometimes stockinette covered), painted features; all in excellent condition. Most commonly found are sailors, Canadian Mounties, Scots and Black Islanders.

Characters:

8in (20cm)	**$ 45—55**
11—12in (28—31cm)	**75—85**
14in (36cm)	**100—125**
16—18in (41—46cm)	**160—185**

Glass eyes:

14in (36cm) white	**125—150**
14in (36cm) black	**150—175**

Children:

Painted eyes,

16—18in (41—46cm)	**350—400**
23in (58cm)	**600—650**

Glass eyes,

16—18in (41—46cm)	**400—500**

13in (33cm) Wellings Indian and Dutch girl, 10½in (27cm) black character. *H&J Foulke, Inc.*

15in (39cm) Norah Wellings child, all original. *Dolly Valk Collection.*

Wislizenus

Maker: Adolf Wislizenus, doll factory, Waltershausen, Thüringia, Germany. Heads made by Bähr & Pröschild, Simon & Halbig and Ernst Heubach.

Date: 1851—on

Material: Bisque head, composition ball-jointed body

Trademarks: Old Glory, Special, Queen Quality

Mark: Germany

A.W.

0

Wislizenus Child Doll: Ca. 1890—on. Perfect bisque head, composition ball-jointed body; good wig; blue or brown sleep eyes, open mouth; dressed; all in good condition.

16—18in (41—46cm)   **$300—350**

22—24in (56—61cm)   **400—450**

Wislizenus Character Doll: Perfect bisque socket head, molded hair, painted eyes, open/closed mouth with molded teeth; composition toddler body; head marked only "115//Germany;" dressed; all in good condition. For photograph see *5th Blue Book of Dolls & Values,* page 341.

12in (31cm)   **$425—450**

**Not enough price samples to compute a reliable range.

Marked A.W. Character: Perfect bisque socket head, good wig, sleep eyes, open/closed mouth with molded tongue and two separated porcelain teeth; bent-limb baby body.

26in (66cm)   **$1100—1200**

**Not enough price samples to compute a reliable range.

26—27in (66—69cm) A.W. character. *Lesley Hurford Collection.*

Wood, German

Maker: Various companies, such as Rudolf Schneider, Sonneberg, Thüringia, Germany
Date: After 1910
Material: All-wood, fully-jointed or wood head and limbs, cloth body
Mark: None

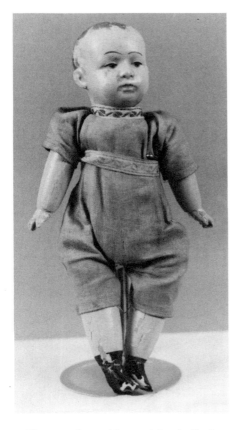

Character boy with wood head. *Ruth Noden Collection.*

"Bébé Tout en Bois" (Doll all of Wood): 1914. Rudolf Schneider. All of wood, fully-jointed; wig, inset glass eyes, open mouth with teeth; appropriate clothes; all in fair to good condition.

16in (41cm)	**$500—600****
21in (53cm)	**750****

**Not enough price samples to compute a reliable range.

Pouty character: Wood head and limbs, cloth body; pouty face with painted hair and eyes, closed mouth; appropriate clothing; all in fair to good condition.

12in (31cm)	**$200—225**

Wood, Swiss

Maker: Various Swiss firms
Date: 20th century
Material: All-wood or wood head and limbs on cloth body
Size: Various, but smaller sizes are more commonly found
Mark: Usually a paper label on wrist or clothes

Swiss Wooden Doll: Wooden head with hand-carved features and hair with good detail (males sometimes have carved hats); all carved wood jointed body; original, usually regional attire; excellent condition.

10in (25cm)   **$175—200**
18—20in (46—51cm)   **450—550**

10½in (27cm) Swiss wood girl with carved hair. *Dolly Valk Collection.*

Glossary

Applied Ears: Ear molded independently and affixed to the head. (On most dolls the ear is included as part of the head mold.)

Bald Head: Head with no crown opening, could be covered by a wig or have painted hair.

Ball-jointed Body: Usually a body of composition or papier-mâché with wooden balls at knees, elbows, hips and shoulders to make swivel joints.

Bébé: French child doll with "dolly face."

Belton-type: A bald head with one, two or three small holes for attaching wig.

Bent-limb Baby Body: Composition body of five pieces with chubby torso and curved arms and legs.

Biskoline: Celluloid-type of substance for making dolls.

Bisque: Unglazed porcelain, usually flesh tinted, used for dolls' heads or all-bisque dolls.

Breather: Dolls with an actual opening in each nostril; also called open nostrils.

Breveté (or Bté): Used on French dolls to indicate that the patent is registered.

Character Doll: Dolls with bisque or composition heads, modeled to look lifelike, such as infants, young or older children, young ladies and so on.

China: Glazed porcelain used for dolls' heads and *Frozen Charlottes*.

Child Dolls: Dolls with a typical "dolly face" which represent a child.

Composition: A material used for dolls' heads and bodies, consisting of such items as wood pulp, glue, sawdust, flour, rags and sundry other substances.

Crown Opening: The cut-away part of a doll head.

DEP: Abbreviation used on German and French dolls claiming registration.

D.R.G.M.: Abbreviation used on German dolls indicating a registered design or patent.

Dolly Face: Typical face used on bisque dolls before 1910 when the character face was developed; "dolly faces" were used also after 1910.

Embossed Mark: Raised letters, numbers or names on the backs of heads or bodies.

Feathered Eyebrows: Eyebrows composed of many tiny painted brush strokes to give a realistic look.

Fixed Eyes: Glass eyes which do not move or sleep.

Flange Neck: A doll's head with a ridge at the base of the neck which contains holes for sewing the head to a cloth body.

Flapper Dolls: Dolls of the 1920s period with bobbed wig or molded hair and slender arms and legs.

Flirting Eyes: Eyes which move from side to side as doll's head is tilted.

Frozen Charlotte: Doll molded all in one piece including arms and legs.

Ges. (Gesch.): Used on German dolls to indicate design is registered or patented.

Googly Eyes: Large, often round, eyes looking to the side; also called roguish or goo goo eyes.

Hard Plastic: Hard material used for making dolls after 1948.

Incised Mark: Letters, numbers or names impressed into the bisque on the back of the head or on the shoulder plate.

Intaglio Eyes: Painted eyes with sunken pupil and iris.

JCB: Jointed composition body. See *ball-jointed body*.

Kid Body: Body of white or pink leather.

Lady Dolls: Dolls with an adult face and a body with adult proportions.

Mohair: Goat's hair widely used in making doll wigs.

Molded Hair: Curls, waves and comb marks which are actually part of the mold and not merely painted onto the head.

Motschmann-type Body: Doll body with cloth midsection and upper limbs with floating joints; hard lower torso and lower limbs.

Open-Mouth: Lips parted with an actual opening in the bisque, usually has teeth either molded in the bisque or set in separately and sometimes a tongue.

Open/Closed Mouth: A mouth molded to appear open, but having no actual slit in the bisque.

Original Clothes: Clothes belonging to a doll during the childhood of the original owner, either commercially or homemade.

Painted Bisque: Bisque covered with a layer of flesh-colored paint, which has not been baked in, so will easily rub or wash off.

Paperweight Eyes: Blown glass eyes which have depth and look real, usually found in French dolls.

Papier-mâché: A material used for dolls' heads and bodies, consisting of paper pulp, sizing, glue, clay or flour.

Pate: A shaped piece of plaster, cork, cardboard or other material which covers the crown opening.

Pierced Ears: Little holes through the doll's earlobes to accommodate earrings.

Pierced-in Ears: A hole at the doll's earlobe which goes into the head to accommodate earrings.

Pink Bisque: A later bisque of about 1920 which was pre-colored pink.

Pink-toned China: China which has been given a pink tint to look more like real flesh color; also called lustered china.

Rembrandt Hair: Hair style parted in center with bangs at front, straight down sides and back and curled at ends.

S.G.D.G.: Used on French dolls to indicate that the patent is registered "without guarantee of the government."

Shoulder Head: A doll's head and shoulders all in one piece.

Shoulder Plate: The actual shoulder portion sometimes molded in one with the head, sometimes a separate piece with a socket in which a head is inserted.

Socket Head: Head and neck which fit into an opening in the shoulder plate or the body.

Solid-dome Head: Head with no crown opening, could have painted hair or be covered by wig.

Stationary Eyes: Glass eyes which do not move or sleep.

Stone Bisque: Coarse white bisque of a lesser quality.

Toddler Body: Usually a chubby ball-jointed composition body with chunky, shorter thighs, and a diagonal hip joint; sometimes has curved instead of jointed arms; sometimes is of five pieces with straight chubby legs.

Topsy-Turvy: Doll with two heads, one usually concealed beneath a skirt.

Turned Shoulder Head: Head and shoulders are one piece, but the head is molded at an angle so that the doll is not looking straight ahead.

Vinyl: Soft plastic material used for making dolls after 1950s.

Watermelon Mouth: Closed line-type mouth curved up at each side in an impish expression.

Wax Over: A doll with head and/or limbs of papier-mâché or composition covered with a layer of wax to give a natural, lifelike finish.

Weighted Eyes: Eyes which can be made to sleep by means of a weight which is attached to the eyes.

Wire Eyes: Eyes which can be made to sleep by means of a wire which protrudes from doll's head.

Selected Bibliography

Anderton, Johana. *Twentieth Century Dolls; More Twentieth Century Dolls*

Angione, Genevieve. *All-Bisque & Half-Bisque Dolls*

Angione & Wharton. *All Dolls Are Collectible*

Borger, Mona. *Chinas/Dolls for Study and Admiration.*

Cieslik, Jürgen & Marianne. *German Doll Encyclopedia 1800-1939*

Coleman, Dorothy, Elizabeth & Evelyn. *The Collector's Encyclopedia of Dolls; The Collector's Book of Dolls' Clothes*

Desmond, Kay. *All Color Book of Dolls*

Foulke, Jan. *Focusing on Effanbee Composition Dolls; Treasury of Madame Alexander Dolls; Focusing on Gebrüder Heubach Dolls - The Art of Gebrüder Heubach: Dolls and Figurines; Kestner, King of Dollmakers; Simon & Halbig Dolls: The Artful Aspect*

Hillier, Mary. *Dolls and Dollmakers*

King, Constance. *Dolls and Doll's Houses; The Collector's History of Dolls*

Merrill, Madelaine. *The Art of Dolls 1700-1940*

Noble, John. *Treasury of Beautiful Dolls*

Richter, Lydia. *The Beloved Käthe-Kruse-Dolls*

Shoemaker, Rhoda. *Compo Dolls Cute and Collectible,* Vols. I, II and III

About the Author

The name Jan Foulke is synonymous with accurate information. As the author of the *Blue Book of Dolls & Values®*, she is the most quoted source on doll information and the most respected and recognized authority on dolls and doll prices in the world.

Born in Burlington, New Jersey, Jan Foulke has always had a fondness for dolls. She recalls, "Many happy hours of my childhood were spent with dolls as companions, since we lived on a quiet country road, and until I was ten, I was an only child." Jan graduated from Columbia Union College, where she was named to the *Who's Who in American Colleges & Universities* and was graduated with high honors. Jan taught for twelve years, in the Montgomery County school system in Maryland and also supervised student teachers in English for the University of Maryland, where she did graduate work.

Jan and her husband, Howard, who photographs the dolls presented in the *Blue Book*, were both fond of antiquing as a hobby, and in 1972 they decided to open a small antique shop of their own. The interest of their daughter, Beth, in dolls sparked their curiosity about the history of old dolls — an interest that quite naturally grew out of their love of heirlooms. The stock in their antique shop gradually changed and evolved into an antique doll shop.

Early in the development of their antique doll shop, Jan and Howard realized that there was a critical need for an accurate and reliable doll identification and price guide resource. In the early 1970's, the Foulkes teamed up with Hobby House Press (publishers of *Doll Reader* Magazine) to produce (along with Thelma Bateman) the first *Blue Book of Dolls & Values*, originally published in 1974. Since that time, the Foulkes have exclusively authored and illustrated the six successive editions, and today the *Blue Book* is regarded by collectors and dealers as the definitive source for doll prices and values.

Jan and Howard Foulke now dedicate all of their professional time to the world of dolls, writing and illustrating books and articles, appraising collections, lecturing on antique dolls, acting as consultants to museums, auction houses and major collectors, and buying and selling dolls both by mail order and through exhibits at major shows throughout the United States.

Mrs. Foulke has appeared on numerous TV talk shows and is often quoted in newspaper and magazine articles as the ultimate source for doll pricing and trends in collecting. In 1985, both "USA Today" and "The Washington Post" observed that the *Blue Book of Dolls & Values* was "the bible of doll collecting."

In addition to her work on the seven editions of the *Blue Book of Dolls & Values*, Jan Foulke has also authored: *Focusing on Effanbee Composition Dolls; A Treasury of Madame Alexander Dolls; Kestner, King of Dollmakers; Simon & Halbig: The Artful Aspect; Focusing on Gebruder Heubach Dolls;* and in August 1986, *Classic Dolls;* among others.

Index

Text references are indicated in alphabetical and numerical order. Often there is a photograph to accompany the text reference. References to illustrations indicate that photographs appear on a different page.